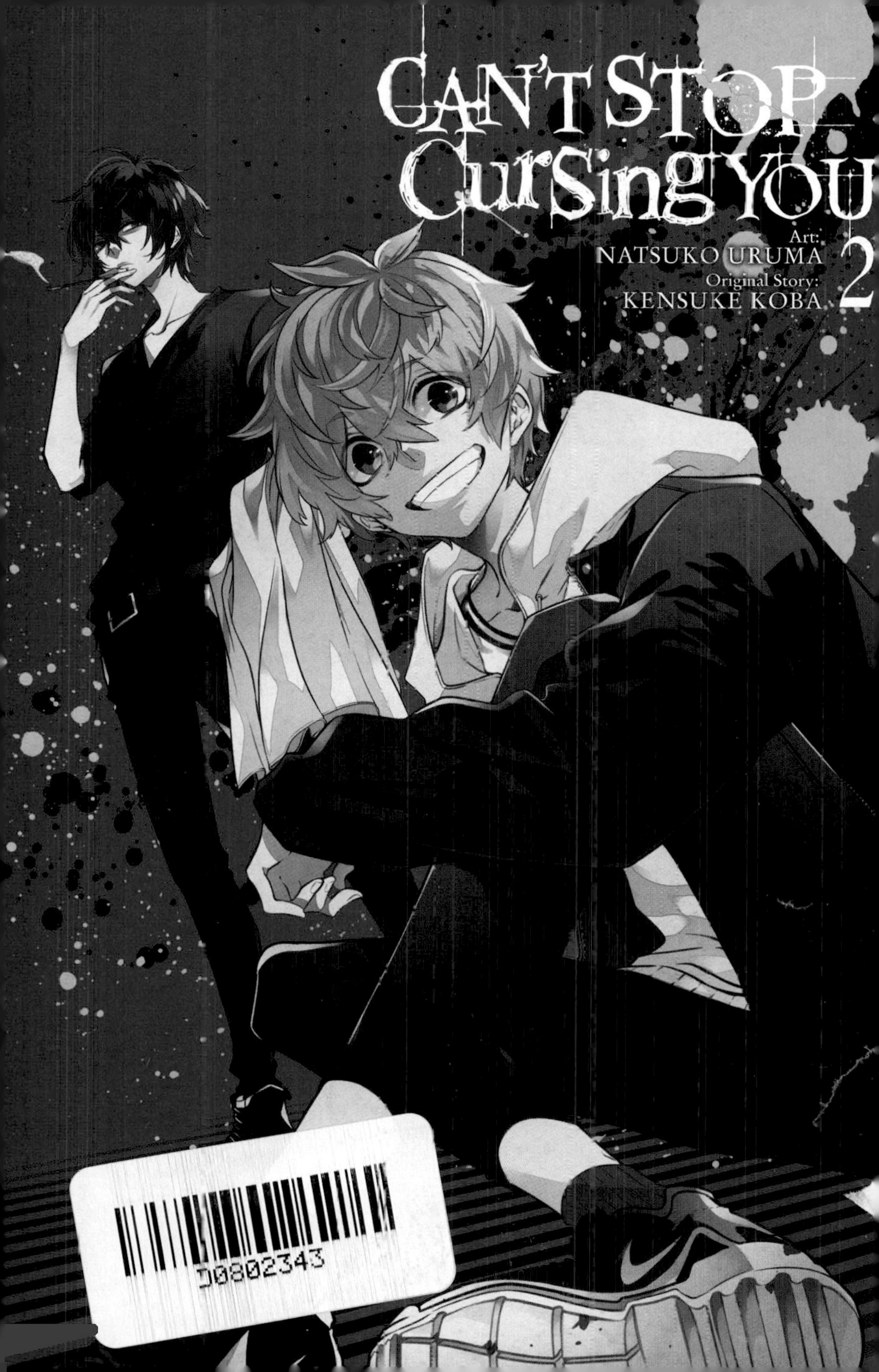
CAN'T STOP CURSING YOU
Art:
NATSUKO URUMA
Original Story:
KENSUKE KOBA
2

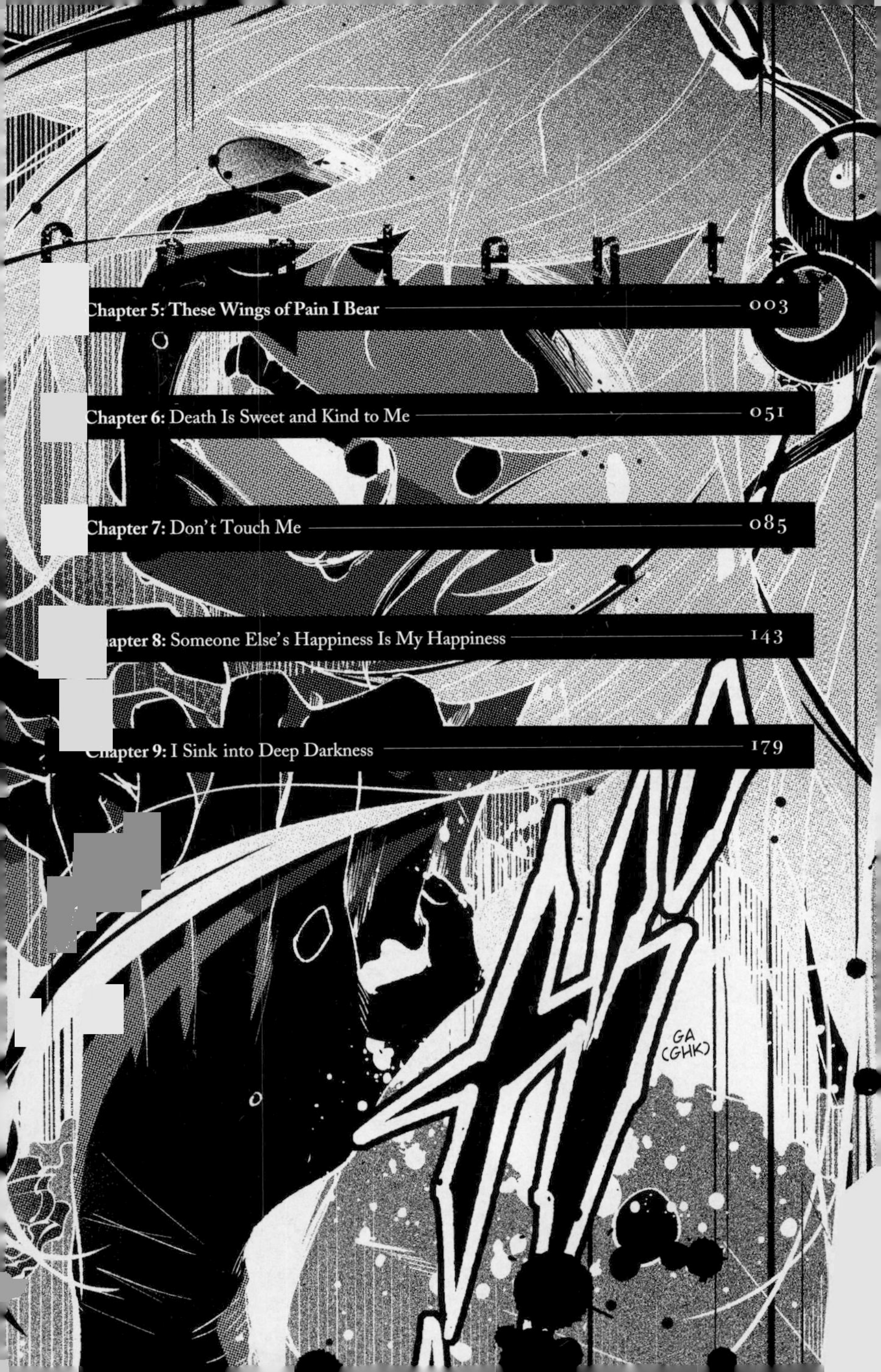
GA
(GHK)

Contents

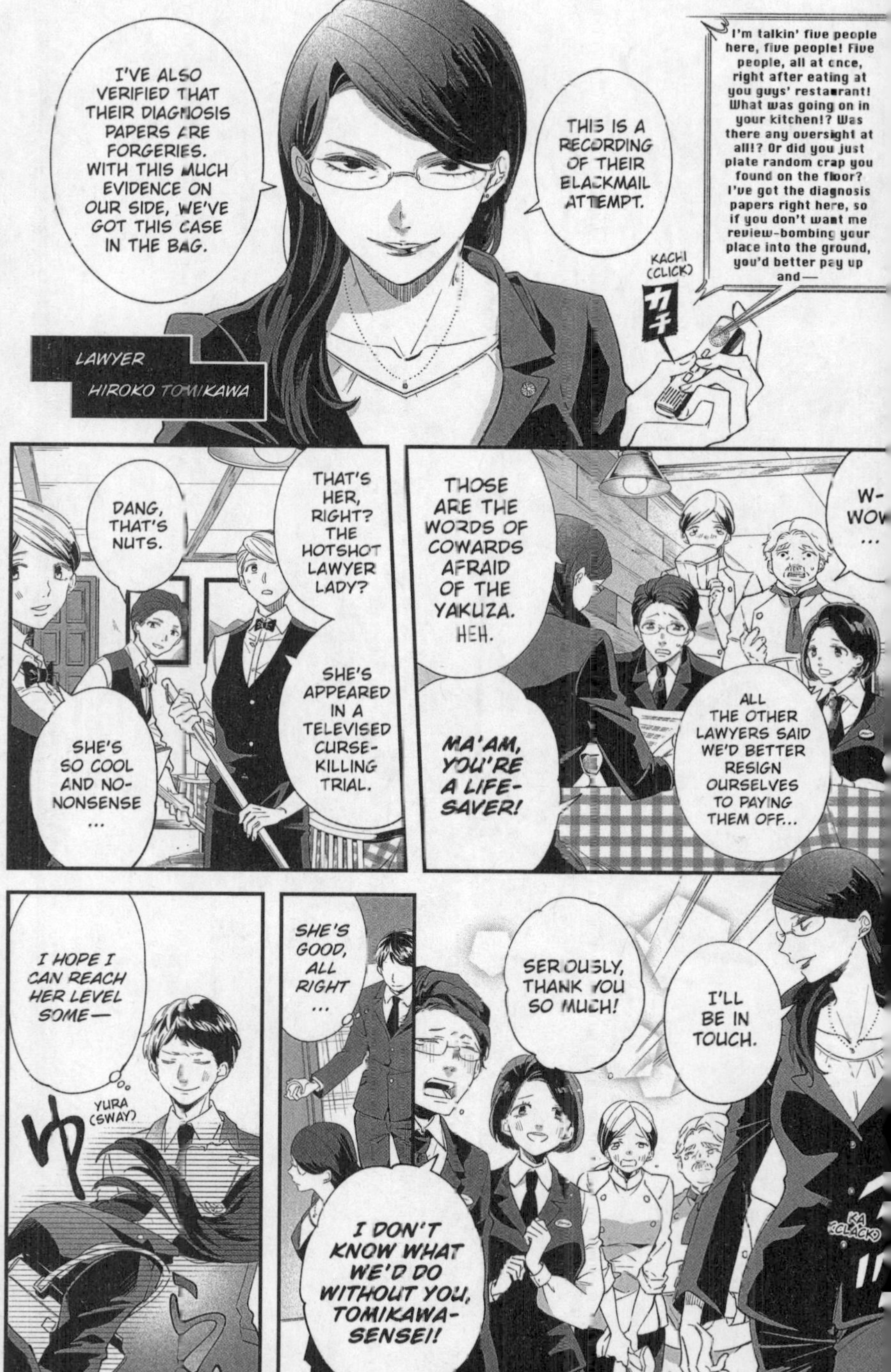
I'm talkin' five people here, five people! Five people, all at once, right after eating at you guys' restaurant! What was going on in your kitchen!? Was there any oversight at all!? Or did you just plate random crap you found on the floor? I've got the diagnosis papers right here, so if you don't want me review-bombing your place into the ground, you'd better pay up and—
KACHI (CLICK)
カチ
THIS IS A RECORDING OF THEIR BLACKMAIL ATTEMPT.
I'VE ALSO VERIFIED THAT THEIR DIAGNOSIS PAPERS ARE FORGERIES. WITH THIS MUCH EVIDENCE ON OUR SIDE, WE'VE GOT THIS CASE IN THE BAG.
LAWYER
HIROKO TOMIKAWA
W-WOW...
THOSE ARE THE WORDS OF COWARDS AFRAID OF THE YAKUZA. HEH.
ALL THE OTHER LAWYERS SAID WE'D BETTER RESIGN OURSELVES TO PAYING THEM OFF...
MA'AM, YOU'RE A LIFE-SAVER!
THAT'S HER, RIGHT? THE HOTSHOT LAWYER LADY?
DANG, THAT'S NUTS.
SHE'S APPEARED IN A TELEVISED CURSE-KILLING TRIAL.
SHE'S SO COOL AND NO-NONSENSE...
I'LL BE IN TOUCH.
KA (CLACK)
SERIOUSLY, THANK YOU SO MUCH!
SHE'S GOOD, ALL RIGHT...
I DON'T KNOW WHAT WE'D DO WITHOUT YOU, TOMIKAWA-SENSEI!
I HOPE I CAN REACH HER LEVEL SOME—
YURA (SWAY)
ゆ

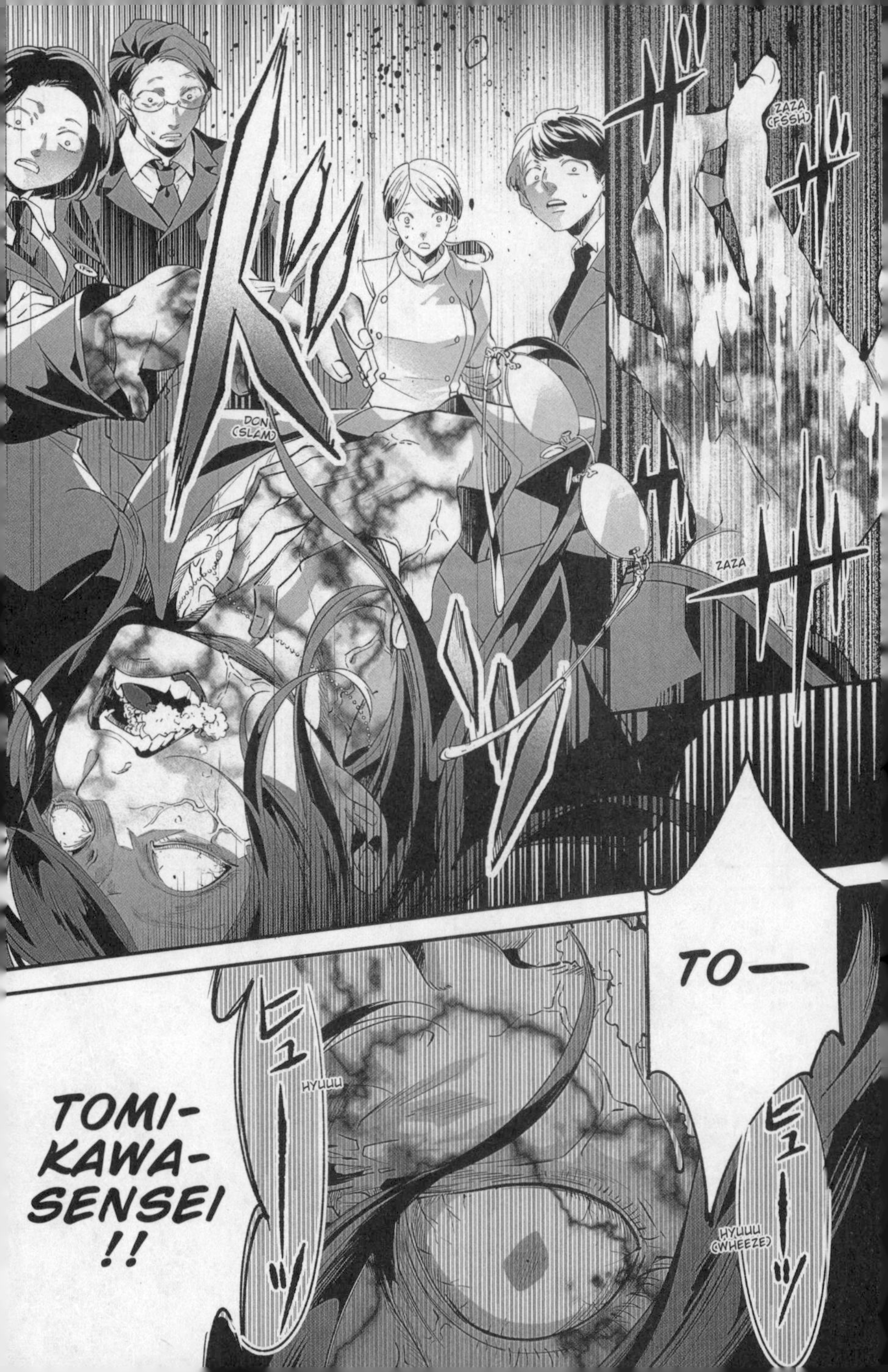
ZAZA (FSSH)
ZAZA
DON (SLAM)
TO—
HYUUU (WHEEZE)
HYUUU
TOMI-KAWA-SENSEI!!

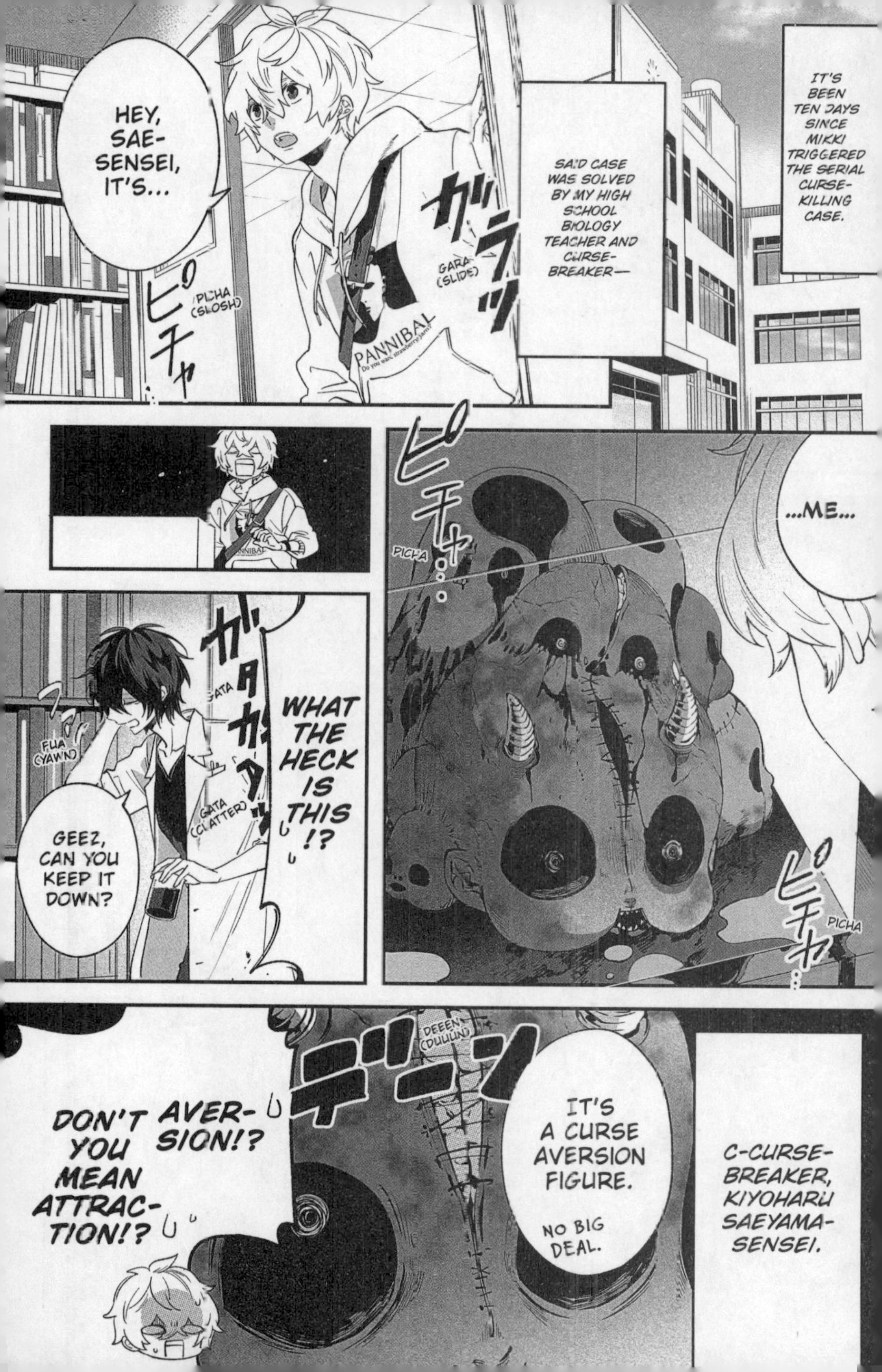
IT'S BEEN TEN DAYS SINCE MIKKI TRIGGERED THE SERIAL CURSE-KILLING CASE.
SAID CASE WAS SOLVED BY MY HIGH SCHOOL BIOLOGY TEACHER AND CURSE-BREAKER—
GARA (SLIDE)
HEY, SAE-SENSEI, IT'S...
PICHA (SLOSH)
...ME...
PICHA
PICHA
WHAT THE HECK IS THIS!?
GATA
GATA (CLATTER)
FUA (YAWN)
GEEZ, CAN YOU KEEP IT DOWN?
C-CURSE-BREAKER, KIYOHARU SAEYAMA-SENSEI.
DEEEN (DUUUN)
IT'S A CURSE AVERSION FIGURE.
NO BIG DEAL.
AVER-SION!?
DON'T YOU MEAN ATTRACTION!?

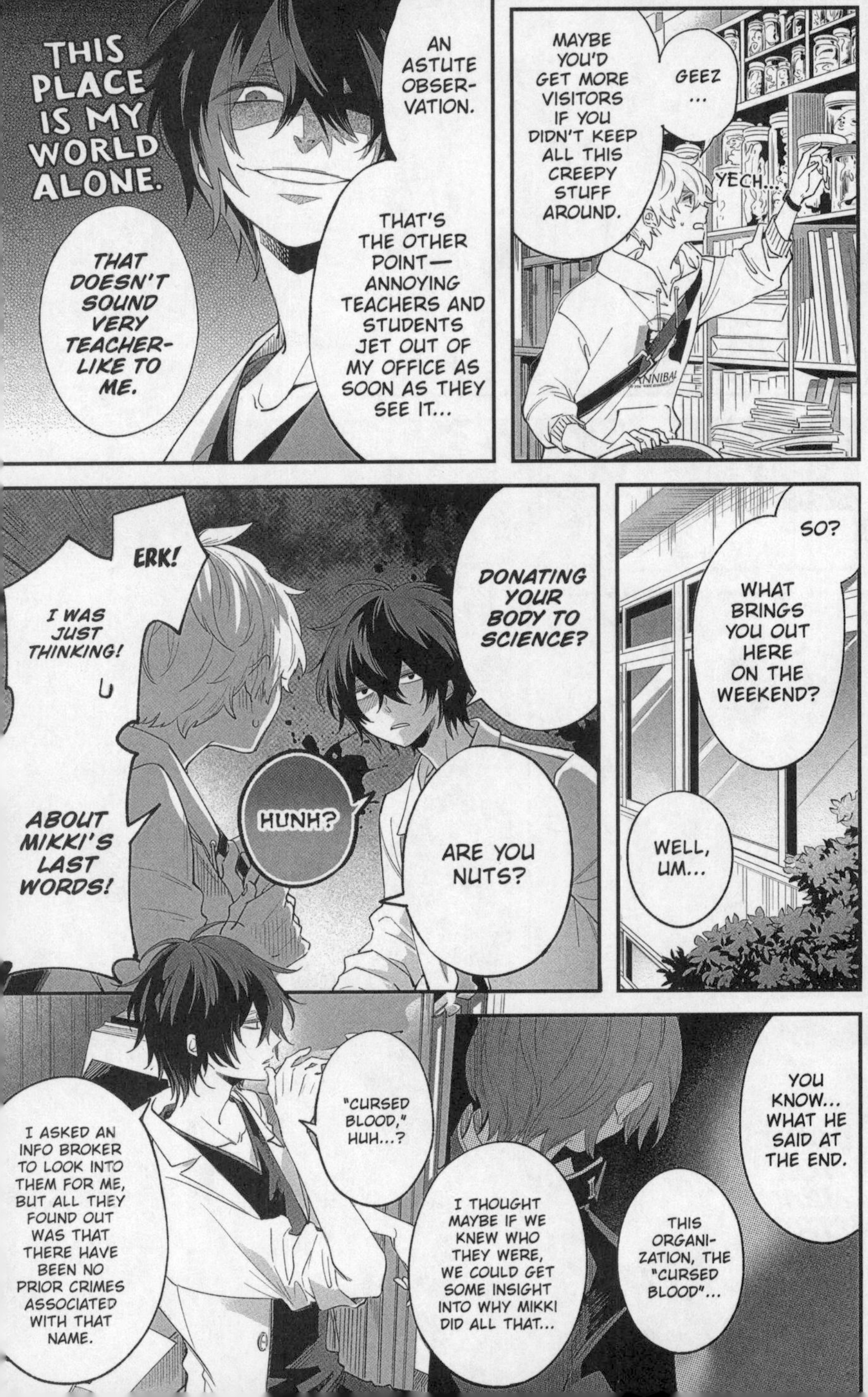
GEEZ...
MAYBE YOU'D GET MORE VISITORS IF YOU DIDN'T KEEP ALL THIS CREEPY STUFF AROUND.
YECH...
AN ASTUTE OBSERVATION.
THAT'S THE OTHER POINT—ANNOYING TEACHERS AND STUDENTS JET OUT OF MY OFFICE AS SOON AS THEY SEE IT...
THIS PLACE IS MY WORLD ALONE.
THAT DOESN'T SOUND VERY TEACHER-LIKE TO ME.
SO?
WHAT BRINGS YOU OUT HERE ON THE WEEKEND?
WELL, UM...
DONATING YOUR BODY TO SCIENCE?
ARE YOU NUTS?
HUNH?
ERK!
I WAS JUST THINKING!
ABOUT MIKKI'S LAST WORDS!
YOU KNOW... WHAT HE SAID AT THE END.
THIS ORGANIZATION, THE "CURSED BLOOD"...
I THOUGHT MAYBE IF WE KNEW WHO THEY WERE, WE COULD GET SOME INSIGHT INTO WHY MIKKI DID ALL THAT...
"CURSED BLOOD," HUH...?
I ASKED AN INFO BROKER TO LOOK INTO THEM FOR ME, BUT ALL THEY FOUND OUT WAS THAT THERE HAVE BEEN NO PRIOR CRIMES ASSOCIATED WITH THAT NAME.

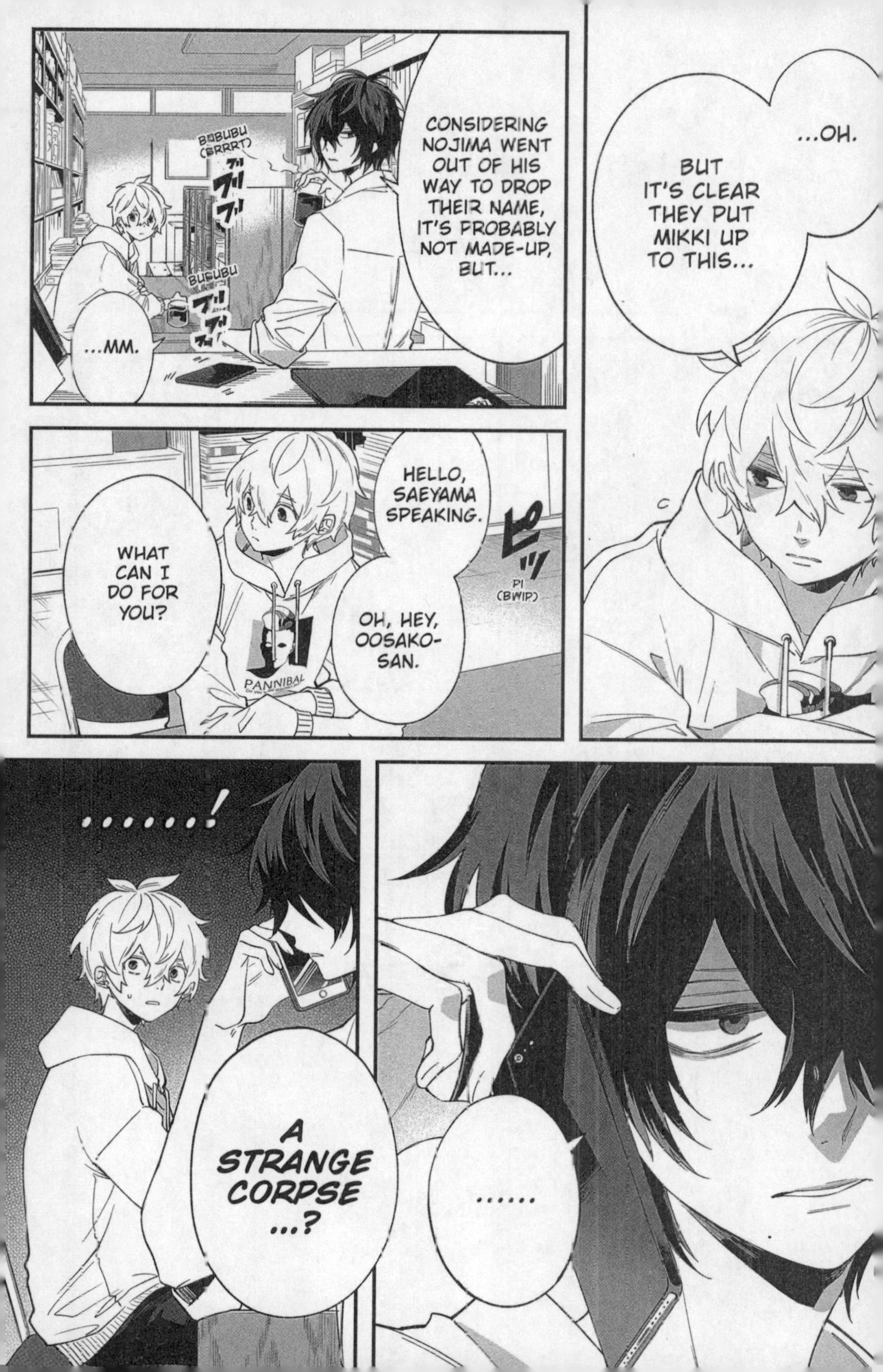
...OH.
BUT IT'S CLEAR THEY PUT MIKKI UP TO THIS...
CONSIDERING NOJIMA WENT OUT OF HIS WAY TO DROP THEIR NAME, IT'S PROBABLY NOT MADE-UP, BUT...
BUBUBU (BRRRT)
BUBUBU
...MM.
PI (BWIP)
HELLO, SAEYAMA SPEAKING.
OH, HEY, OOSAKO-SAN.
WHAT CAN I DO FOR YOU?
PANNIBAL
......
.......!
A STRANGE CORPSE ...?

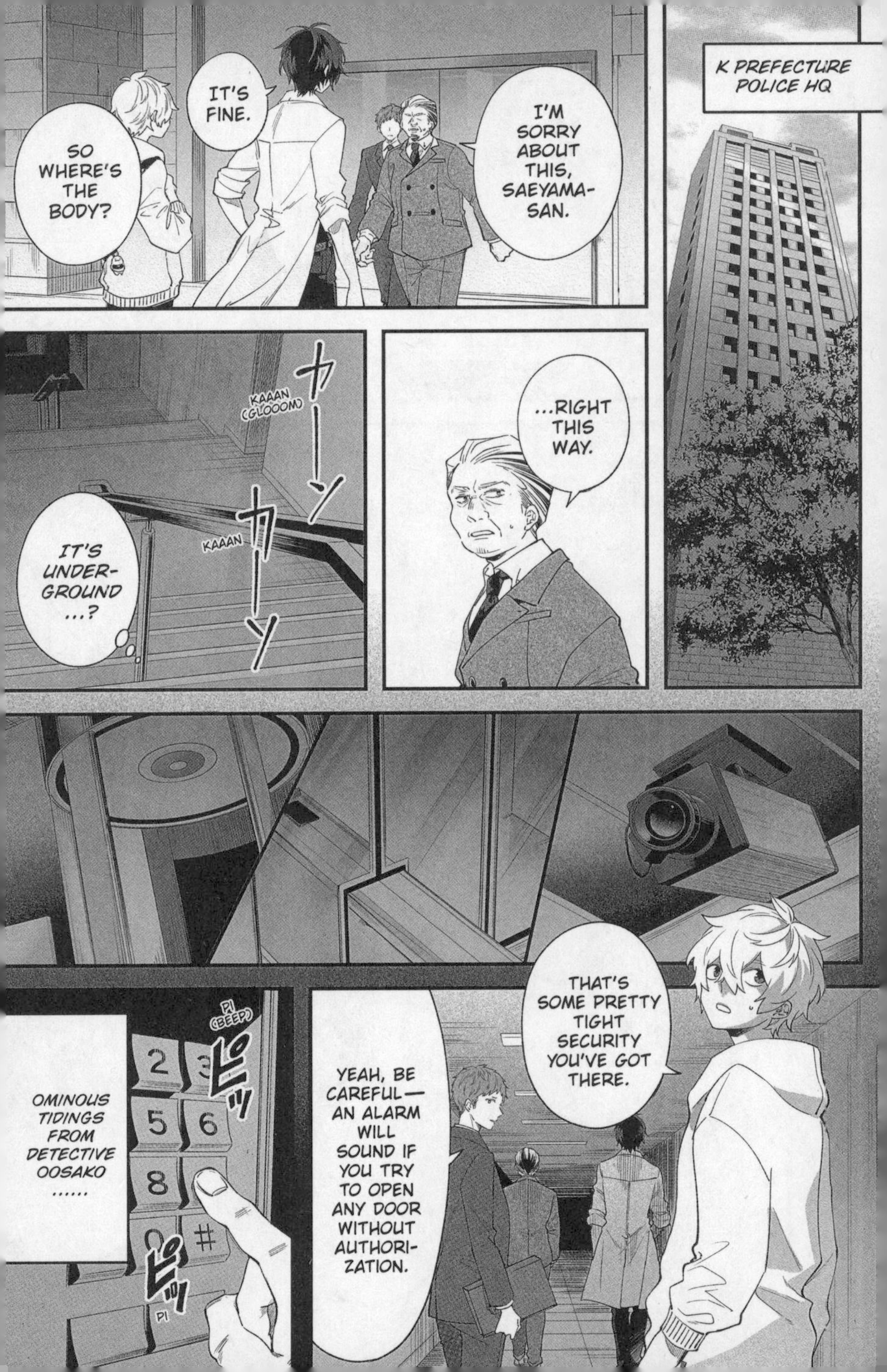
K PREFECTURE POLICE HQ
I'M SORRY ABOUT THIS, SAEYAMA-SAN.
IT'S FINE.
SO WHERE'S THE BODY?
...RIGHT THIS WAY.
KAAAN (GLOOOM)
KAAAN
IT'S UNDER-GROUND ...?
THAT'S SOME PRETTY TIGHT SECURITY YOU'VE GOT THERE.
YEAH, BE CAREFUL—AN ALARM WILL SOUND IF YOU TRY TO OPEN ANY DOOR WITHOUT AUTHORI-ZATION.
PI (BEEP)
PI
OMINOUS TIDINGS FROM DETECTIVE OOSAKO ......

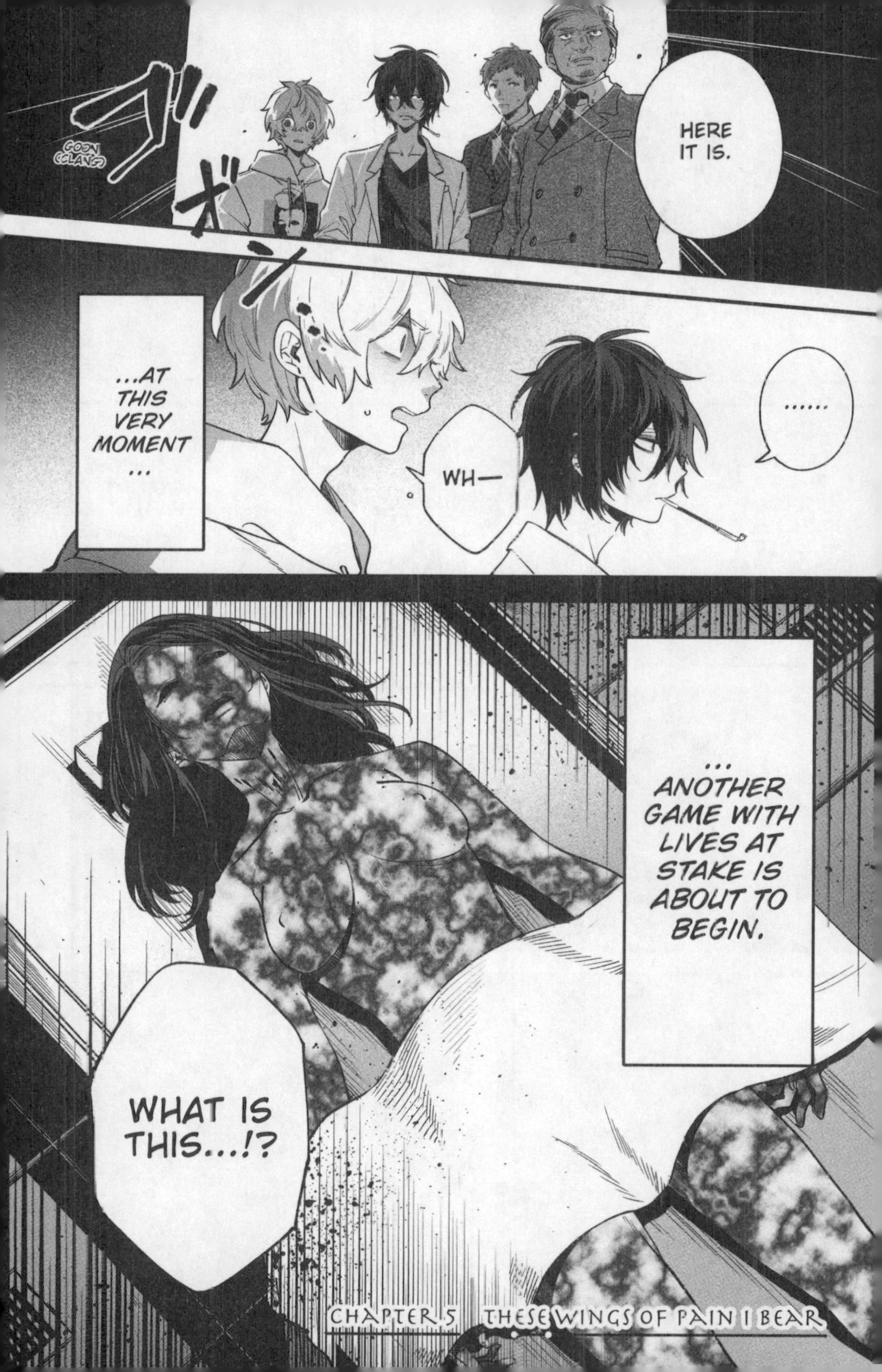
HERE IT IS.
GOON (CLANG)
......
WH—
...AT THIS VERY MOMENT ...
... ANOTHER GAME WITH LIVES AT STAKE IS ABOUT TO BEGIN.
WHAT IS THIS...!?
CHAPTER 5 THESE WINGS OF PAIN I BEAR

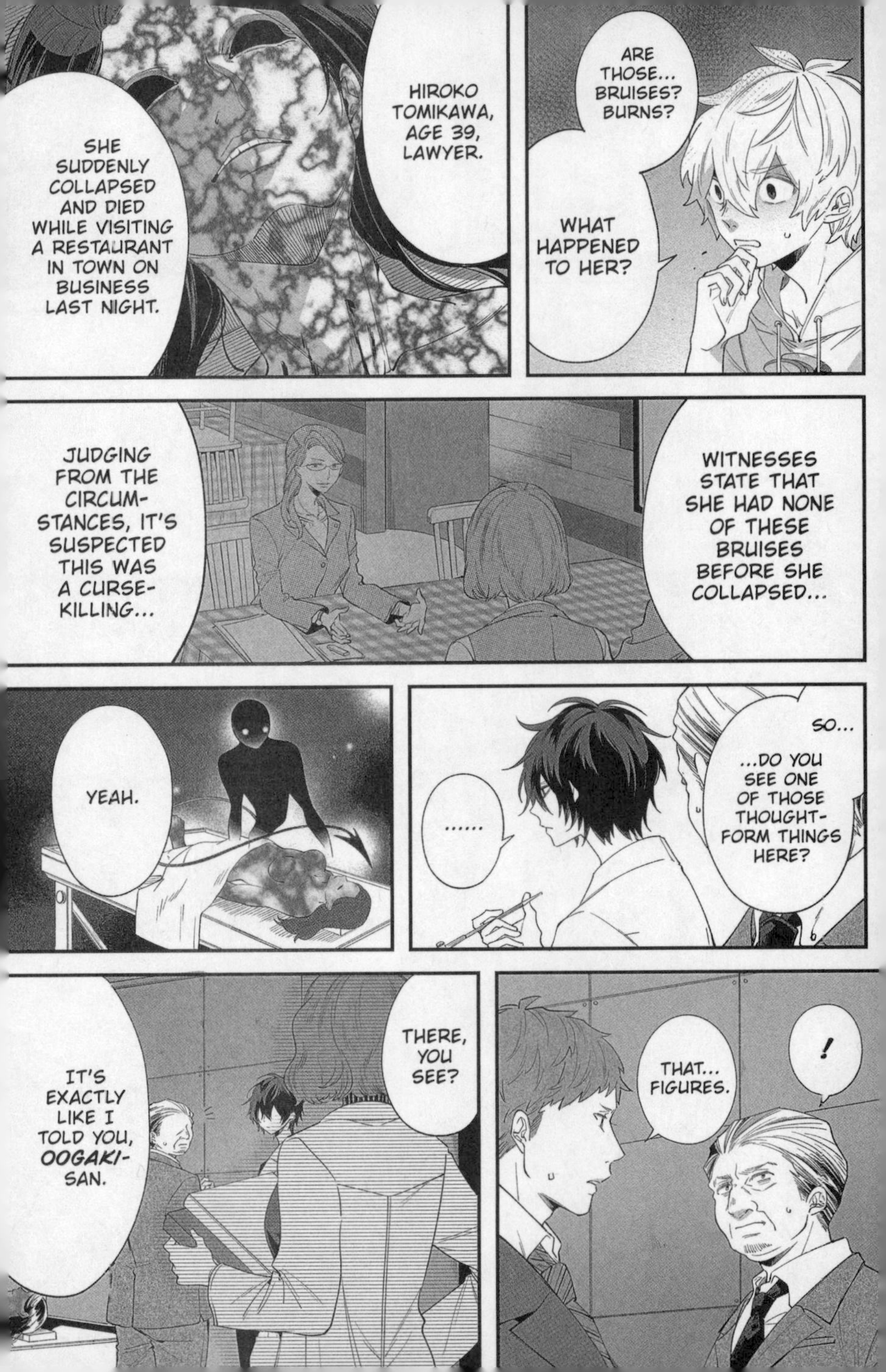
ARE THOSE... BRUISES? BURNS?
WHAT HAPPENED TO HER?
HIROKO TOMIKAWA, AGE 39, LAWYER.
SHE SUDDENLY COLLAPSED AND DIED WHILE VISITING A RESTAURANT IN TOWN ON BUSINESS LAST NIGHT.
WITNESSES STATE THAT SHE HAD NONE OF THESE BRUISES BEFORE SHE COLLAPSED...
JUDGING FROM THE CIRCUMSTANCES, IT'S SUSPECTED THIS WAS A CURSE-KILLING...
SO...
...DO YOU SEE ONE OF THOSE THOUGHT-FORM THINGS HERE?
......
YEAH.
!
THAT... FIGURES.
THERE, YOU SEE?
IT'S EXACTLY LIKE I TOLD YOU, *OOGAKI*-SAN.

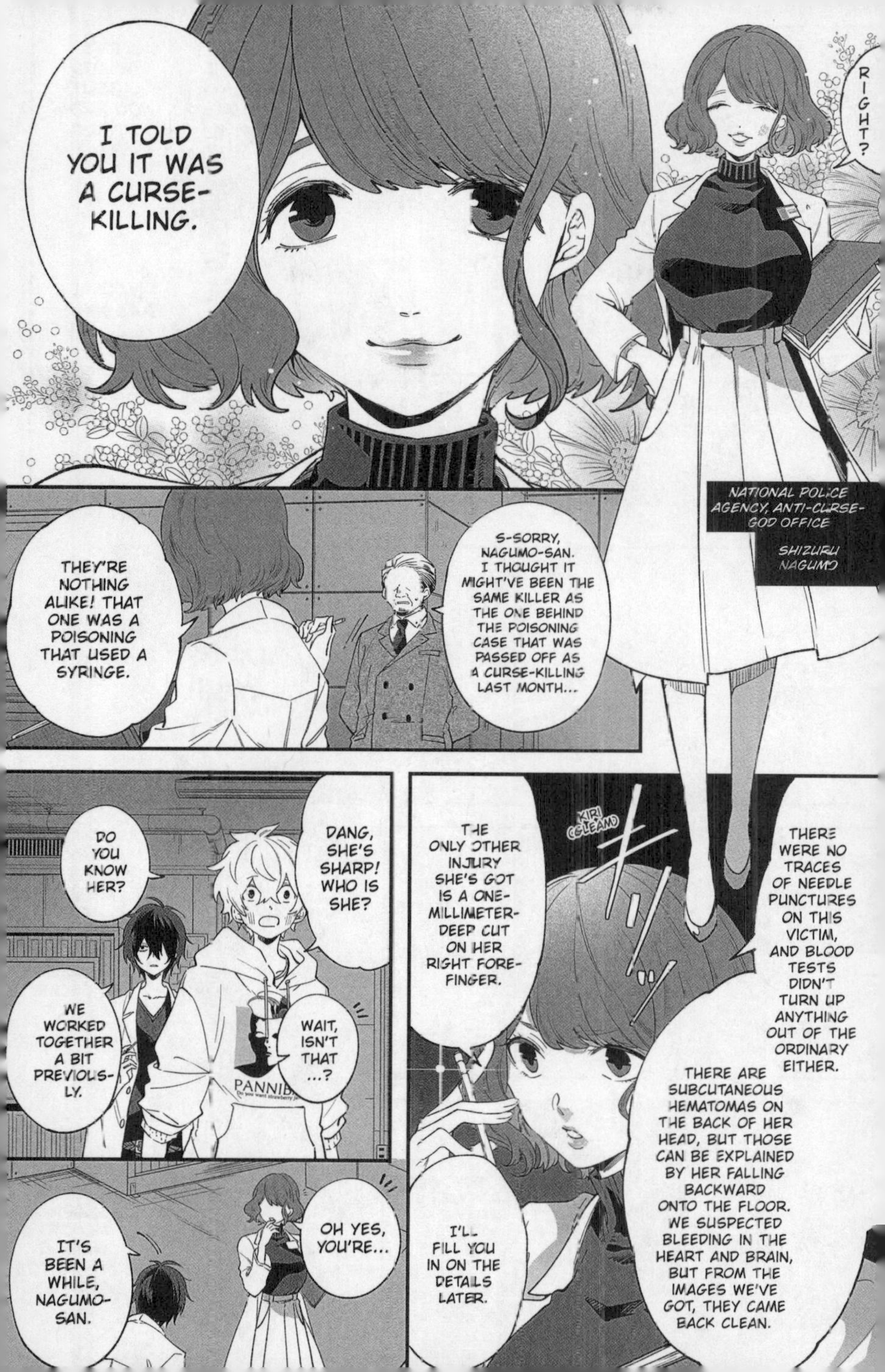
RIGHT?
NATIONAL POLICE AGENCY, ANTI-CURSE-GOD OFFICE
SHIZURU NAGUMO
I TOLD YOU IT WAS A CURSE-KILLING.
S-SORRY, NAGUMO-SAN. I THOUGHT IT MIGHT'VE BEEN THE SAME KILLER AS THE ONE BEHIND THE POISONING CASE THAT WAS PASSED OFF AS A CURSE-KILLING LAST MONTH...
THEY'RE NOTHING ALIKE! THAT ONE WAS A POISONING THAT USED A SYRINGE.
KIRI (GLEAM)
THERE WERE NO TRACES OF NEEDLE PUNCTURES ON THIS VICTIM, AND BLOOD TESTS DIDN'T TURN UP ANYTHING OUT OF THE ORDINARY EITHER.
THE ONLY OTHER INJURY SHE'S GOT IS A ONE-MILLIMETER-DEEP CUT ON HER RIGHT FORE-FINGER.
THERE ARE SUBCUTANEOUS HEMATOMAS ON THE BACK OF HER HEAD, BUT THOSE CAN BE EXPLAINED BY HER FALLING BACKWARD ONTO THE FLOOR. WE SUSPECTED BLEEDING IN THE HEART AND BRAIN, BUT FROM THE IMAGES WE'VE GOT, THEY CAME BACK CLEAN.
I'LL FILL YOU IN ON THE DETAILS LATER.
DANG, SHE'S SHARP! WHO IS SHE?
DO YOU KNOW HER?
WAIT, ISN'T THAT ...?
WE WORKED TOGETHER A BIT PREVIOUS-LY.
OH YES, YOU'RE...
IT'S BEEN A WHILE, NAGUMO-SAN.

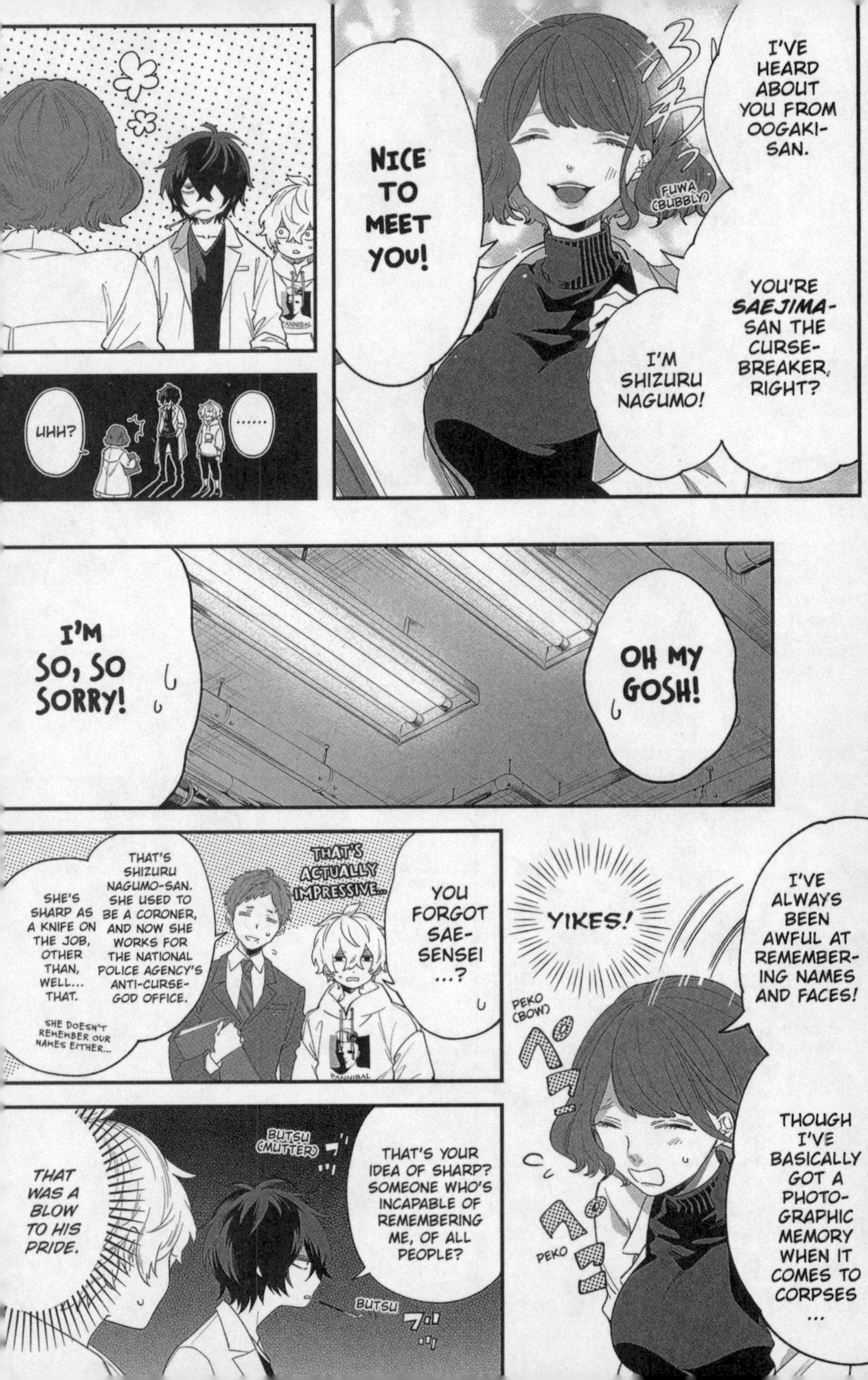
I'VE HEARD ABOUT YOU FROM OOGAKI-SAN.
FUWA (BUBBLY)
NICE TO MEET YOU!
YOU'RE SAEJIMA-SAN THE CURSE-BREAKER, RIGHT?
I'M SHIZURU NAGUMO!
......
UHH?
OH MY GOSH!
I'M SO, SO SORRY!
I'VE ALWAYS BEEN AWFUL AT REMEMBERING NAMES AND FACES!
YIKES!
PEKO (BOW)
PEKO
THOUGH I'VE BASICALLY GOT A PHOTOGRAPHIC MEMORY WHEN IT COMES TO CORPSES...
YOU FORGOT SAE-SENSEI...?
THAT'S ACTUALLY IMPRESSIVE...
THAT'S SHIZURU NAGUMO-SAN. SHE USED TO BE A CORONER, AND NOW SHE WORKS FOR THE NATIONAL POLICE AGENCY'S ANTI-CURSE-GOD OFFICE.
SHE'S SHARP AS A KNIFE ON THE JOB, OTHER THAN, WELL... THAT.
SHE DOESN'T REMEMBER OUR NAMES EITHER...
BUTSU (MUTTER)
THAT'S YOUR IDEA OF SHARP? SOMEONE WHO'S INCAPABLE OF REMEMBERING ME, OF ALL PEOPLE?
BUTSU
THAT WAS A BLOW TO HIS PRIDE.

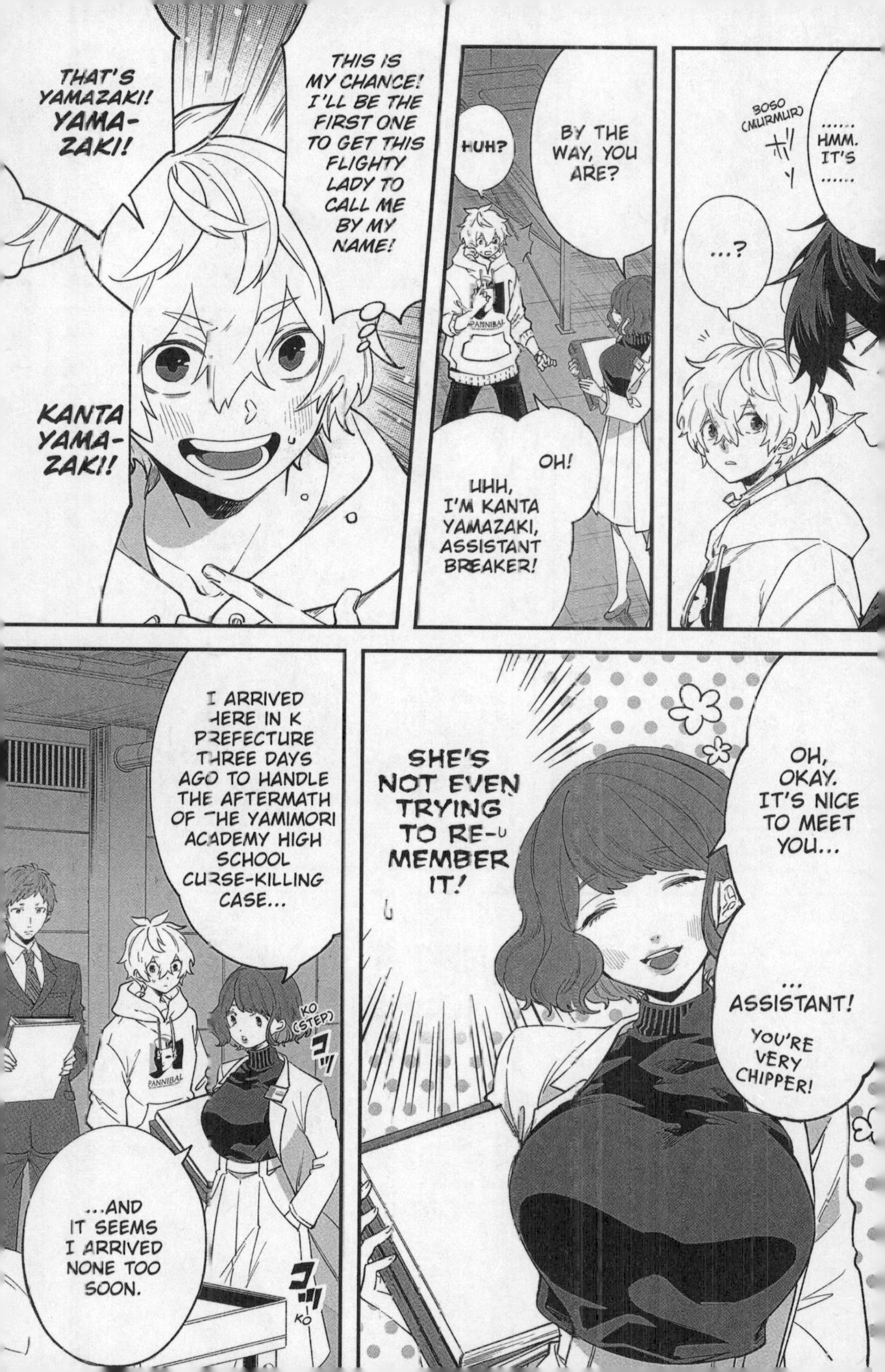
...... HMM. IT'S ......
BOSO (MURMUR)
...?
BY THE WAY, YOU ARE?
HUH?
OH!
UHH, I'M KANTA YAMAZAKI, ASSISTANT BREAKER!
THIS IS MY CHANCE! I'LL BE THE FIRST ONE TO GET THIS FLIGHTY LADY TO CALL ME BY MY NAME!
THAT'S YAMAZAKI! YAMA-ZAKI!
KANTA YAMA-ZAKI!
OH, OKAY. IT'S NICE TO MEET YOU...
... ASSISTANT!
YOU'RE VERY CHIPPER!
SHE'S NOT EVEN TRYING TO RE-MEMBER IT!
I ARRIVED HERE IN K PREFECTURE THREE DAYS AGO TO HANDLE THE AFTERMATH OF THE YAMIMORI ACADEMY HIGH SCHOOL CURSE-KILLING CASE...
KO (STEP)
...AND IT SEEMS I ARRIVED NONE TOO SOON.
KO

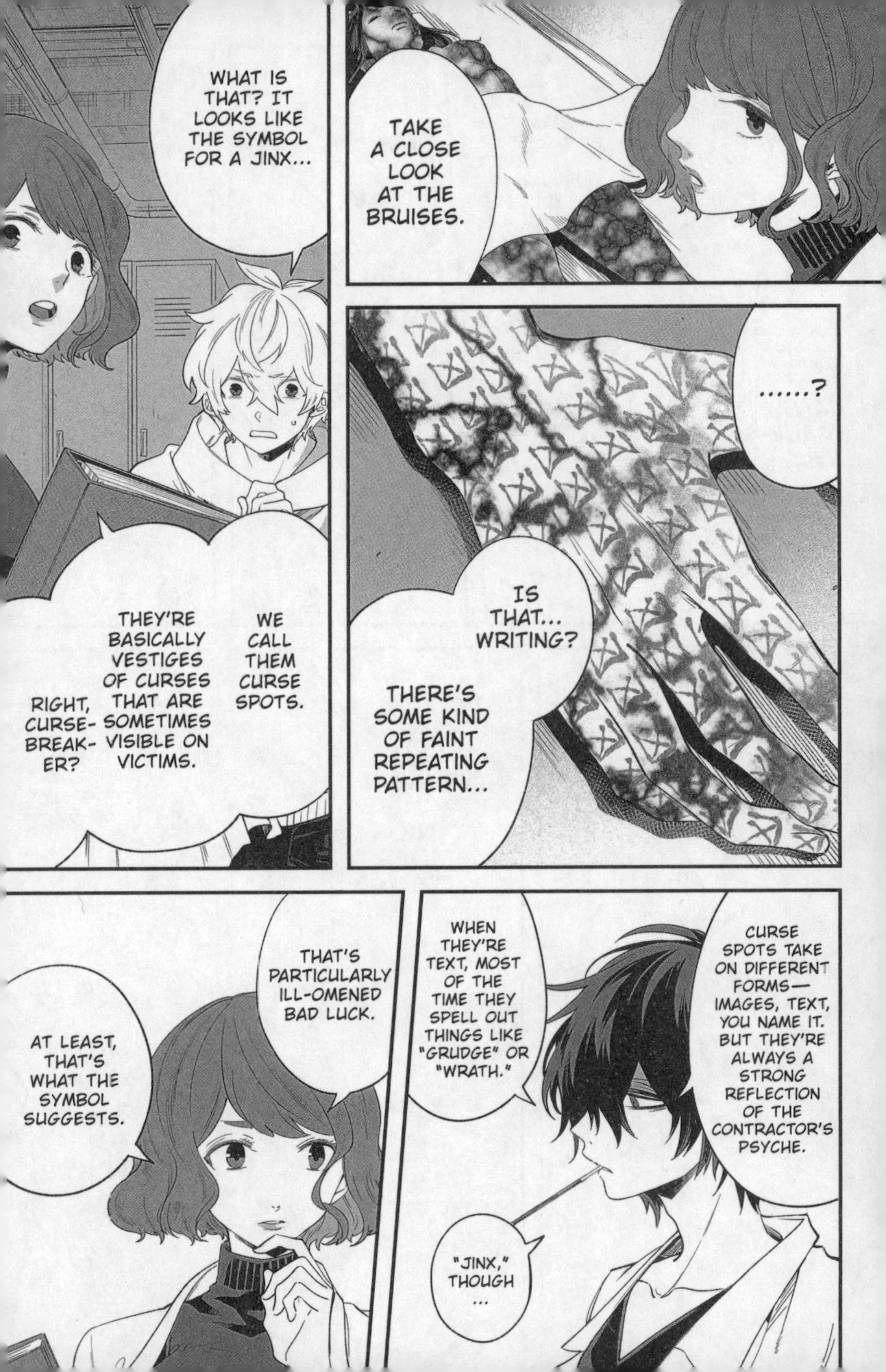
TAKE A CLOSE LOOK AT THE BRUISES.
......?
IS THAT... WRITING?
THERE'S SOME KIND OF FAINT REPEATING PATTERN...
WHAT IS THAT? IT LOOKS LIKE THE SYMBOL FOR A JINX...
WE CALL THEM CURSE SPOTS.
THEY'RE BASICALLY VESTIGES OF CURSES THAT ARE SOMETIMES VISIBLE ON VICTIMS.
RIGHT, CURSE-BREAKER?
CURSE SPOTS TAKE ON DIFFERENT FORMS—IMAGES, TEXT, YOU NAME IT. BUT THEY'RE ALWAYS A STRONG REFLECTION OF THE CONTRACTOR'S PSYCHE.
WHEN THEY'RE TEXT, MOST OF THE TIME THEY SPELL OUT THINGS LIKE "GRUDGE" OR "WRATH."
"JINX," THOUGH ...
THAT'S PARTICULARLY ILL-OMENED BAD LUCK.
AT LEAST, THAT'S WHAT THE SYMBOL SUGGESTS.

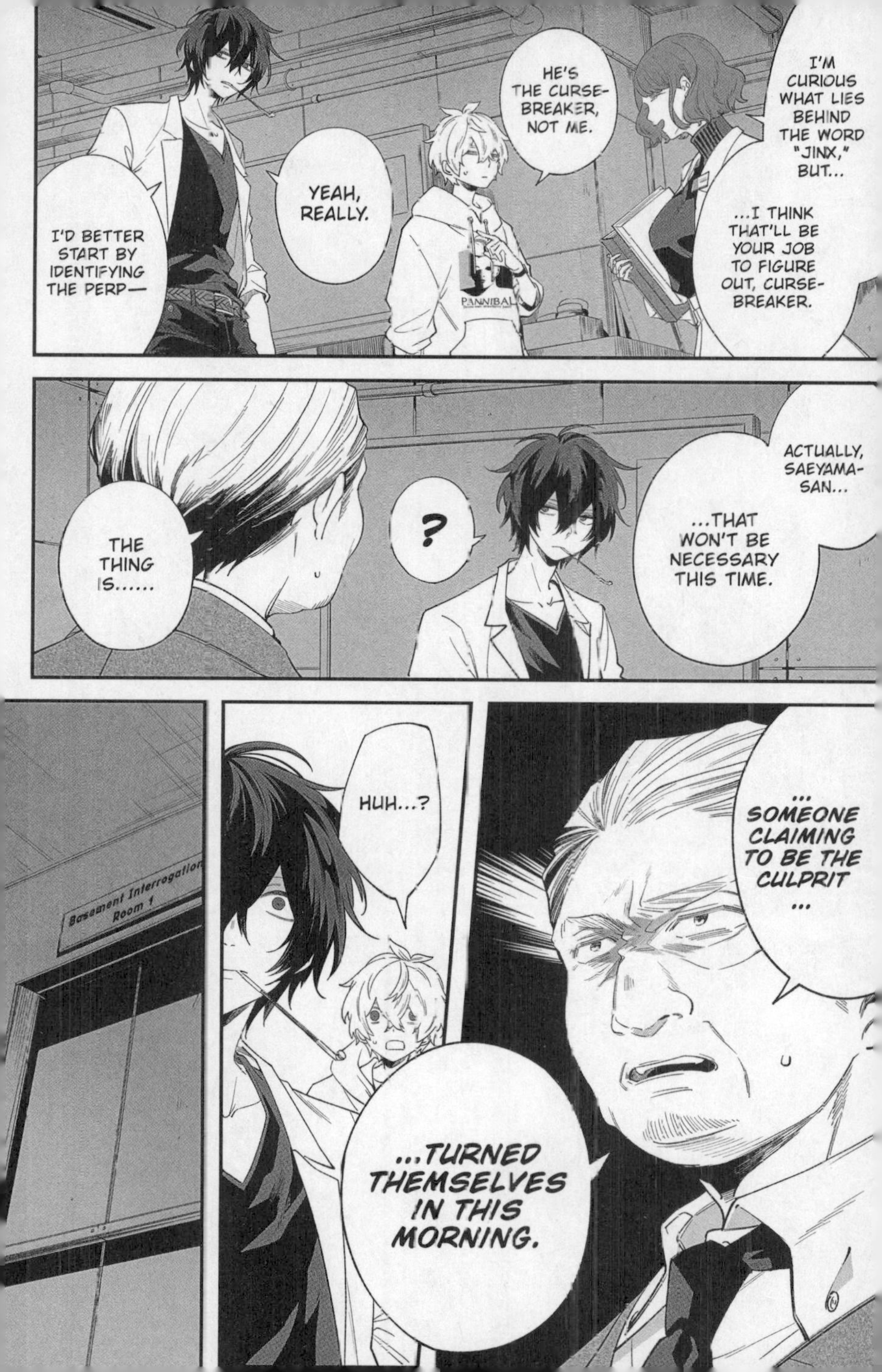
I'M CURIOUS WHAT LIES BEHIND THE WORD "JINX," BUT...
...I THINK THAT'LL BE YOUR JOB TO FIGURE OUT, CURSE-BREAKER.
HE'S THE CURSE-BREAKER, NOT ME.
YEAH, REALLY.
I'D BETTER START BY IDENTIFYING THE PERP—
ACTUALLY, SAEYAMA-SAN...
...THAT WON'T BE NECESSARY THIS TIME.
?
THE THING IS......
...SOMEONE CLAIMING TO BE THE CULPRIT...
...TURNED THEMSELVES IN THIS MORNING.
HUH...?
Basement Interrogation Room 1

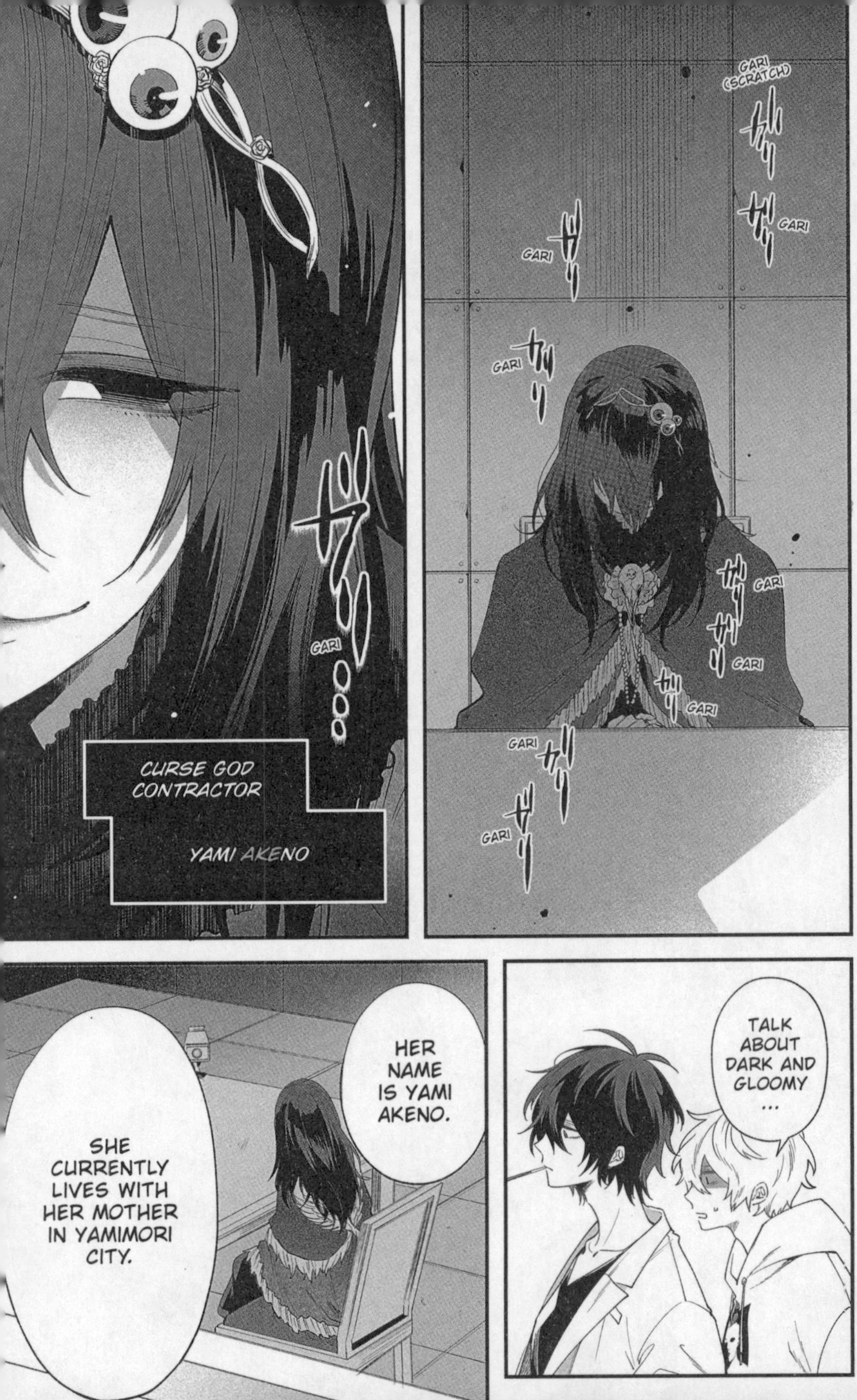
GARI (SCRATCH)
GARI
GARI
GARI
GARI
GARI
GARI
GARI
GARI
GARI
CURSE GOD CONTRACTOR
YAMI AKENO
TALK ABOUT DARK AND GLOOMY ...
HER NAME IS YAMI AKENO.
SHE CURRENTLY LIVES WITH HER MOTHER IN YAMIMORI CITY.

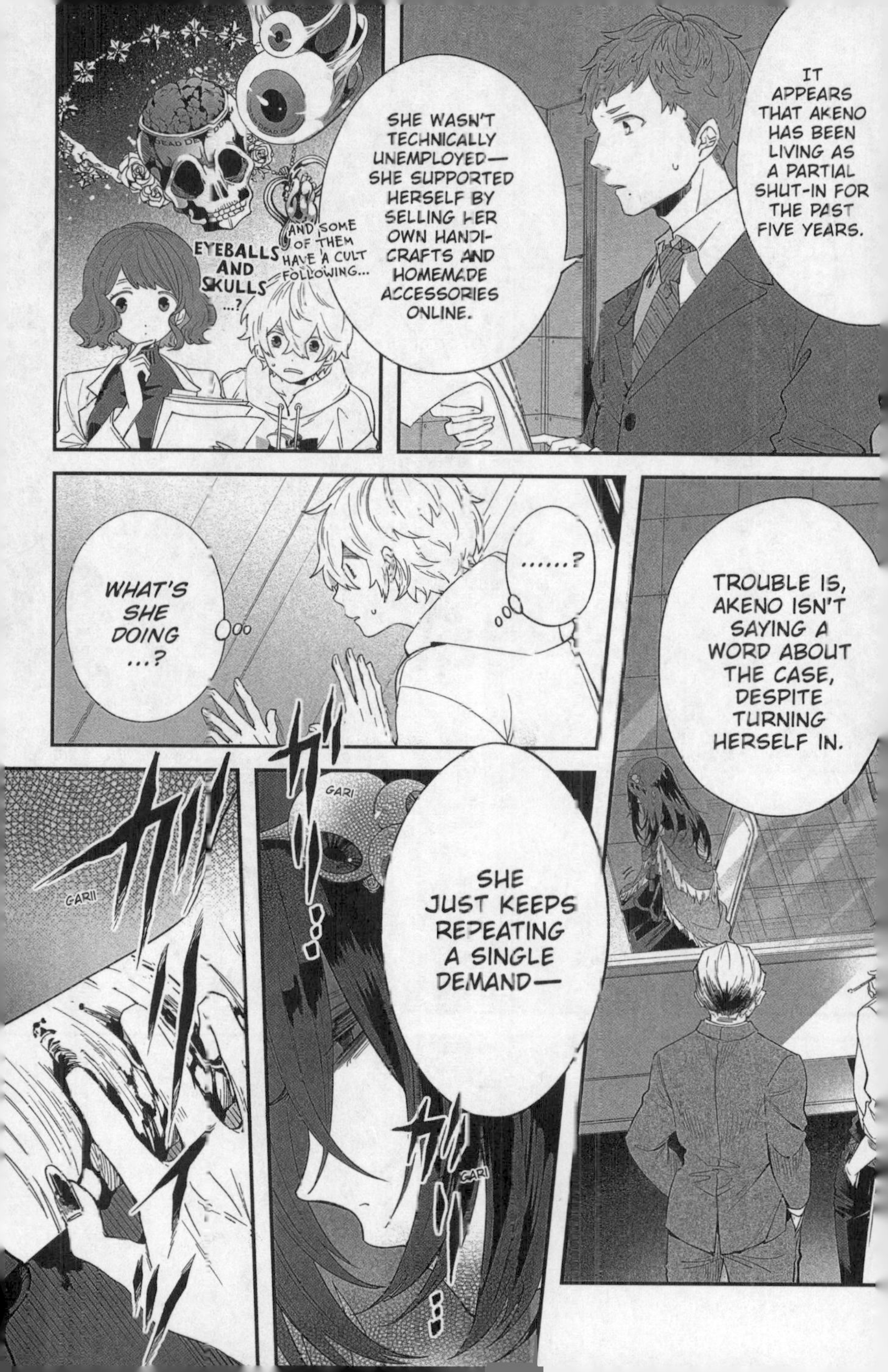
IT APPEARS THAT AKENO HAS BEEN LIVING AS A PARTIAL SHUT-IN FOR THE PAST FIVE YEARS.
SHE WASN'T TECHNICALLY UNEMPLOYED—SHE SUPPORTED HERSELF BY SELLING HER OWN HANDI-CRAFTS AND HOMEMADE ACCESSORIES ONLINE.
AND SOME OF THEM HAVE A CULT FOLLOWING...
EYEBALLS AND SKULLS ...?
TROUBLE IS, AKENO ISN'T SAYING A WORD ABOUT THE CASE, DESPITE TURNING HERSELF IN.
......?
WHAT'S SHE DOING ...?
SHE JUST KEEPS REPEATING A SINGLE DEMAND—
GARI
GARI
GARII

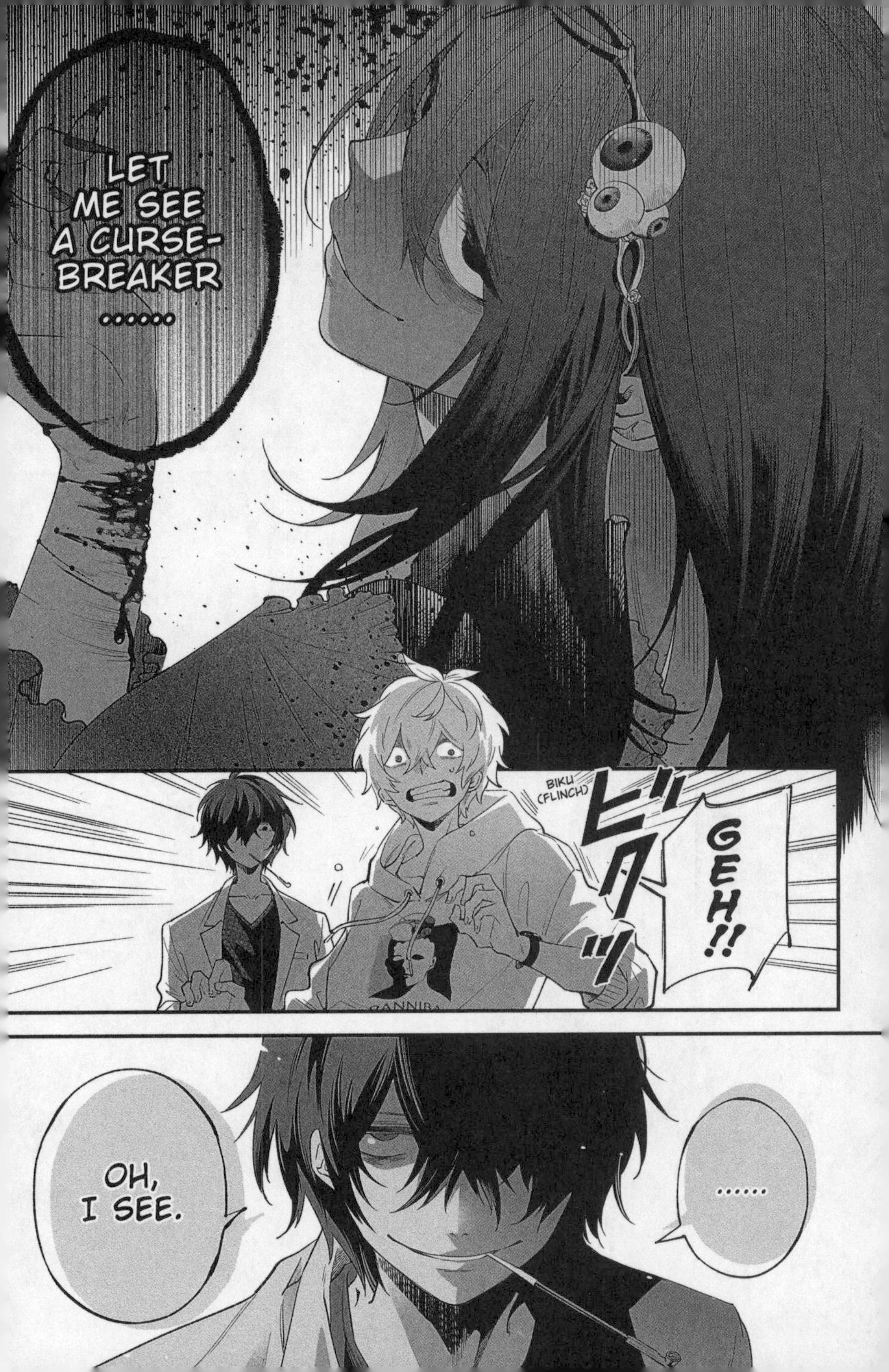
LET ME SEE A CURSE-BREAKER ......
GEH!!
BIKU (FLINCH)
......
OH, I SEE.

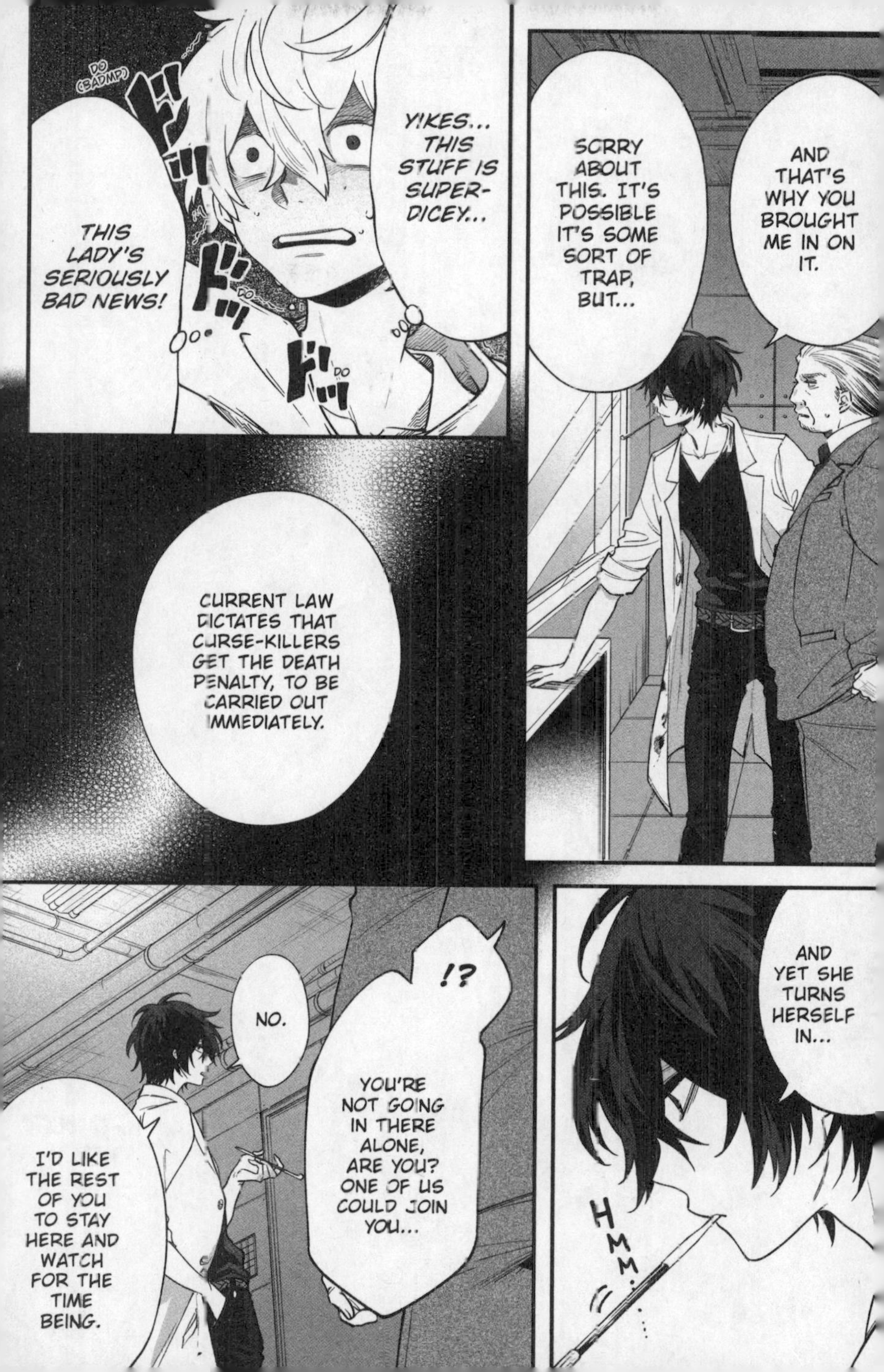
AND THAT'S WHY YOU BROUGHT ME IN ON IT.
SORRY ABOUT THIS. IT'S POSSIBLE IT'S SOME SORT OF TRAP, BUT...
DO (BADMP)
YIKES... THIS STUFF IS SUPER-DICEY...
THIS LADY'S SERIOUSLY BAD NEWS!
DO
DO
CURRENT LAW DICTATES THAT CURSE-KILLERS GET THE DEATH PENALTY, TO BE CARRIED OUT IMMEDIATELY.
AND YET SHE TURNS HERSELF IN...
HMM...
!?
YOU'RE NOT GOING IN THERE ALONE, ARE YOU? ONE OF US COULD JOIN YOU...
NO.
I'D LIKE THE REST OF YOU TO STAY HERE AND WATCH FOR THE TIME BEING.

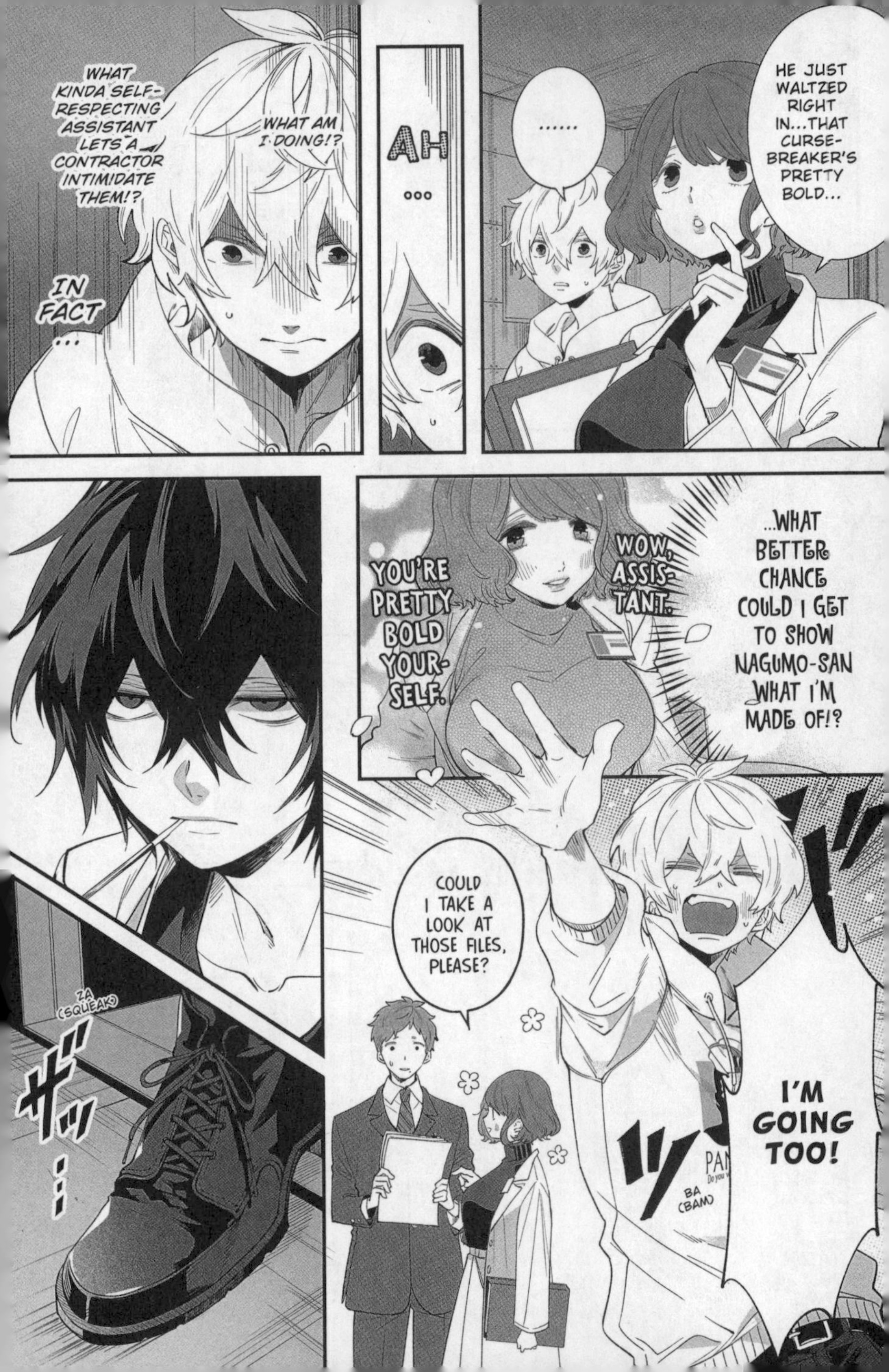
HE JUST WALTZED RIGHT IN...THAT CURSE-BREAKER'S PRETTY BOLD...
......
AH ...
WHAT AM I DOING!?
WHAT KINDA SELF-RESPECTING ASSISTANT LETS A CONTRACTOR INTIMIDATE THEM!?
IN FACT ...
...WHAT BETTER CHANCE COULD I GET TO SHOW NAGUMO-SAN WHAT I'M MADE OF!?
WOW, ASSISTANT.
YOU'RE PRETTY BOLD YOURSELF.
I'M GOING TOO!
BA (BAM)
COULD I TAKE A LOOK AT THOSE FILES, PLEASE?
ZA (SQUEAK)

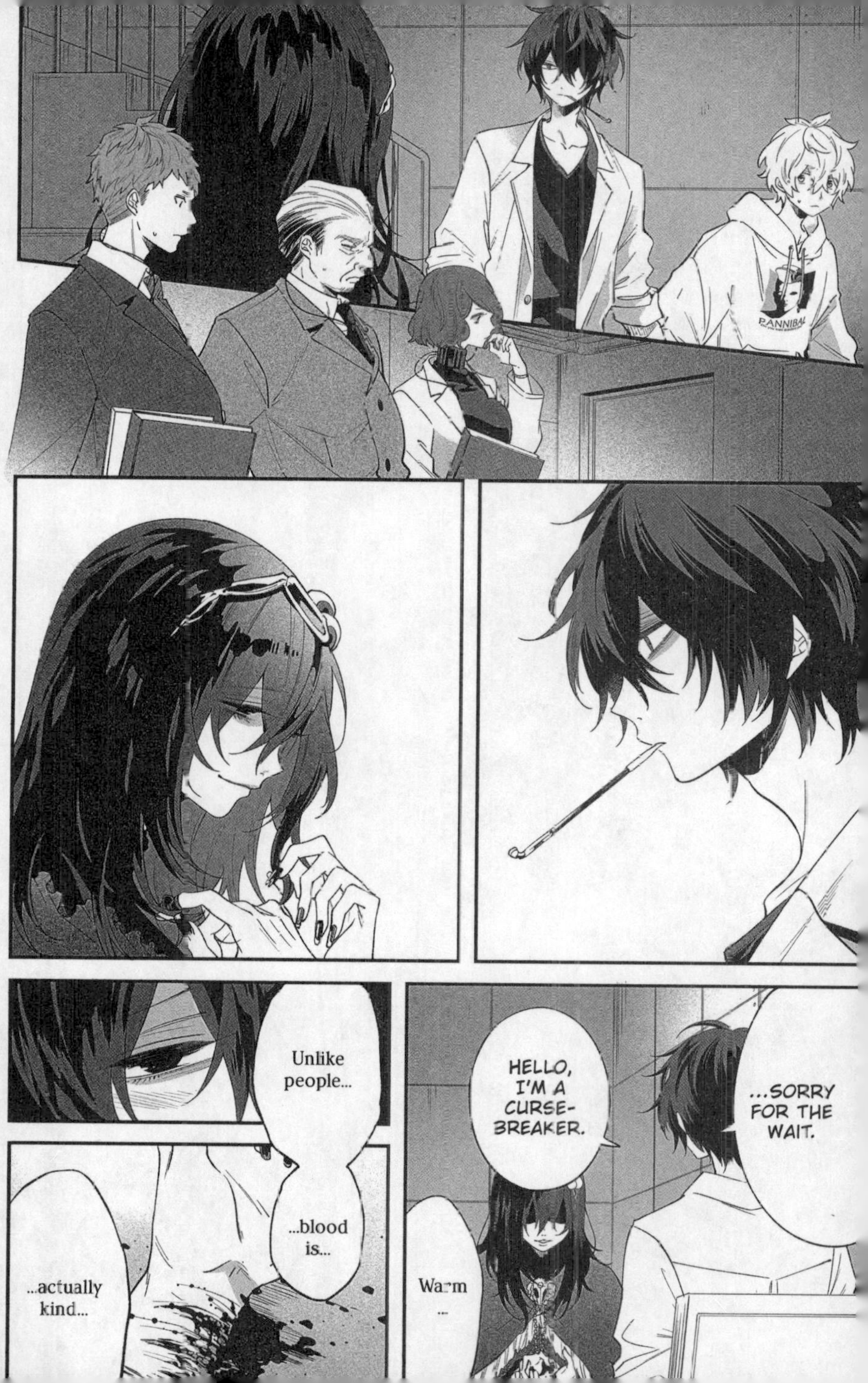
PANNIBAL
...SORRY FOR THE WAIT.
HELLO, I'M A CURSE-BREAKER.
Warm ...
Unlike people...
...blood is...
...actually kind...

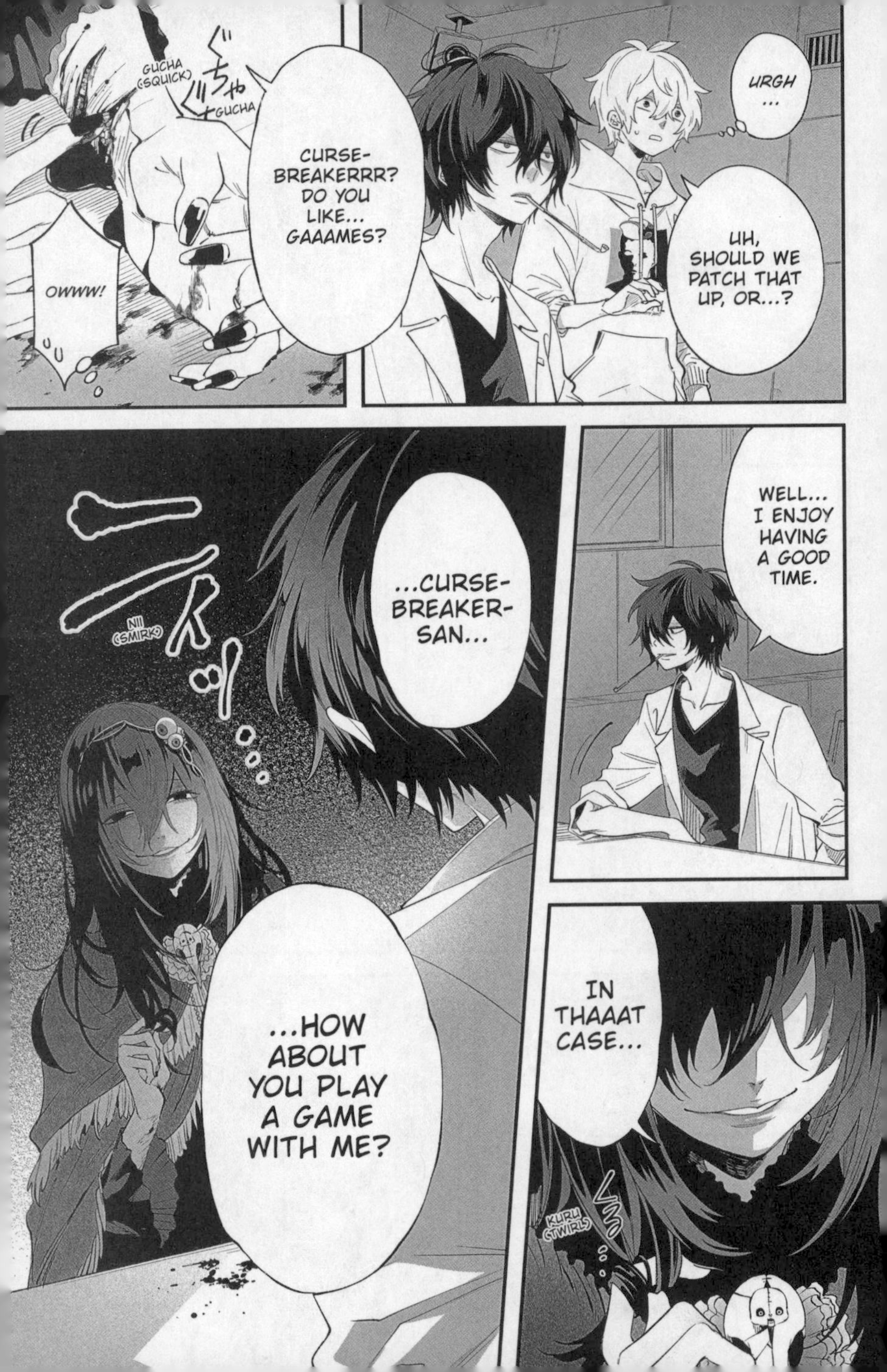
URGH ...
UH, SHOULD WE PATCH THAT UP, OR...?
CURSE-BREAKERRR? DO YOU LIKE... GAAAMES?
ぐちゃ
GUCHA (SQUICK)
ぐちゃ
GUCHA
OWWW!
WELL... I ENJOY HAVING A GOOD TIME.
IN THAAAT CASE...
KURU (TWIRL)
...CURSE-BREAKER-SAN...
ニイッ
NII (SMIRK)
...HOW ABOUT YOU PLAY A GAME WITH ME?

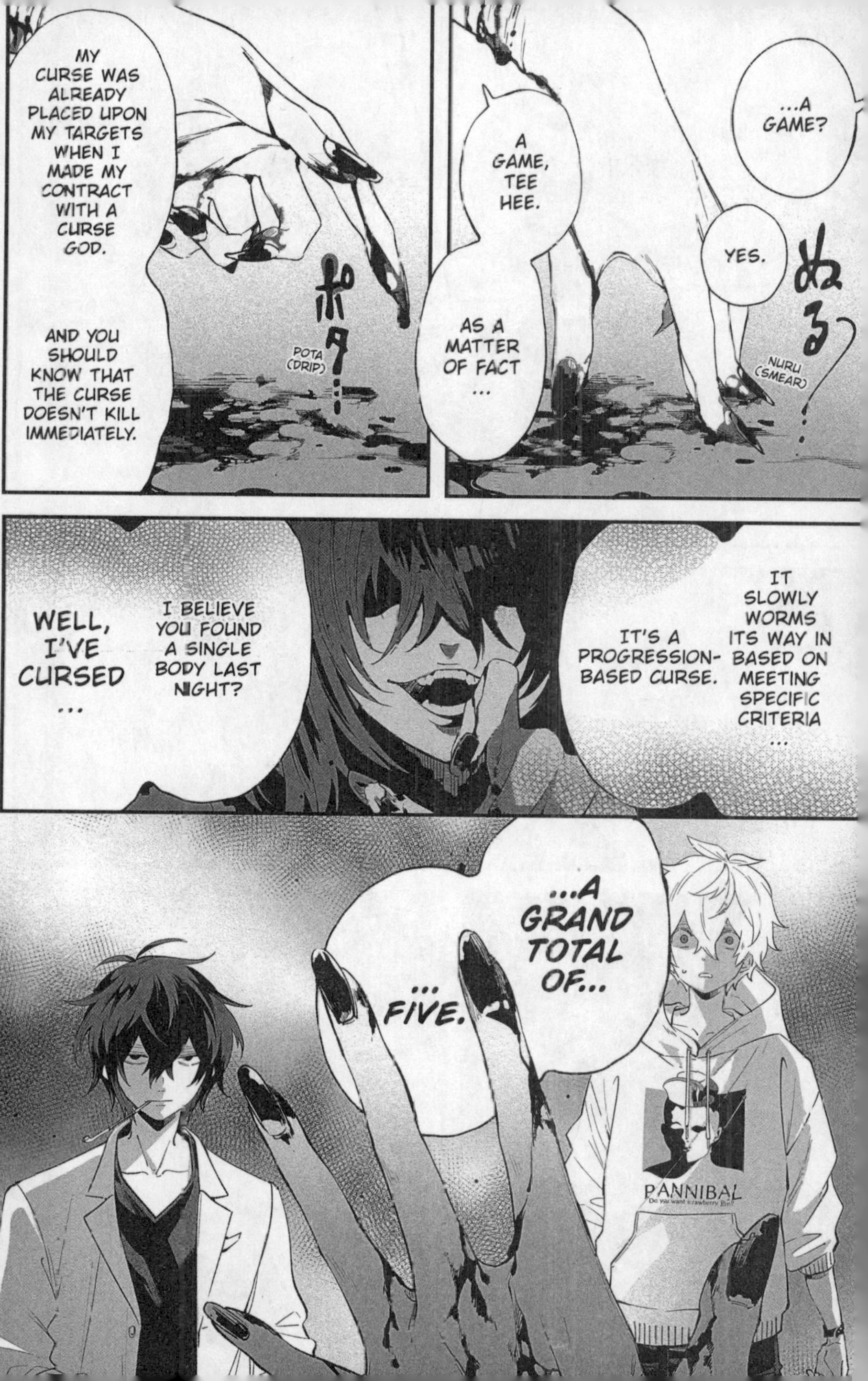
...A GAME?
A GAME, TEE HEE.
YES.
ぬる
NURU (SMEAR)
AS A MATTER OF FACT ...
MY CURSE WAS ALREADY PLACED UPON MY TARGETS WHEN I MADE MY CONTRACT WITH A CURSE GOD.
ポタ...
POTA (DRIP)
AND YOU SHOULD KNOW THAT THE CURSE DOESN'T KILL IMMEDIATELY.
IT SLOWLY WORMS ITS WAY IN BASED ON MEETING SPECIFIC CRITERIA ...
IT'S A PROGRESSION-BASED CURSE.
I BELIEVE YOU FOUND A SINGLE BODY LAST NIGHT?
WELL, I'VE CURSED ...
...A GRAND TOTAL OF...
... FIVE.
PANNIBAL

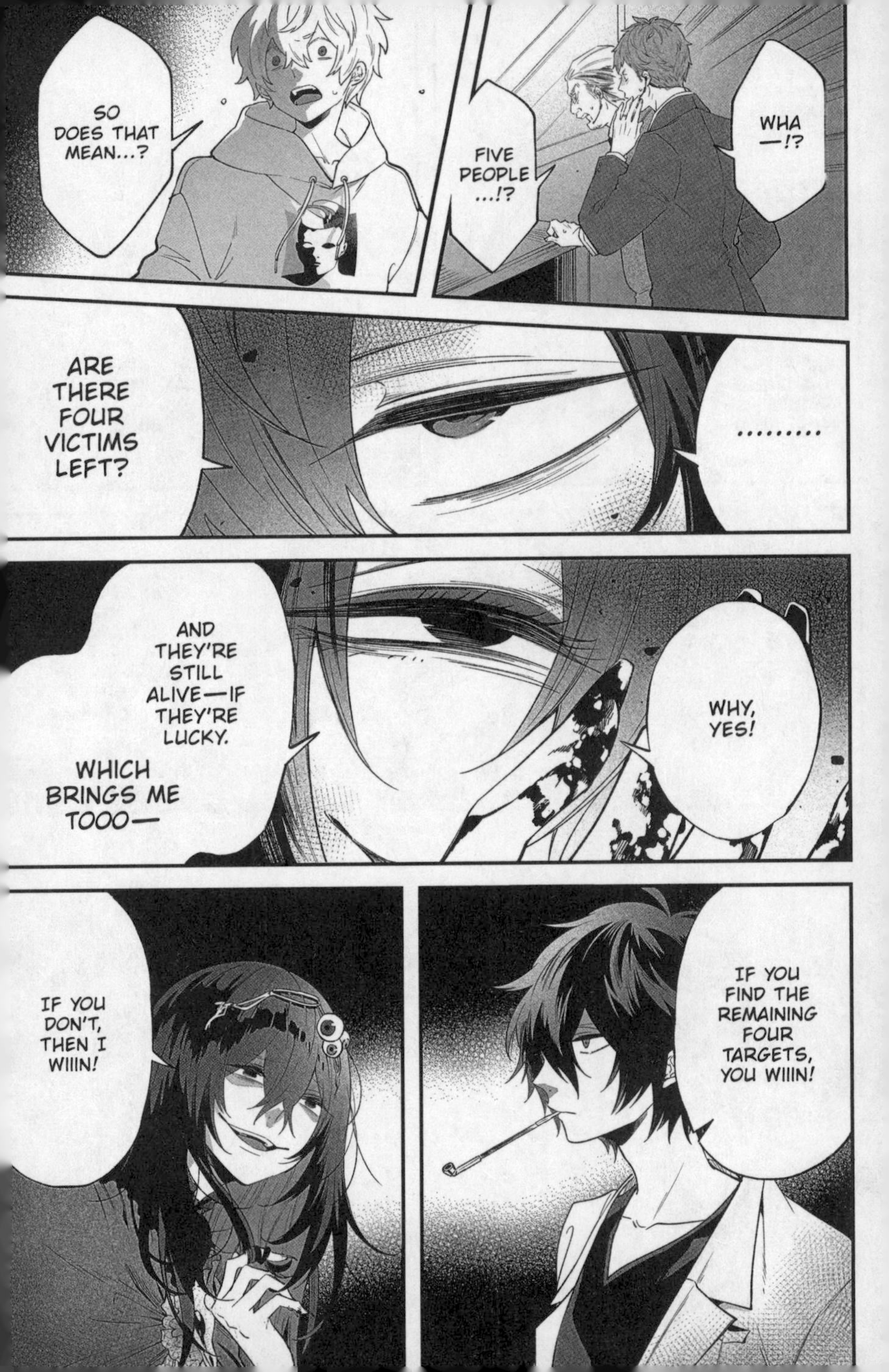
WHA—!?
FIVE PEOPLE...!?
SO DOES THAT MEAN...?
....
ARE THERE FOUR VICTIMS LEFT?
WHY, YES!
AND THEY'RE STILL ALIVE—IF THEY'RE LUCKY.
WHICH BRINGS ME TOOO—
IF YOU FIND THE REMAINING FOUR TARGETS, YOU WIIIN!
IF YOU DON'T, THEN I WIIIN!

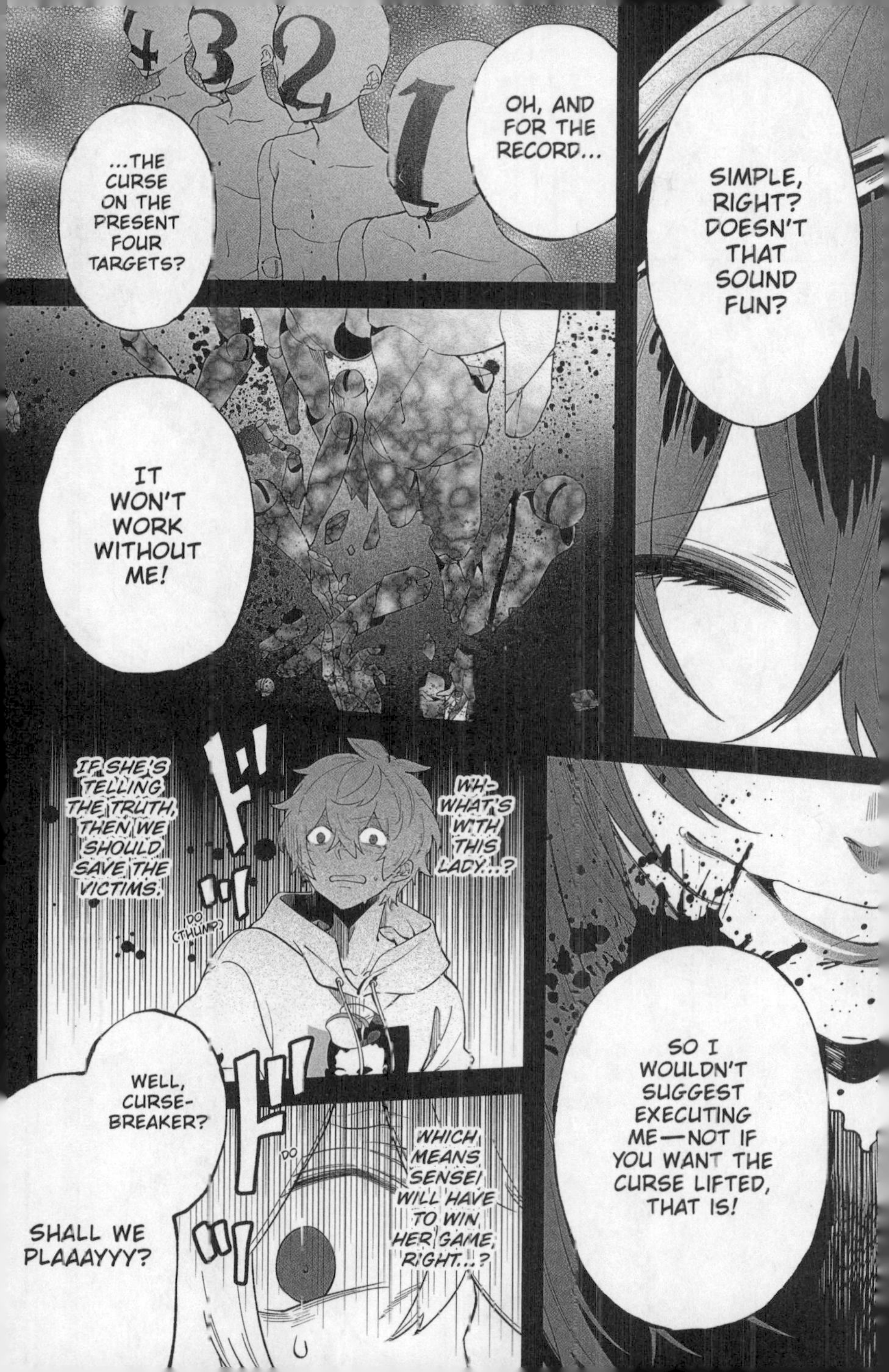
SIMPLE, RIGHT? DOESN'T THAT SOUND FUN?
OH, AND FOR THE RECORD...
...THE CURSE ON THE PRESENT FOUR TARGETS?
IT WON'T WORK WITHOUT ME!
SO I WOULDN'T SUGGEST EXECUTING ME—NOT IF YOU WANT THE CURSE LIFTED, THAT IS!
WH-WHAT'S WITH THIS LADY...?
IF SHE'S TELLING THE TRUTH, THEN WE SHOULD SAVE THE VICTIMS.
DO (THUMP)
WHICH MEANS SENSEI WILL HAVE TO WIN HER GAME, RIGHT...?
WELL, CURSE-BREAKER?
DO
SHALL WE PLAAAYYY?

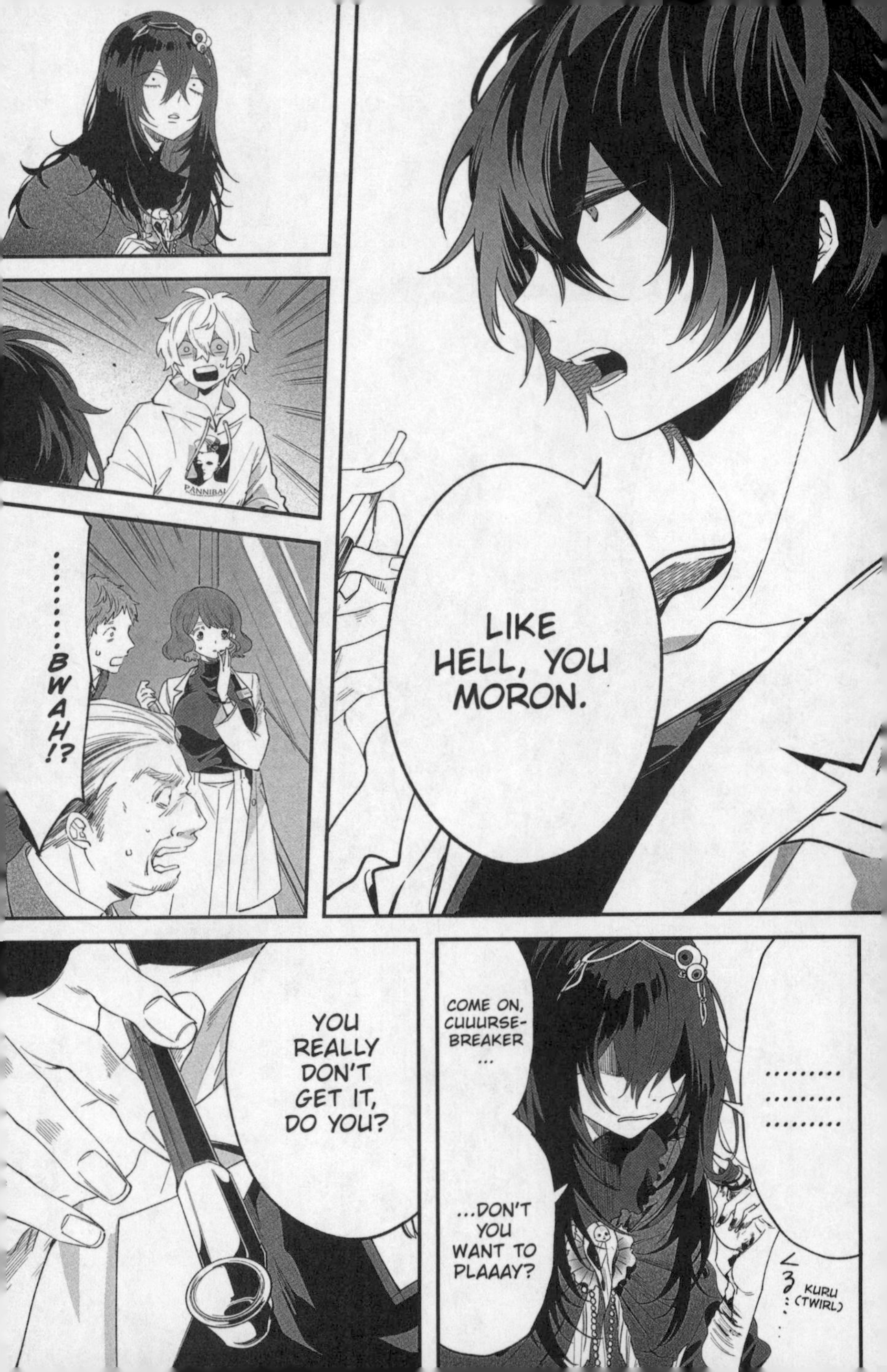
LIKE HELL, YOU MORON.
......BWAH!?
COME ON, CUUURSE-BREAKER...
....
...DON'T YOU WANT TO PLAAAY?
KURU (TWIRL)
YOU REALLY DON'T GET IT, DO YOU?

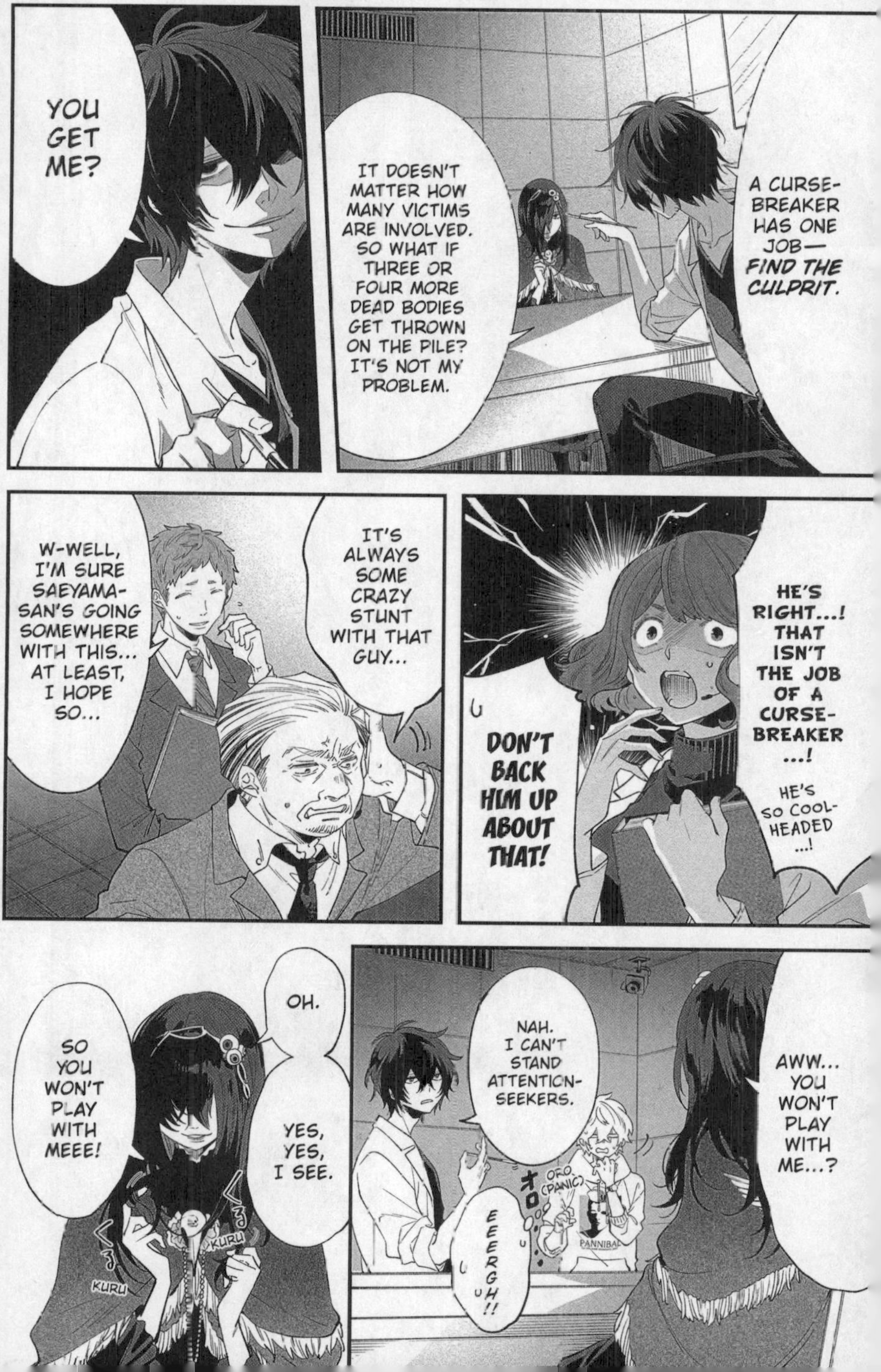
A CURSE-BREAKER HAS ONE JOB— *FIND THE CULPRIT.*
IT DOESN'T MATTER HOW MANY VICTIMS ARE INVOLVED. SO WHAT IF THREE OR FOUR MORE DEAD BODIES GET THROWN ON THE PILE? IT'S NOT MY PROBLEM.
YOU GET ME?
HE'S RIGHT...! THAT ISN'T THE JOB OF A CURSE-BREAKER ...!
HE'S SO COOL-HEADED ...!
DON'T BACK HIM UP ABOUT THAT!
IT'S ALWAYS SOME CRAZY STUNT WITH THAT GUY...
W-WELL, I'M SURE SAEYAMA-SAN'S GOING SOMEWHERE WITH THIS... AT LEAST, I HOPE SO...
AWW... YOU WON'T PLAY WITH ME...?
NAH. I CAN'T STAND ATTENTION-SEEKERS.
ORO (PANIC)
EEERGH!!
OH.
YES, YES, I SEE.
SO YOU WON'T PLAY WITH MEEE!
KURU
KURU

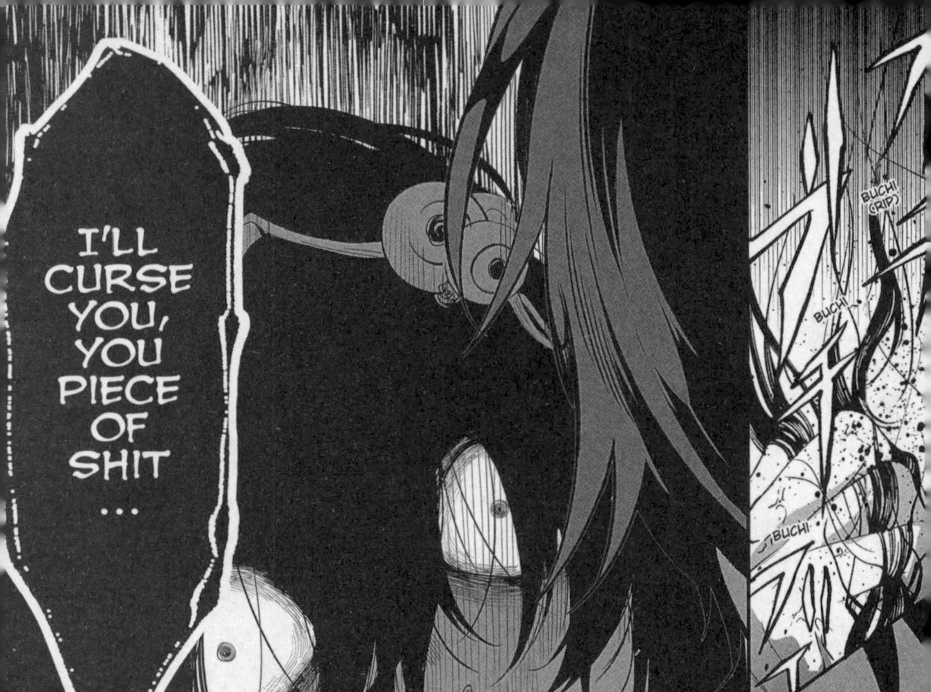
BUCHI (RIP)
BUCHI
BUCHI
I'LL CURSE YOU, YOU PIECE OF SHIT...
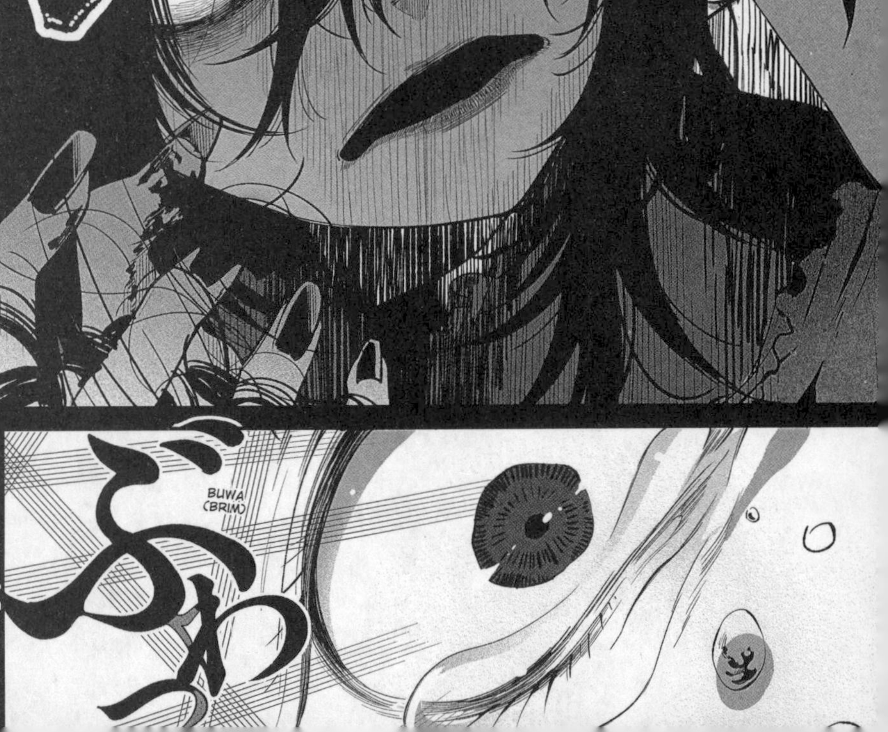
BUWA (BRIM)

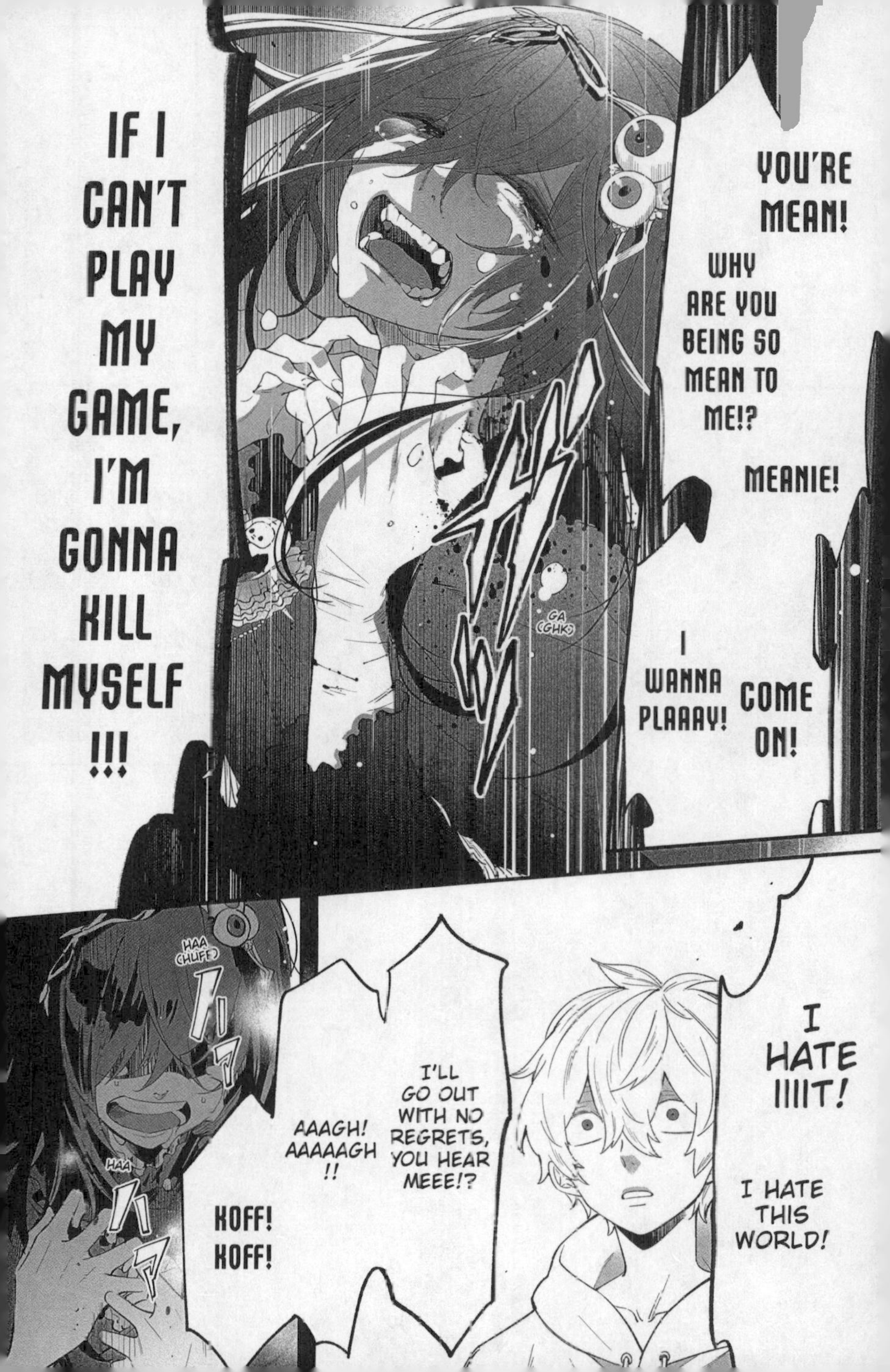
YOU'RE MEAN!
WHY ARE YOU BEING SO MEAN TO ME!?
MEANIE!
COME ON!
I WANNA PLAAAY!
GA (GHK)
IF I CAN'T PLAY MY GAME, I'M GONNA KILL MYSELF!!!
I HATE IIIIT!
I HATE THIS WORLD!
I'LL GO OUT WITH NO REGRETS, YOU HEAR MEEE!?
AAAGH! AAAAAGH!!
KOFF! KOFF!
HAA (HUFF)
HAA

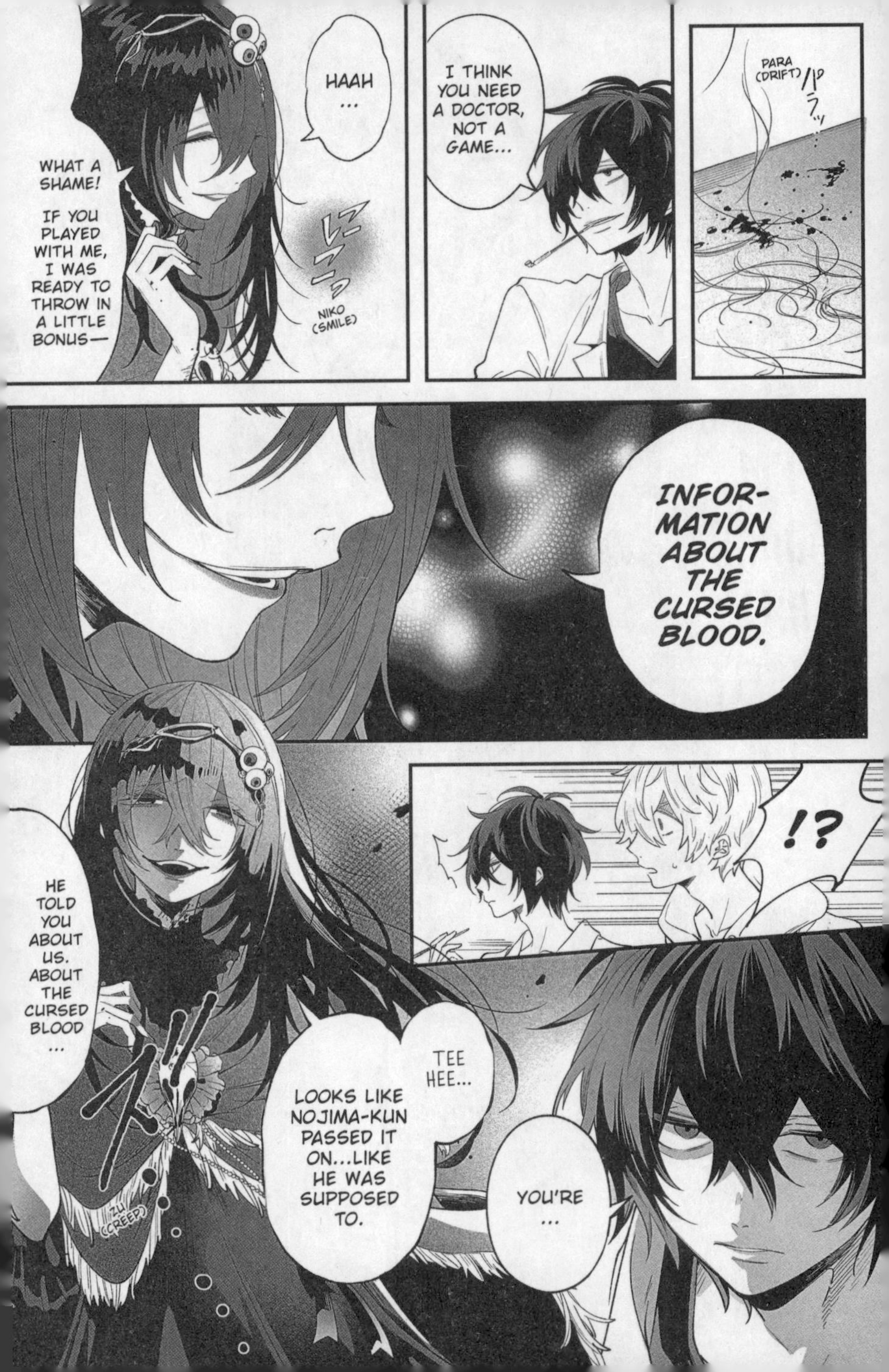

PARA (DRIFT)
I THINK YOU NEED A DOCTOR, NOT A GAME...
HAAH ...
WHAT A SHAME!
IF YOU PLAYED WITH ME, I WAS READY TO THROW IN A LITTLE BONUS—
NIKO (SMILE)
INFORMATION ABOUT THE CURSED BLOOD.
!?
YOU'RE ...
TEE HEE...
LOOKS LIKE NOJIMA-KUN PASSED IT ON...LIKE HE WAS SUPPOSED TO.
HE TOLD YOU ABOUT US. ABOUT THE CURSED BLOOD ...
ZU (CREEP)

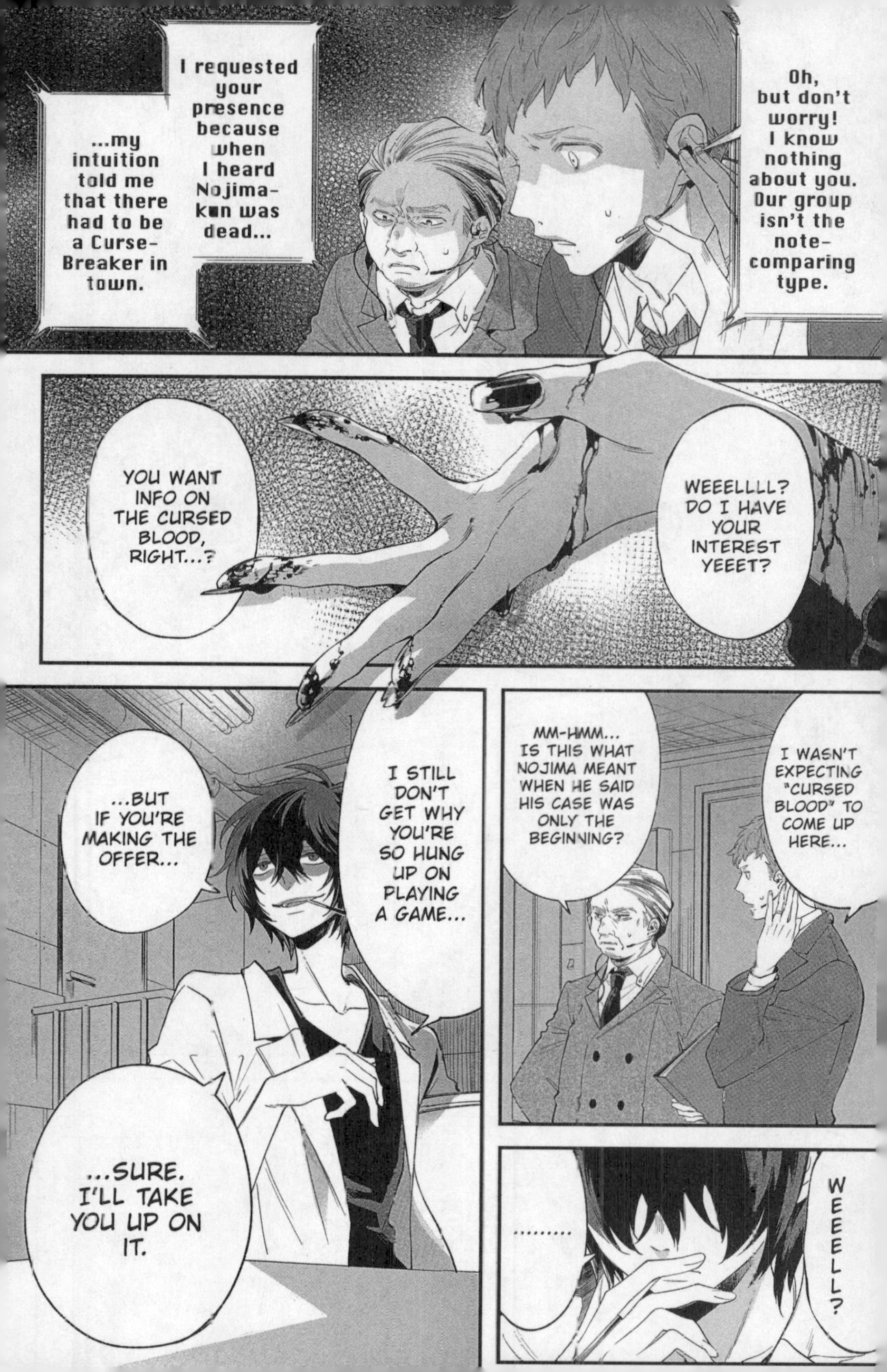
Oh, but don't worry! I know nothing about you. Our group isn't the note-comparing type.
I requested your presence because when I heard Nojima-kun was dead...
...my intuition told me that there had to be a Curse-Breaker in town.
WEEELLLL? DO I HAVE YOUR INTEREST YEEET?
YOU WANT INFO ON THE CURSED BLOOD, RIGHT...?
I WASN'T EXPECTING "CURSED BLOOD" TO COME UP HERE...
MM-HMM... IS THIS WHAT NOJIMA MEANT WHEN HE SAID HIS CASE WAS ONLY THE BEGINNING?
WEEELL?
....
I STILL DON'T GET WHY YOU'RE SO HUNG UP ON PLAYING A GAME...
...BUT IF YOU'RE MAKING THE OFFER...
...SURE. I'LL TAKE YOU UP ON IT.

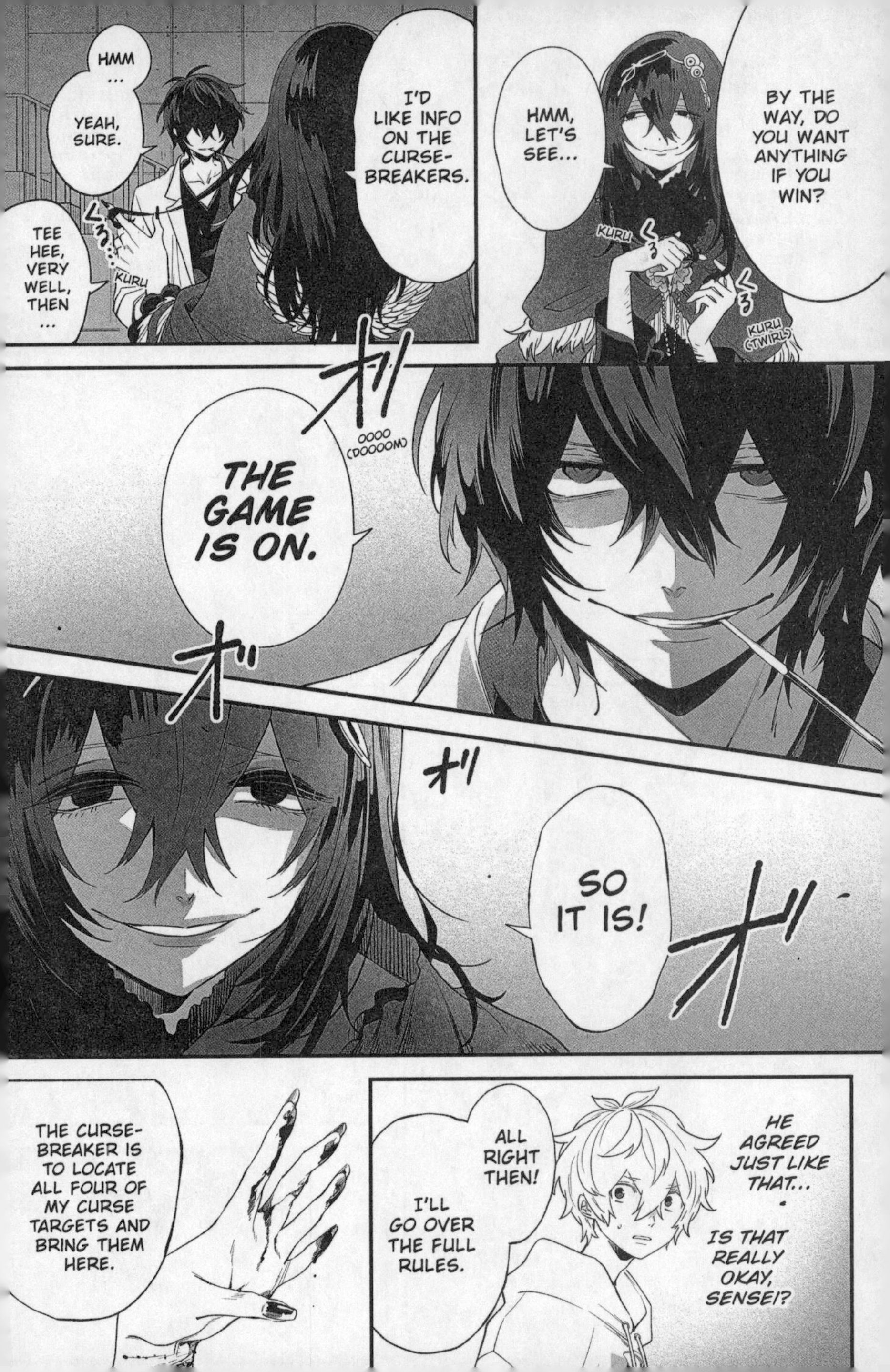
BY THE WAY, DO YOU WANT ANYTHING IF YOU WIN?
HMM, LET'S SEE...
KURU
KURU (TWIRL)
I'D LIKE INFO ON THE CURSE-BREAKERS.
HMM... YEAH, SURE.
TEE HEE, VERY WELL, THEN...
KURU
OOOO (DOOOOM)
THE GAME IS ON.
SO IT IS!
HE AGREED JUST LIKE THAT...
IS THAT REALLY OKAY, SENSEI?
ALL RIGHT THEN!
I'LL GO OVER THE FULL RULES.
THE CURSE-BREAKER IS TO LOCATE ALL FOUR OF MY CURSE TARGETS AND BRING THEM HERE.

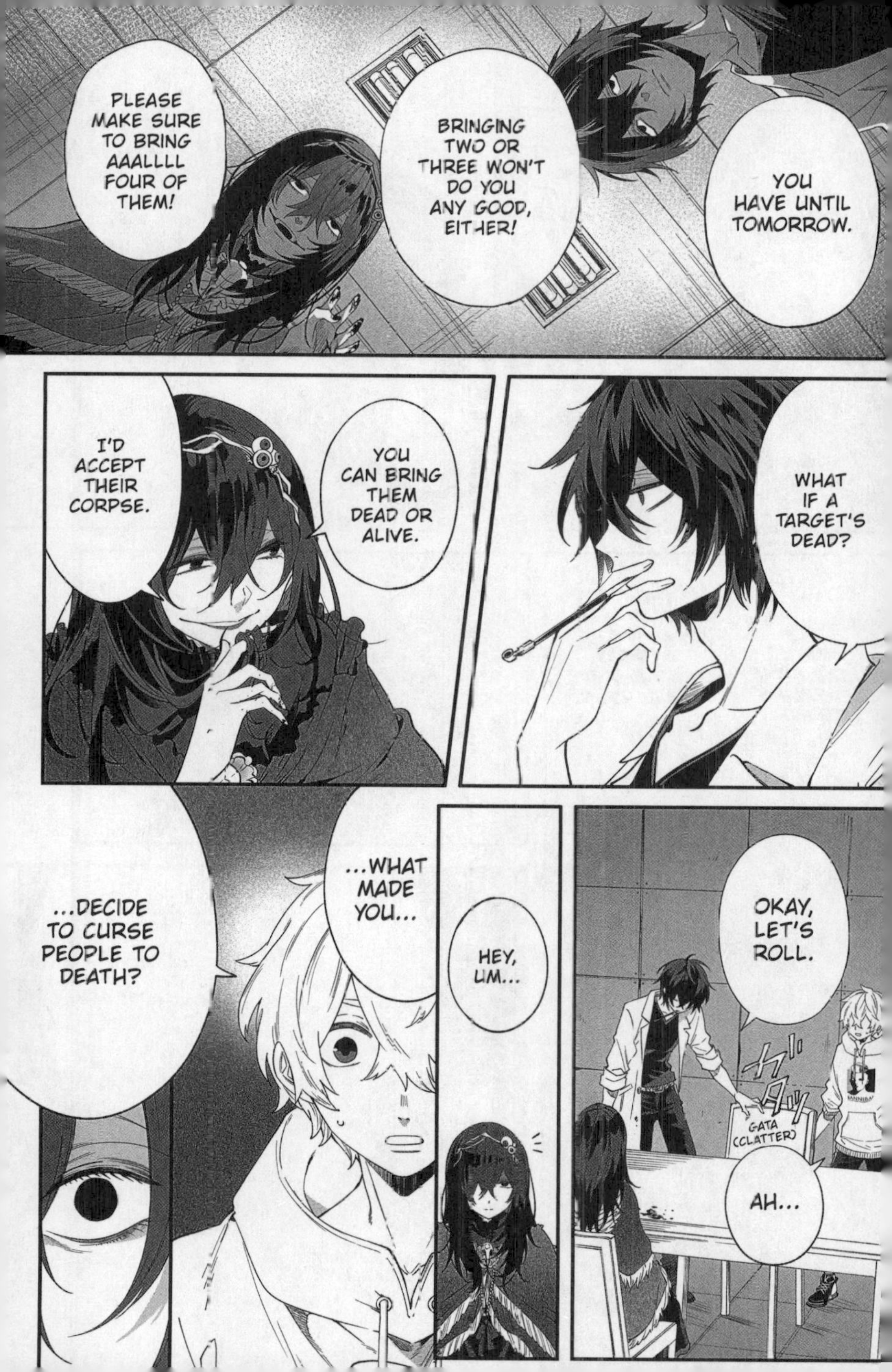
YOU HAVE UNTIL TOMORROW.
BRINGING TWO OR THREE WON'T DO YOU ANY GOOD, EITHER!
PLEASE MAKE SURE TO BRING AAALLLL FOUR OF THEM!
WHAT IF A TARGET'S DEAD?
YOU CAN BRING THEM DEAD OR ALIVE.
I'D ACCEPT THEIR CORPSE.
OKAY, LET'S ROLL.
GATA (CLATTER)
AH...
HEY, UM...
...WHAT MADE YOU...
...DECIDE TO CURSE PEOPLE TO DEATH?

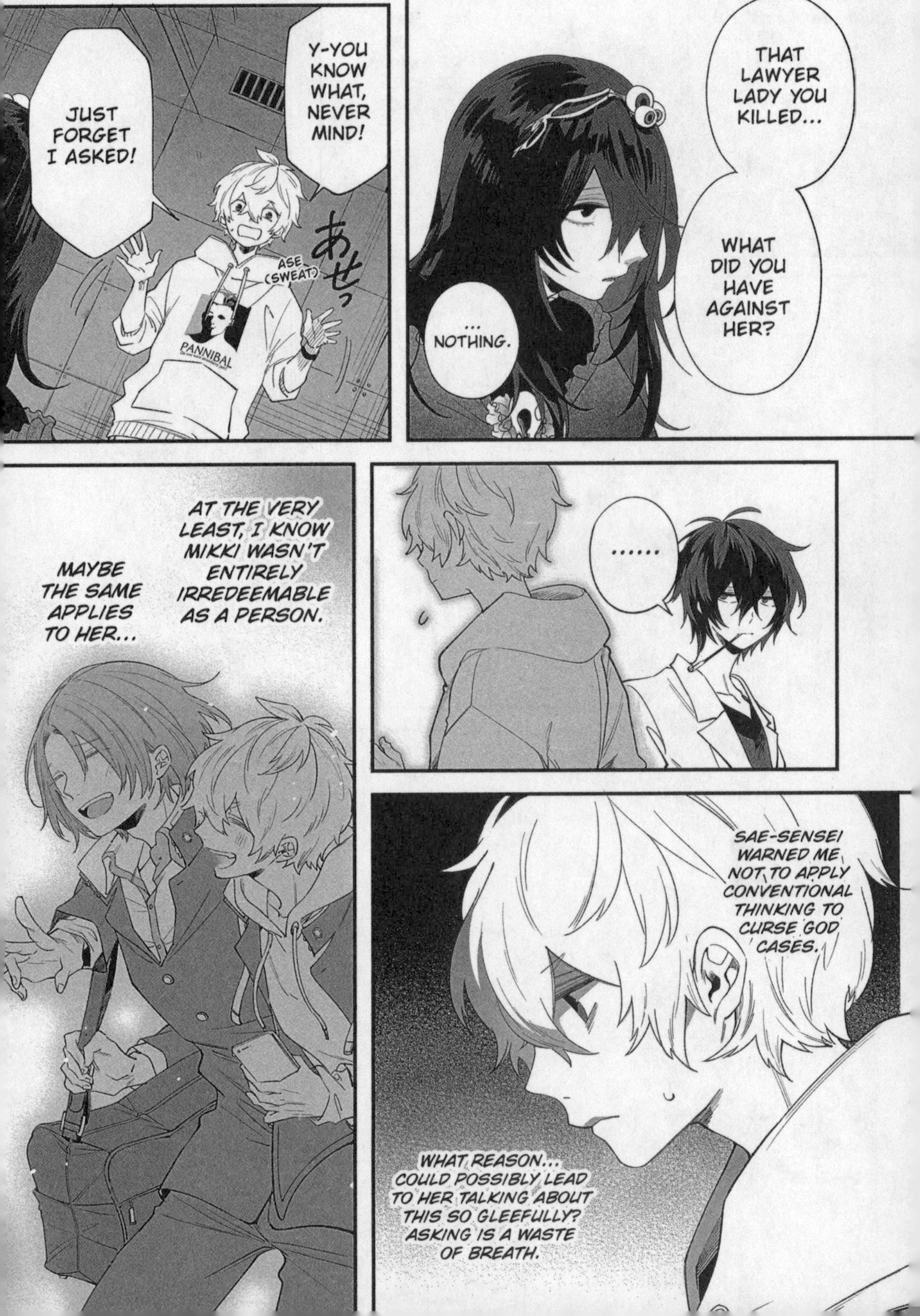
THAT LAWYER LADY YOU KILLED...
WHAT DID YOU HAVE AGAINST HER?
... NOTHING.
Y-YOU KNOW WHAT, NEVER MIND!
JUST FORGET I ASKED!
あせっ
ASE (SWEAT)
PANNIBAL
......
SAE-SENSEI WARNED ME NOT TO APPLY CONVENTIONAL THINKING TO CURSE GOD CASES.
WHAT REASON... COULD POSSIBLY LEAD TO HER TALKING ABOUT THIS SO GLEEFULLY? ASKING IS A WASTE OF BREATH.
AT THE VERY LEAST, I KNOW MIKKI WASN'T ENTIRELY IRREDEEMABLE AS A PERSON.
MAYBE THE SAME APPLIES TO HER...

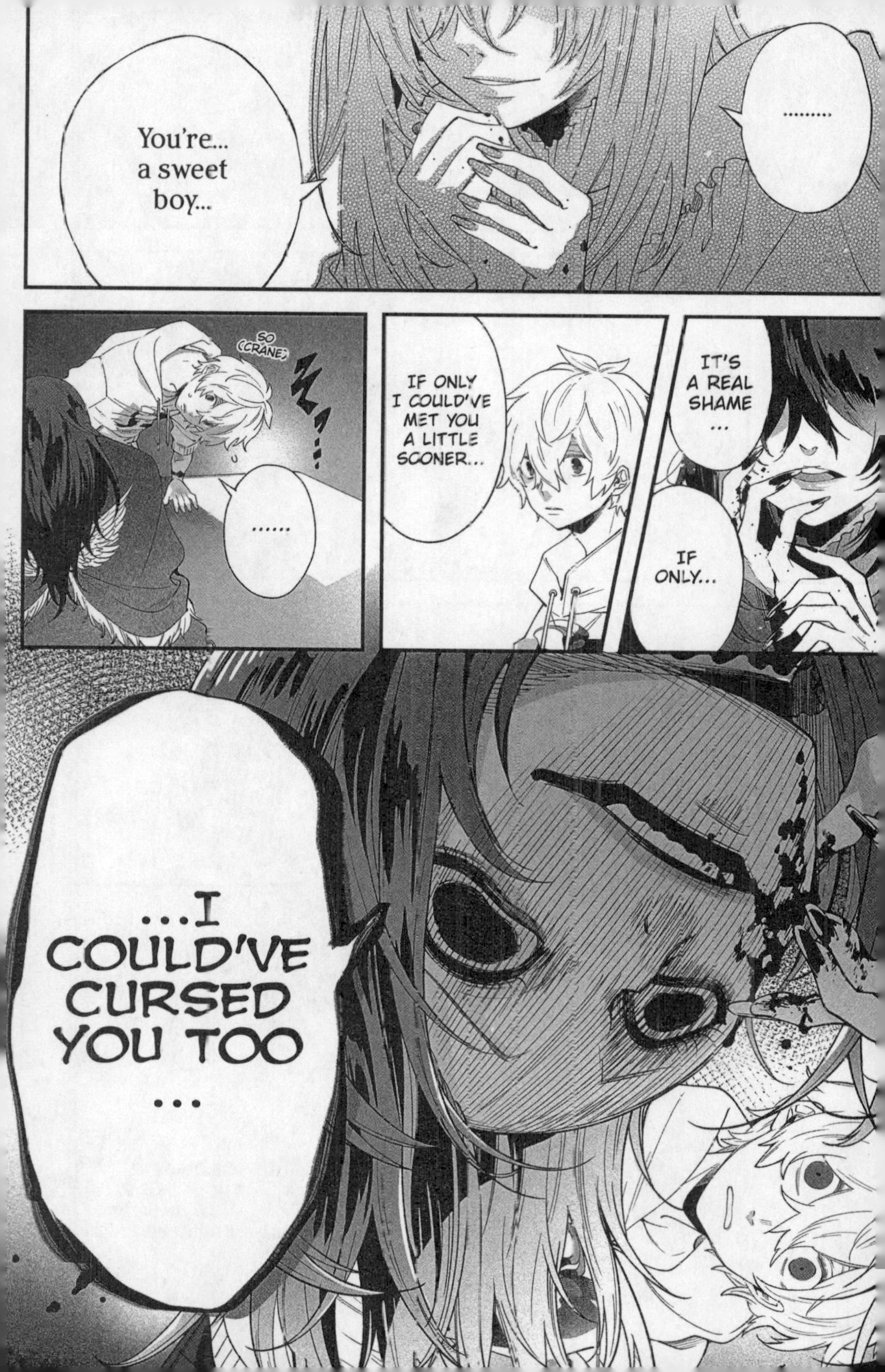
....
You're... a sweet boy...
IT'S A REAL SHAME ...
IF ONLY...
IF ONLY I COULD'VE MET YOU A LITTLE SOONER...
SO (CRANE)
......
...I COULD'VE CURSED YOU TOO ...

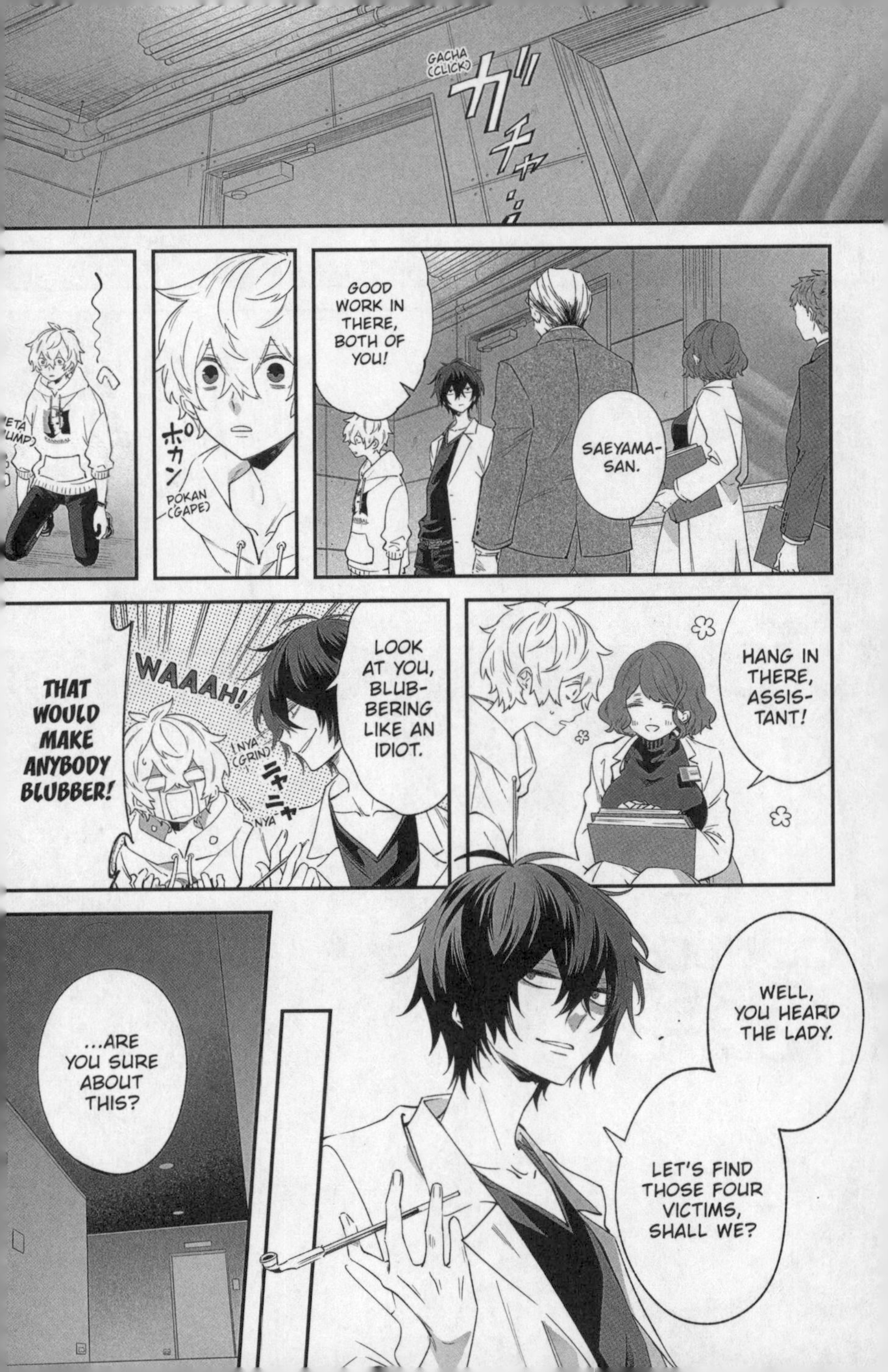
GACHA (CLICK)
ガチャ
GOOD WORK IN THERE, BOTH OF YOU!
SAEYAMA-SAN.
ポカン
POKAN (GAPE)
HANG IN THERE, ASSISTANT!
LOOK AT YOU, BLUBBERING LIKE AN IDIOT.
NYA (GRIN)
ニャニャ
NYA
WAAAH!
THAT WOULD MAKE ANYBODY BLUBBER!
WELL, YOU HEARD THE LADY.
LET'S FIND THOSE FOUR VICTIMS, SHALL WE?
...ARE YOU SURE ABOUT THIS?

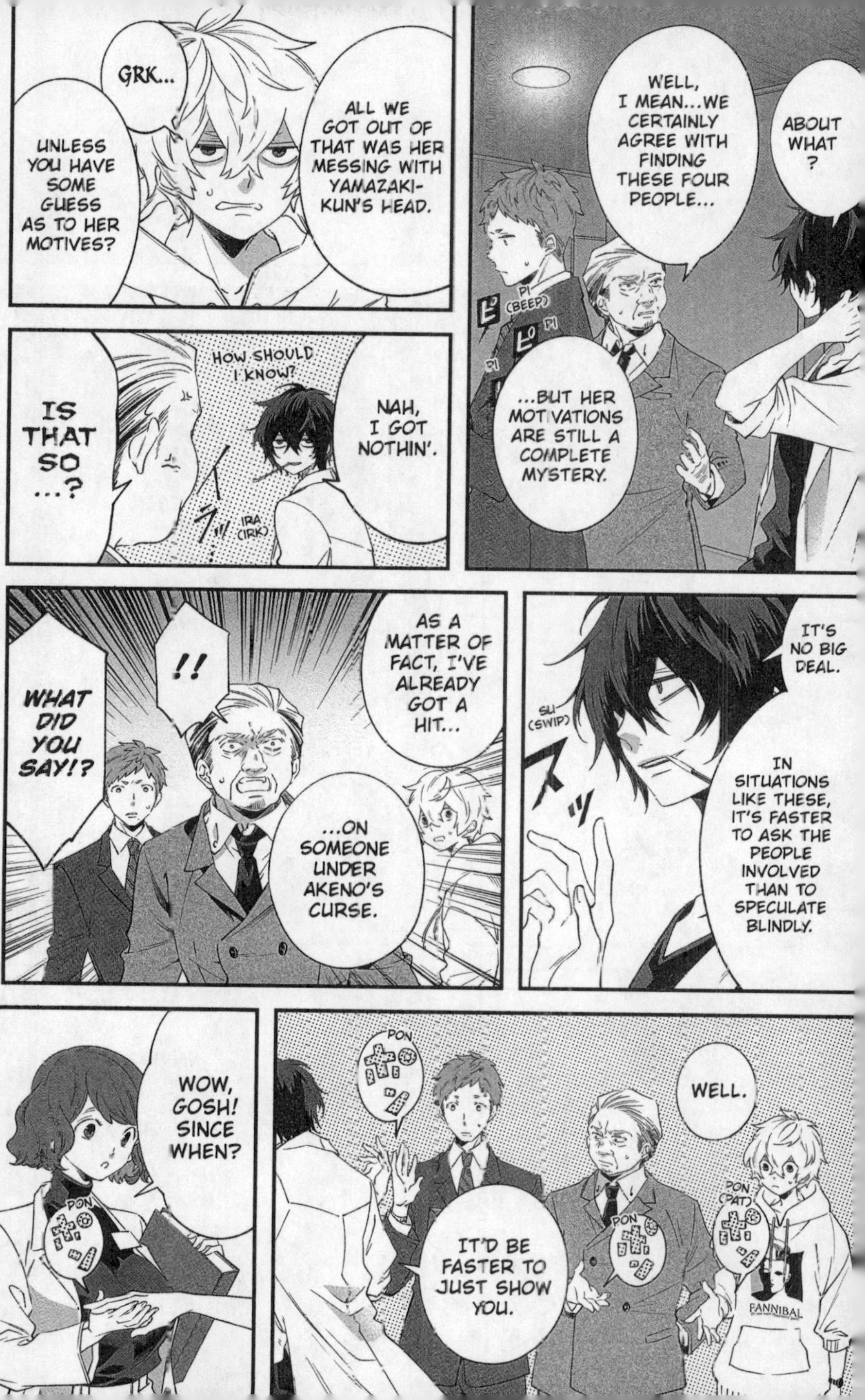
ABOUT WHAT?
WELL, I MEAN...WE CERTAINLY AGREE WITH FINDING THESE FOUR PEOPLE...
PI (BEEP)
PI
PI
...BUT HER MOTIVATIONS ARE STILL A COMPLETE MYSTERY.
ALL WE GOT OUT OF THAT WAS HER MESSING WITH YAMAZAKI-KUN'S HEAD.
GRK...
UNLESS YOU HAVE SOME GUESS AS TO HER MOTIVES?
NAH, I GOT NOTHIN'.
HOW SHOULD I KNOW?
IRA (IRK)
IS THAT SO ...?
IT'S NO BIG DEAL.
SU (SWIP)
IN SITUATIONS LIKE THESE, IT'S FASTER TO ASK THE PEOPLE INVOLVED THAN TO SPECULATE BLINDLY.
AS A MATTER OF FACT, I'VE ALREADY GOT A HIT...
!!
...ON SOMEONE UNDER AKENO'S CURSE.
WHAT DID YOU SAY!?
WELL.
PON (PAT)
FANNIBAL
PON
IT'D BE FASTER TO JUST SHOW YOU.
PON
WOW, GOSH! SINCE WHEN?
PON

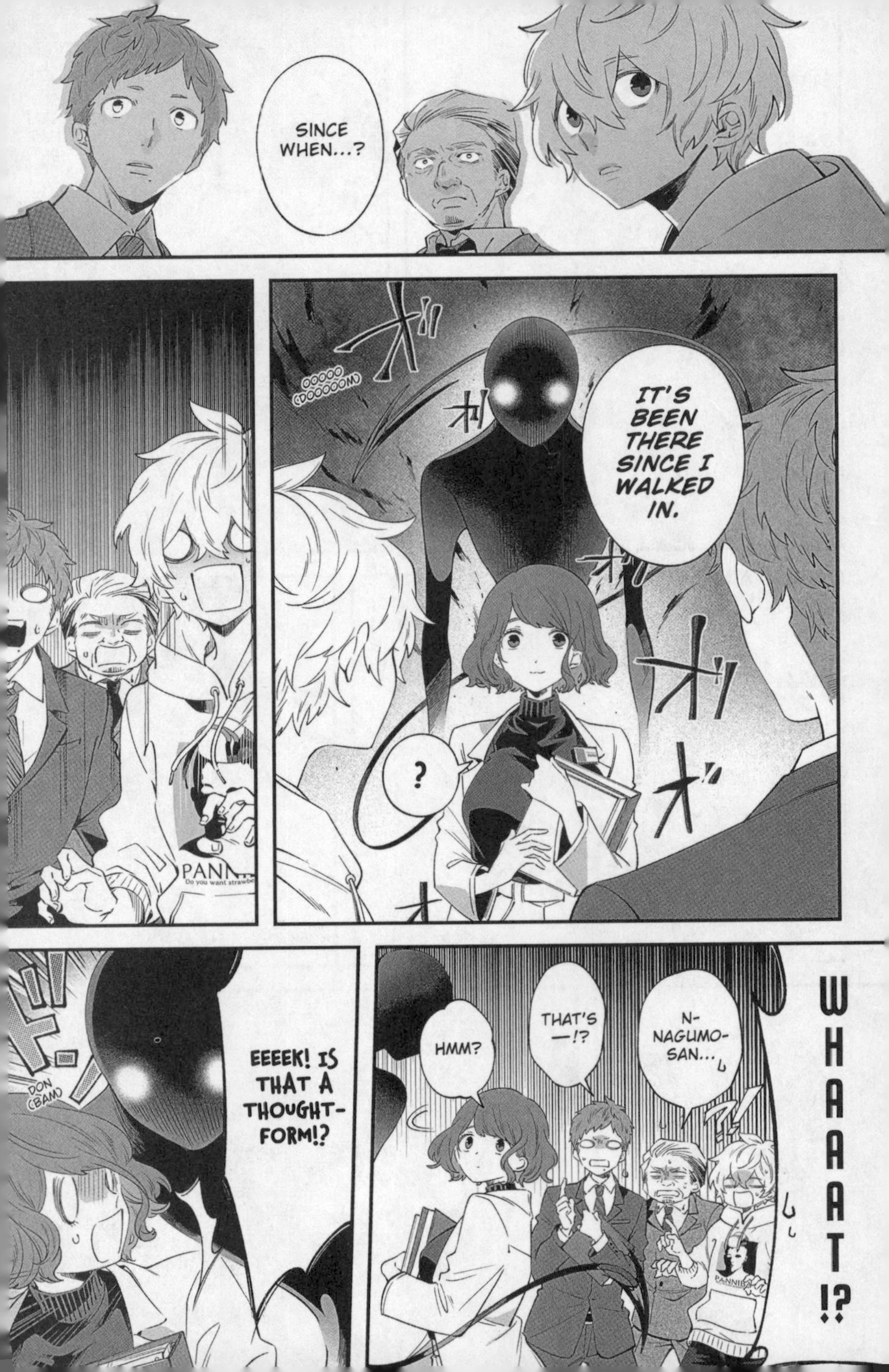
SINCE WHEN...?
IT'S BEEN THERE SINCE I WALKED IN.
OOOOO (DOOOOOM)
?
WHAAAT!?
N-NAGUMO-SAN...
THAT'S—!?
HMM?
DON (BAM)
EEEEK! IS THAT A THOUGHT-FORM!?

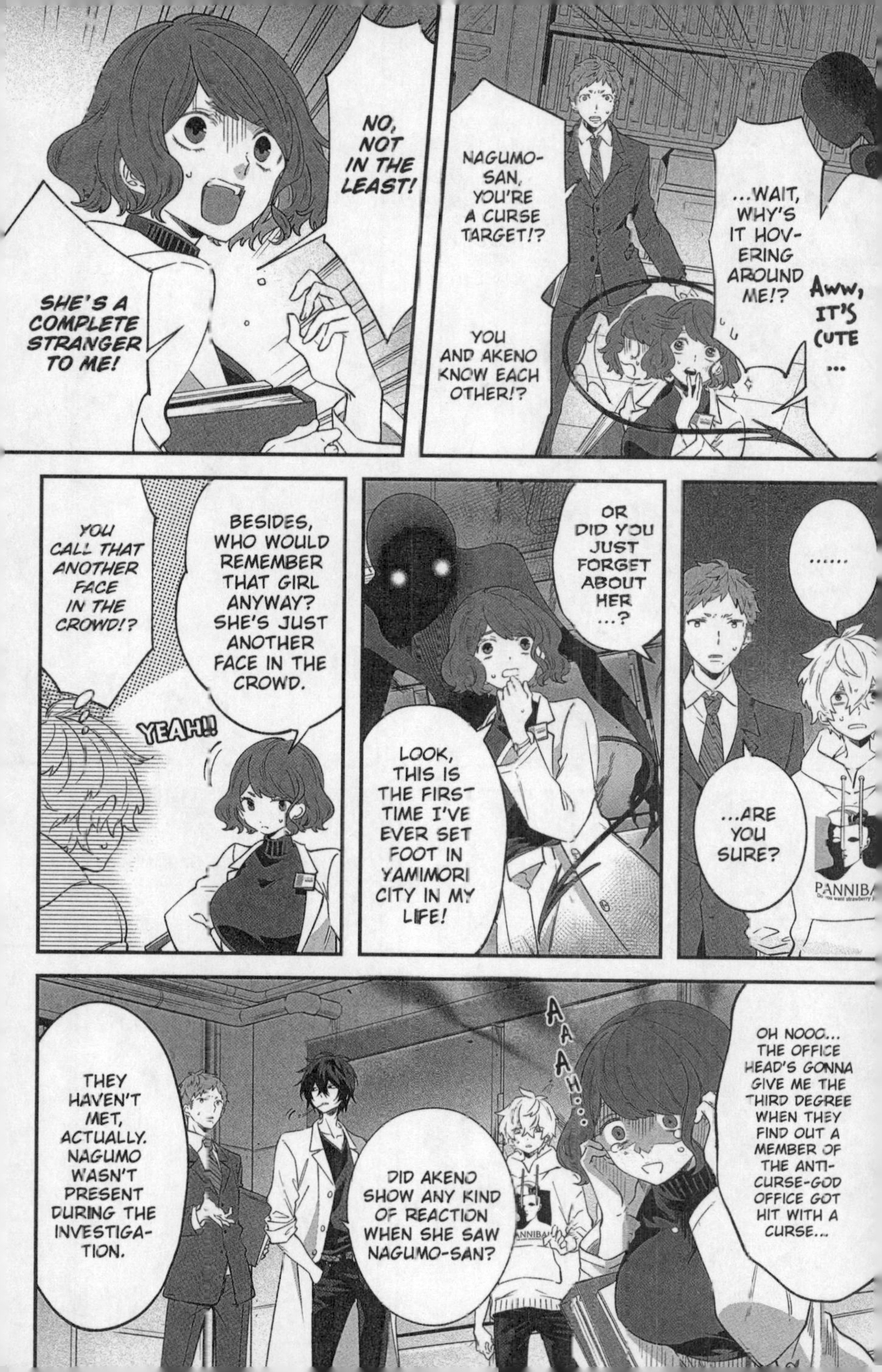
...WAIT, WHY'S IT HOV-ERING AROUND ME!?
Aww, IT'S CUTE...
NAGUMO-SAN, YOU'RE A CURSE TARGET!?
YOU AND AKENO KNOW EACH OTHER!?
NO, NOT IN THE LEAST!
SHE'S A COMPLETE STRANGER TO ME!
......
...ARE YOU SURE?
PANNIBA
OR DID YOU JUST FORGET ABOUT HER...?
LOOK, THIS IS THE FIRST-TIME I'VE EVER SET FOOT IN YAMIMORI CITY IN MY LIFE!
BESIDES, WHO WOULD REMEMBER THAT GIRL ANYWAY? SHE'S JUST ANOTHER FACE IN THE CROWD.
YEAH!!
YOU CALL THAT ANOTHER FACE IN THE CROWD!?
OH NOOO... THE OFFICE HEAD'S GONNA GIVE ME THE THIRD DEGREE WHEN THEY FIND OUT A MEMBER OF THE ANTI-CURSE-GOD OFFICE GOT HIT WITH A CURSE...
AAAAH...
DID AKENO SHOW ANY KIND OF REACTION WHEN SHE SAW NAGUMO-SAN?
THEY HAVEN'T MET, ACTUALLY. NAGUMO WASN'T PRESENT DURING THE INVESTIGA-TION.

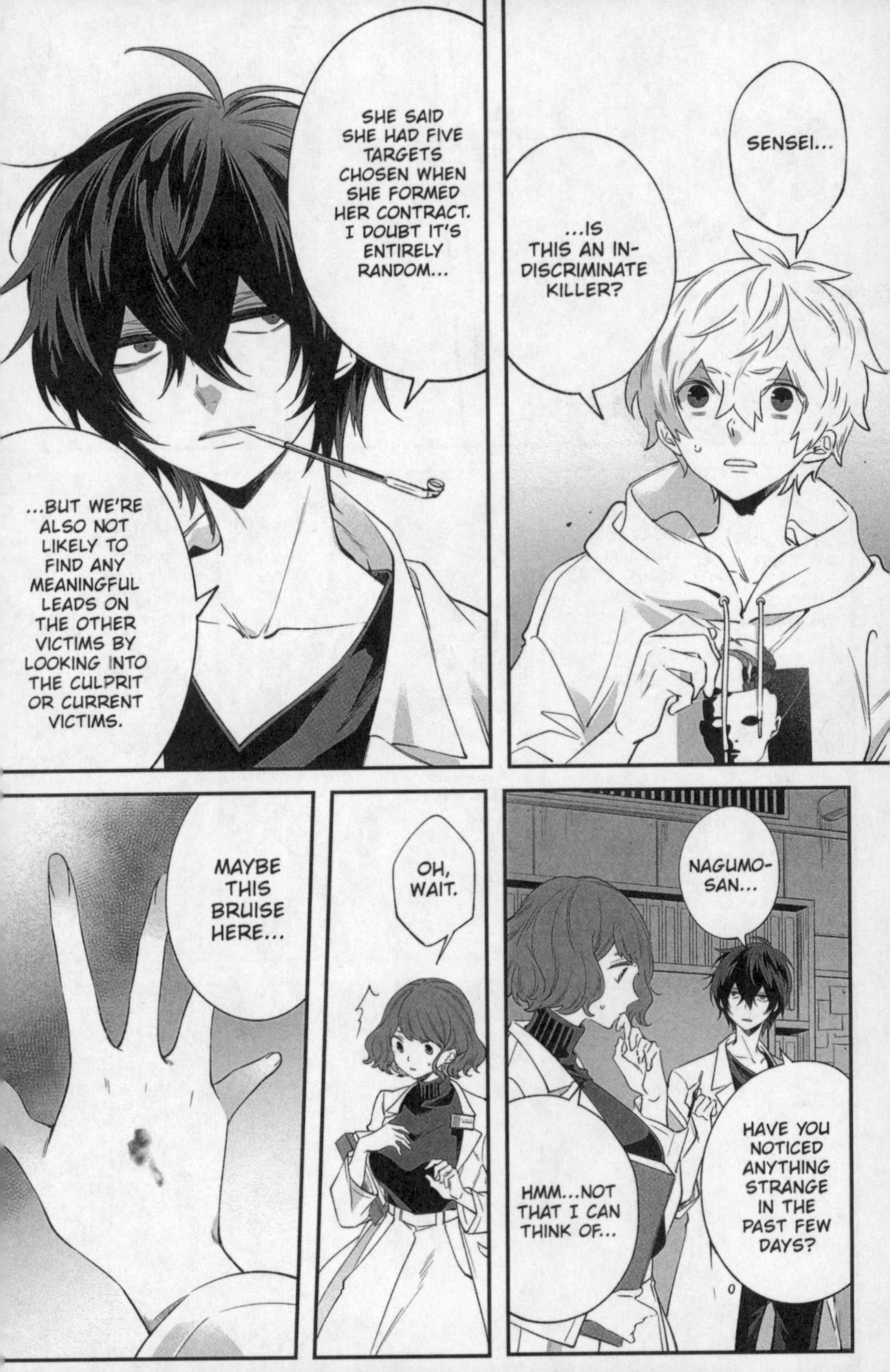
SENSEI...
...IS THIS AN IN-DISCRIMINATE KILLER?
SHE SAID SHE HAD FIVE TARGETS CHOSEN WHEN SHE FORMED HER CONTRACT. I DOUBT IT'S ENTIRELY RANDOM...
...BUT WE'RE ALSO NOT LIKELY TO FIND ANY MEANINGFUL LEADS ON THE OTHER VICTIMS BY LOOKING INTO THE CULPRIT OR CURRENT VICTIMS.
NAGUMO-SAN...
HAVE YOU NOTICED ANYTHING STRANGE IN THE PAST FEW DAYS?
HMM...NOT THAT I CAN THINK OF...
OH, WAIT.
MAYBE THIS BRUISE HERE...

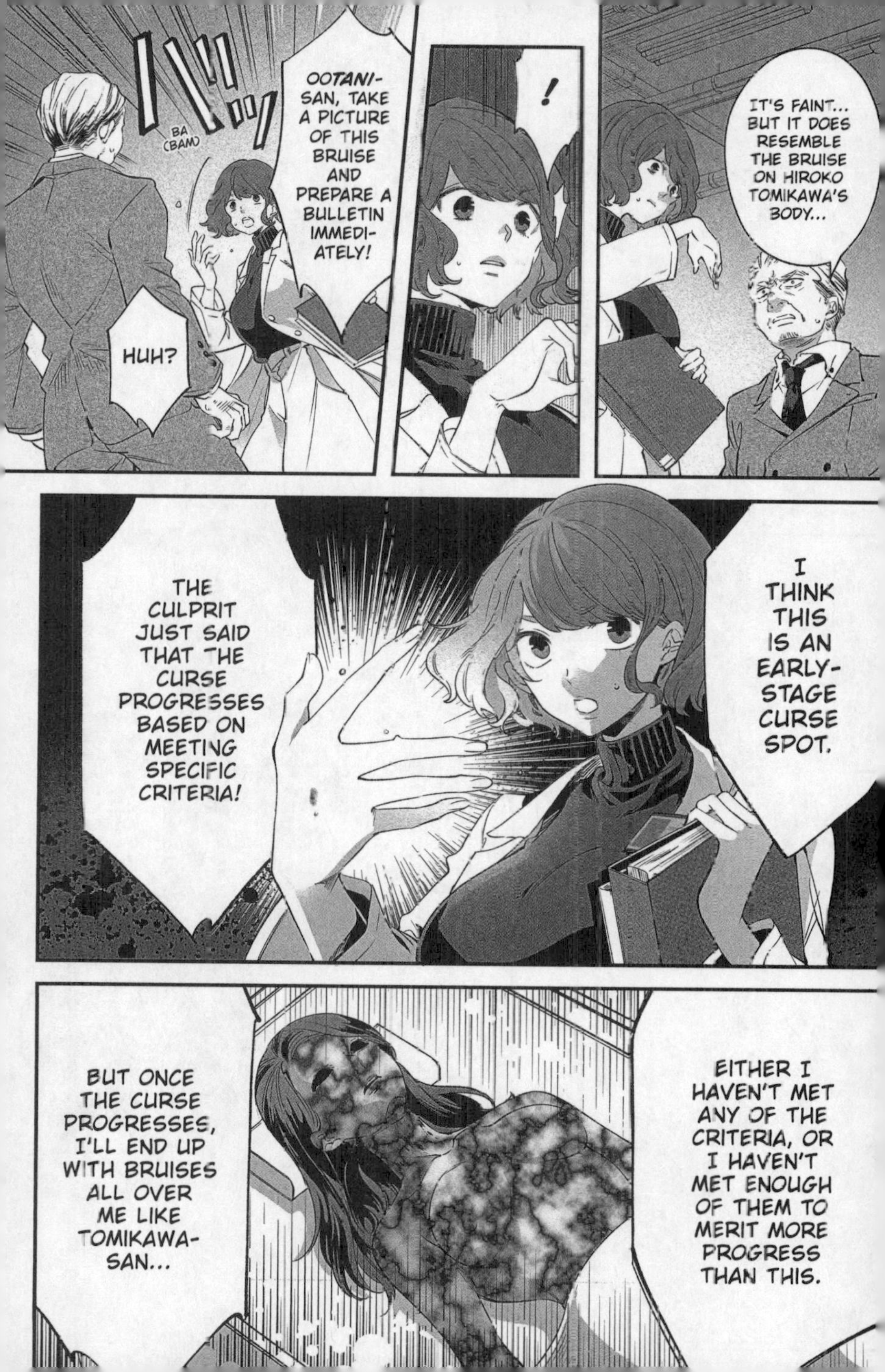
IT'S FAINT... BUT IT DOES RESEMBLE THE BRUISE ON HIROKO TOMIKAWA'S BODY...
!
OOTANI-SAN, TAKE A PICTURE OF THIS BRUISE AND PREPARE A BULLETIN IMMEDIATELY!
BA (BAM)
HUH?
I THINK THIS IS AN EARLY-STAGE CURSE SPOT.
THE CULPRIT JUST SAID THAT THE CURSE PROGRESSES BASED ON MEETING SPECIFIC CRITERIA!
EITHER I HAVEN'T MET ANY OF THE CRITERIA, OR I HAVEN'T MET ENOUGH OF THEM TO MERIT MORE PROGRESS THAN THIS.
BUT ONCE THE CURSE PROGRESSES, I'LL END UP WITH BRUISES ALL OVER ME LIKE TOMIKAWA-SAN...

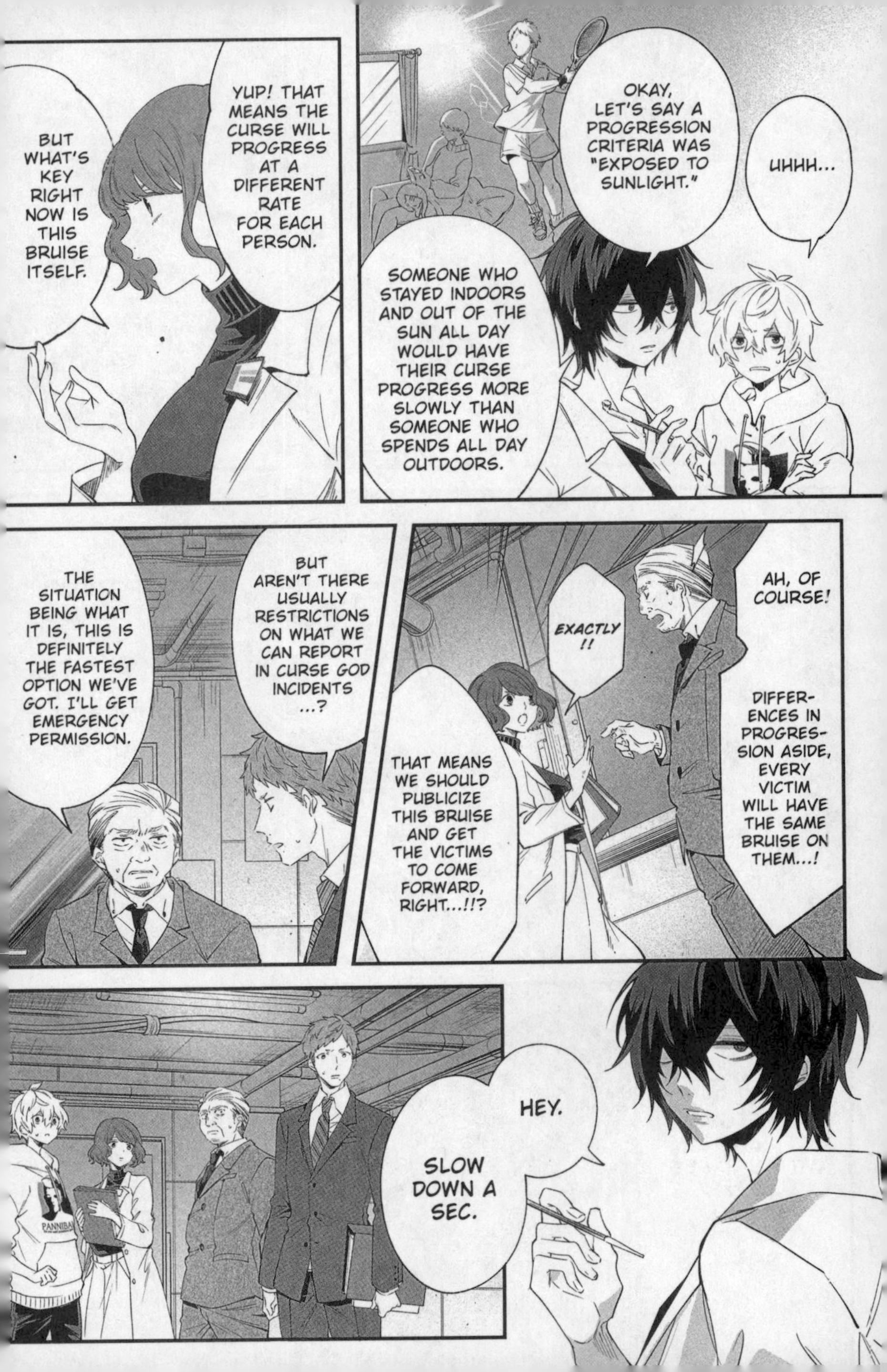
UHHH...
OKAY, LET'S SAY A PROGRESSION CRITERIA WAS "EXPOSED TO SUNLIGHT."
SOMEONE WHO STAYED INDOORS AND OUT OF THE SUN ALL DAY WOULD HAVE THEIR CURSE PROGRESS MORE SLOWLY THAN SOMEONE WHO SPENDS ALL DAY OUTDOORS.
YUP! THAT MEANS THE CURSE WILL PROGRESS AT A DIFFERENT RATE FOR EACH PERSON.
BUT WHAT'S KEY RIGHT NOW IS THIS BRUISE ITSELF.
AH, OF COURSE!
DIFFERENCES IN PROGRESSION ASIDE, EVERY VICTIM WILL HAVE THE SAME BRUISE ON THEM...!
EXACTLY!!
THAT MEANS WE SHOULD PUBLICIZE THIS BRUISE AND GET THE VICTIMS TO COME FORWARD, RIGHT...!!?
BUT AREN'T THERE USUALLY RESTRICTIONS ON WHAT WE CAN REPORT IN CURSE GOD INCIDENTS ...?
THE SITUATION BEING WHAT IT IS, THIS IS DEFINITELY THE FASTEST OPTION WE'VE GOT. I'LL GET EMERGENCY PERMISSION.
HEY.
SLOW DOWN A SEC.

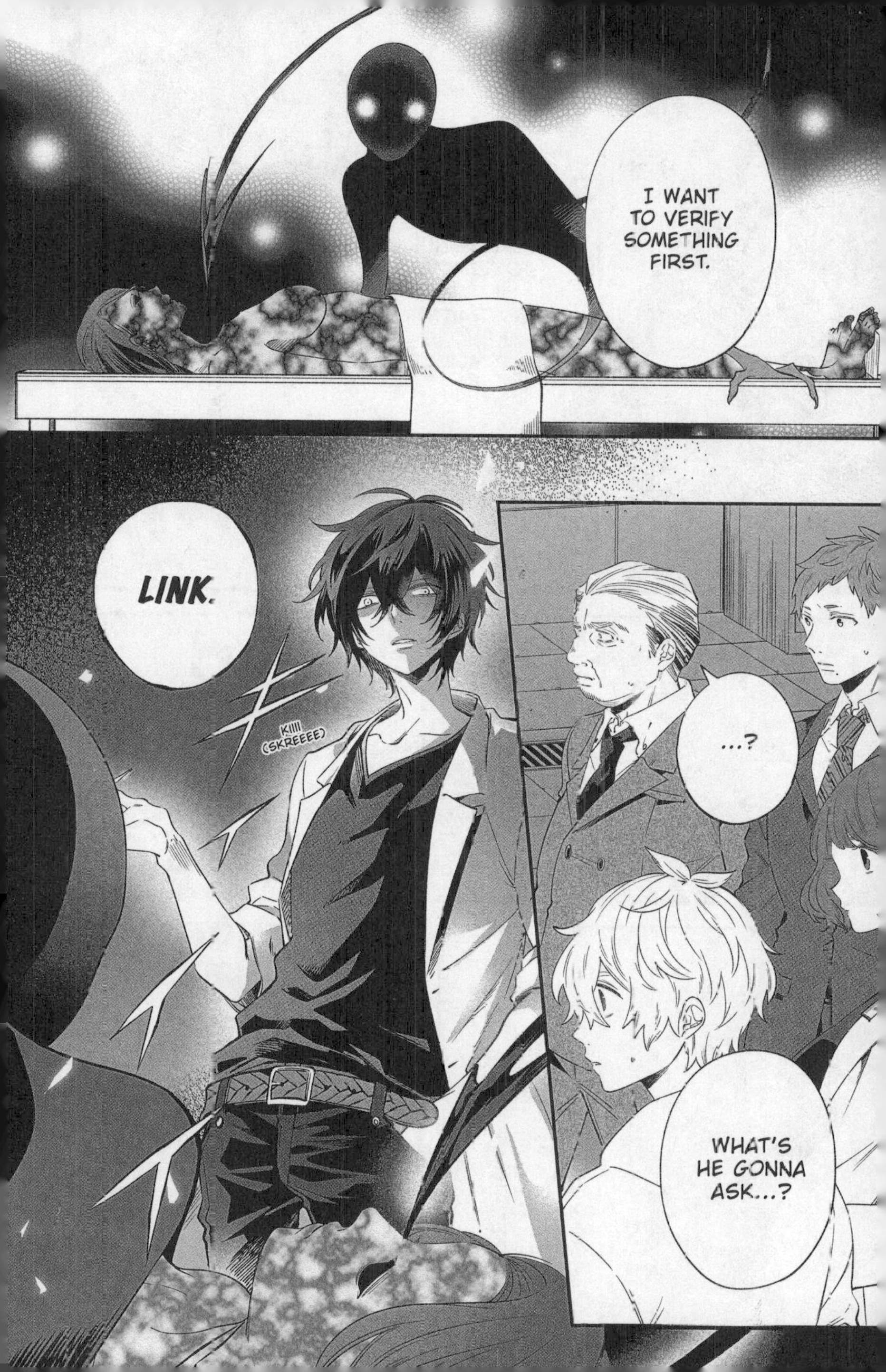
I WANT TO VERIFY SOMETHING FIRST.
...?
WHAT'S HE GONNA ASK...?
LINK.
KIIII (SKREEEE)

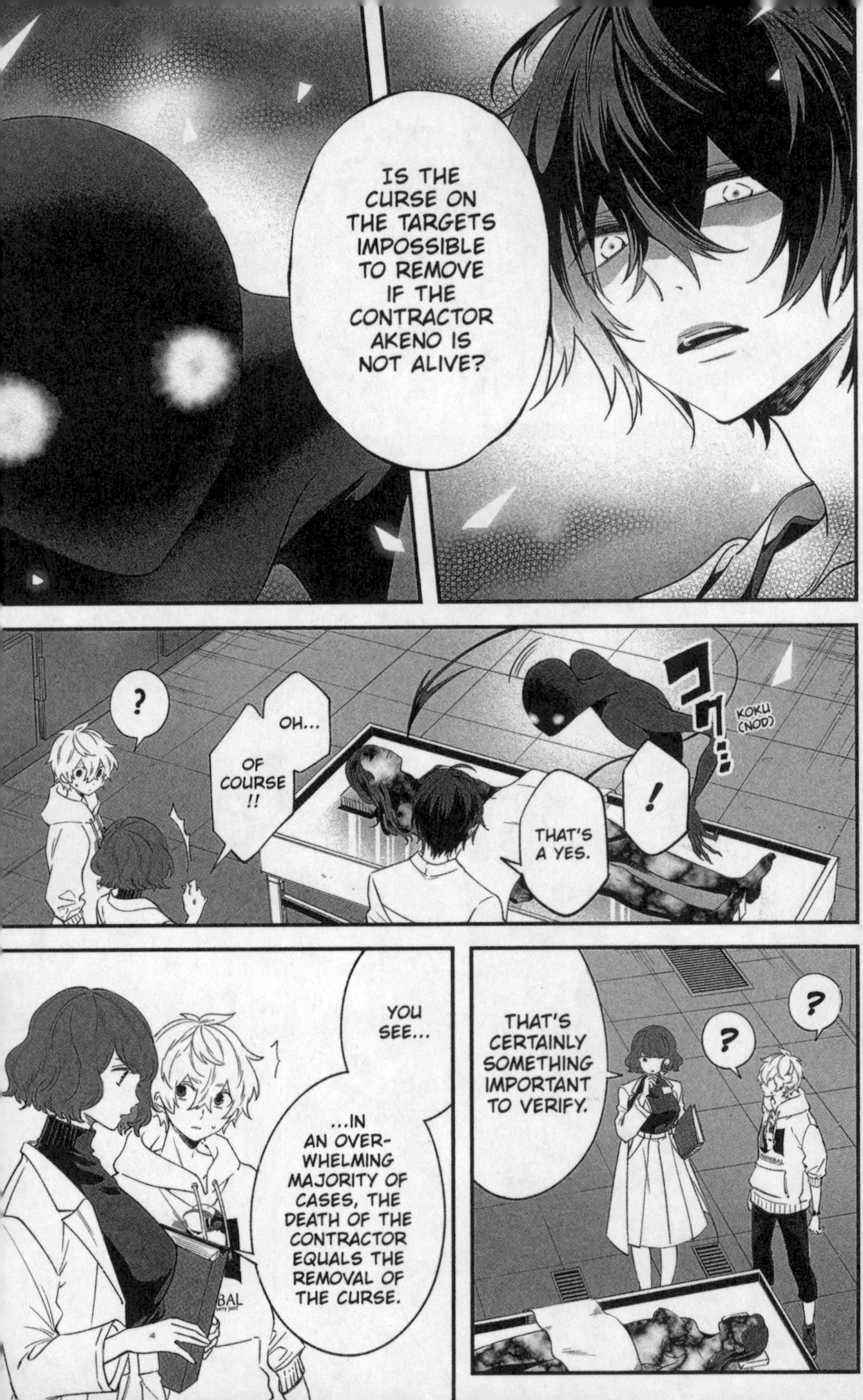
IS THE CURSE ON THE TARGETS IMPOSSIBLE TO REMOVE IF THE CONTRACTOR AKENO IS NOT ALIVE?
KOKU (NOD)
!
THAT'S A YES.
OH...
OF COURSE!!
?
THAT'S CERTAINLY SOMETHING IMPORTANT TO VERIFY.
?
?
YOU SEE...
...IN AN OVER-WHELMING MAJORITY OF CASES, THE DEATH OF THE CONTRACTOR EQUALS THE REMOVAL OF THE CURSE.

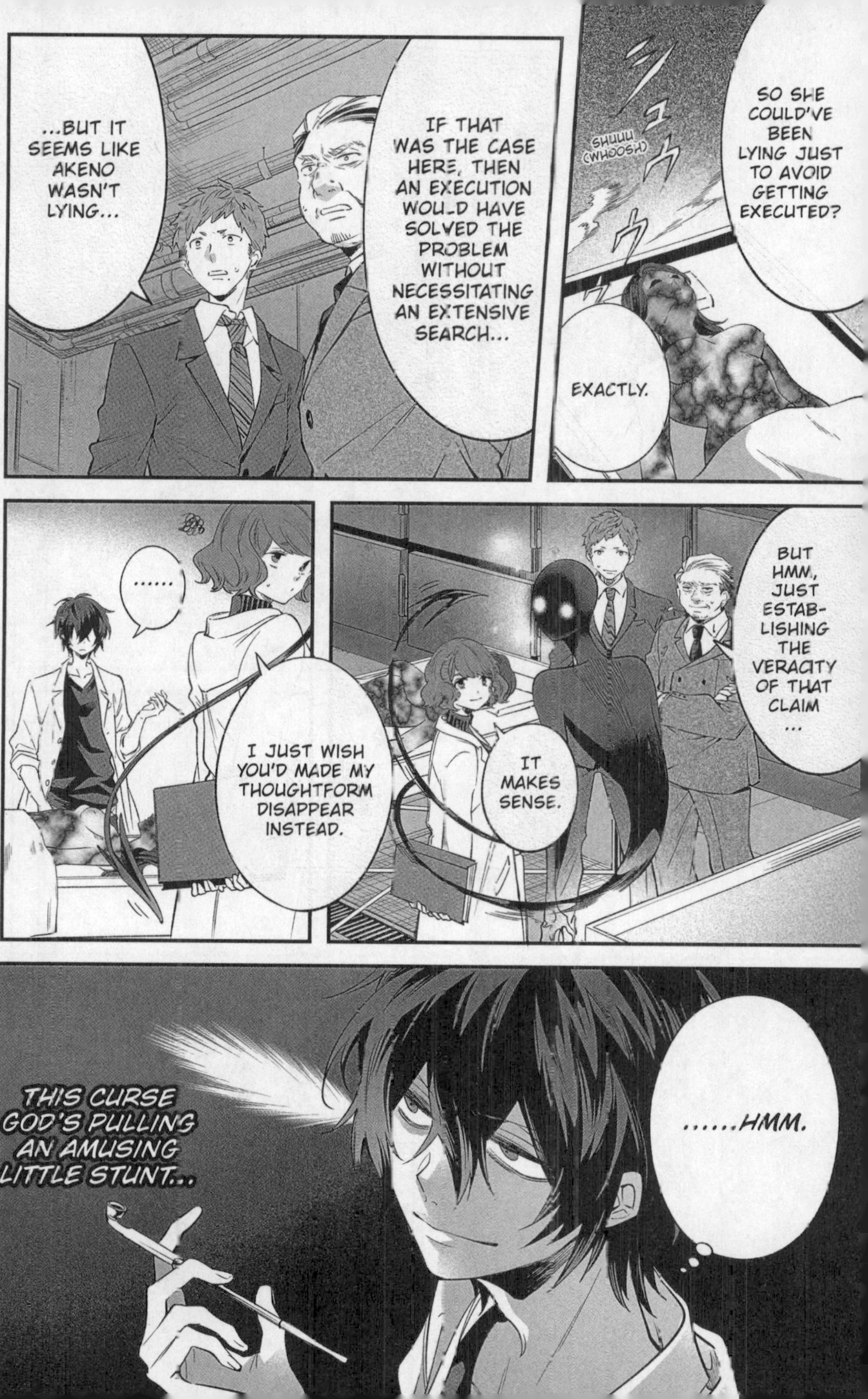
SO SHE COULD'VE BEEN LYING JUST TO AVOID GETTING EXECUTED?
SHUUU (WHOOSH)
EXACTLY.
IF THAT WAS THE CASE HERE, THEN AN EXECUTION WOULD HAVE SOLVED THE PROBLEM WITHOUT NECESSITATING AN EXTENSIVE SEARCH...
...BUT IT SEEMS LIKE AKENO WASN'T LYING...
BUT HMM, JUST ESTAB-LISHING THE VERACITY OF THAT CLAIM ...
IT MAKES SENSE.
......
I JUST WISH YOU'D MADE MY THOUGHTFORM DISAPPEAR INSTEAD.
......HMM.
THIS CURSE GOD'S PULLING AN AMUSING LITTLE STUNT...

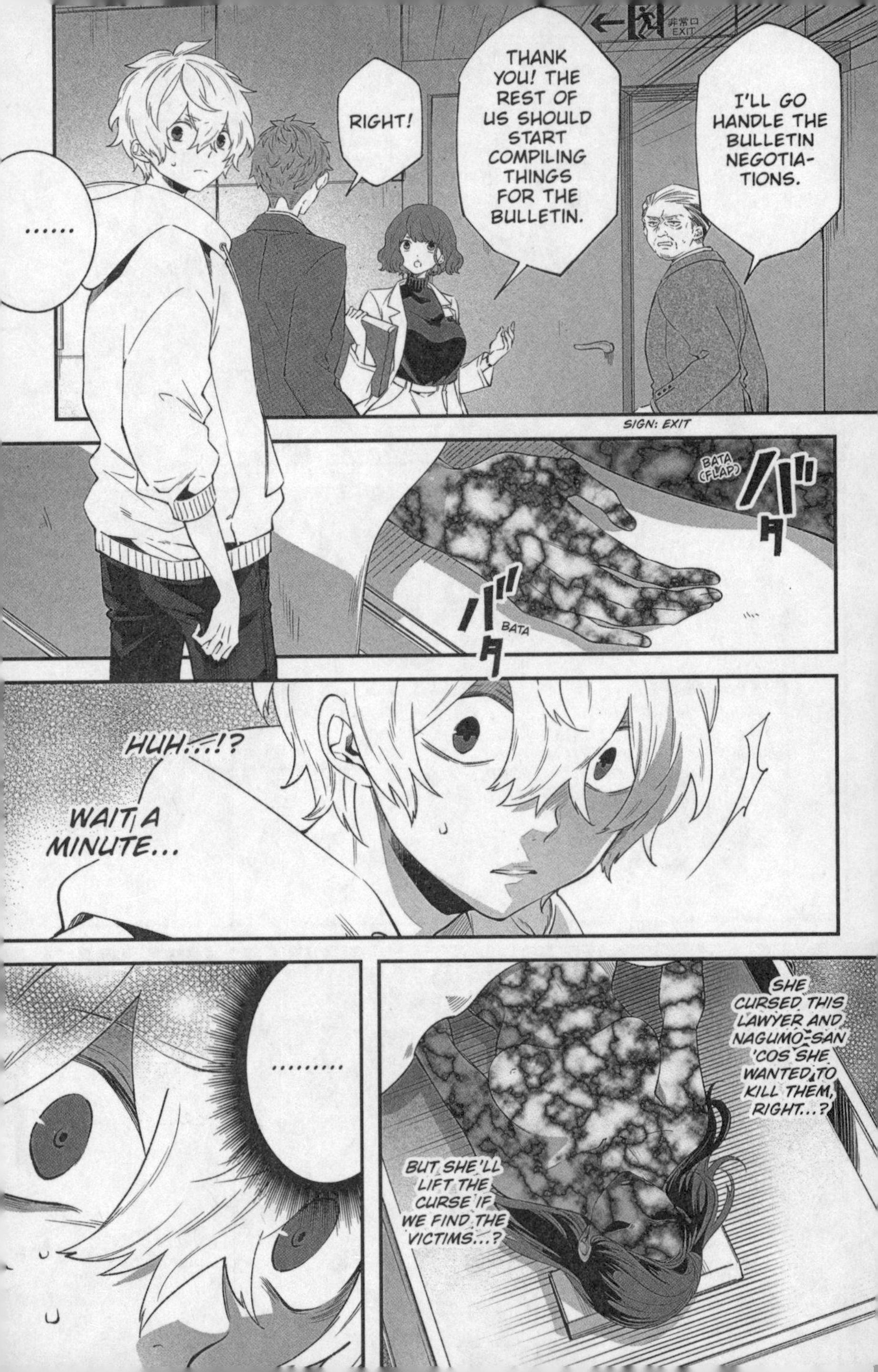

非常口
EXIT
I'LL GO HANDLE THE BULLETIN NEGOTIATIONS.
THANK YOU! THE REST OF US SHOULD START COMPILING THINGS FOR THE BULLETIN.
RIGHT!
......
SIGN: EXIT
バタ
BATA (FLAP)
バタ
BATA
HUH...!?
WAIT A MINUTE...
SHE CURSED THIS LAWYER AND NAGUMO-SAN 'COS SHE WANTED TO KILL THEM, RIGHT...?
BUT SHE'LL LIFT THE CURSE IF WE FIND THE VICTIMS...?
....

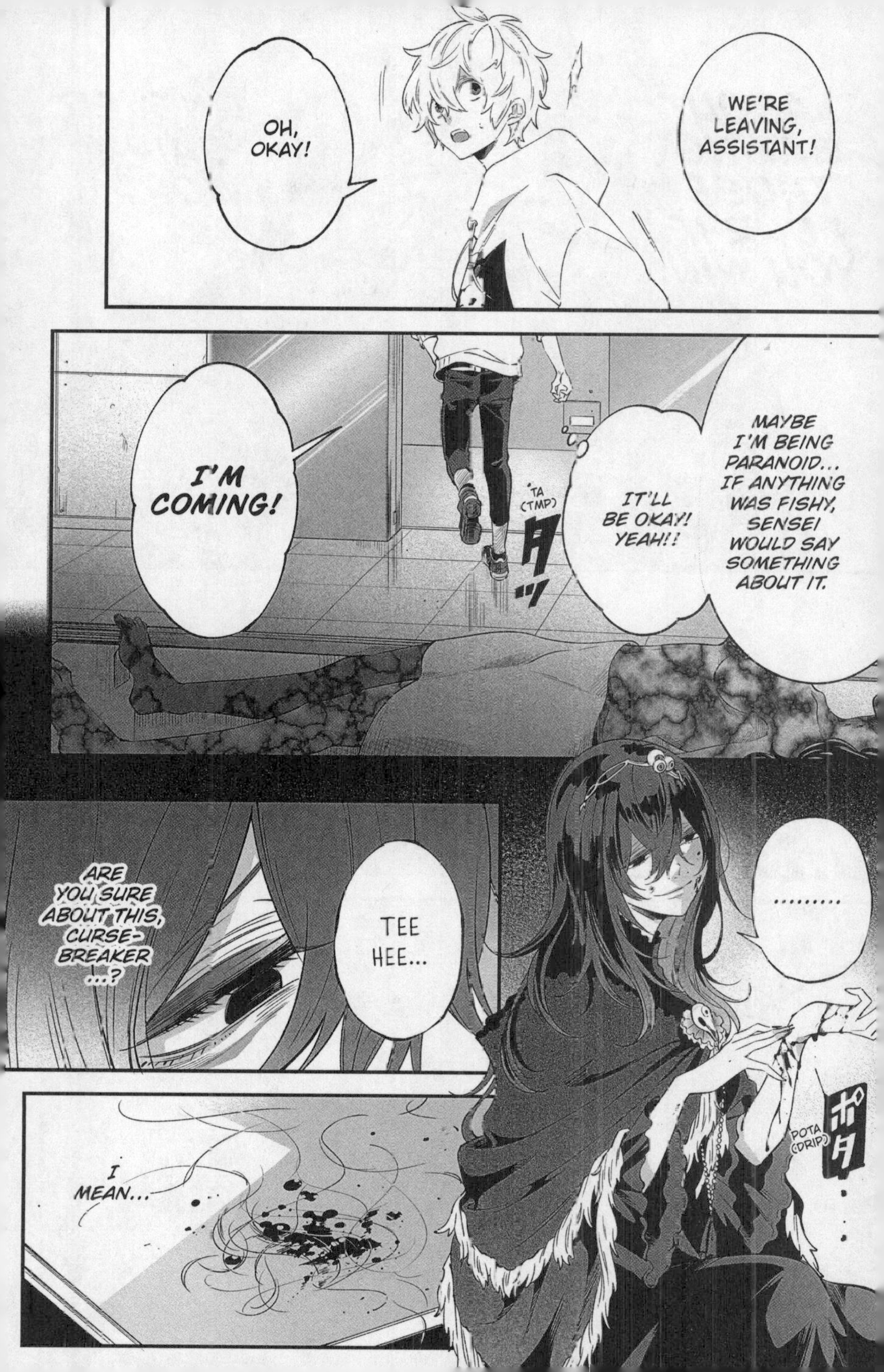
WE'RE LEAVING, ASSISTANT!
OH, OKAY!
MAYBE I'M BEING PARANOID... IF ANYTHING WAS FISHY, SENSEI WOULD SAY SOMETHING ABOUT IT.
IT'LL BE OKAY! YEAH!!
TA (TMP)
I'M COMING!
....
POTA (DRIP)
TEE HEE...
ARE YOU SURE ABOUT THIS, CURSE-BREAKER ...?
I MEAN...

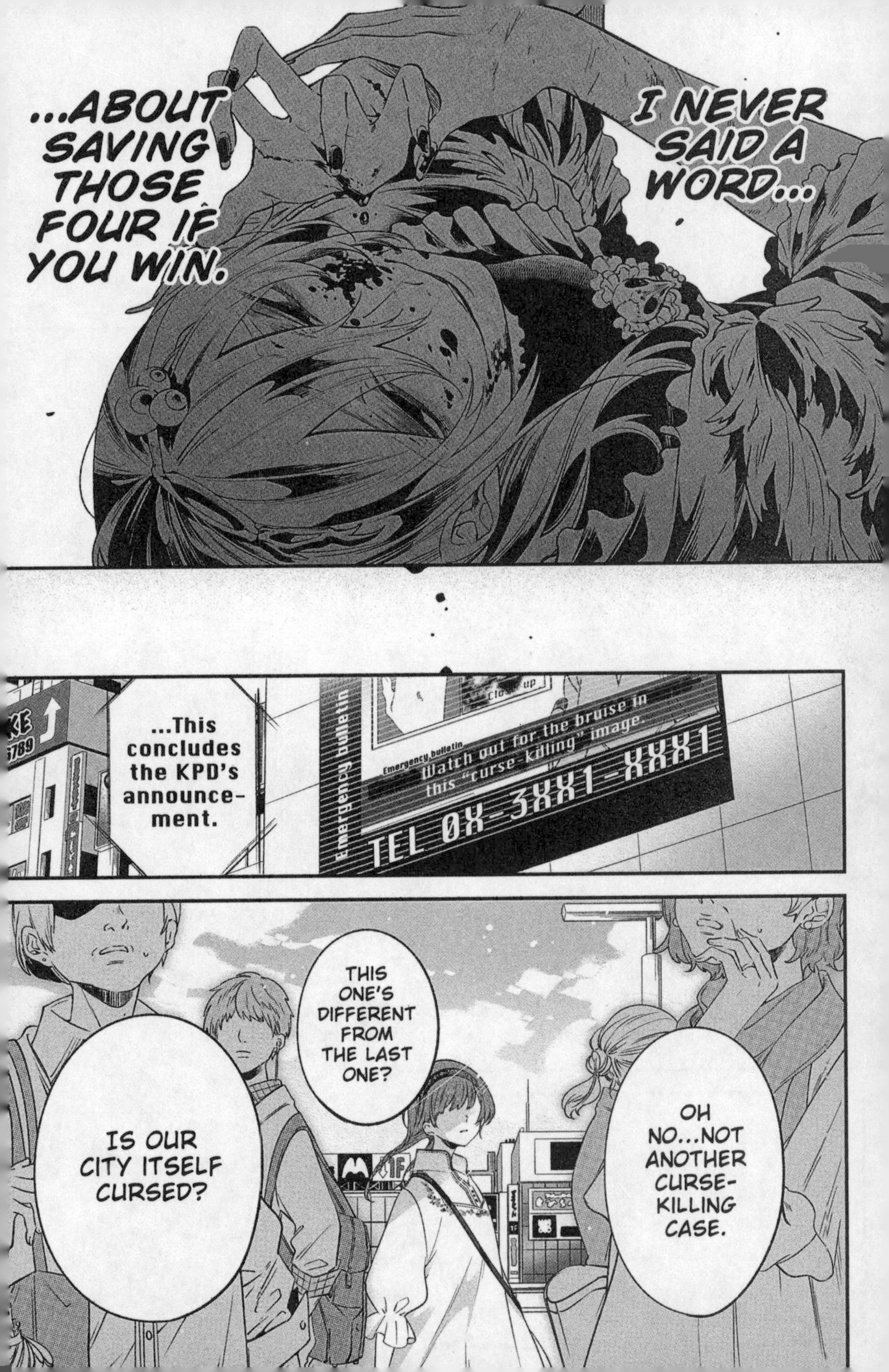
I NEVER SAID A WORD...
...ABOUT SAVING THOSE FOUR IF YOU WIN.
Emergency bulletin
Watch out for the bruise in this "curse-killing" image.
TEL 0X-3XX1-XXX1
...This concludes the KPD's announcement.
OH NO...NOT ANOTHER CURSE-KILLING CASE.
THIS ONE'S DIFFERENT FROM THE LAST ONE?
IS OUR CITY ITSELF CURSED?

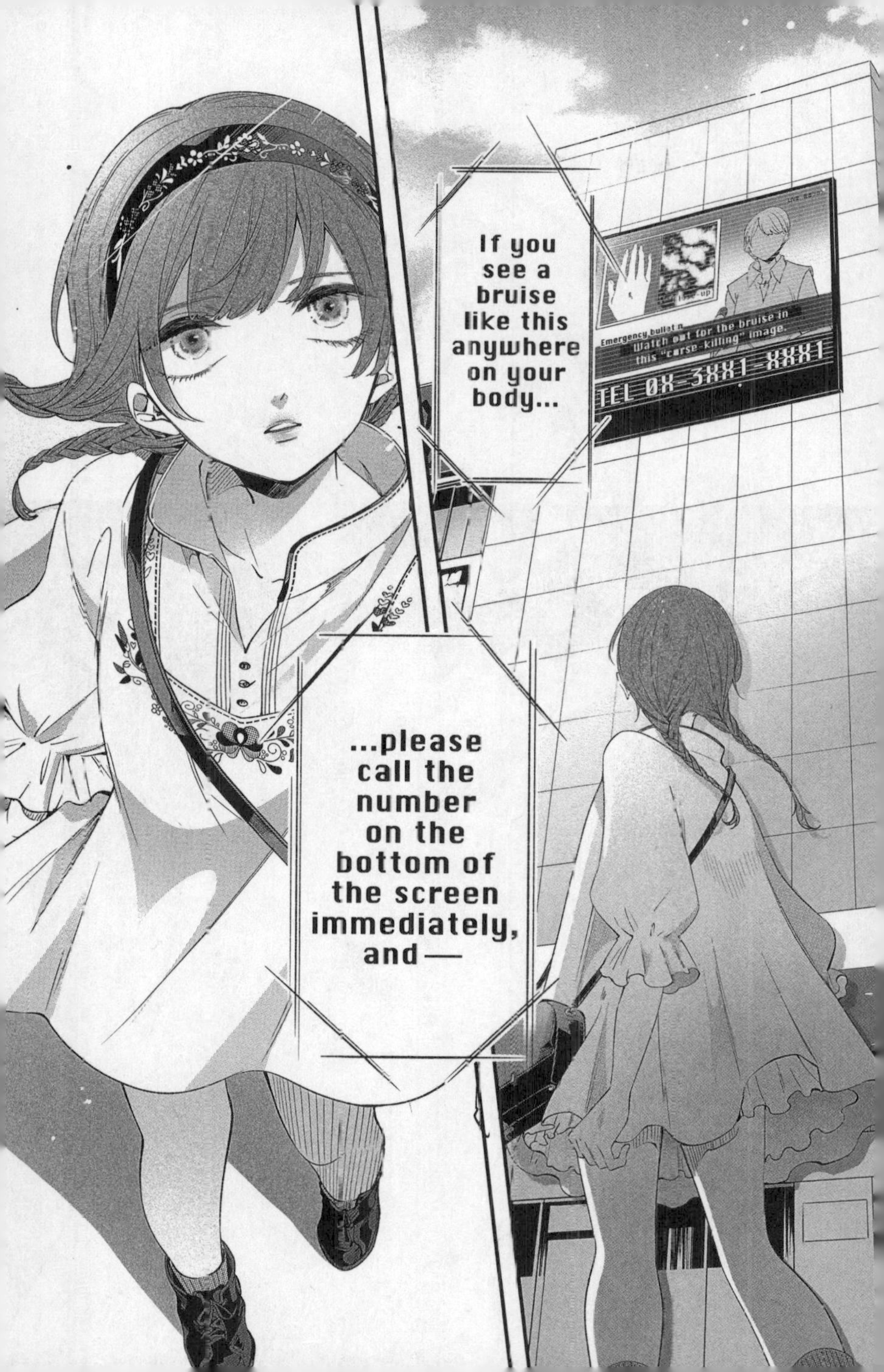
Emergency bulletin
Watch out for the bruise in this "curse-killing" image.
TEL 0X-3XX1-XXX1
If you see a bruise like this anywhere on your body...
...please call the number on the bottom of the screen immediately, and—

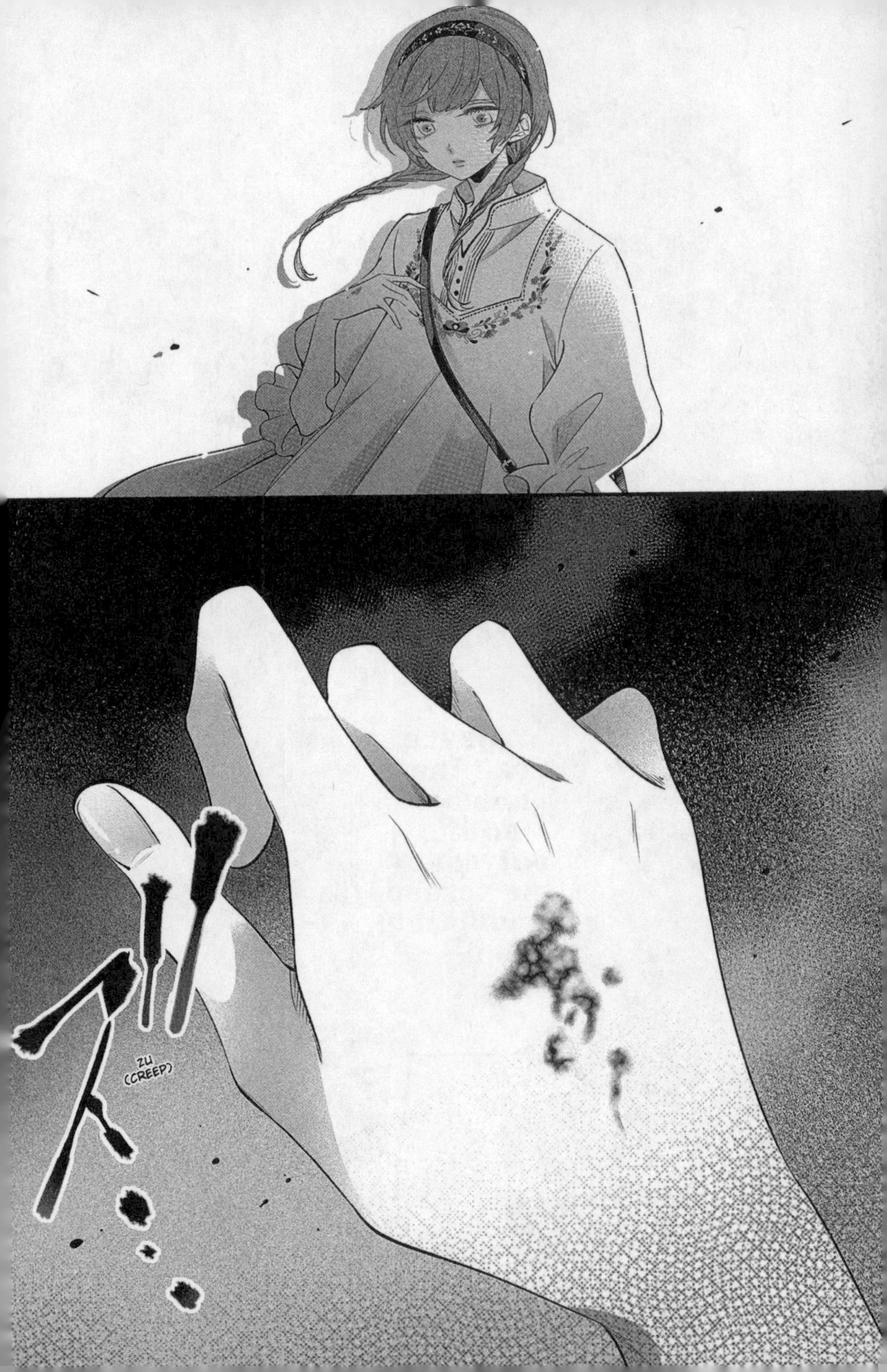
ZU
(CREEP)

CHAPTER 6

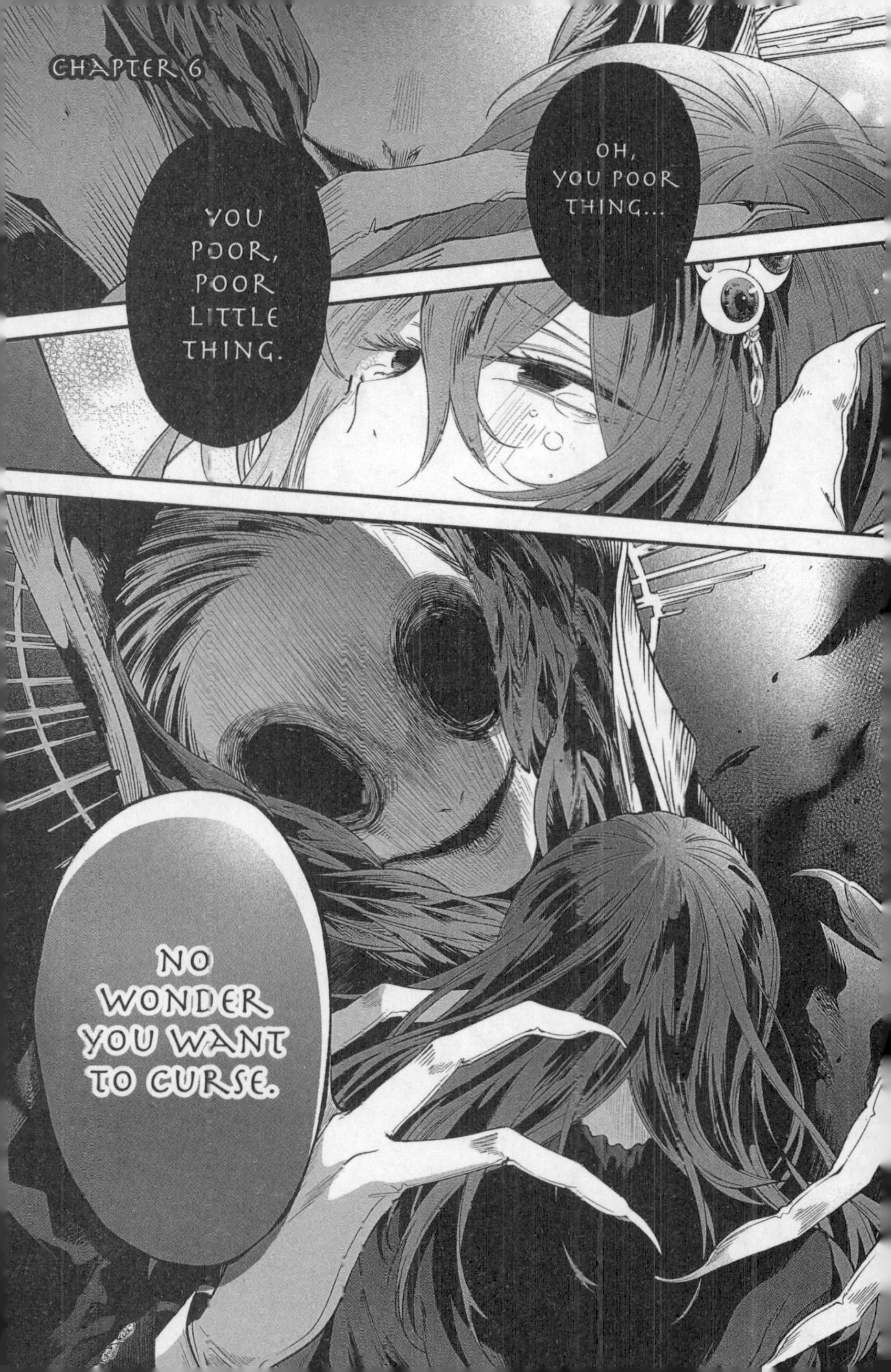
OH, YOU POOR THING...
YOU POOR, POOR LITTLE THING.
NO WONDER YOU WANT TO CURSE.

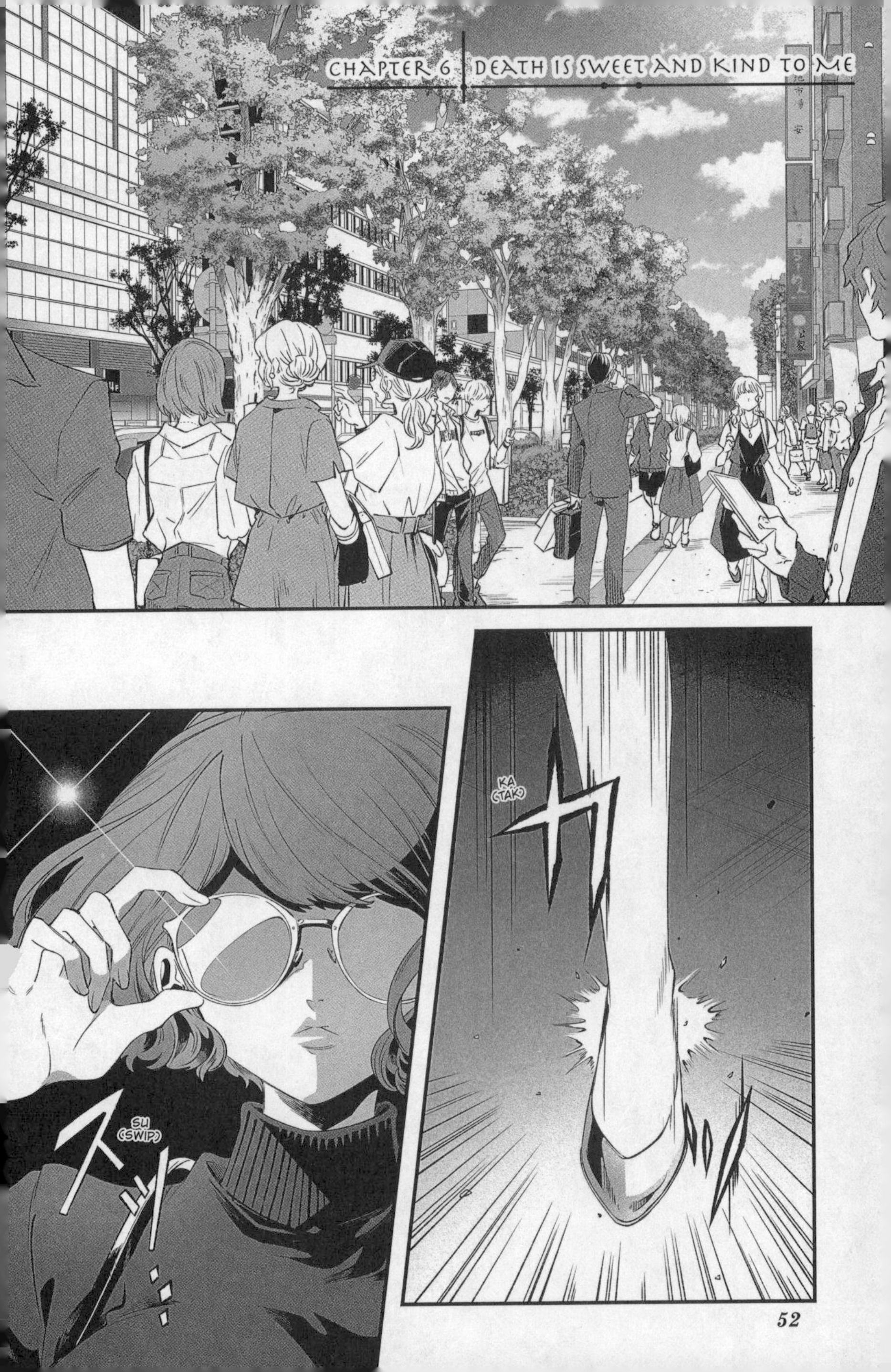
CHAPTER 6 DEATH IS SWEET AND KIND TO ME
KA (TAK)
SU (SWIP)

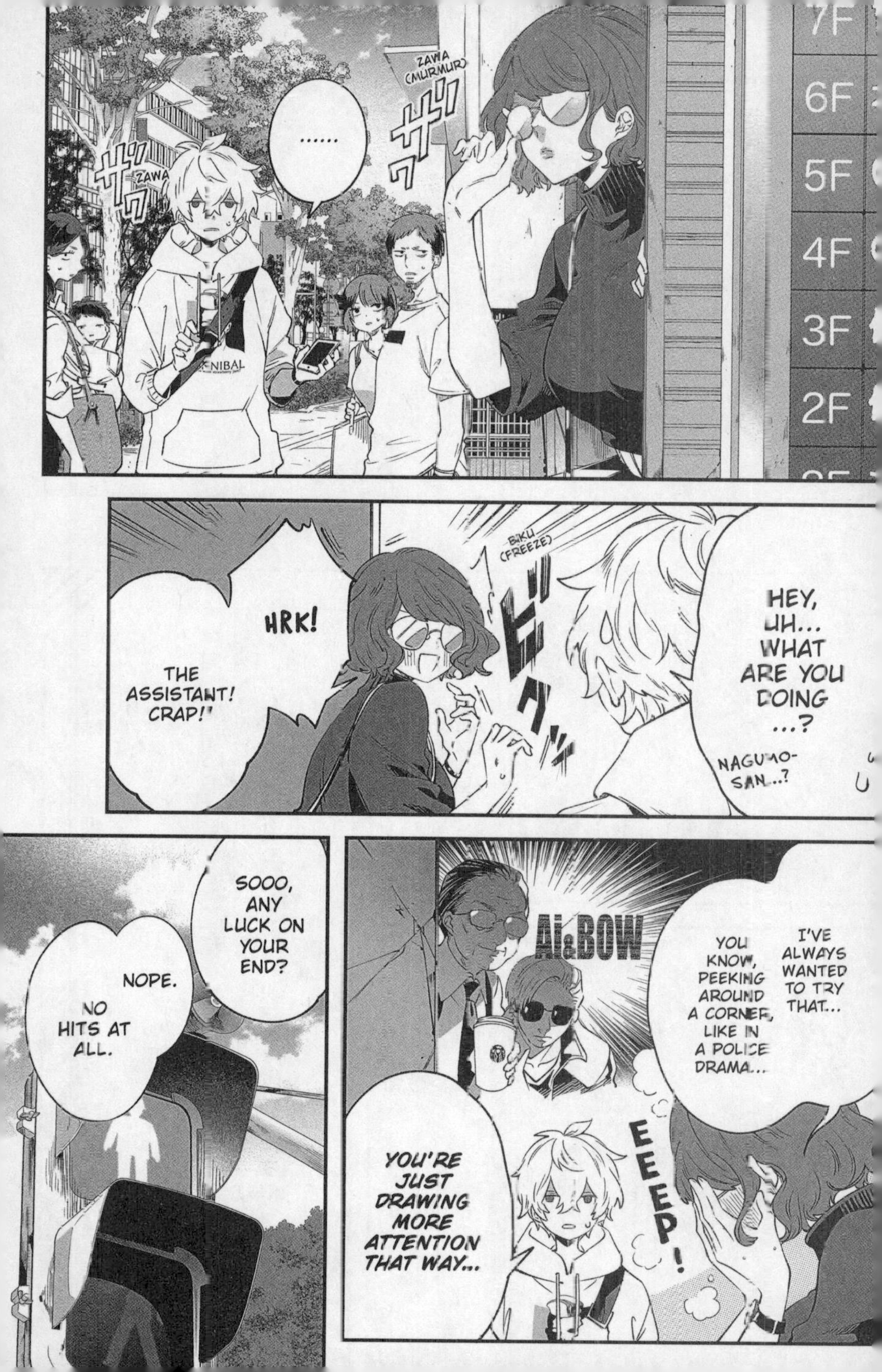
7F 6F 5F 4F 3F 2F
ZAWA (MURMUR)
......
ZAWA
HEY, UH... WHAT ARE YOU DOING ...?
NAGUMO-SAN...?
BIKU (FREEZE)
HRK!
THE ASSISTANT! CRAP!
I'VE ALWAYS WANTED TO TRY THAT...
YOU KNOW, PEEKING AROUND A CORNER, LIKE IN A POLICE DRAMA...
Ai&BOW
EEEP!
YOU'RE JUST DRAWING MORE ATTENTION THAT WAY...
SOOO, ANY LUCK ON YOUR END?
NOPE.
NO HITS AT ALL.

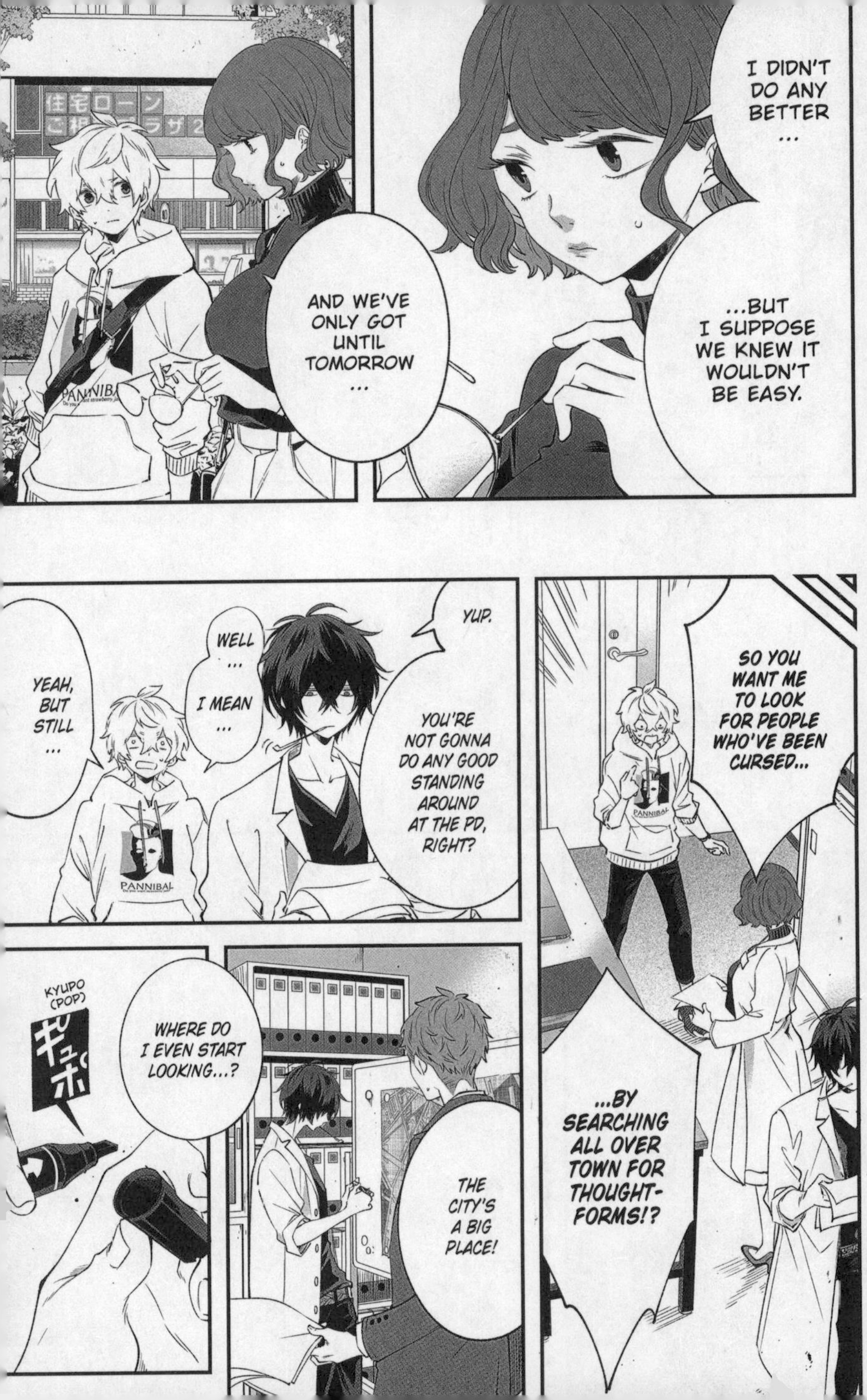
I DIDN'T DO ANY BETTER ...
...BUT I SUPPOSE WE KNEW IT WOULDN'T BE EASY.
AND WE'VE ONLY GOT UNTIL TOMORROW ...
SO YOU WANT ME TO LOOK FOR PEOPLE WHO'VE BEEN CURSED...
...BY SEARCHING ALL OVER TOWN FOR THOUGHT-FORMS!?
YUP.
YOU'RE NOT GONNA DO ANY GOOD STANDING AROUND AT THE PD, RIGHT?
WELL ... I MEAN ...
YEAH, BUT STILL ...
THE CITY'S A BIG PLACE!
WHERE DO I EVEN START LOOKING...?
KYUPO (POP)
キュポ

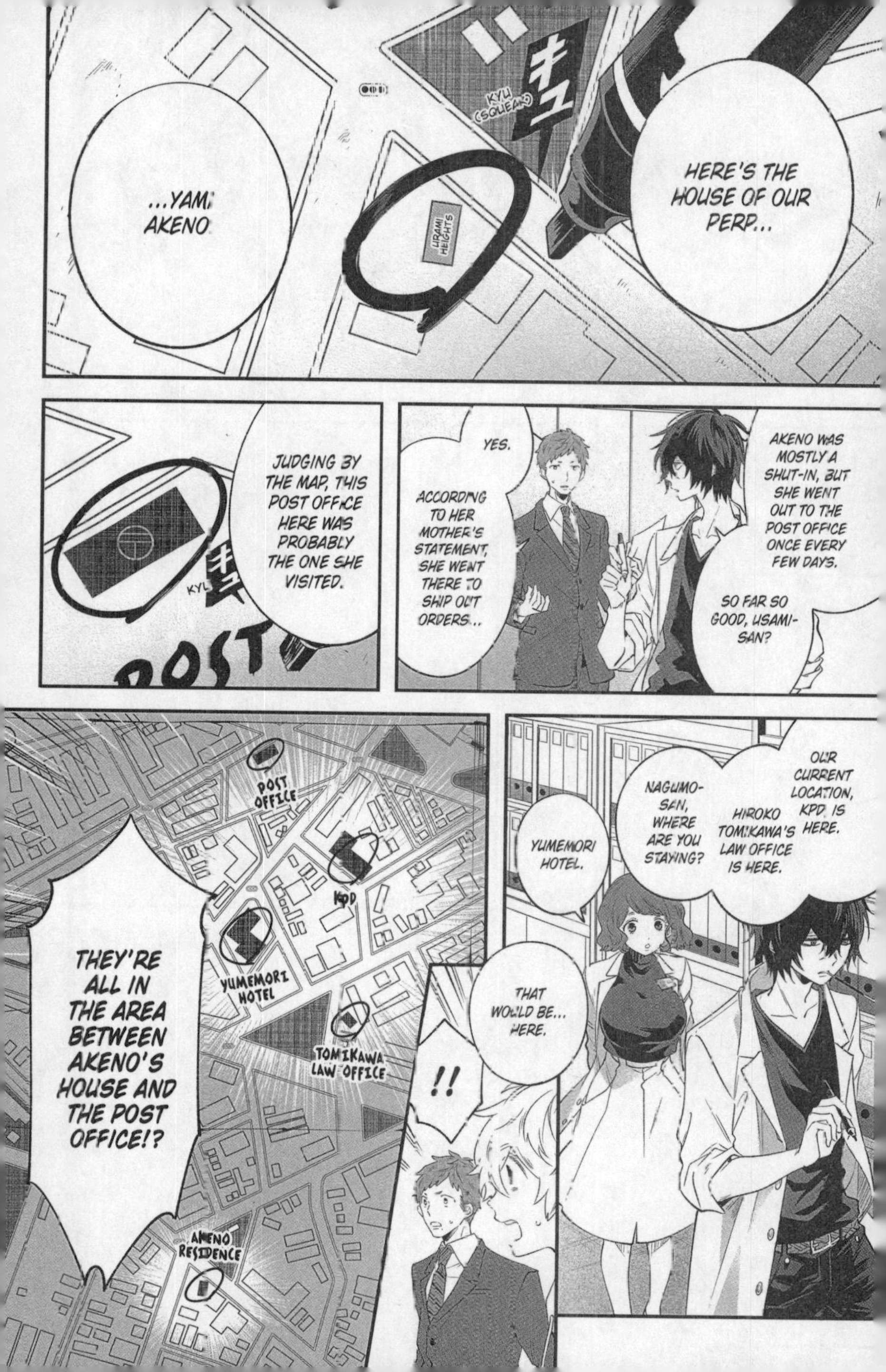
HERE'S THE HOUSE OF OUR PERP...
KYU (SQUEAK)
URAMI HEIGHTS
...YAMI AKENO.
AKENO WAS MOSTLY A SHUT-IN, BUT SHE WENT OUT TO THE POST OFFICE ONCE EVERY FEW DAYS.
SO FAR SO GOOD, USAMI-SAN?
YES.
ACCORDING TO HER MOTHER'S STATEMENT, SHE WENT THERE TO SHIP OUT ORDERS...
JUDGING BY THE MAP, THIS POST OFFICE HERE WAS PROBABLY THE ONE SHE VISITED.
KYU
OUR CURRENT LOCATION, KPD, IS HERE.
HIROKO TOMIKAWA'S LAW OFFICE IS HERE.
NAGUMO-SAN, WHERE ARE YOU STAYING?
YUMEMORI HOTEL.
THAT WOULD BE... HERE.
!!
POST OFFICE
KPD
YUMEMORI HOTEL
TOMIKAWA LAW OFFICE
AKENO RESIDENCE
THEY'RE ALL IN THE AREA BETWEEN AKENO'S HOUSE AND THE POST OFFICE!?

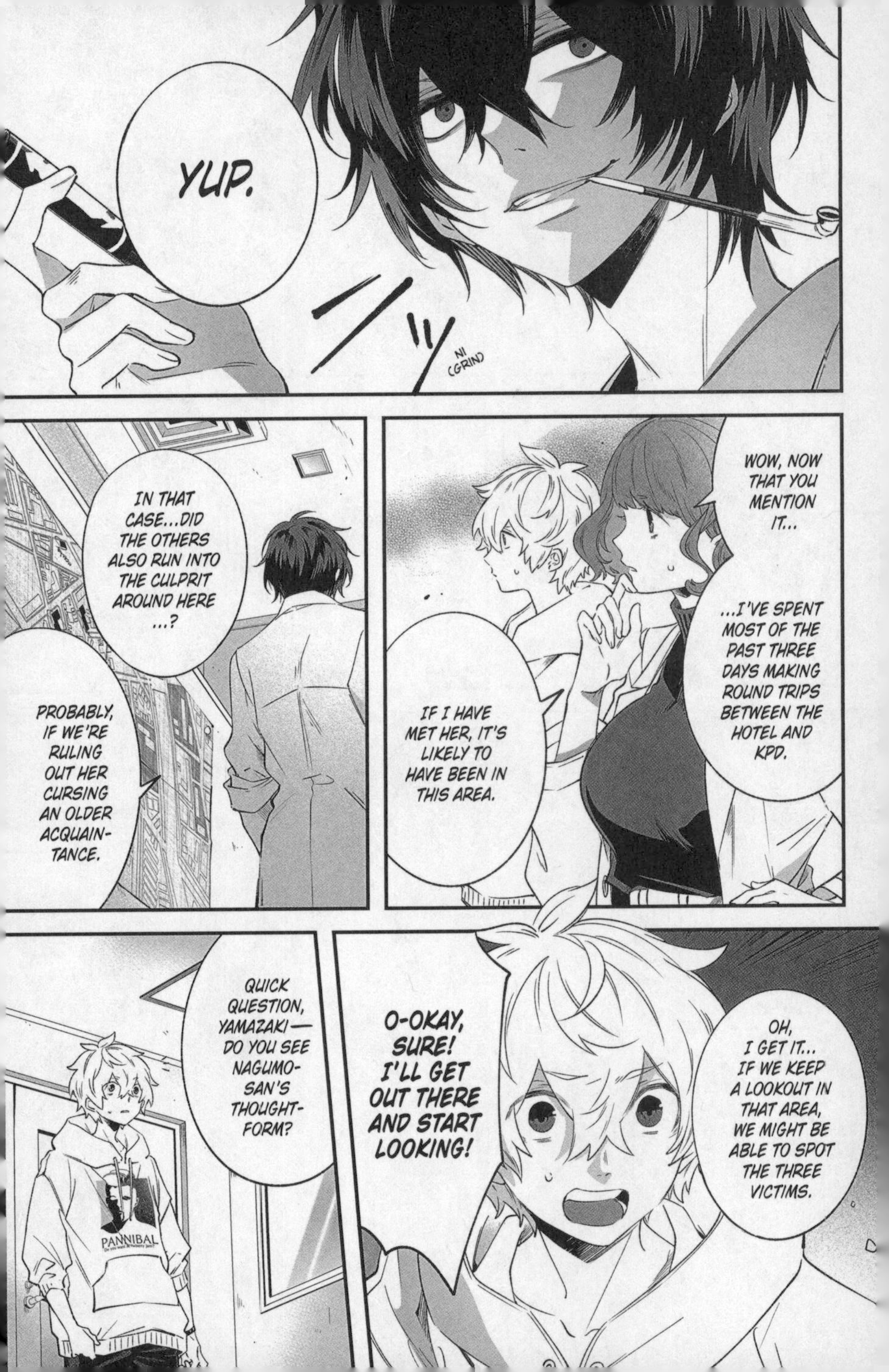
YUP.
NI (GRIND)
WOW, NOW THAT YOU MENTION IT...
...I'VE SPENT MOST OF THE PAST THREE DAYS MAKING ROUND TRIPS BETWEEN THE HOTEL AND KPD.
IF I HAVE MET HER, IT'S LIKELY TO HAVE BEEN IN THIS AREA.
IN THAT CASE...DID THE OTHERS ALSO RUN INTO THE CULPRIT AROUND HERE ...?
PROBABLY, IF WE'RE RULING OUT HER CURSING AN OLDER ACQUAIN-TANCE.
OH, I GET IT... IF WE KEEP A LOOKOUT IN THAT AREA, WE MIGHT BE ABLE TO SPOT THE THREE VICTIMS.
O-OKAY, SURE! I'LL GET OUT THERE AND START LOOKING!
QUICK QUESTION, YAMAZAKI— DO YOU SEE NAGUMO-SAN'S THOUGHT-FORM?
PANNIBAL

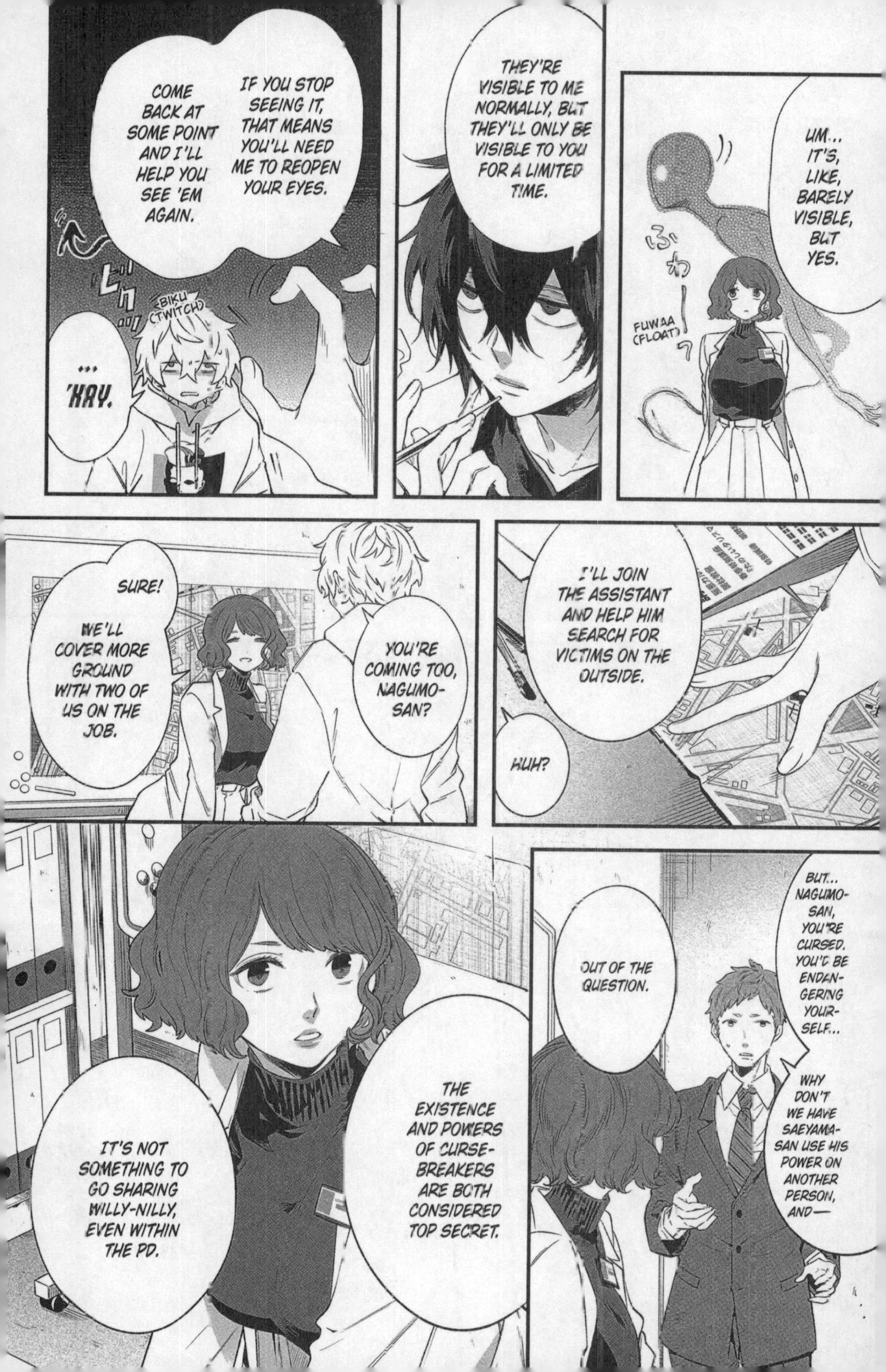
UM... IT'S, LIKE, BARELY VISIBLE, BUT YES.
FUWAA (FLOAT)
THEY'RE VISIBLE TO ME NORMALLY, BUT THEY'LL ONLY BE VISIBLE TO YOU FOR A LIMITED TIME.
IF YOU STOP SEEING IT, THAT MEANS YOU'LL NEED ME TO REOPEN YOUR EYES.
COME BACK AT SOME POINT AND I'LL HELP YOU SEE 'EM AGAIN.
BIKU (TWITCH)
...'KAY.
I'LL JOIN THE ASSISTANT AND HELP HIM SEARCH FOR VICTIMS ON THE OUTSIDE.
HUH?
YOU'RE COMING TOO, NAGUMO-SAN?
SURE!
WE'LL COVER MORE GROUND WITH TWO OF US ON THE JOB.
BUT... NAGUMO-SAN, YOU'RE CURSED. YOU'D BE ENDANGERING YOURSELF...
WHY DON'T WE HAVE SAEYAMA-SAN USE HIS POWER ON ANOTHER PERSON, AND—
OUT OF THE QUESTION.
THE EXISTENCE AND POWERS OF CURSE-BREAKERS ARE BOTH CONSIDERED TOP SECRET.
IT'S NOT SOMETHING TO GO SHARING WILLY-NILLY, EVEN WITHIN THE PD.

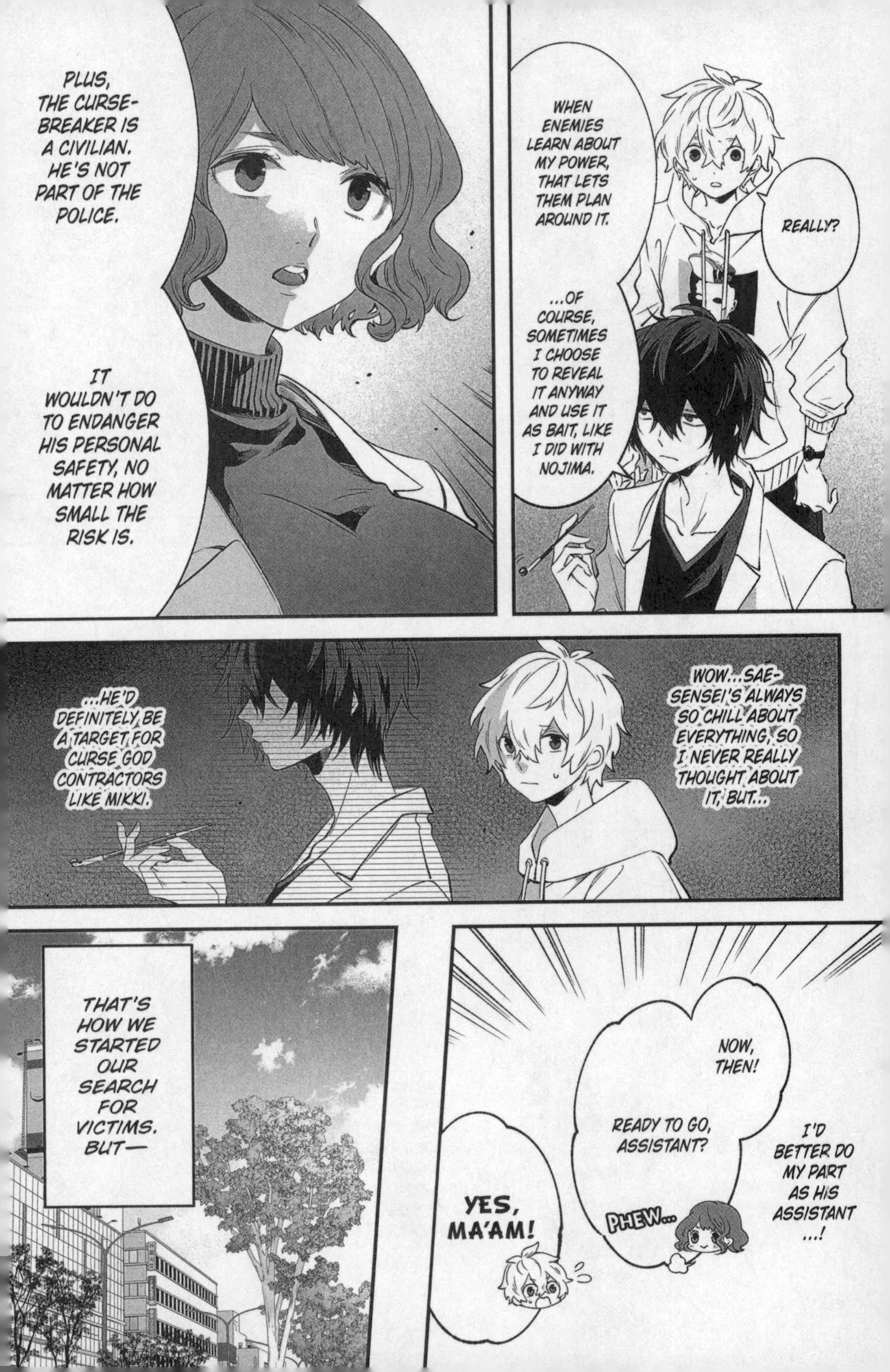
WHEN ENEMIES LEARN ABOUT MY POWER, THAT LETS THEM PLAN AROUND IT.
REALLY?
...OF COURSE, SOMETIMES I CHOOSE TO REVEAL IT ANYWAY AND USE IT AS BAIT, LIKE I DID WITH NOJIMA.
PLUS, THE CURSE-BREAKER IS A CIVILIAN. HE'S NOT PART OF THE POLICE.
IT WOULDN'T DO TO ENDANGER HIS PERSONAL SAFETY, NO MATTER HOW SMALL THE RISK IS.
WOW...SAE-SENSEI'S ALWAYS SO CHILL ABOUT EVERYTHING, SO I NEVER REALLY THOUGHT ABOUT IT, BUT...
...HE'D DEFINITELY BE A TARGET FOR CURSE GOD CONTRACTORS LIKE MIKKI.
NOW, THEN!
READY TO GO, ASSISTANT?
I'D BETTER DO MY PART AS HIS ASSISTANT ...!
PHEW...
YES, MA'AM!
THAT'S HOW WE STARTED OUR SEARCH FOR VICTIMS. BUT—

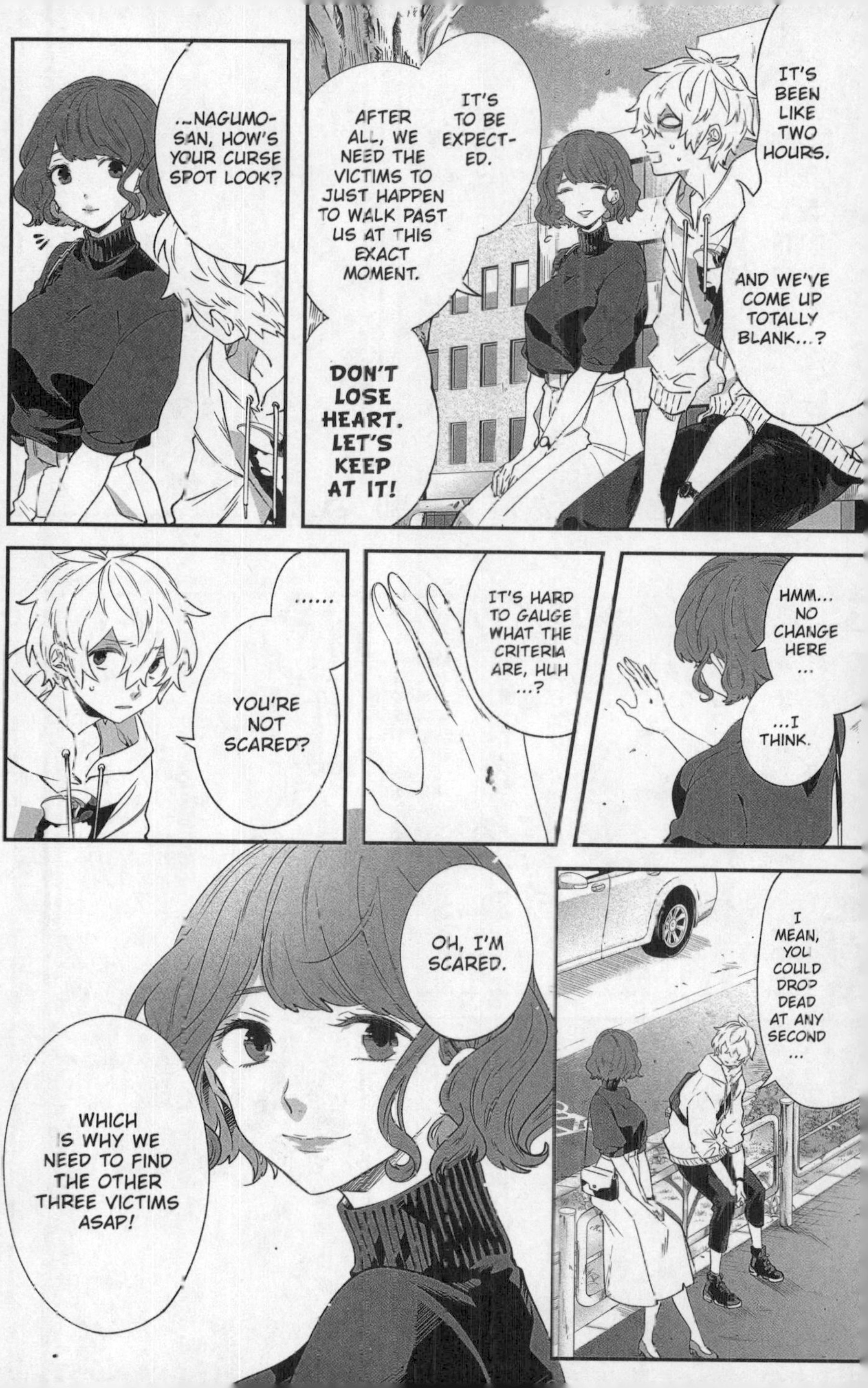
IT'S BEEN LIKE TWO HOURS.
AND WE'VE COME UP TOTALLY BLANK...?
IT'S TO BE EXPECTED.
AFTER ALL, WE NEED THE VICTIMS TO JUST HAPPEN TO WALK PAST US AT THIS EXACT MOMENT.
DON'T LOSE HEART. LET'S KEEP AT IT!
...NAGUMO-SAN, HOW'S YOUR CURSE SPOT LOOK?
HMM... NO CHANGE HERE...
...I THINK.
IT'S HARD TO GAUGE WHAT THE CRITERIA ARE, HUH...?
......
YOU'RE NOT SCARED?
I MEAN, YOU COULD DROP DEAD AT ANY SECOND...
OH, I'M SCARED.
WHICH IS WHY WE NEED TO FIND THE OTHER THREE VICTIMS ASAP!

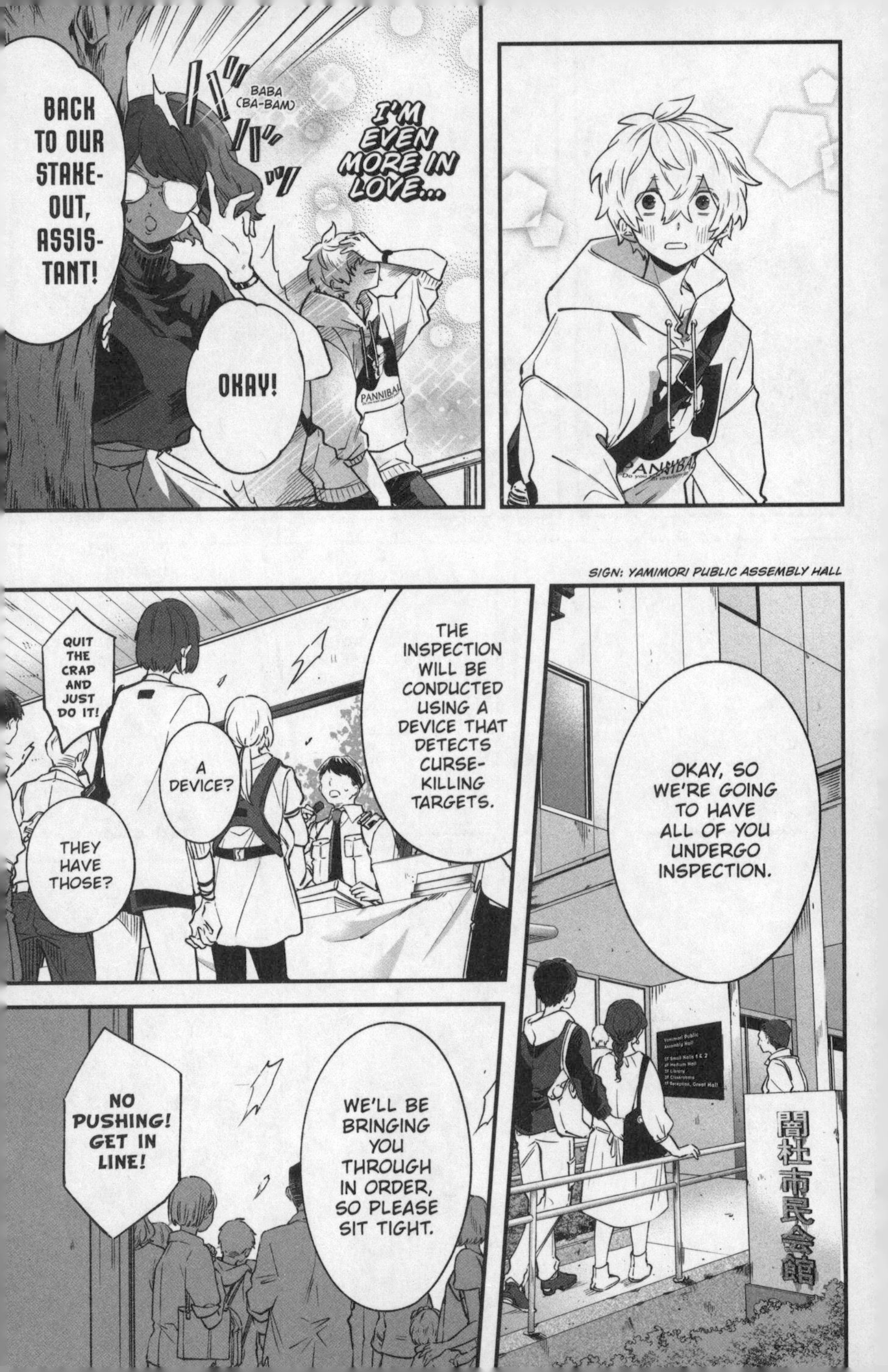
I'M EVEN MORE IN LOVE...
BABA (BA-BAM)
BACK TO OUR STAKE-OUT, ASSISTANT!
OKAY!
SIGN: YAMIMORI PUBLIC ASSEMBLY HALL
闇杜市民会館
OKAY, SO WE'RE GOING TO HAVE ALL OF YOU UNDERGO INSPECTION.
THE INSPECTION WILL BE CONDUCTED USING A DEVICE THAT DETECTS CURSE-KILLING TARGETS.
A DEVICE?
QUIT THE CRAP AND JUST DO IT!
THEY HAVE THOSE?
WE'LL BE BRINGING YOU THROUGH IN ORDER, SO PLEASE SIT TIGHT.
NO PUSHING! GET IN LINE!

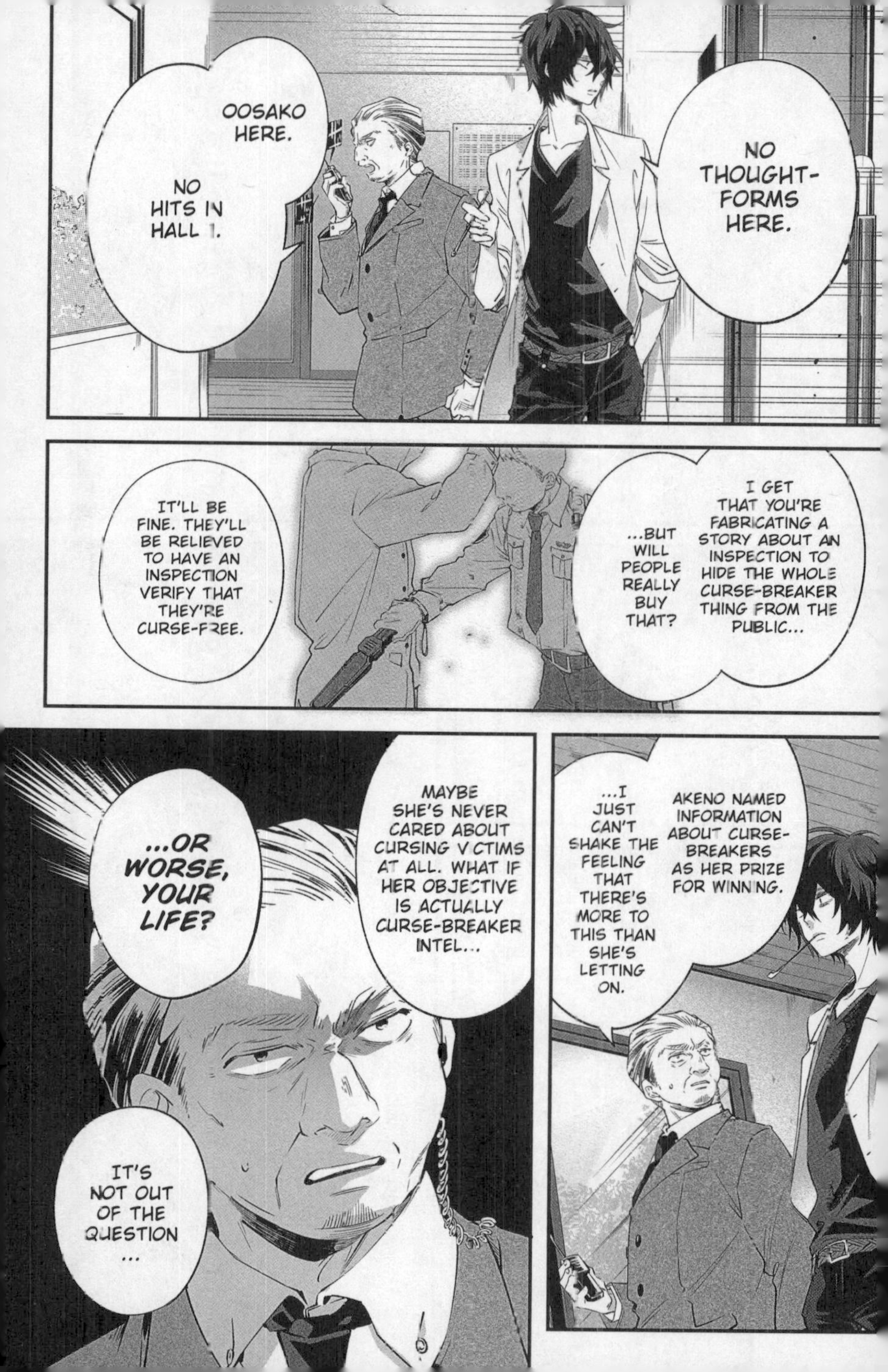
NO THOUGHT-FORMS HERE.
OOSAKO HERE.
NO HITS IN HALL 1.
I GET THAT YOU'RE FABRICATING A STORY ABOUT AN INSPECTION TO HIDE THE WHOLE CURSE-BREAKER THING FROM THE PUBLIC...
...BUT WILL PEOPLE REALLY BUY THAT?
IT'LL BE FINE. THEY'LL BE RELIEVED TO HAVE AN INSPECTION VERIFY THAT THEY'RE CURSE-FREE.
AKENO NAMED INFORMATION ABOUT CURSE-BREAKERS AS HER PRIZE FOR WINNING.
...I JUST CAN'T SHAKE THE FEELING THAT THERE'S MORE TO THIS THAN SHE'S LETTING ON.
MAYBE SHE'S NEVER CARED ABOUT CURSING VICTIMS AT ALL. WHAT IF HER OBJECTIVE IS ACTUALLY CURSE-BREAKER INTEL...
...OR WORSE, YOUR LIFE?
IT'S NOT OUT OF THE QUESTION ...

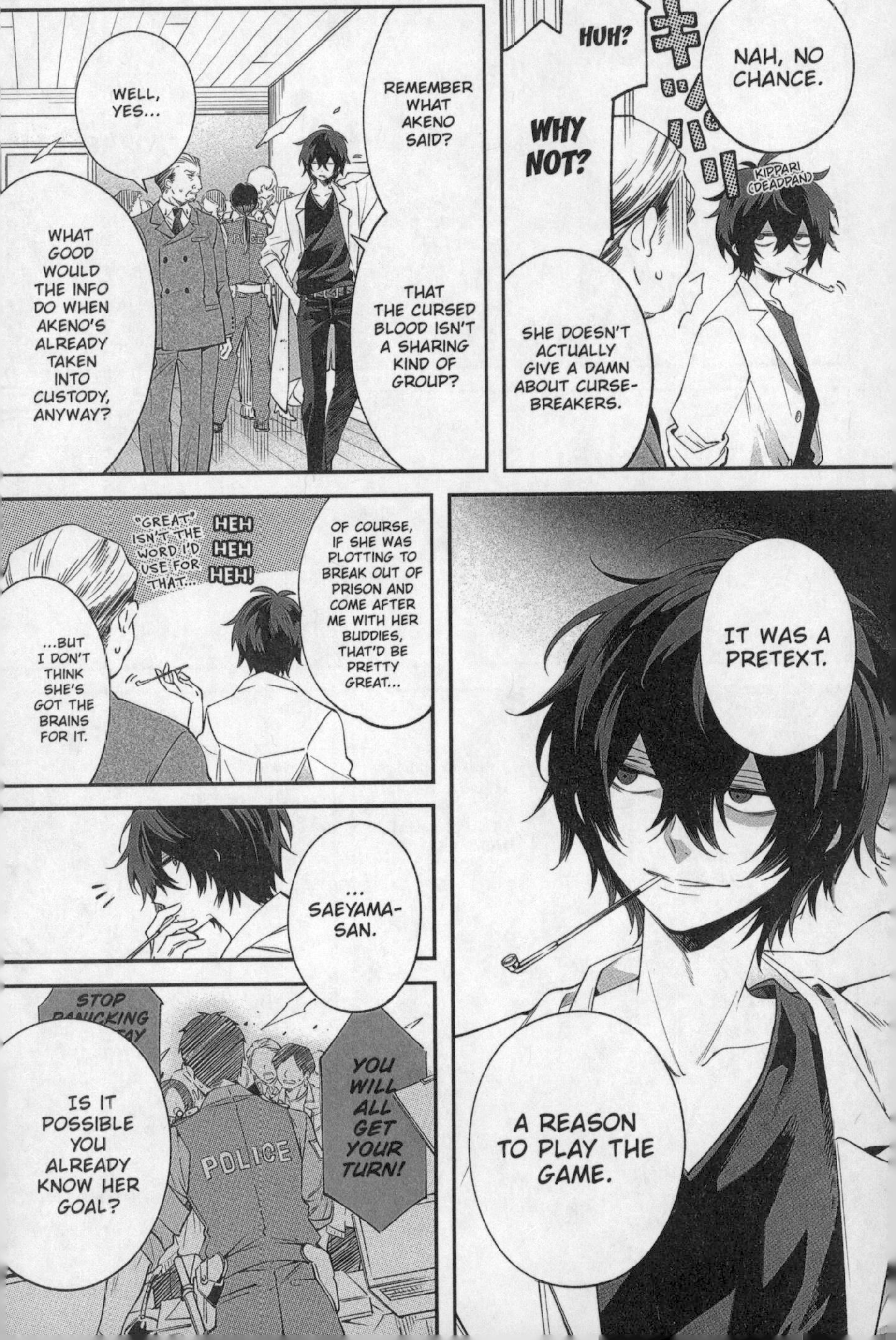

NAH, NO CHANCE.
HUH?
WHY NOT?
KIPPARI (DEADPAN)
SHE DOESN'T ACTUALLY GIVE A DAMN ABOUT CURSE-BREAKERS.
REMEMBER WHAT AKENO SAID?
THAT THE CURSED BLOOD ISN'T A SHARING KIND OF GROUP?
WELL, YES...
WHAT GOOD WOULD THE INFO DO WHEN AKENO'S ALREADY TAKEN INTO CUSTODY, ANYWAY?
IT WAS A PRETEXT.
A REASON TO PLAY THE GAME.
OF COURSE, IF SHE WAS PLOTTING TO BREAK OUT OF PRISON AND COME AFTER ME WITH HER BUDDIES, THAT'D BE PRETTY GREAT...
HEH HEH HEH!
"GREAT" ISN'T THE WORD I'D USE FOR THAT...
...BUT I DON'T THINK SHE'S GOT THE BRAINS FOR IT.
... SAEYAMA-SAN.
YOU WILL ALL GET YOUR TURN!
STOP
POLICE
IS IT POSSIBLE YOU ALREADY KNOW HER GOAL?

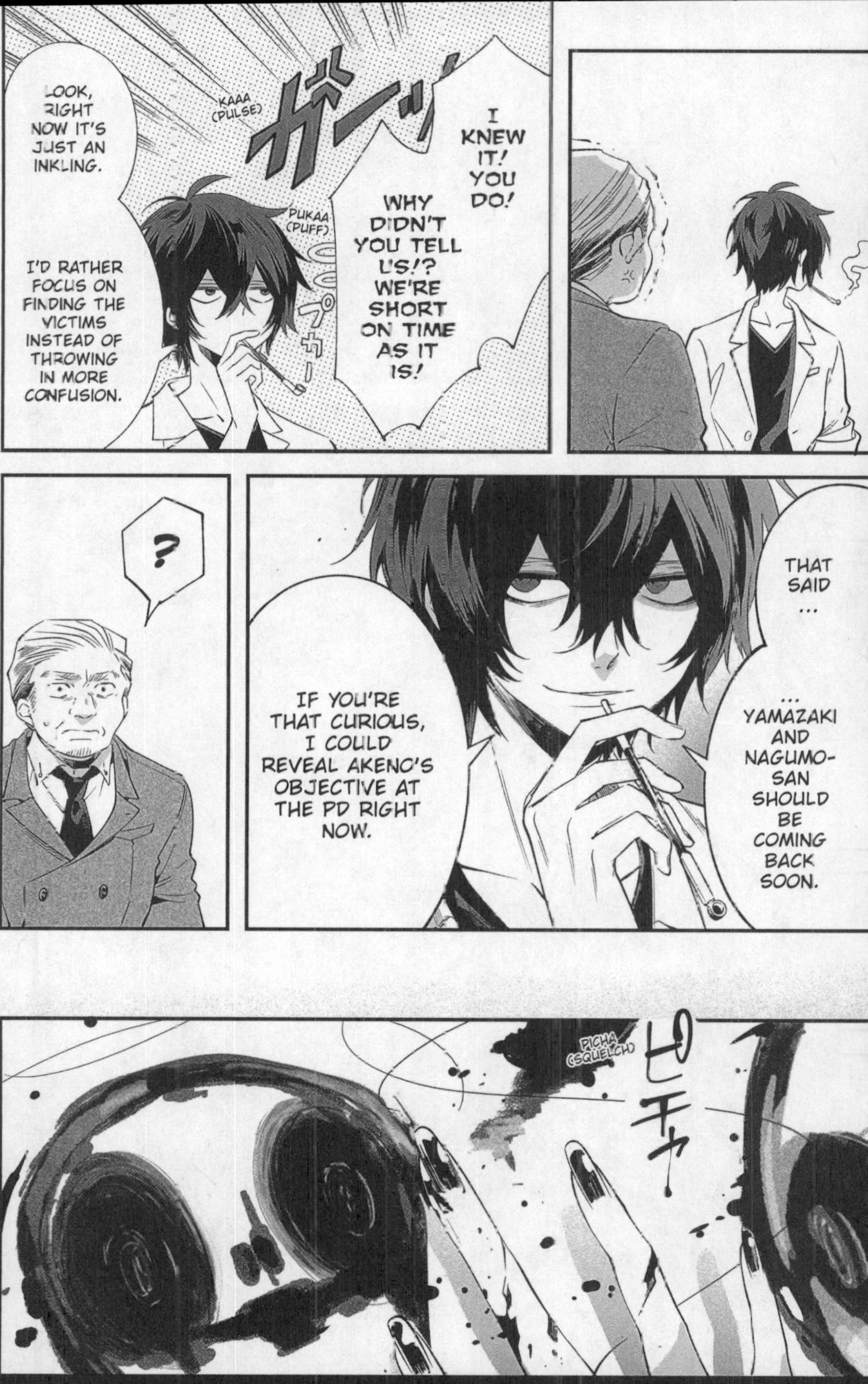
I KNEW IT! YOU DO!
WHY DIDN'T YOU TELL US!? WE'RE SHORT ON TIME AS IT IS!
KAAA (PULSE)
PUKAA (PUFF)
LOOK, RIGHT NOW IT'S JUST AN INKLING.
I'D RATHER FOCUS ON FINDING THE VICTIMS INSTEAD OF THROWING IN MORE CONFUSION.
THAT SAID ...
... YAMAZAKI AND NAGUMO-SAN SHOULD BE COMING BACK SOON.
IF YOU'RE THAT CURIOUS, I COULD REVEAL AKENO'S OBJECTIVE AT THE PD RIGHT NOW.
?
PICHA (SQUELCH)

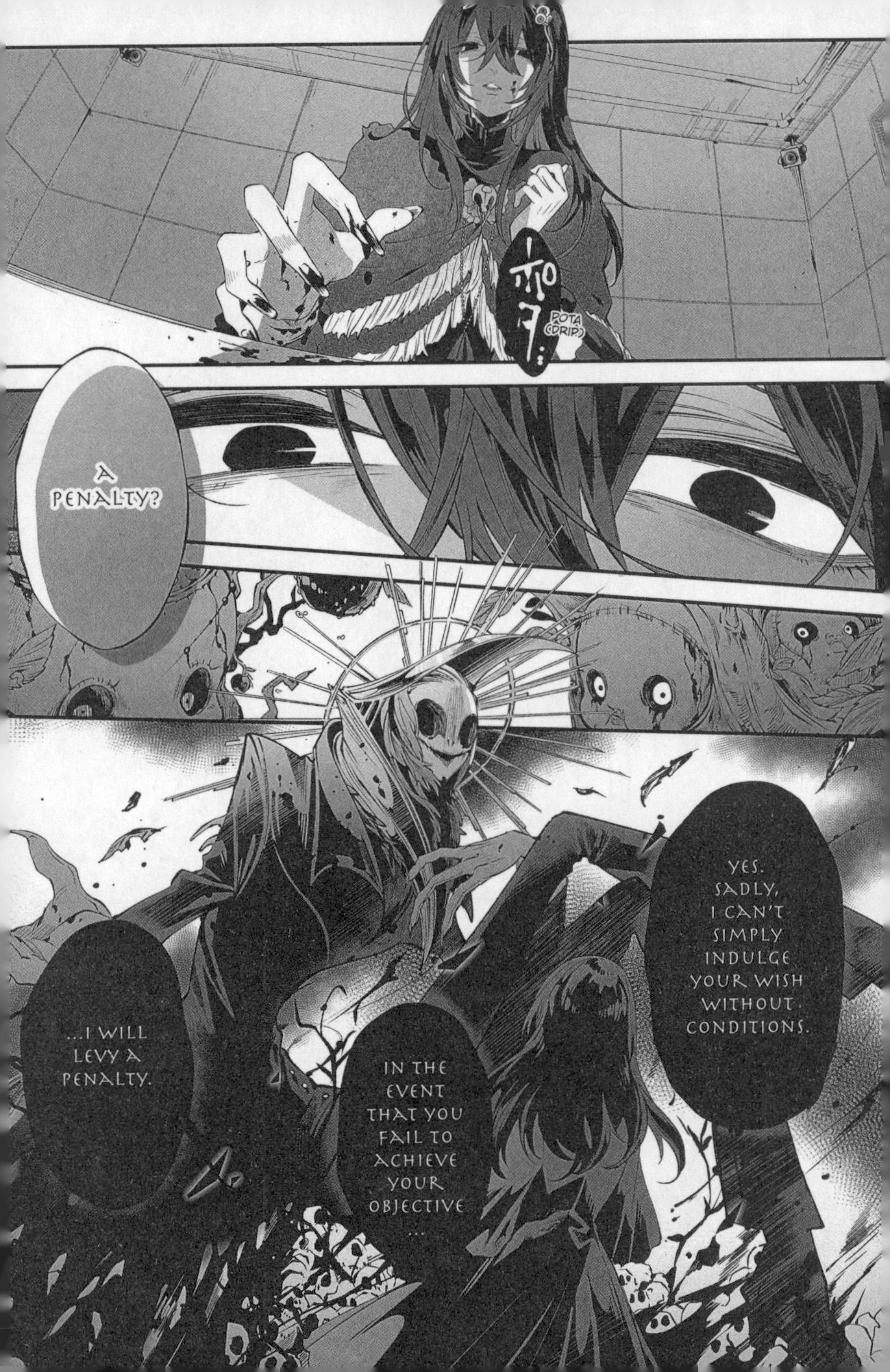
POTA (DRIP)
A PENALTY?
YES. SADLY, I CAN'T SIMPLY INDULGE YOUR WISH WITHOUT CONDITIONS.
IN THE EVENT THAT YOU FAIL TO ACHIEVE YOUR OBJECTIVE ...
...I WILL LEVY A PENALTY.

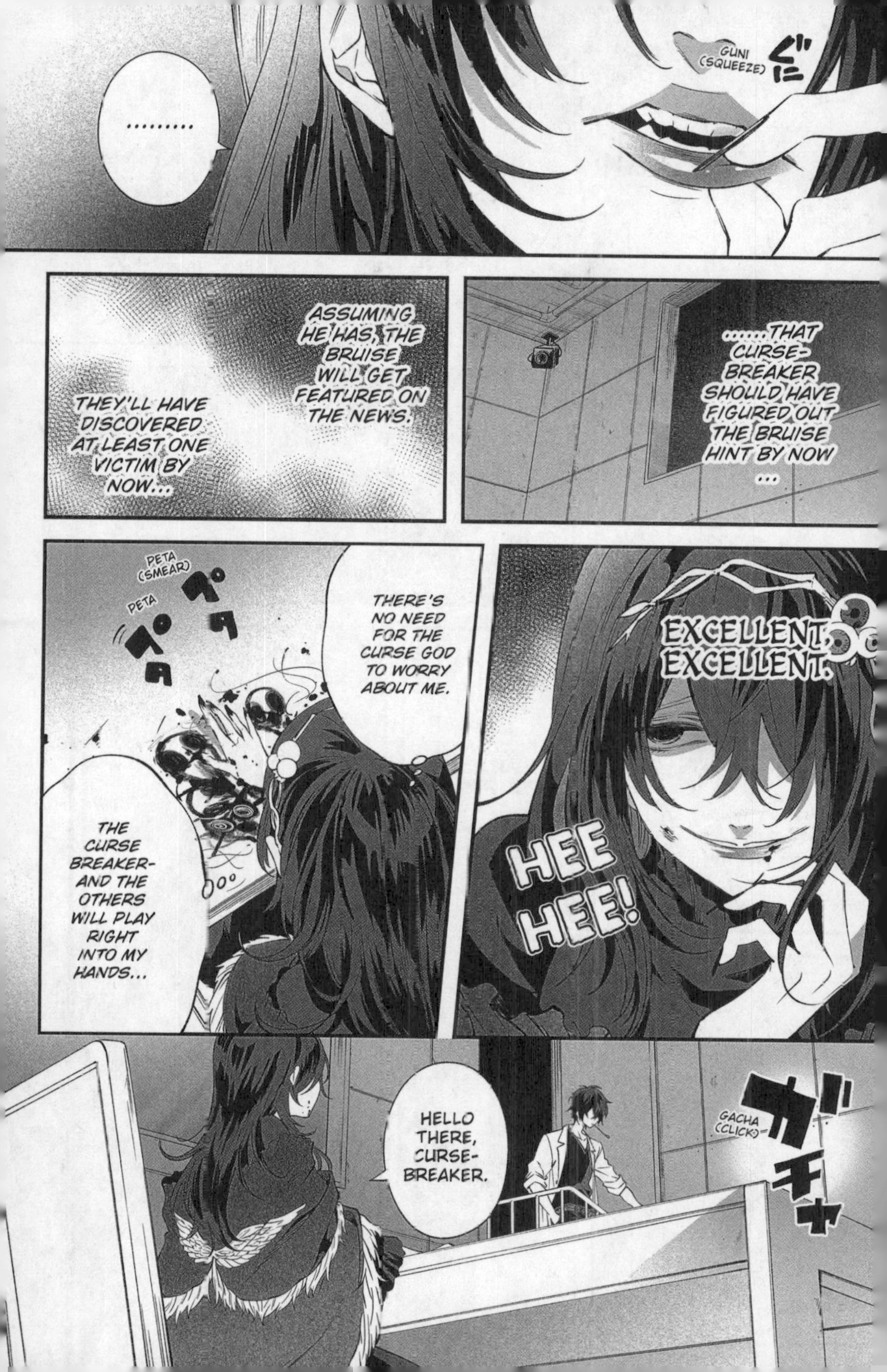
ぐに
GUNI (SQUEEZE)
....
......THAT CURSE-BREAKER SHOULD HAVE FIGURED OUT THE BRUISE HINT BY NOW ...
ASSUMING HE HAS, THE BRUISE WILL GET FEATURED ON THE NEWS.
THEY'LL HAVE DISCOVERED AT LEAST ONE VICTIM BY NOW...
EXCELLENT, EXCELLENT.
HEE HEE!
THERE'S NO NEED FOR THE CURSE GOD TO WORRY ABOUT ME.
ペタ
PETA (SMEAR)
ペタ
PETA
THE CURSE BREAKER- AND THE OTHERS WILL PLAY RIGHT INTO MY HANDS...
ガチャ
GACHA (CLICK)
HELLO THERE, CURSE-BREAKER.

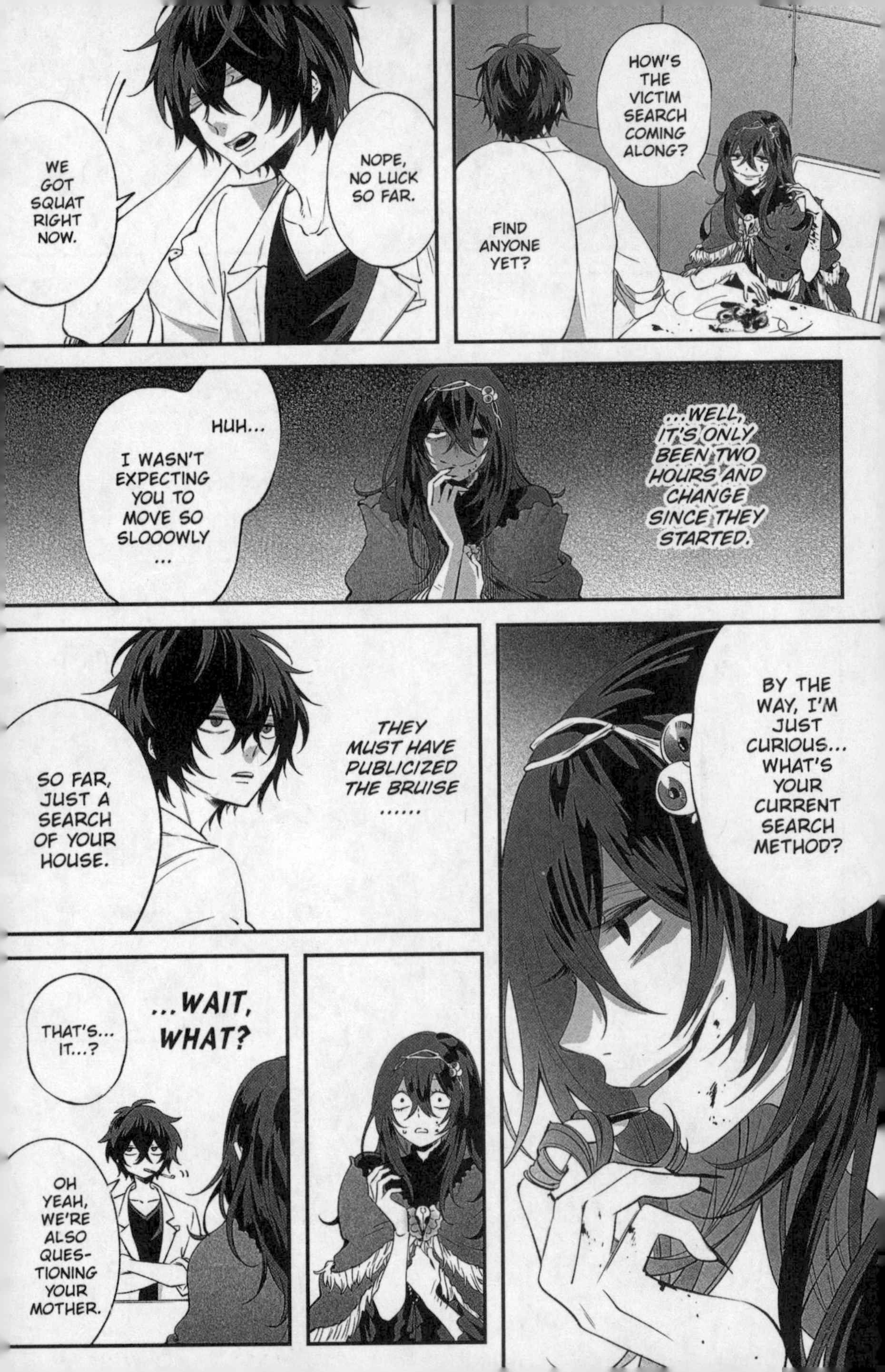
HOW'S THE VICTIM SEARCH COMING ALONG?
FIND ANYONE YET?
NOPE, NO LUCK SO FAR.
WE GOT SQUAT RIGHT NOW.
...WELL, IT'S ONLY BEEN TWO HOURS AND CHANGE SINCE THEY STARTED.
HUH...
I WASN'T EXPECTING YOU TO MOVE SO SLOOOWLY...
BY THE WAY, I'M JUST CURIOUS... WHAT'S YOUR CURRENT SEARCH METHOD?
THEY MUST HAVE PUBLICIZED THE BRUISE......
SO FAR, JUST A SEARCH OF YOUR HOUSE.
...WAIT, WHAT?
THAT'S... IT...?
OH YEAH, WE'RE ALSO QUES-TIONING YOUR MOTHER.

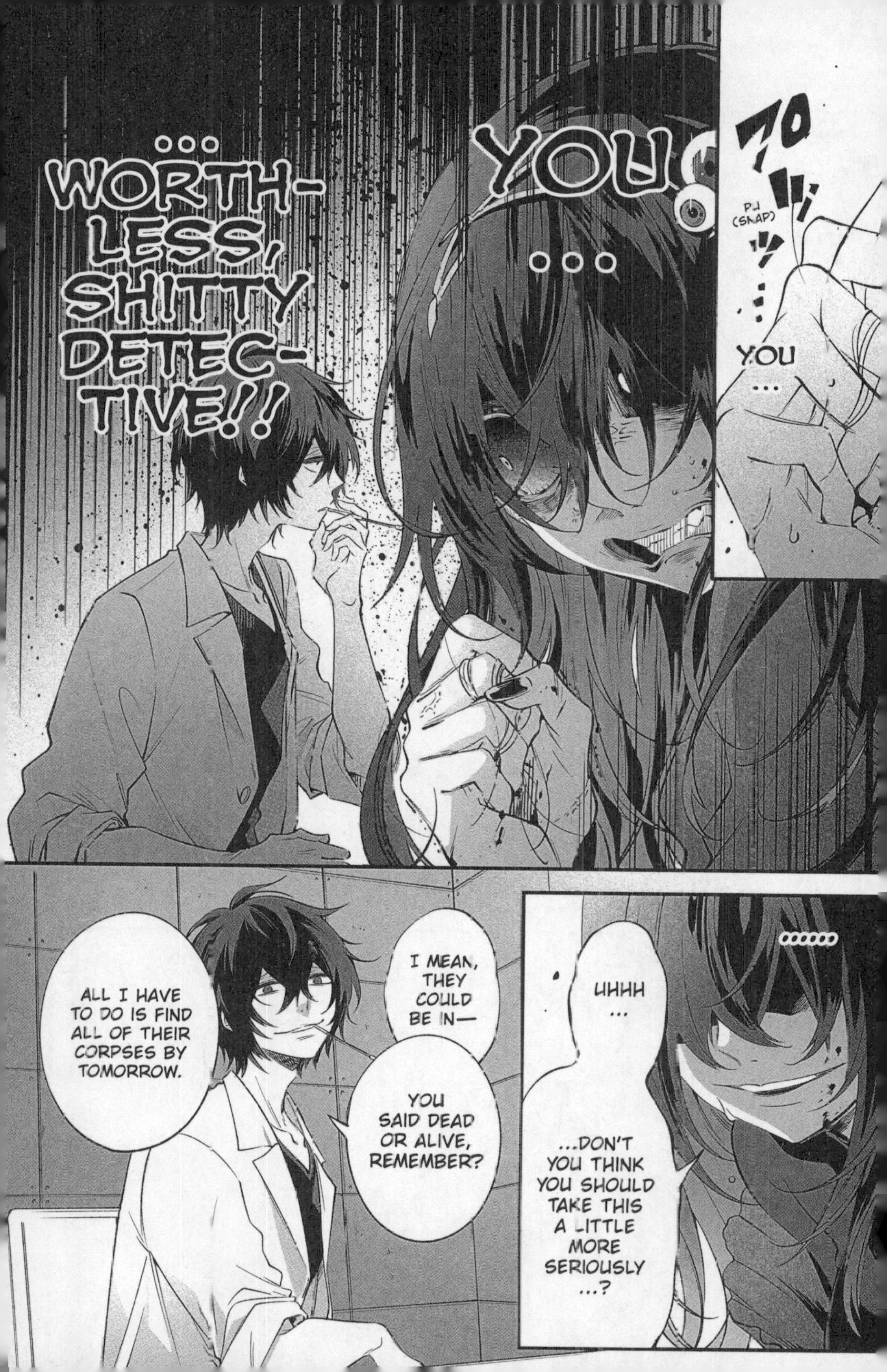
PJ (SNAP)
YOU ...
YOU...
...WORTH-LESS, SHITTY DETEC-TIVE!!
......
UHHH ...
...DON'T YOU THINK YOU SHOULD TAKE THIS A LITTLE MORE SERIOUSLY ...?
I MEAN, THEY COULD BE IN—
ALL I HAVE TO DO IS FIND ALL OF THEIR CORPSES BY TOMORROW.
YOU SAID DEAD OR ALIVE, REMEMBER?

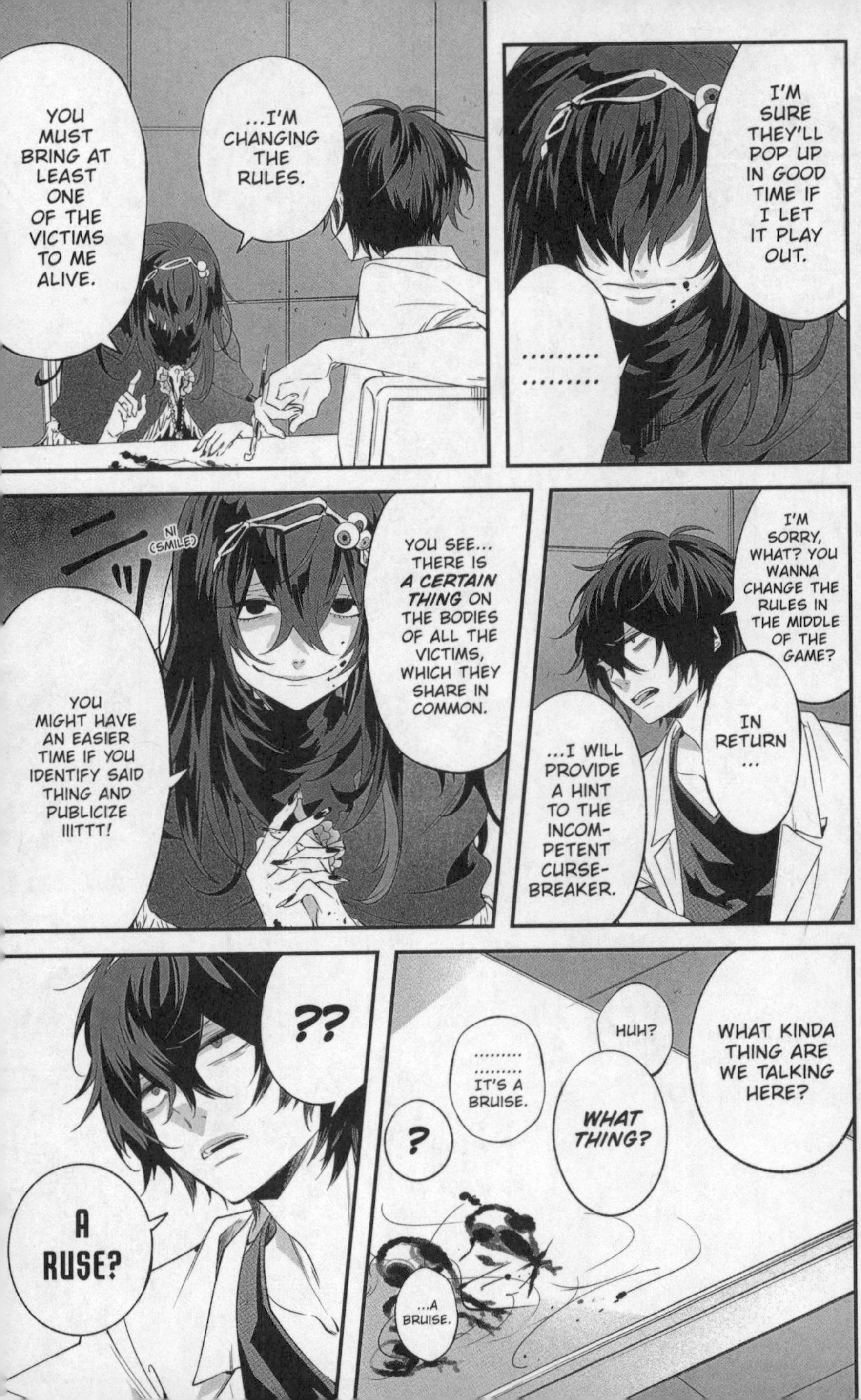
I'M SURE THEY'LL POP UP IN GOOD TIME IF I LET IT PLAY OUT.
....
....
...I'M CHANGING THE RULES.
YOU MUST BRING AT LEAST ONE OF THE VICTIMS TO ME ALIVE.
I'M SORRY, WHAT? YOU WANNA CHANGE THE RULES IN THE MIDDLE OF THE GAME?
IN RETURN...
...I WILL PROVIDE A HINT TO THE INCOMPETENT CURSE-BREAKER.
NI (SMILE)
YOU SEE... THERE IS *A CERTAIN THING* ON THE BODIES OF ALL THE VICTIMS, WHICH THEY SHARE IN COMMON.
YOU MIGHT HAVE AN EASIER TIME IF YOU IDENTIFY SAID THING AND PUBLICIZE IIITTT!
WHAT KINDA THING ARE WE TALKING HERE?
HUH?
....
....
IT'S A BRUISE.
WHAT THING?
?
...A BRUISE.
??
A RUSE?

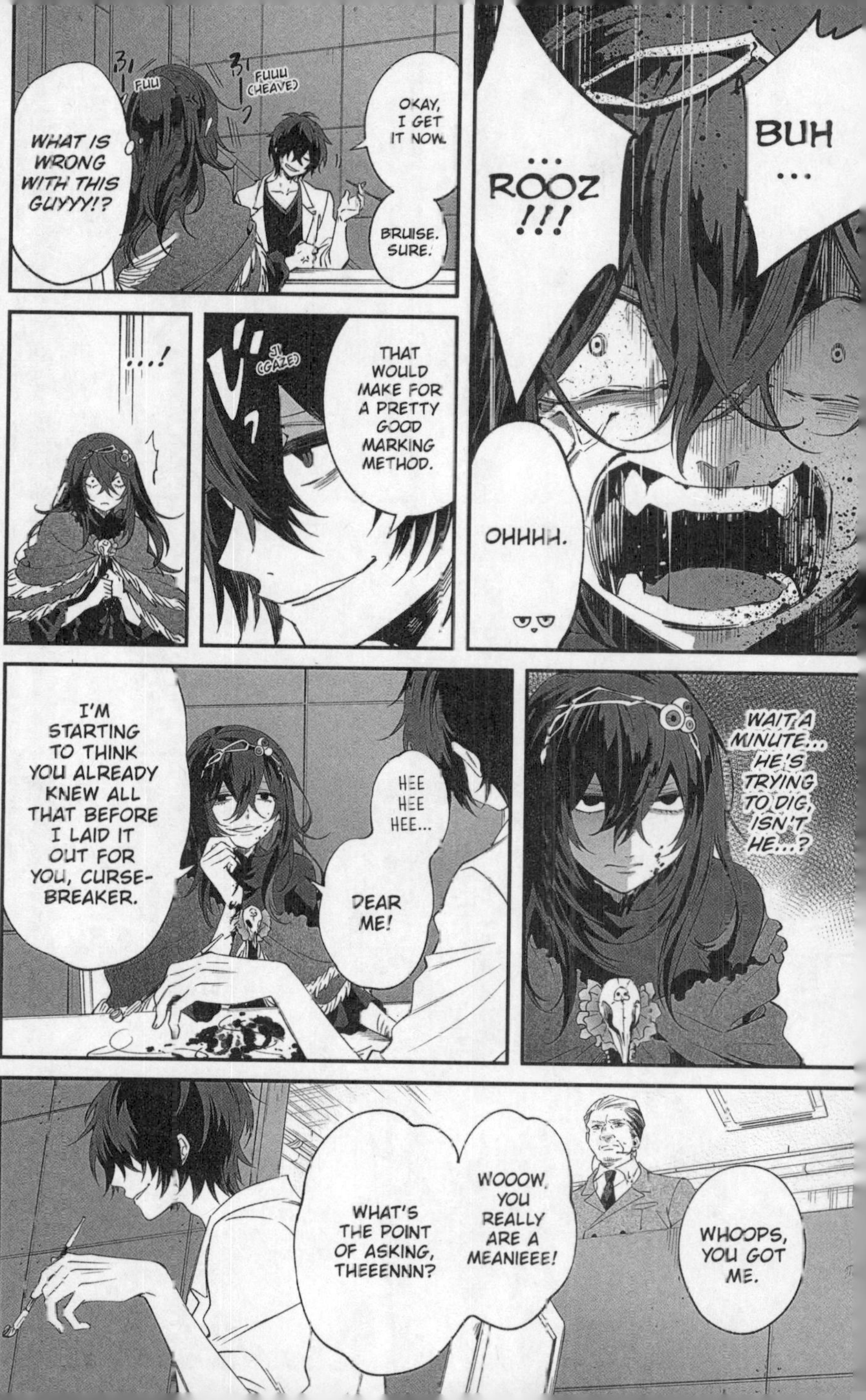
BUH...
...ROOZ!!!
OHHHH.
OKAY, I GET IT NOW.
BRUISE. SURE!
FUUU (HEAVE)
FUU
WHAT IS WRONG WITH THIS GUYYY!?
JI (GAZE)
THAT WOULD MAKE FOR A PRETTY GOOD MARKING METHOD.
...!
WAIT A MINUTE... HE'S TRYING TO DIG, ISN'T HE...?
I'M STARTING TO THINK YOU ALREADY KNEW ALL THAT BEFORE I LAID IT OUT FOR YOU, CURSE-BREAKER.
HEE HEE HEE...
DEAR ME!
WHOOPS, YOU GOT ME.
WOOOW, YOU REALLY ARE A MEANIEEE!
WHAT'S THE POINT OF ASKING, THEEENNN?

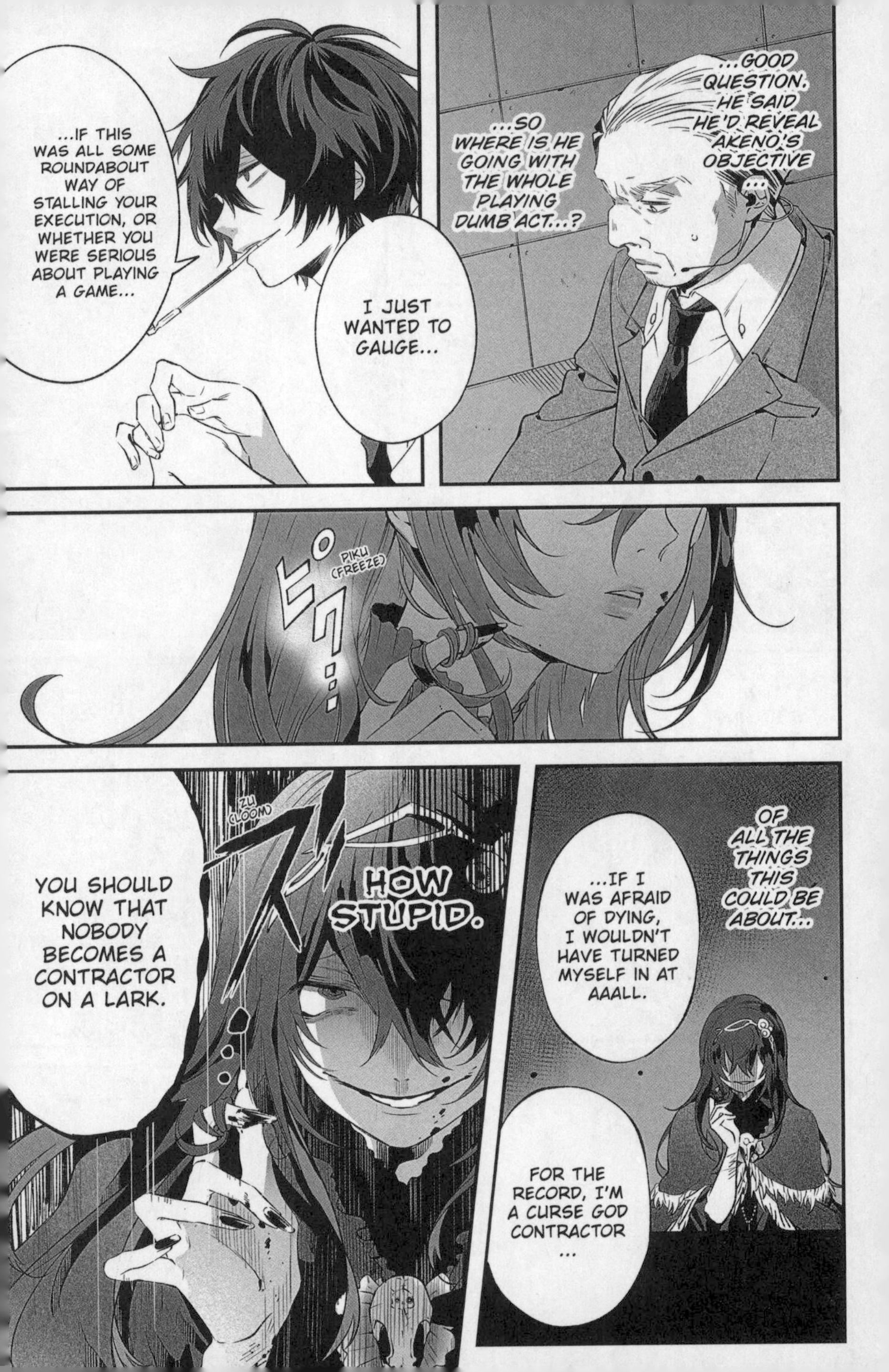
...SO WHERE IS HE GOING WITH THE WHOLE PLAYING DUMB ACT...?
...GOOD QUESTION. HE SAID HE'D REVEAL AKENO'S OBJECTIVE ...
...IF THIS WAS ALL SOME ROUNDABOUT WAY OF STALLING YOUR EXECUTION, OR WHETHER YOU WERE SERIOUS ABOUT PLAYING A GAME...
I JUST WANTED TO GAUGE...
PIKU (FREEZE)
OF ALL THE THINGS THIS COULD BE ABOUT...
...IF I WAS AFRAID OF DYING, I WOULDN'T HAVE TURNED MYSELF IN AT AAALL.
FOR THE RECORD, I'M A CURSE GOD CONTRACTOR ...
ZU (LOOM)
HOW STUPID.
YOU SHOULD KNOW THAT NOBODY BECOMES A CONTRACTOR ON A LARK.

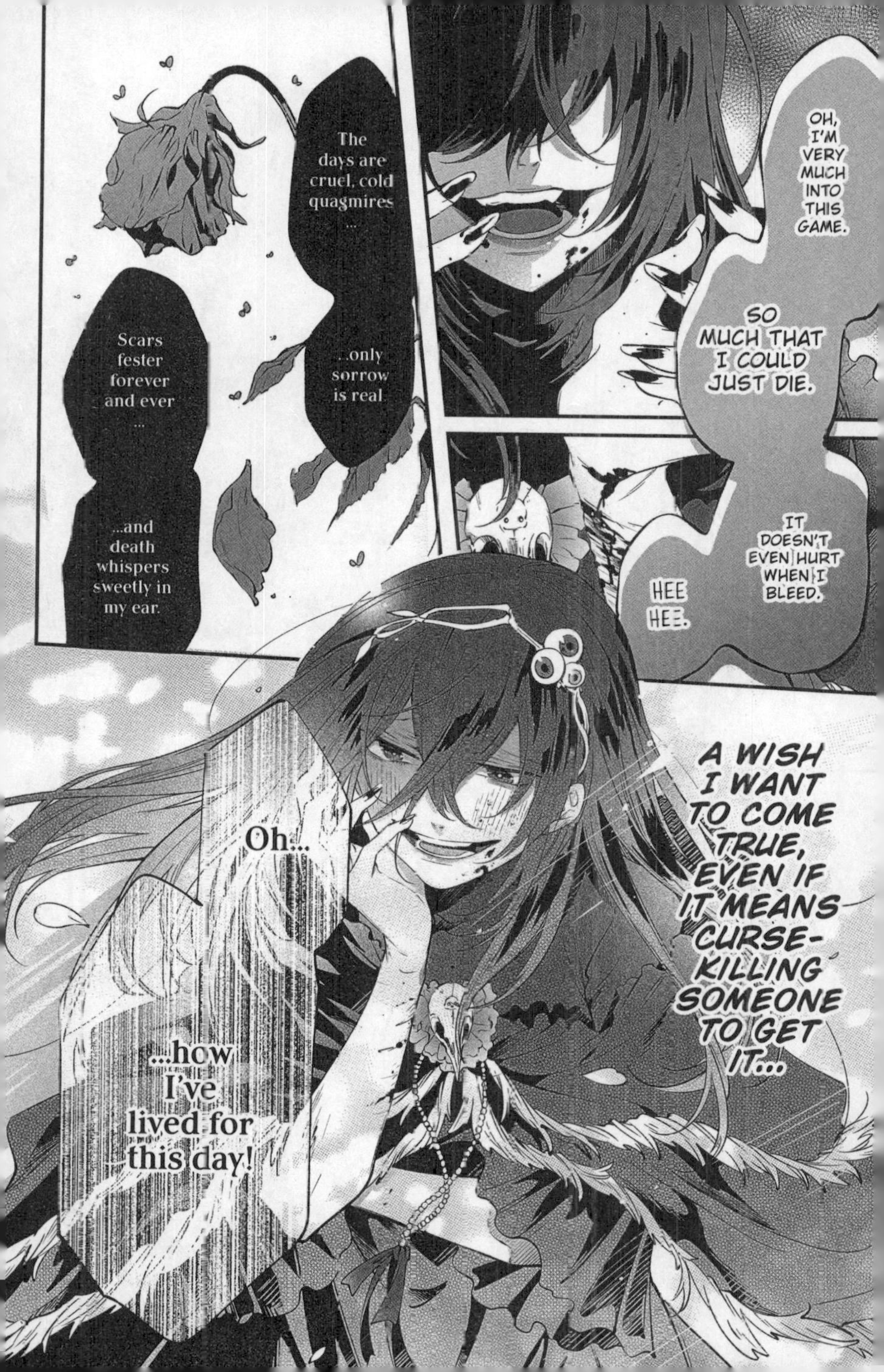
OH, I'M VERY MUCH INTO THIS GAME.
SO MUCH THAT I COULD JUST DIE.
IT DOESN'T EVEN HURT WHEN I BLEED.
HEE HEE.
The days are cruel, cold quagmires...
...only sorrow is real.
Scars fester forever and ever...
...and death whispers sweetly in my ear.
A WISH I WANT TO COME TRUE, EVEN IF IT MEANS CURSE-KILLING SOMEONE TO GET IT...
Oh...
...how I've lived for this day!

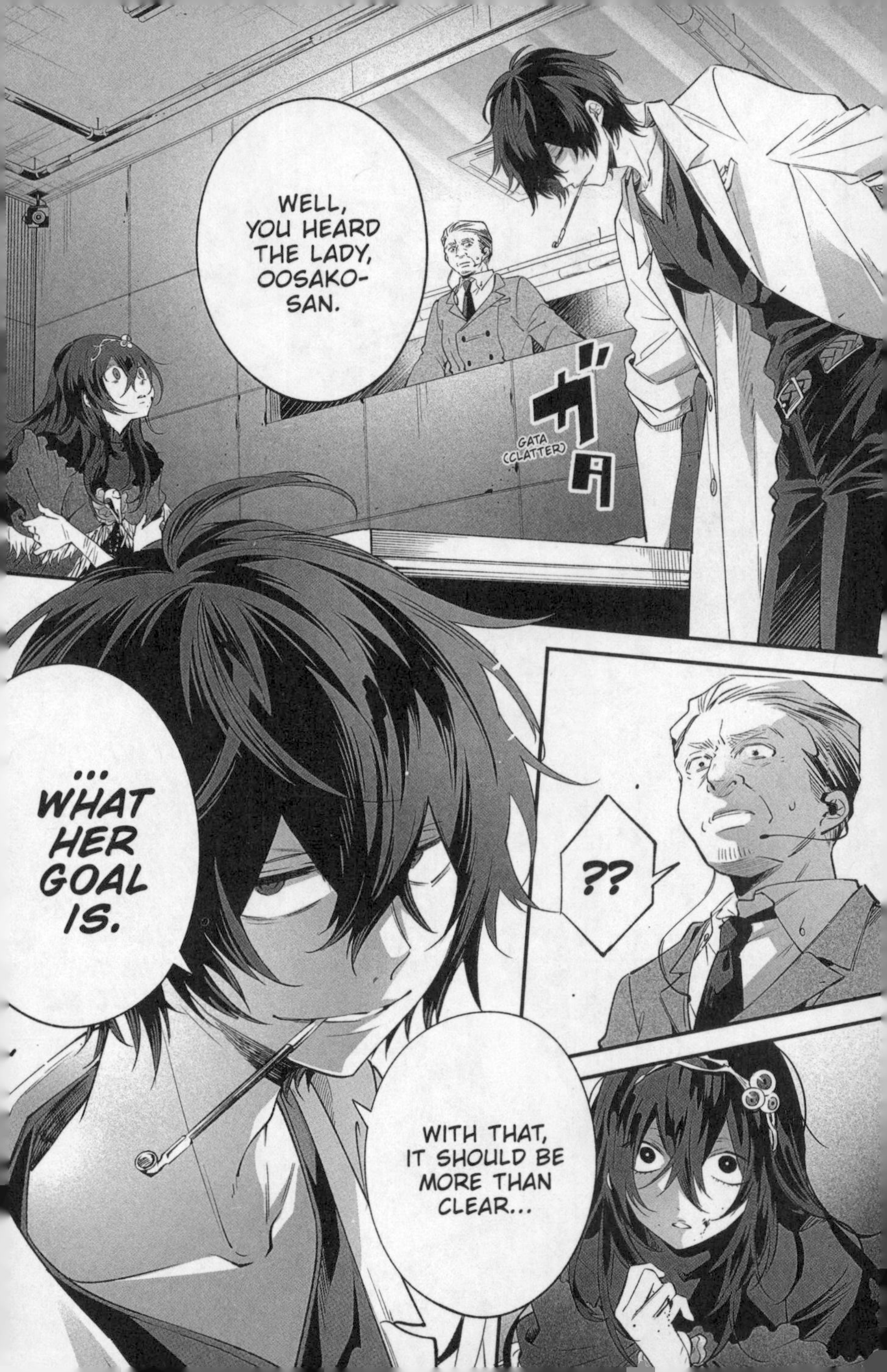
WELL, YOU HEARD THE LADY, OOSAKO-SAN.
GATA (CLATTER)
??
WITH THAT, IT SHOULD BE MORE THAN CLEAR...
...WHAT HER GOAL IS.

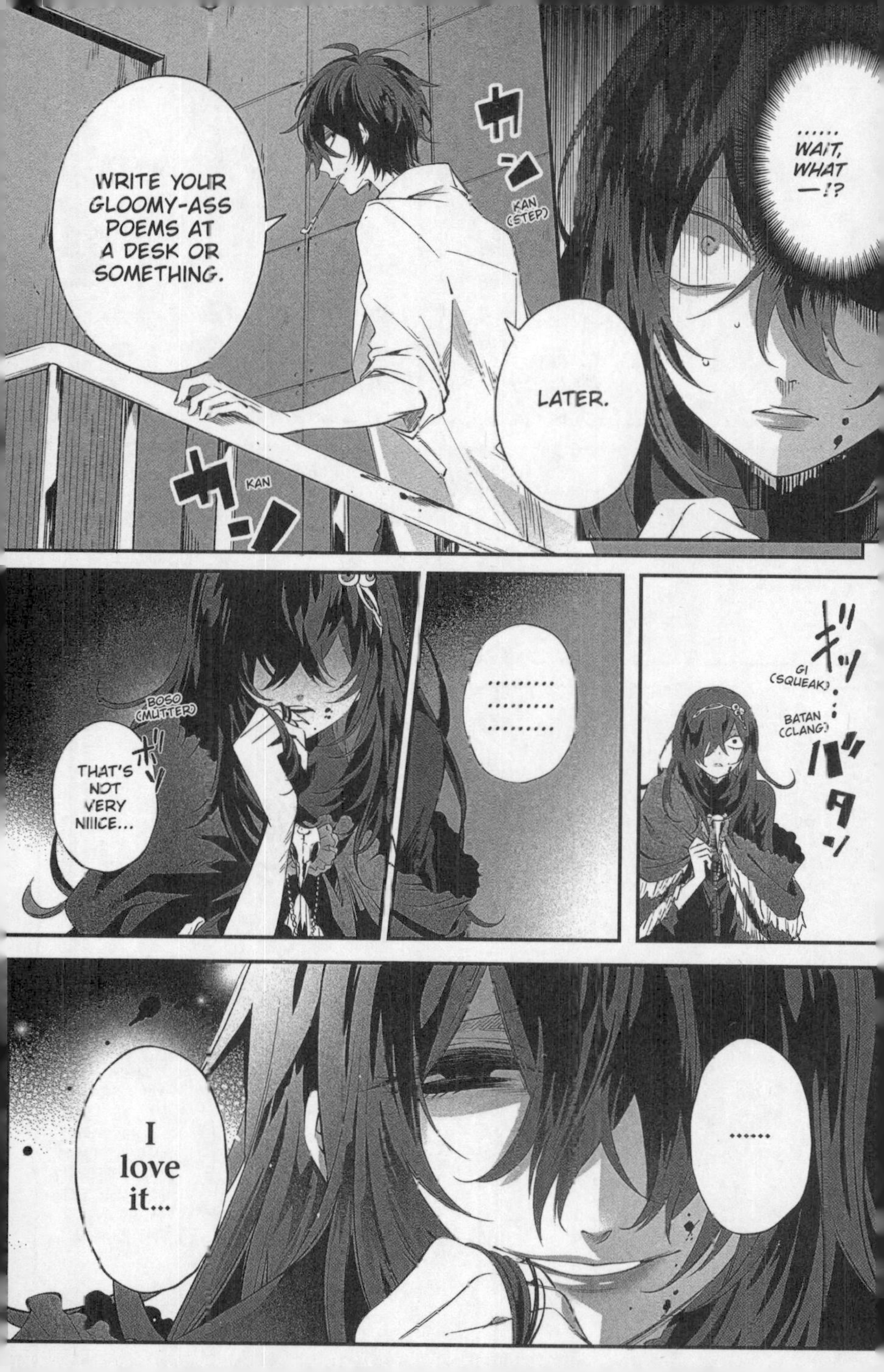
KAN (STEP)
WRITE YOUR GLOOMY-ASS POEMS AT A DESK OR SOMETHING.
LATER.
KAN
......WAIT, WHAT—!?
GI (SQUEAK)
BATAN (CLANG)
....
....
....
BOSO (MUTTER)
THAT'S NOT VERY NIIICE...
......
I love it...

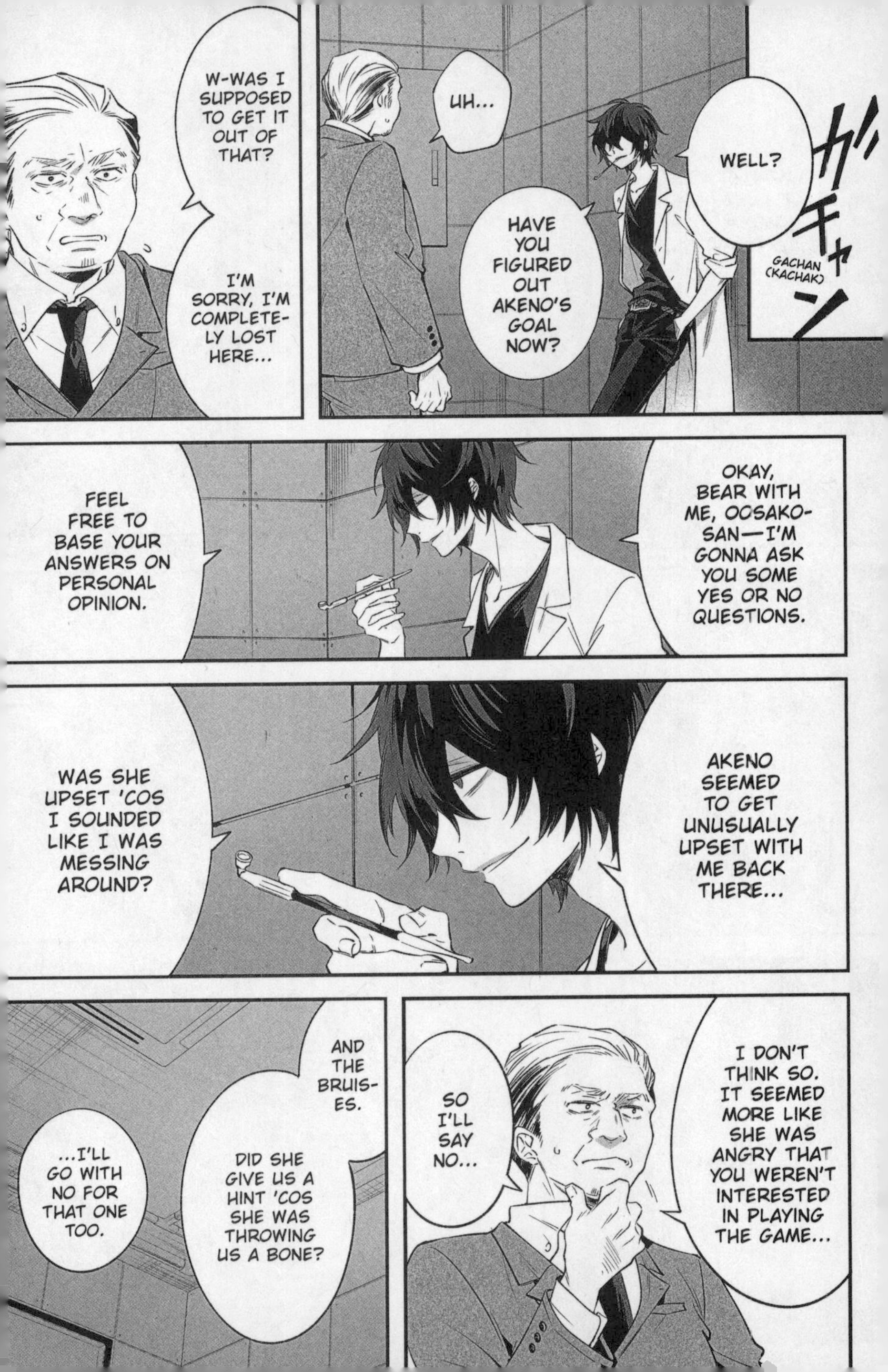
ガチャン
GACHAN (KACHAK)
WELL?
HAVE YOU FIGURED OUT AKENO'S GOAL NOW?
UH...
W-WAS I SUPPOSED TO GET IT OUT OF THAT?
I'M SORRY, I'M COMPLETE-LY LOST HERE...
OKAY, BEAR WITH ME, OOSAKO-SAN—I'M GONNA ASK YOU SOME YES OR NO QUESTIONS.
FEEL FREE TO BASE YOUR ANSWERS ON PERSONAL OPINION.
AKENO SEEMED TO GET UNUSUALLY UPSET WITH ME BACK THERE...
WAS SHE UPSET 'COS I SOUNDED LIKE I WAS MESSING AROUND?
I DON'T THINK SO. IT SEEMED MORE LIKE SHE WAS ANGRY THAT YOU WEREN'T INTERESTED IN PLAYING THE GAME...
SO I'LL SAY NO...
AND THE BRUIS-ES.
DID SHE GIVE US A HINT 'COS SHE WAS THROWING US A BONE?
...I'LL GO WITH NO FOR THAT ONE TOO.

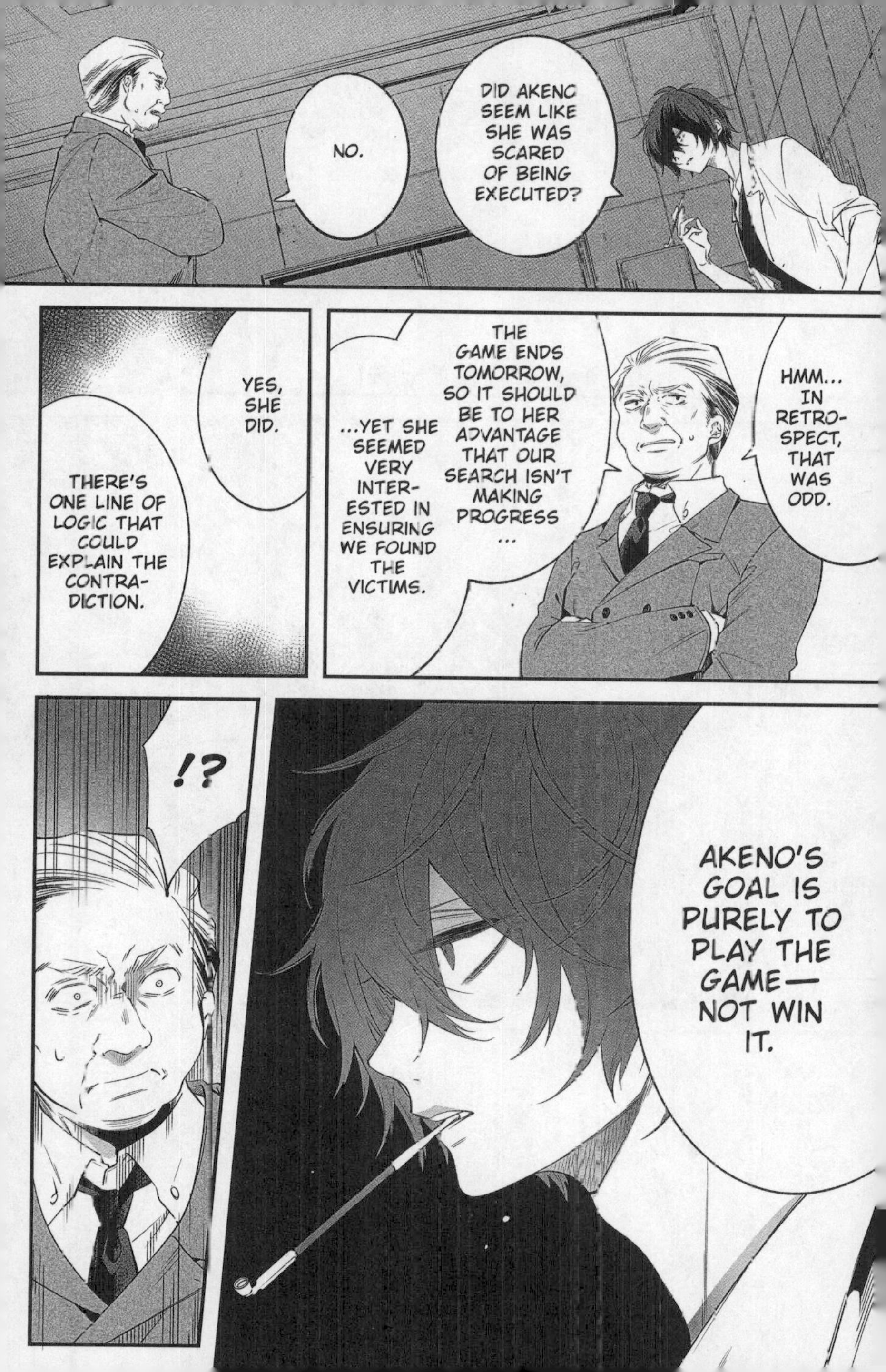
DID AKENO SEEM LIKE SHE WAS SCARED OF BEING EXECUTED?
NO.
HMM... IN RETROSPECT, THAT WAS ODD.
THE GAME ENDS TOMORROW, SO IT SHOULD BE TO HER ADVANTAGE THAT OUR SEARCH ISN'T MAKING PROGRESS...
...YET SHE SEEMED VERY INTERESTED IN ENSURING WE FOUND THE VICTIMS.
YES, SHE DID.
THERE'S ONE LINE OF LOGIC THAT COULD EXPLAIN THE CONTRADICTION.
AKENO'S GOAL IS PURELY TO PLAY THE GAME—NOT WIN IT.
!?

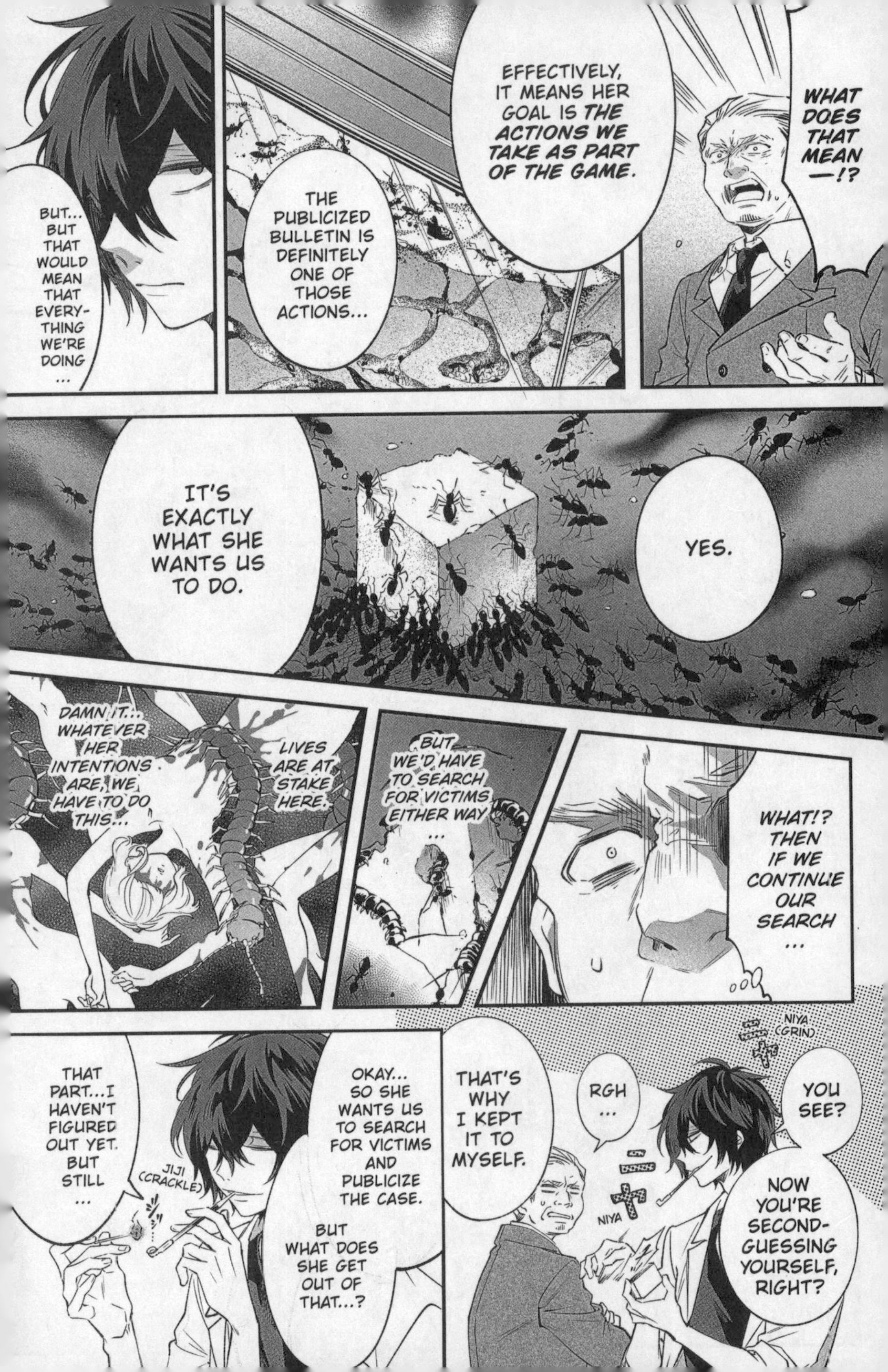
WHAT DOES THAT MEAN—!?
EFFECTIVELY, IT MEANS HER GOAL IS *THE ACTIONS WE TAKE AS PART OF THE GAME*.
THE PUBLICIZED BULLETIN IS DEFINITELY ONE OF THOSE ACTIONS...
BUT... BUT THAT WOULD MEAN THAT EVERYTHING WE'RE DOING...
YES.
IT'S EXACTLY WHAT SHE WANTS US TO DO.
WHAT!? THEN IF WE CONTINUE OUR SEARCH...
BUT WE'D HAVE TO SEARCH FOR VICTIMS EITHER WAY...
LIVES ARE AT STAKE HERE.
DAMN IT... WHATEVER HER INTENTIONS ARE, WE HAVE TO DO THIS...
NIYA (GRIN)
YOU SEE?
NOW YOU'RE SECOND-GUESSING YOURSELF, RIGHT?
RGH...
NIYA
THAT'S WHY I KEPT IT TO MYSELF.
OKAY... SO SHE WANTS US TO SEARCH FOR VICTIMS AND PUBLICIZE THE CASE.
BUT WHAT DOES SHE GET OUT OF THAT...?
THAT PART...I HAVEN'T FIGURED OUT YET. BUT STILL...
JIJI (CRACKLE)

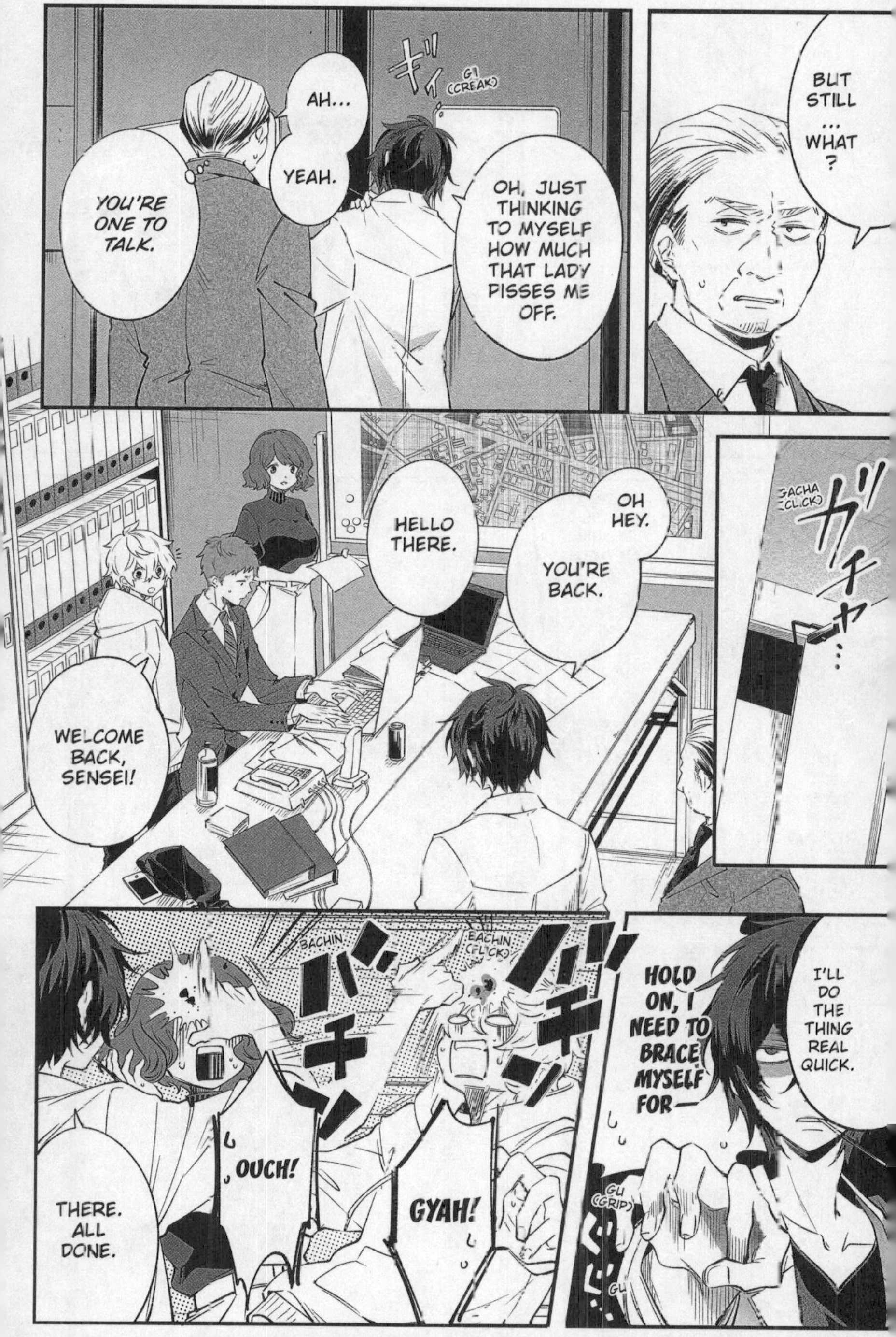
BUT STILL ... WHAT?
OH, JUST THINKING TO MYSELF HOW MUCH THAT LADY PISSES ME OFF.
YOU'RE ONE TO TALK.
AH...
YEAH.
GI (CREAK)
GACHA (CLICK)
OH HEY.
YOU'RE BACK.
HELLO THERE.
WELCOME BACK, SENSEI!
I'LL DO THE THING REAL QUICK.
HOLD ON, I NEED TO BRACE MYSELF FOR—
GU (GRIP)
GU
BACHIN (FLICK)
GYAH!
BACHIN
OUCH!
THERE. ALL DONE.

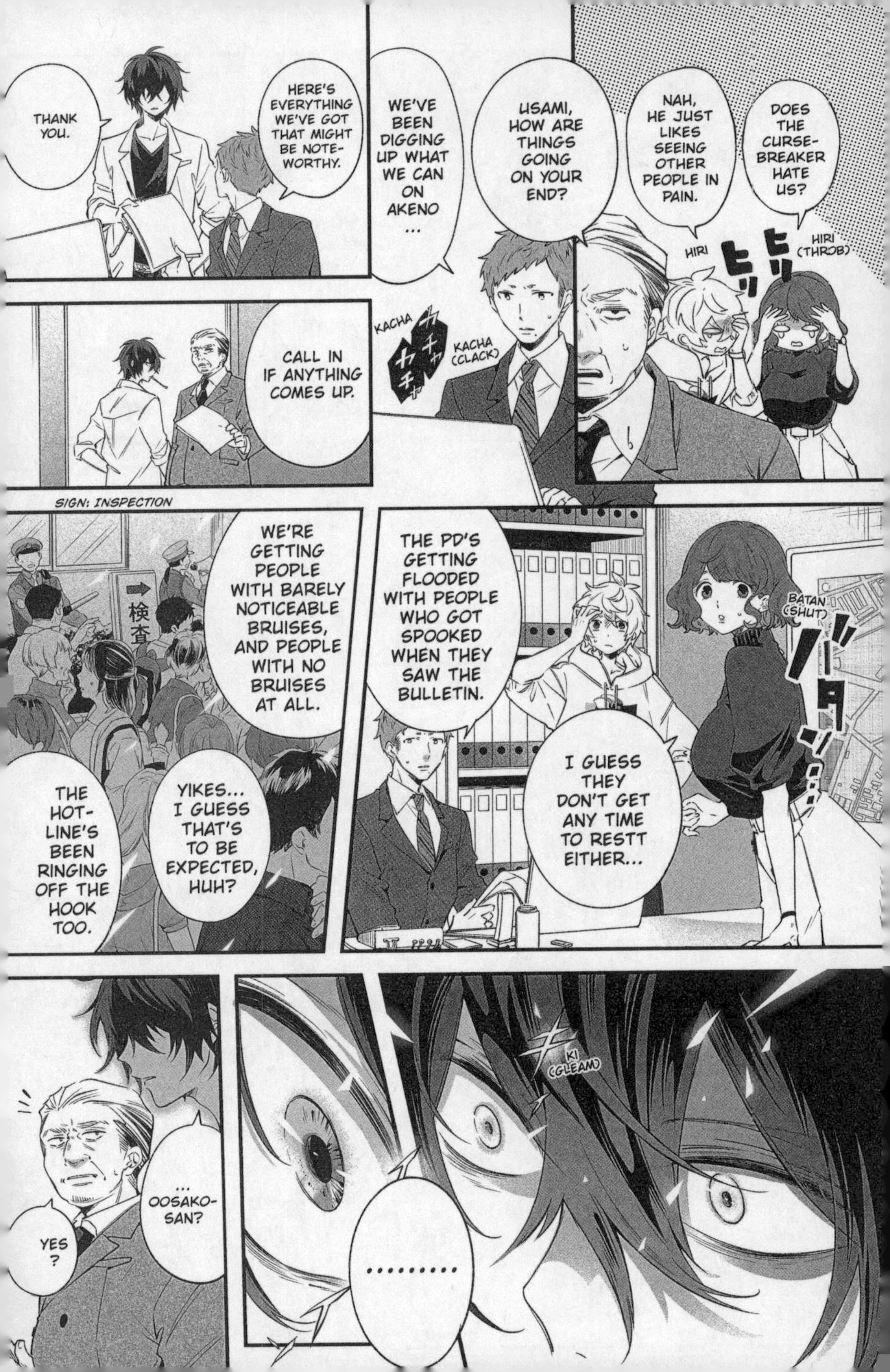
DOES THE CURSE-BREAKER HATE US?
NAH, HE JUST LIKES SEEING OTHER PEOPLE IN PAIN.
HIRI (THROB)
HIRI
USAMI, HOW ARE THINGS GOING ON YOUR END?
WE'VE BEEN DIGGING UP WHAT WE CAN ON AKENO ...
KACHA (CLACK)
KACHA
HERE'S EVERYTHING WE'VE GOT THAT MIGHT BE NOTE-WORTHY.
THANK YOU.
CALL IN IF ANYTHING COMES UP.
BATAN (SHUT)
THE PD'S GETTING FLOODED WITH PEOPLE WHO GOT SPOOKED WHEN THEY SAW THE BULLETIN.
I GUESS THEY DON'T GET ANY TIME TO RESTT EITHER...
SIGN: INSPECTION
検査
WE'RE GETTING PEOPLE WITH BARELY NOTICEABLE BRUISES, AND PEOPLE WITH NO BRUISES AT ALL.
YIKES... I GUESS THAT'S TO BE EXPECTED, HUH?
THE HOT-LINE'S BEEN RINGING OFF THE HOOK TOO.
KI (GLEAM)
....
... OOSAKO-SAN?
YES?

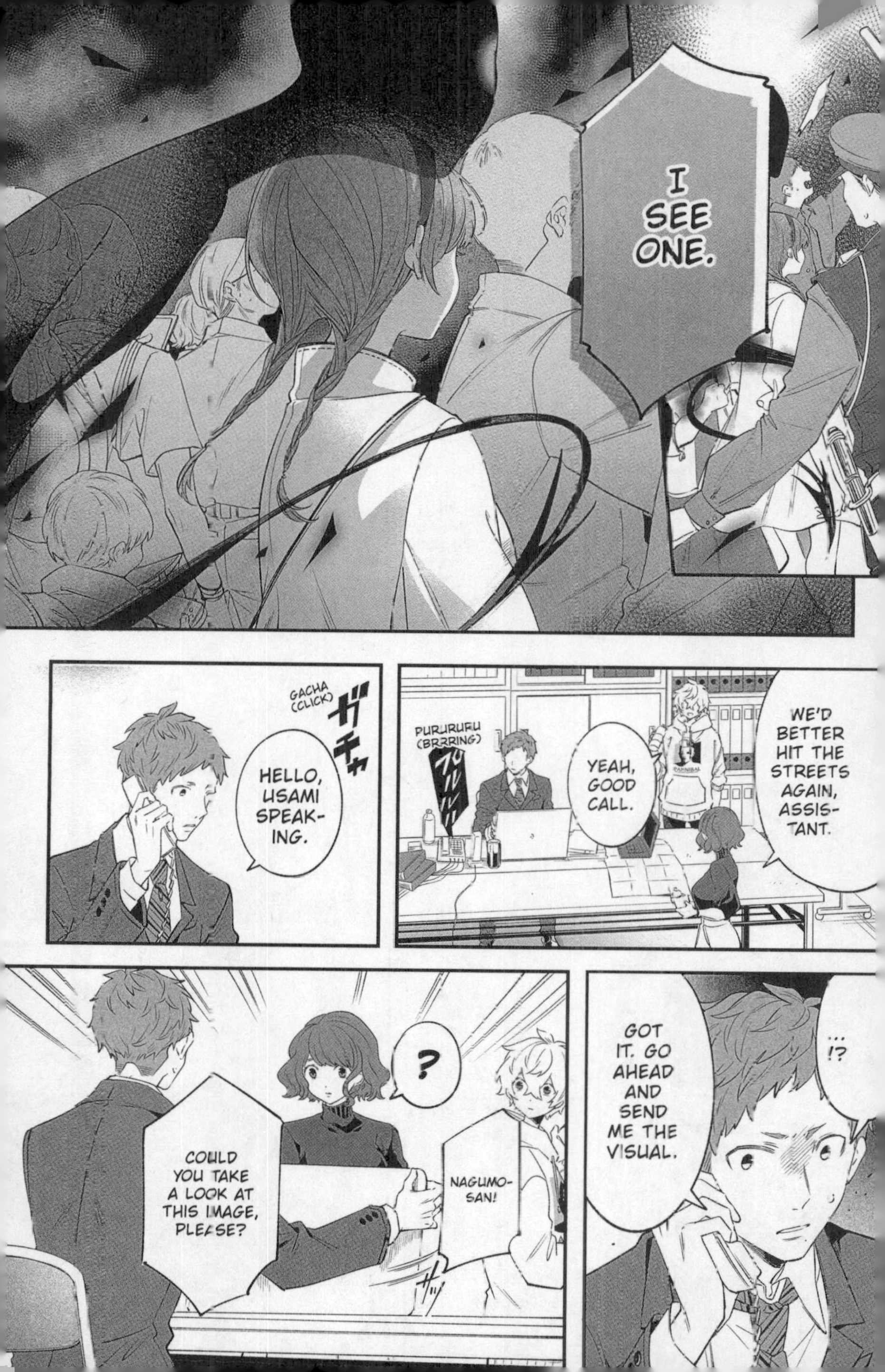
I SEE ONE.
WE'D BETTER HIT THE STREETS AGAIN, ASSISTANT.
YEAH, GOOD CALL.
PURURURU (BRRRING)
GACHA (CLICK)
HELLO, USAMI SPEAKING.
...!?
GOT IT. GO AHEAD AND SEND ME THE VISUAL.
NAGUMO-SAN!
COULD YOU TAKE A LOOK AT THIS IMAGE, PLEASE?
?

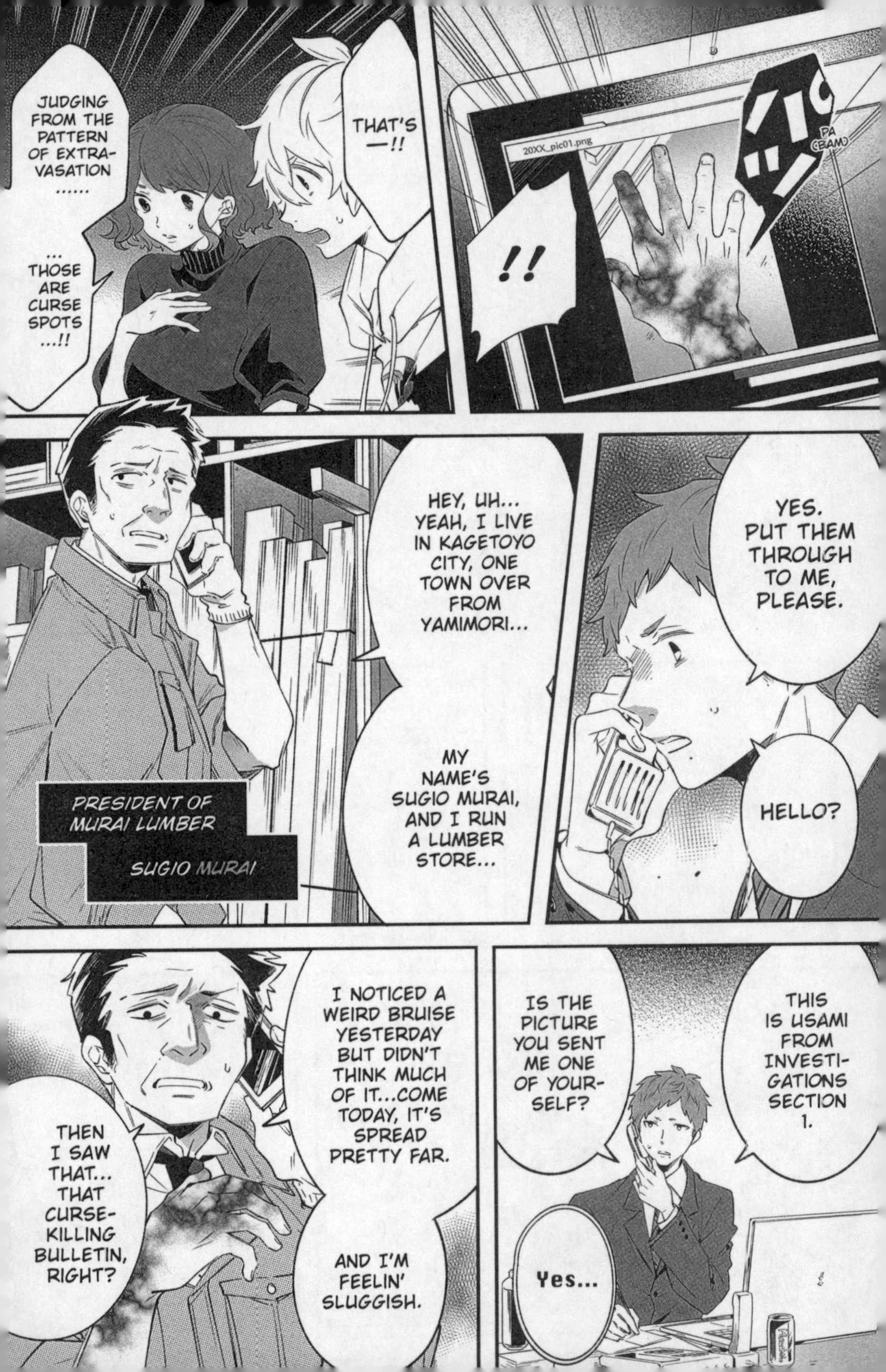
PA (BAM)
20XX_pic01.png
!!
THAT'S—!!
JUDGING FROM THE PATTERN OF EXTRA-VASATION......
...THOSE ARE CURSE SPOTS...!!
YES. PUT THEM THROUGH TO ME, PLEASE.
HELLO?
HEY, UH... YEAH, I LIVE IN KAGETOYO CITY, ONE TOWN OVER FROM YAMIMORI...
MY NAME'S SUGIO MURAI, AND I RUN A LUMBER STORE...
PRESIDENT OF MURAI LUMBER
SUGIO MURAI
THIS IS USAMI FROM INVESTI-GATIONS SECTION 1.
IS THE PICTURE YOU SENT ME ONE OF YOUR-SELF?
Yes...
I NOTICED A WEIRD BRUISE YESTERDAY BUT DIDN'T THINK MUCH OF IT...COME TODAY, IT'S SPREAD PRETTY FAR.
AND I'M FEELIN' SLUGGISH.
THEN I SAW THAT... THAT CURSE-KILLING BULLETIN, RIGHT?

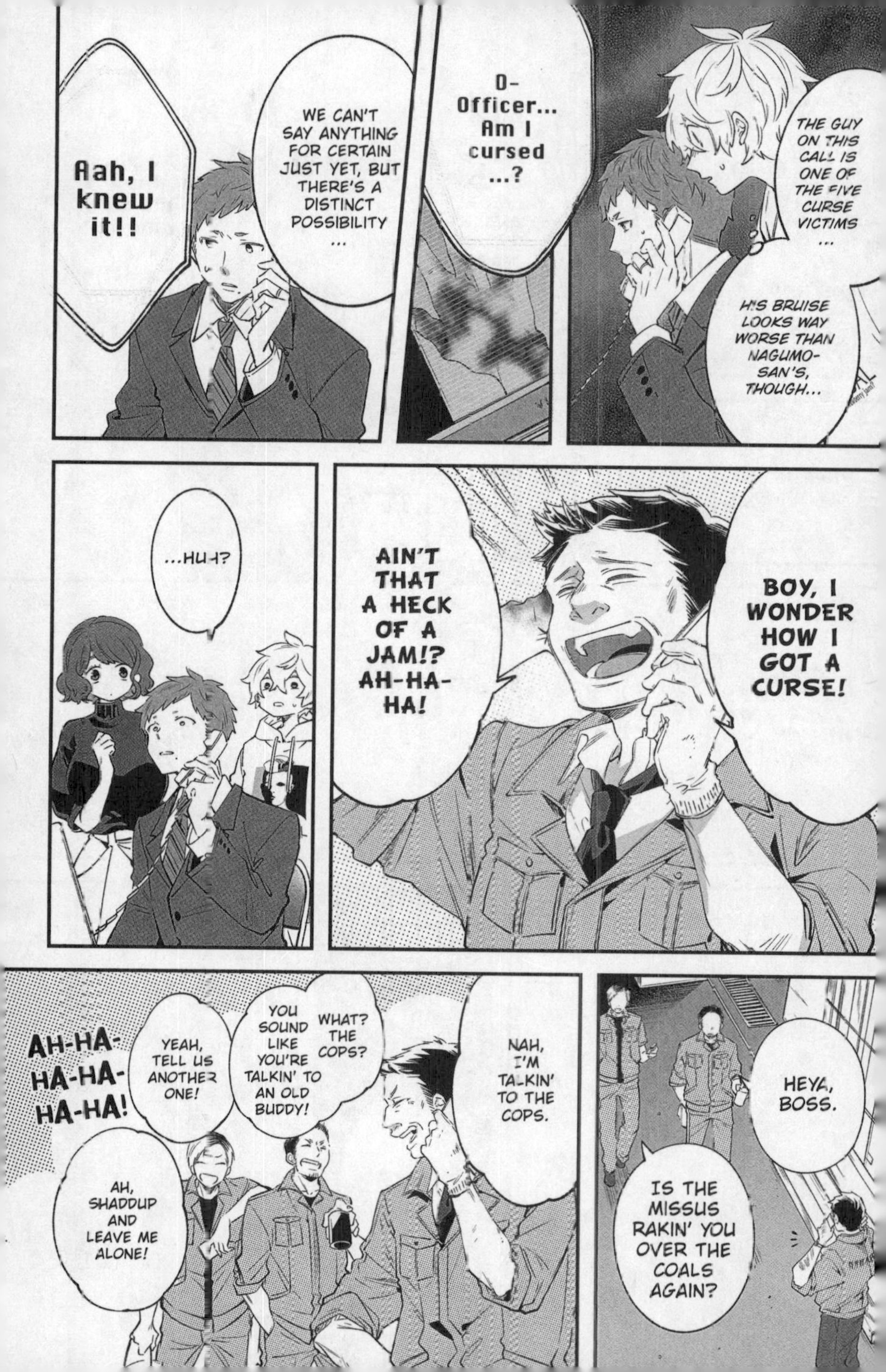
THE GUY ON THIS CALL IS ONE OF THE FIVE CURSE VICTIMS...
HIS BRUISE LOOKS WAY WORSE THAN NAGUMO-SAN'S, THOUGH...
D-Officer... Am I cursed...?
WE CAN'T SAY ANYTHING FOR CERTAIN JUST YET, BUT THERE'S A DISTINCT POSSIBILITY...
Aah, I knew it!!
BOY, I WONDER HOW I GOT A CURSE!
AIN'T THAT A HECK OF A JAM!? AH-HA-HA!
...HUH?
HEYA, BOSS.
IS THE MISSUS RAKIN' YOU OVER THE COALS AGAIN?
NAH, I'M TALKIN' TO THE COPS.
WHAT? THE COPS?
YOU SOUND LIKE YOU'RE TALKIN' TO AN OLD BUDDY!
YEAH, TELL US ANOTHER ONE!
AH-HA-HA-HA-HA-HA!
AH, SHADDUP AND LEAVE ME ALONE!

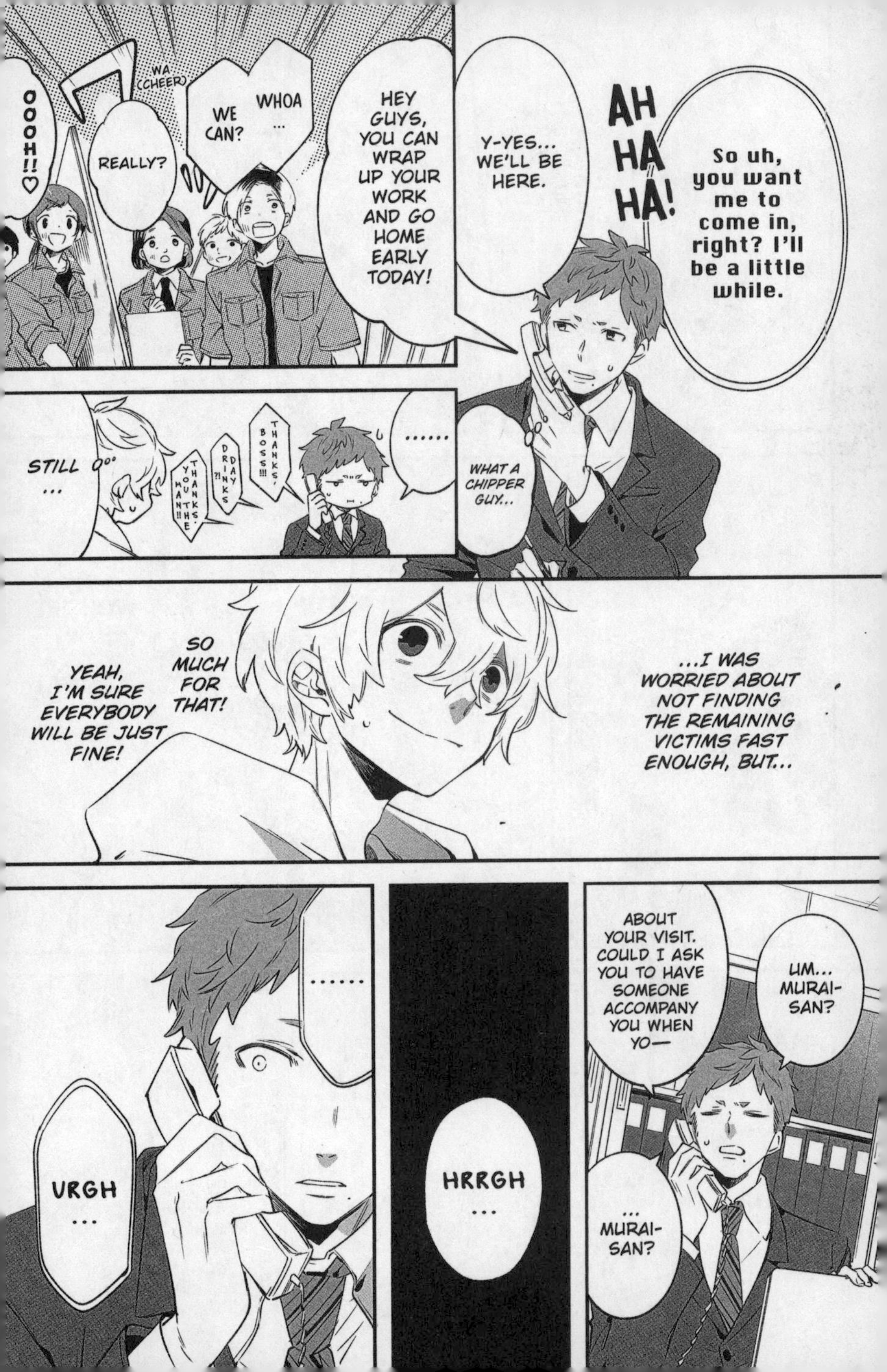
AH HA HA!
So uh, you want me to come in, right? I'll be a little while.
Y-YES... WE'LL BE HERE.
HEY GUYS, YOU CAN WRAP UP YOUR WORK AND GO HOME EARLY TODAY!
WHOA ...
WE CAN?
WA (CHEER)
REALLY?
OOOH!!♡
WHAT A CHIPPER GUY...
......
THANKS, BOSS!!!
DAY DRINKS?!
THANKS, YOU THE MAN!!
STILL ...
...I WAS WORRIED ABOUT NOT FINDING THE REMAINING VICTIMS FAST ENOUGH, BUT...
SO MUCH FOR THAT!
YEAH, I'M SURE EVERYBODY WILL BE JUST FINE!
UM... MURAI-SAN?
ABOUT YOUR VISIT. COULD I ASK YOU TO HAVE SOMEONE ACCOMPANY YOU WHEN YO—
...MURAI-SAN?
HRRGH ...
......
URGH ...

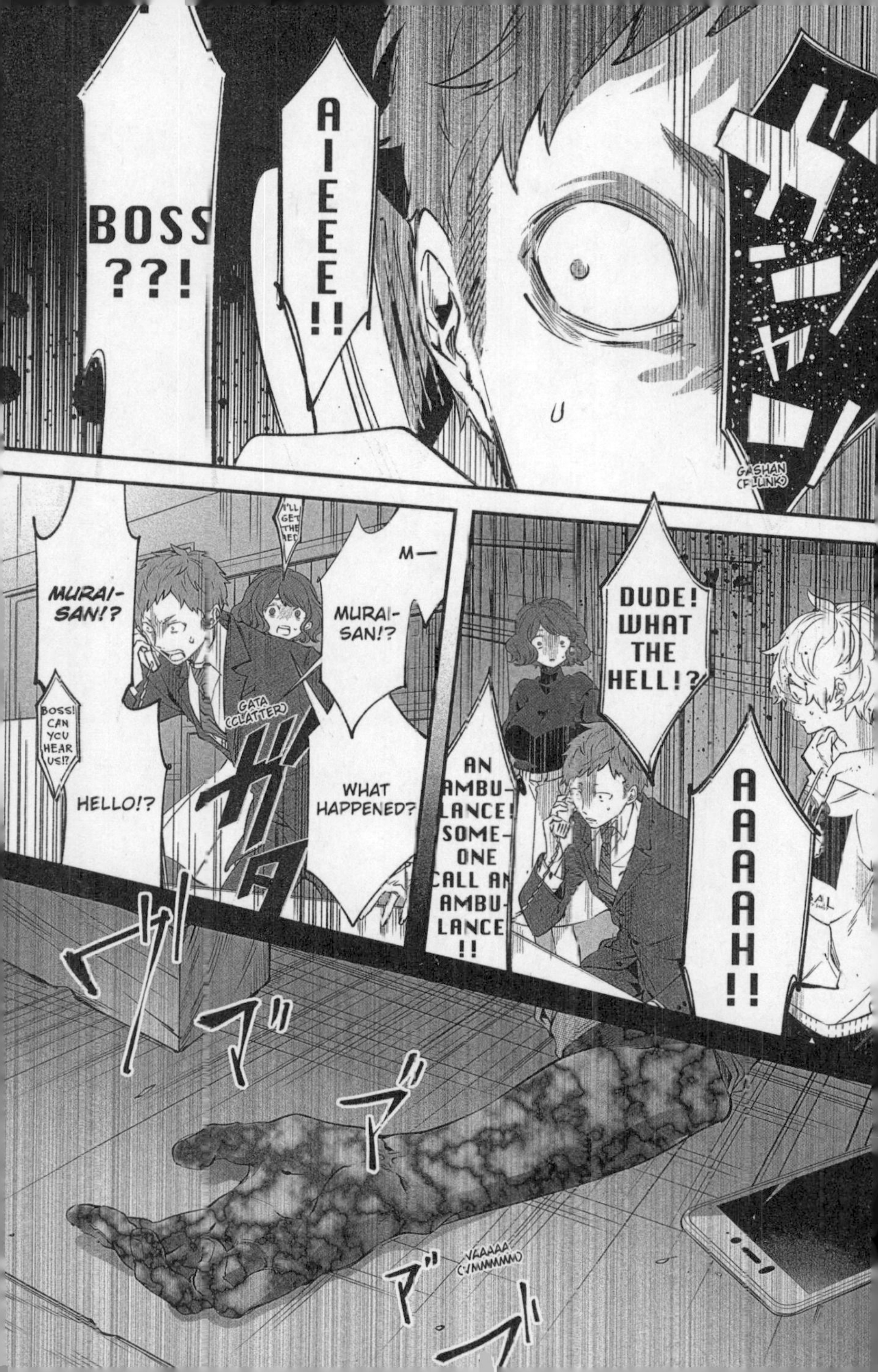
GASHAN (CLINK)
AIEEE!!
BOSS??!
DUDE! WHAT THE HELL!?
AAAAAH!!
AN AMBULANCE! SOME-ONE CALL AN AMBULANCE!!
M— MURAI-SAN!?
WHAT HAPPENED?
I'LL GET THE REC
MURAI-SAN!?
GATA (CLATTER)
BOSS! CAN YOU HEAR US!?
HELLO!?
VAAAAA (VMMMMMM)

A HEARTWARMING DISMEMBERMENT COMEDY

SLICEY-SAN

AMPUTATING THE TIES THAT BIND YOU
SATURDAYS AT 5 A.M., ONLY ON YAMIMORI TV

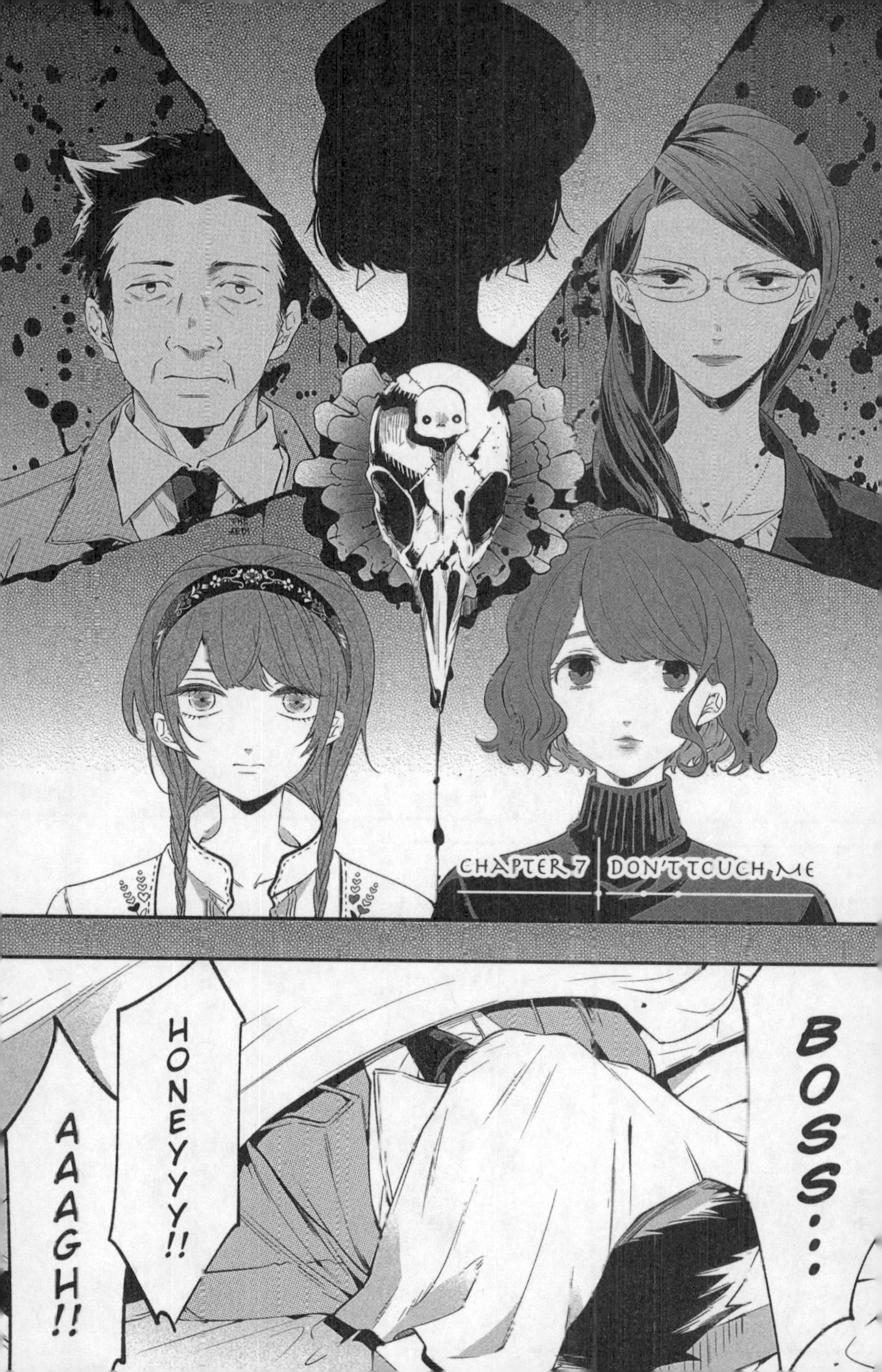
CHAPTER 7 DON'T TOUCH ME
BOSS...
HONEYYY!!
AAAGH!!

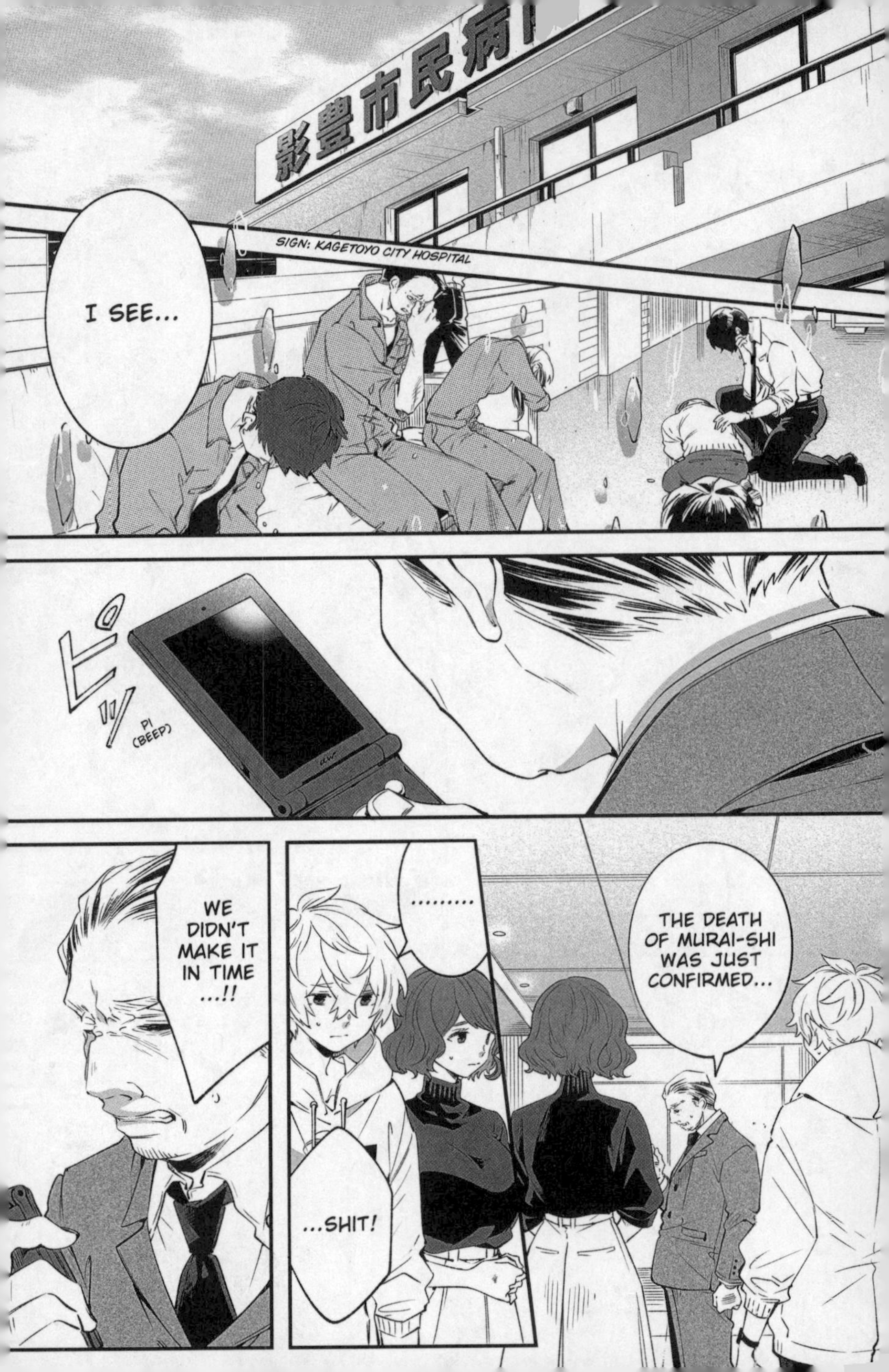
影豊市民病
SIGN: KAGETOYO CITY HOSPITAL
I SEE...
ピッ
PI (BEEP)
THE DEATH OF MURAI-SHI WAS JUST CONFIRMED...
....
...SHIT!
WE DIDN'T MAKE IT IN TIME ...!!

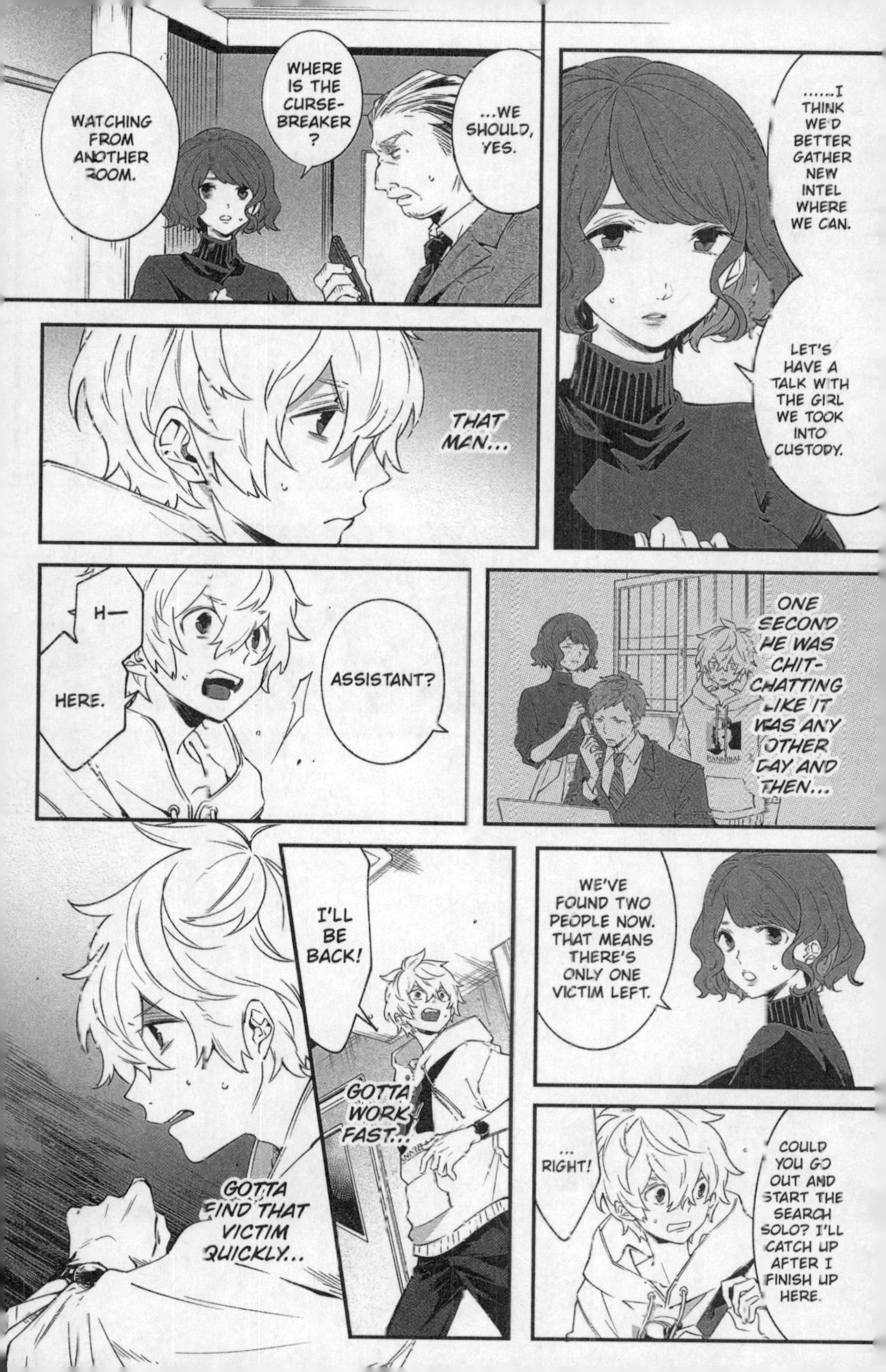
......I THINK WE'D BETTER GATHER NEW INTEL WHERE WE CAN.
LET'S HAVE A TALK WITH THE GIRL WE TOOK INTO CUSTODY.
...WE SHOULD, YES.
WHERE IS THE CURSE-BREAKER?
WATCHING FROM ANOTHER ROOM.
THAT MAN...
ONE SECOND HE WAS CHIT-CHATTING LIKE IT WAS ANY OTHER DAY AND THEN...
ASSISTANT?
H— HERE.
WE'VE FOUND TWO PEOPLE NOW. THAT MEANS THERE'S ONLY ONE VICTIM LEFT.
COULD YOU GO OUT AND START THE SEARCH SOLO? I'LL CATCH UP AFTER I FINISH UP HERE.
...RIGHT!
I'LL BE BACK!
GOTTA WORK FAST...
GOTTA FIND THAT VICTIM QUICKLY...

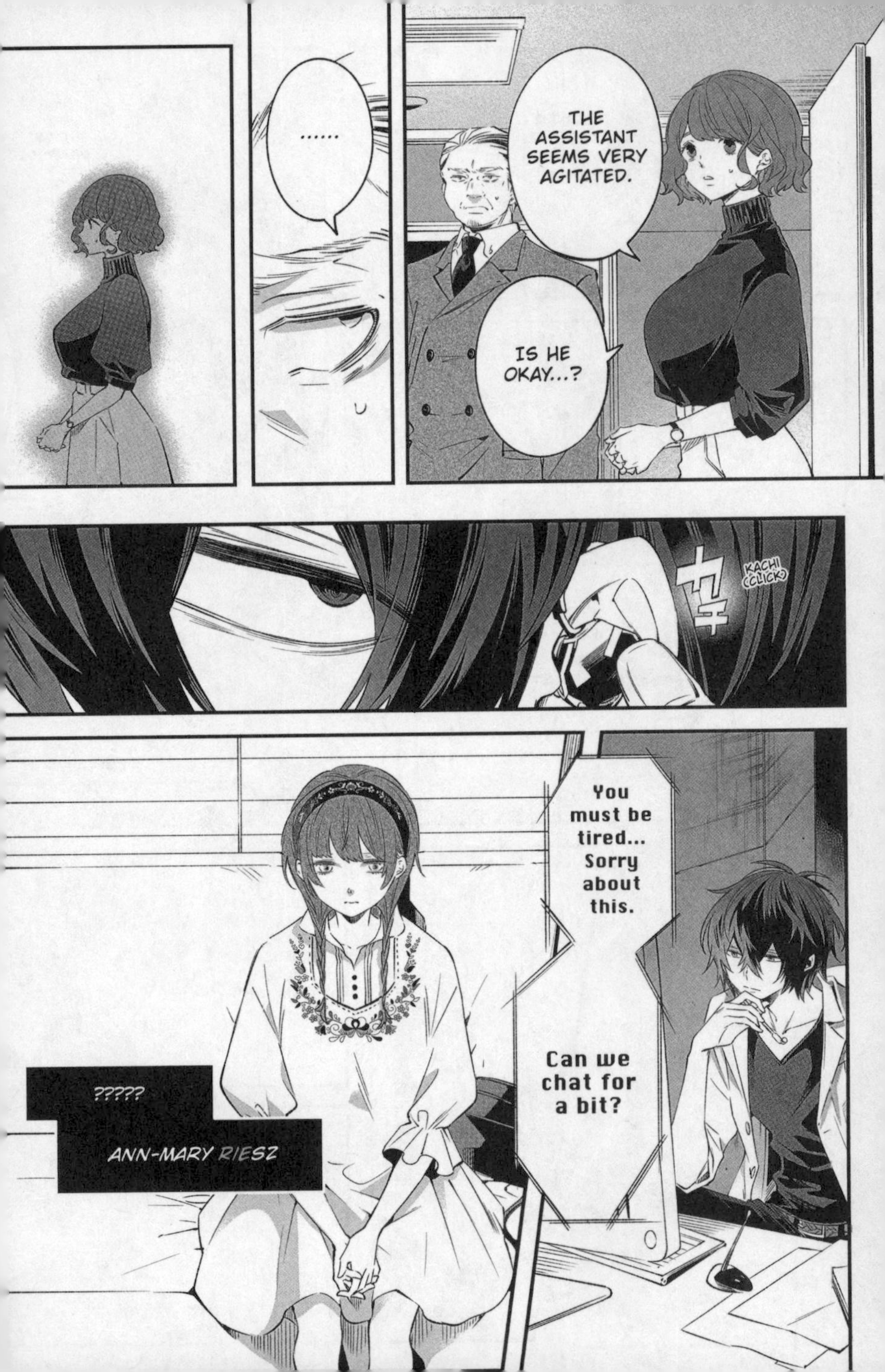
THE ASSISTANT SEEMS VERY AGITATED.
IS HE OKAY...?
......
KACHI (CLICK)
You must be tired... Sorry about this.
Can we chat for a bit?
?????
ANN-MARY RIESZ

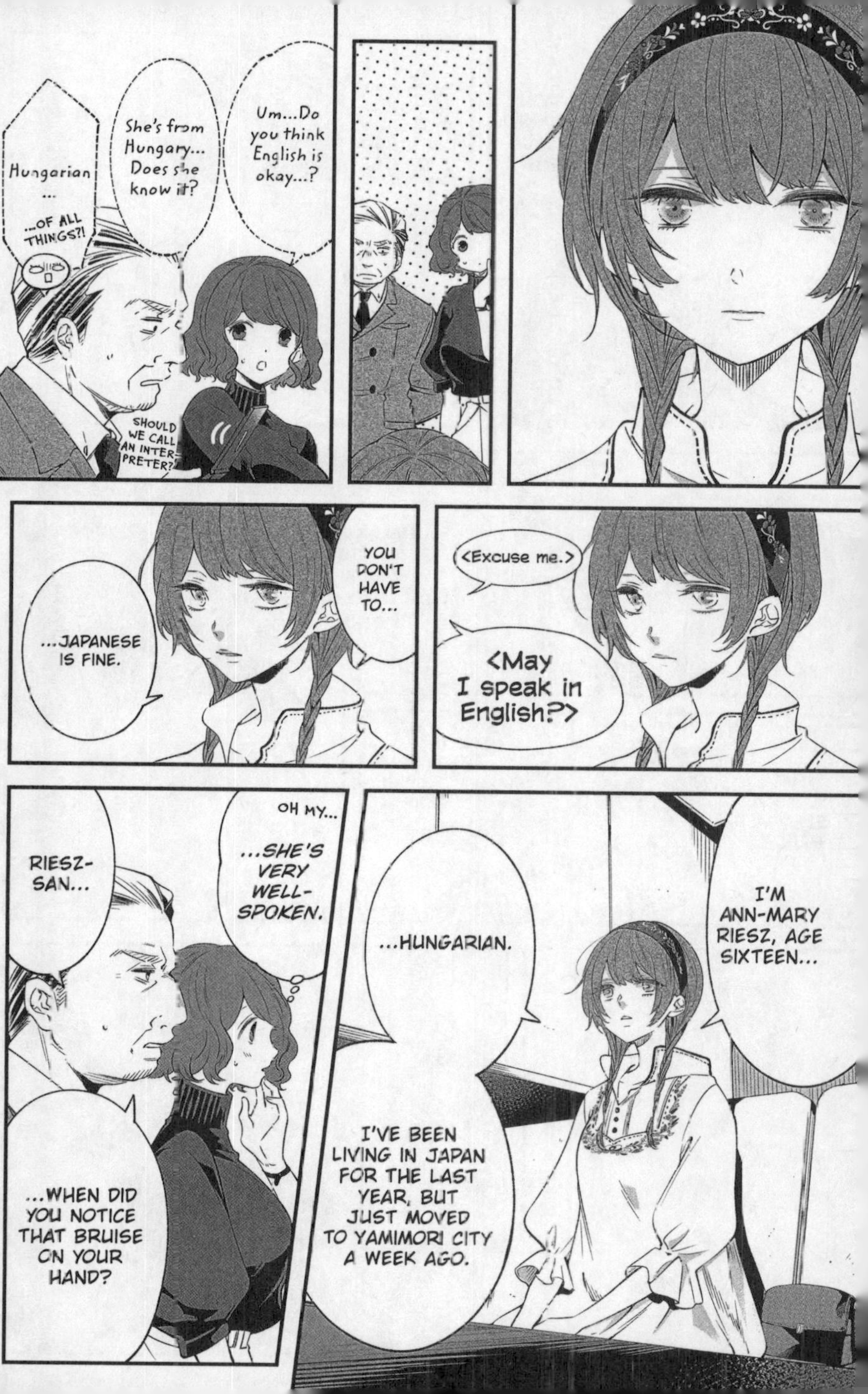
Um...Do you think English is okay...?
She's from Hungary... Does she know it?
Hungarian ... ...OF ALL THINGS?!
SHOULD WE CALL AN INTERPRETER?
<Excuse me.>
<May I speak in English?>
YOU DON'T HAVE TO...
...JAPANESE IS FINE.
I'M ANN-MARY RIESZ, AGE SIXTEEN...
...HUNGARIAN.
I'VE BEEN LIVING IN JAPAN FOR THE LAST YEAR, BUT JUST MOVED TO YAMIMORI CITY A WEEK AGO.
OH MY... ...SHE'S VERY WELL-SPOKEN.
RIESZ-SAN...
...WHEN DID YOU NOTICE THAT BRUISE ON YOUR HAND?

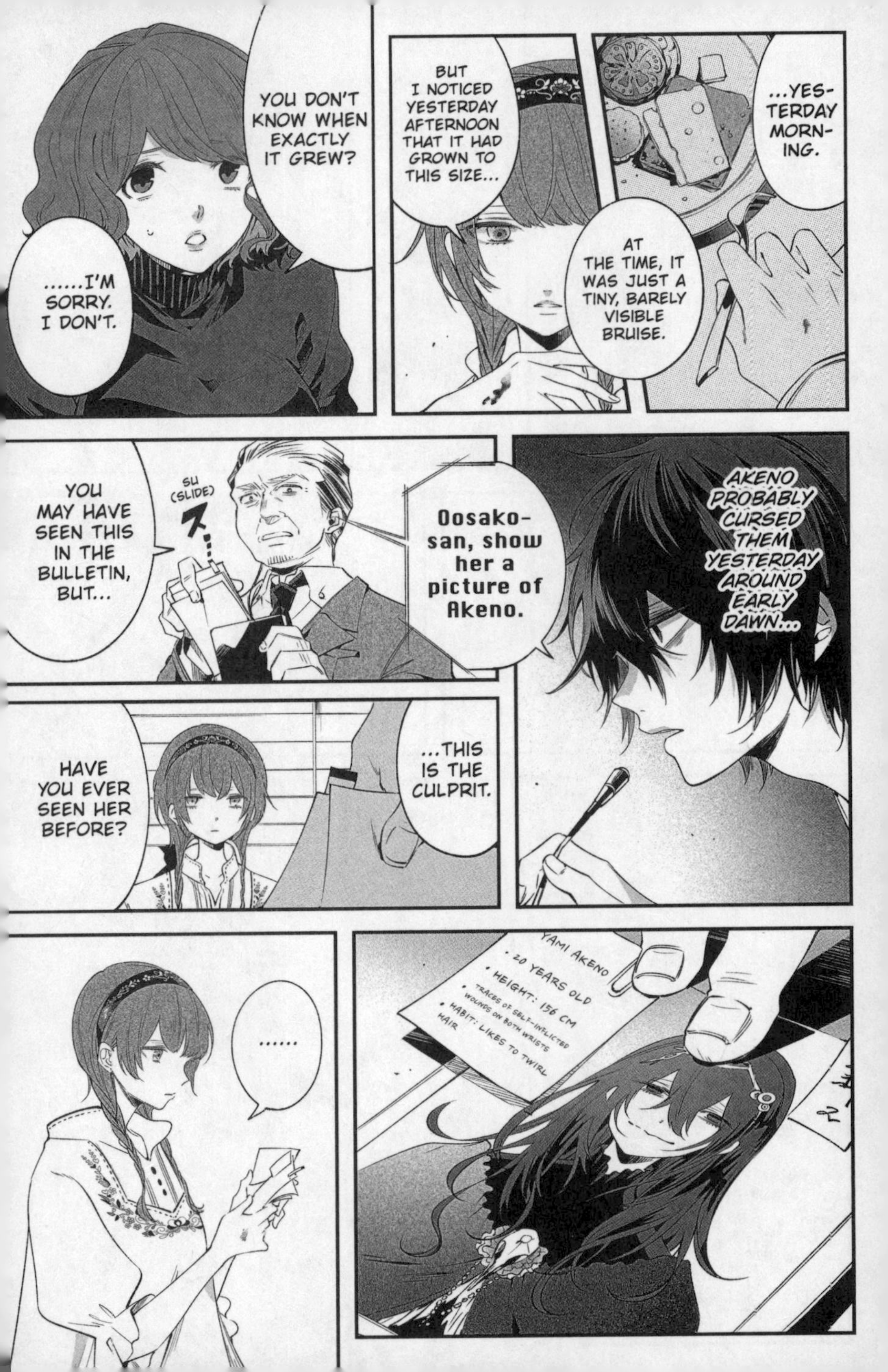
...YES-TERDAY MORNING.
AT THE TIME, IT WAS JUST A TINY, BARELY VISIBLE BRUISE.
BUT I NOTICED YESTERDAY AFTERNOON THAT IT HAD GROWN TO THIS SIZE...
YOU DON'T KNOW WHEN EXACTLY IT GREW?
......I'M SORRY. I DON'T.
AKENO PROBABLY CURSED THEM YESTERDAY AROUND EARLY DAWN...
Oosako-san, show her a picture of Akeno.
SU (SLIDE)
YOU MAY HAVE SEEN THIS IN THE BULLETIN, BUT...
...THIS IS THE CULPRIT.
HAVE YOU EVER SEEN HER BEFORE?
YAMI AKENO
• 20 YEARS OLD
• HEIGHT: 156 CM
• TRACES OF SELF-INFLICTED WOUNDS ON BOTH WRISTS
• HABIT: LIKES TO TWIRL HAIR
......

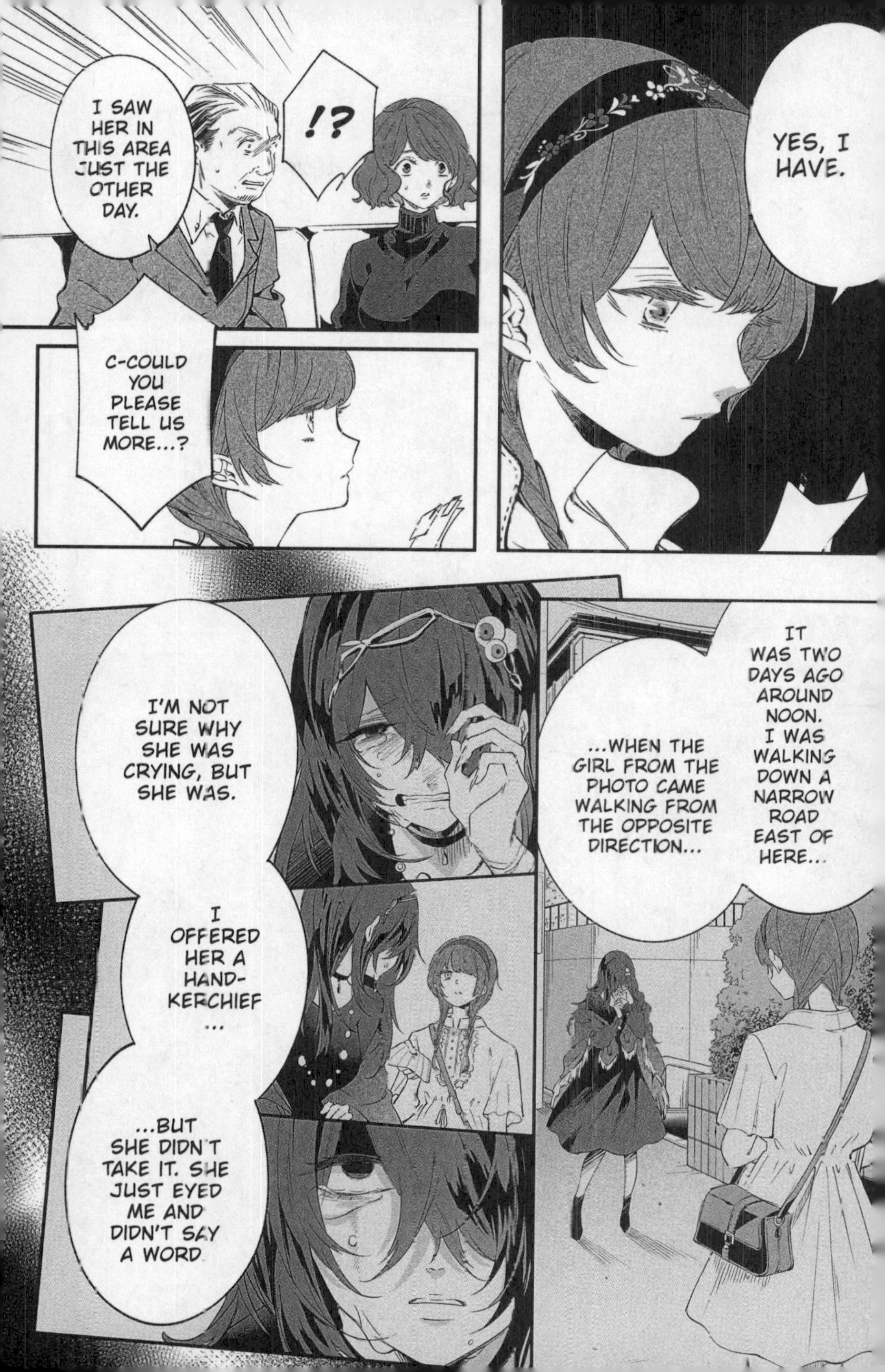
YES, I HAVE.
!?
I SAW HER IN THIS AREA JUST THE OTHER DAY.
C-COULD YOU PLEASE TELL US MORE...?
IT WAS TWO DAYS AGO AROUND NOON. I WAS WALKING DOWN A NARROW ROAD EAST OF HERE...
...WHEN THE GIRL FROM THE PHOTO CAME WALKING FROM THE OPPOSITE DIRECTION...
I'M NOT SURE WHY SHE WAS CRYING, BUT SHE WAS.
I OFFERED HER A HAND-KERCHIEF...
...BUT SHE DIDN'T TAKE IT. SHE JUST EYED ME AND DIDN'T SAY A WORD.

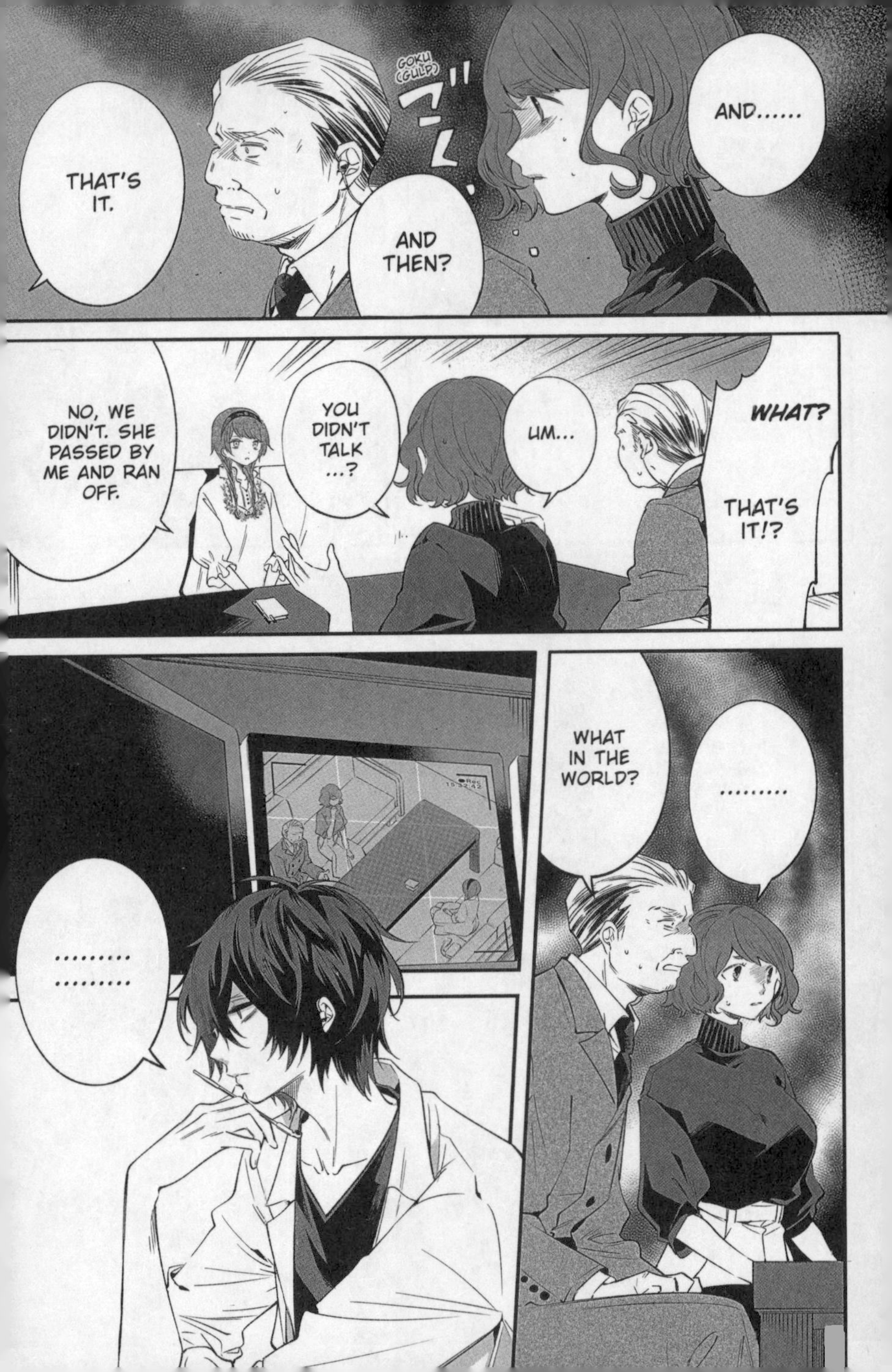
AND......
GOKU (GULP)
AND THEN?
THAT'S IT.
WHAT?
THAT'S IT!?
UM...
YOU DIDN'T TALK ...?
NO, WE DIDN'T. SHE PASSED BY ME AND RAN OFF.
....
WHAT IN THE WORLD?
....

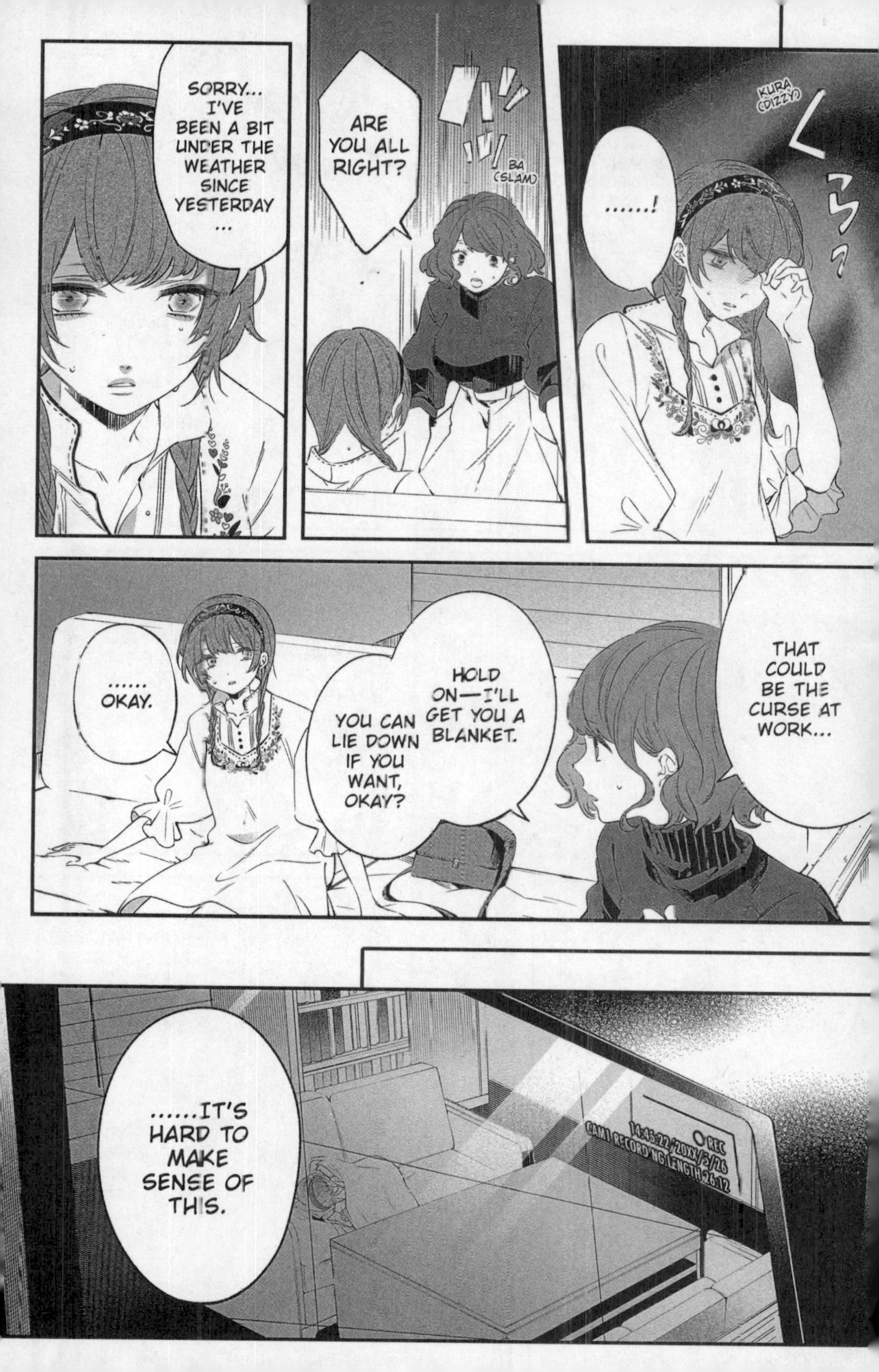
KURA (DIZZY)
......!
BA (SLAM)
ARE YOU ALL RIGHT?
SORRY... I'VE BEEN A BIT UNDER THE WEATHER SINCE YESTERDAY ...
THAT COULD BE THE CURSE AT WORK...
HOLD ON—I'LL GET YOU A BLANKET.
YOU CAN LIE DOWN IF YOU WANT, OKAY?
...... OKAY.
REC
14:45:22 20XX/3/26
CAM1 RECORDING LENGTH 26:12
......IT'S HARD TO MAKE SENSE OF THIS.

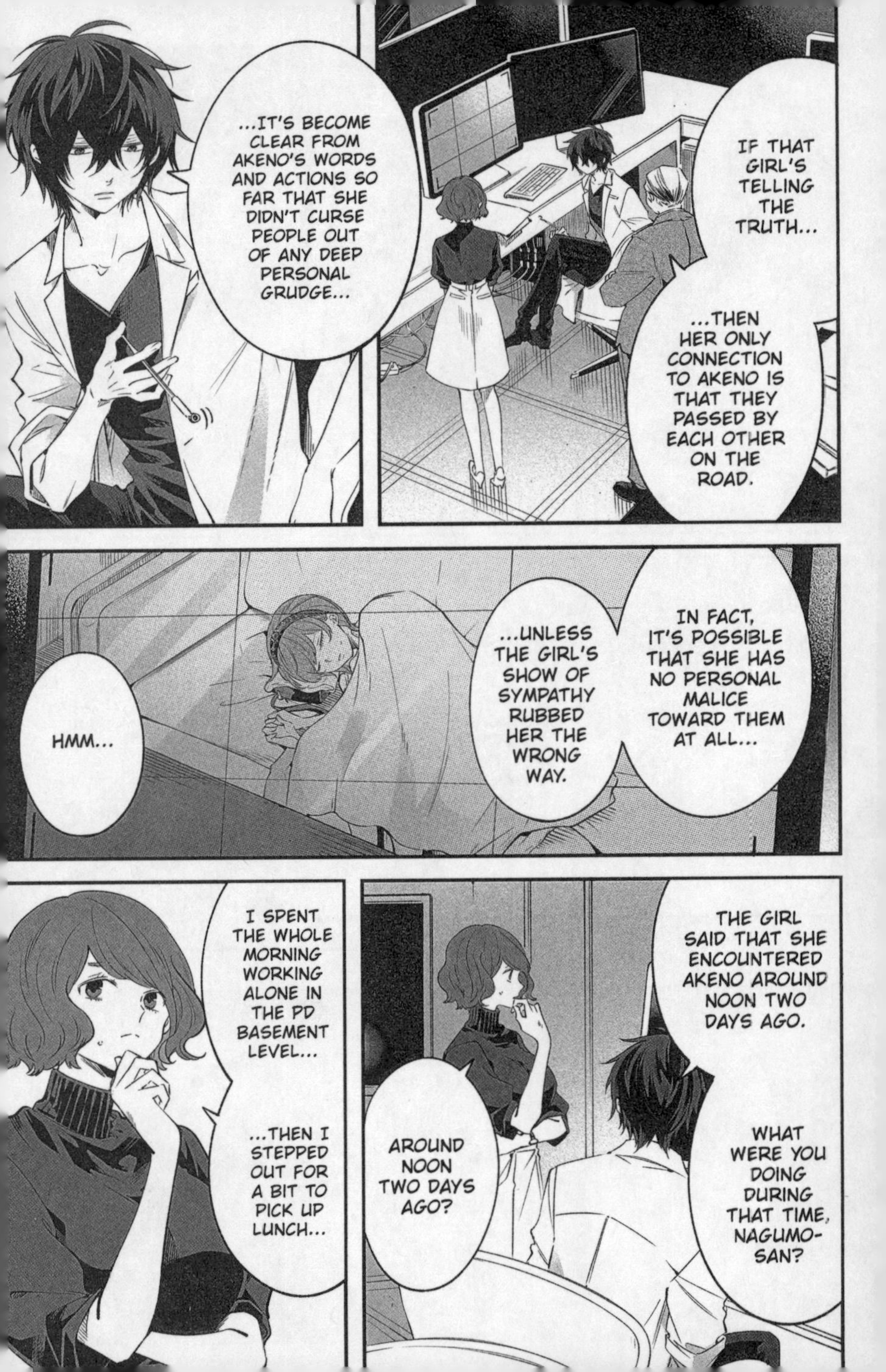
IF THAT GIRL'S TELLING THE TRUTH...
...THEN HER ONLY CONNECTION TO AKENO IS THAT THEY PASSED BY EACH OTHER ON THE ROAD.
...IT'S BECOME CLEAR FROM AKENO'S WORDS AND ACTIONS SO FAR THAT SHE DIDN'T CURSE PEOPLE OUT OF ANY DEEP PERSONAL GRUDGE...
IN FACT, IT'S POSSIBLE THAT SHE HAS NO PERSONAL MALICE TOWARD THEM AT ALL...
...UNLESS THE GIRL'S SHOW OF SYMPATHY RUBBED HER THE WRONG WAY.
HMM...
THE GIRL SAID THAT SHE ENCOUNTERED AKENO AROUND NOON TWO DAYS AGO.
WHAT WERE YOU DOING DURING THAT TIME, NAGUMO-SAN?
AROUND NOON TWO DAYS AGO?
I SPENT THE WHOLE MORNING WORKING ALONE IN THE PD BASEMENT LEVEL...
...THEN I STEPPED OUT FOR A BIT TO PICK UP LUNCH...

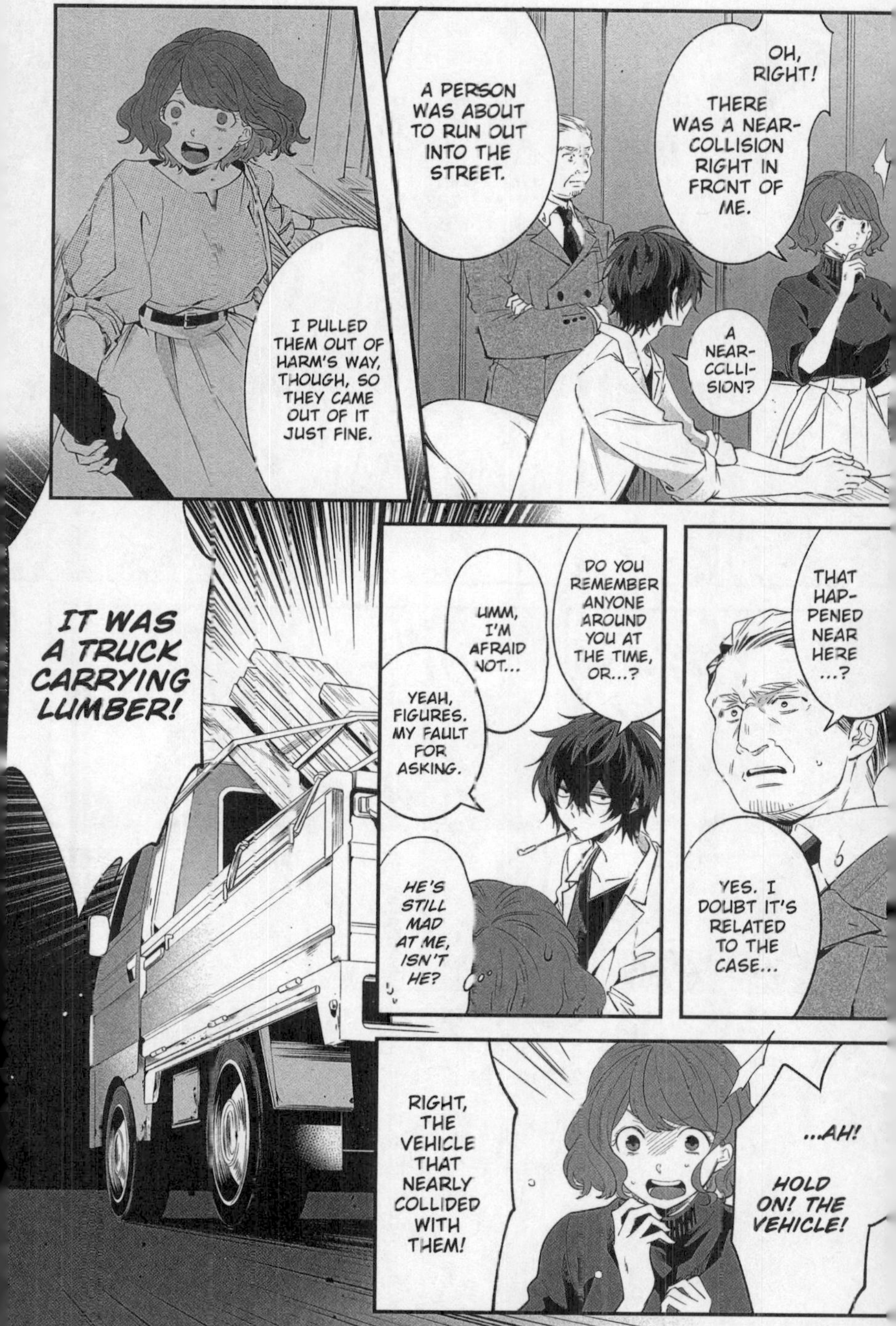
OH, RIGHT! THERE WAS A NEAR-COLLISION RIGHT IN FRONT OF ME.
A PERSON WAS ABOUT TO RUN OUT INTO THE STREET.
A NEAR-COLLISION?
I PULLED THEM OUT OF HARM'S WAY, THOUGH, SO THEY CAME OUT OF IT JUST FINE.
THAT HAPPENED NEAR HERE...?
YES. I DOUBT IT'S RELATED TO THE CASE...
DO YOU REMEMBER ANYONE AROUND YOU AT THE TIME, OR...?
UMM, I'M AFRAID NOT...
YEAH, FIGURES. MY FAULT FOR ASKING.
HE'S STILL MAD AT ME, ISN'T HE?
...AH!
HOLD ON! THE VEHICLE!
RIGHT, THE VEHICLE THAT NEARLY COLLIDED WITH THEM!
IT WAS A TRUCK CARRYING LUMBER!

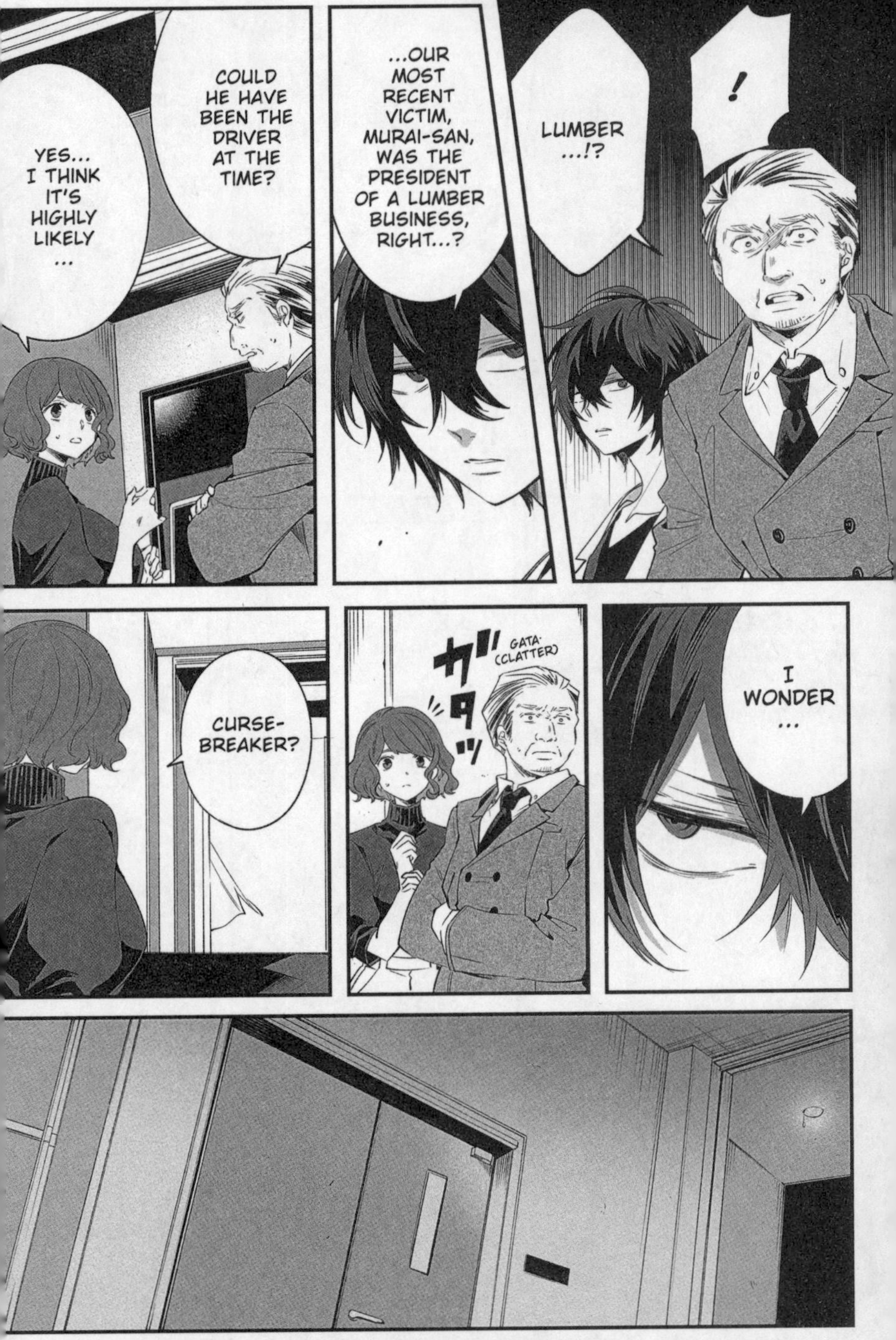
!
LUMBER ...!?
...OUR MOST RECENT VICTIM, MURAI-SAN, WAS THE PRESIDENT OF A LUMBER BUSINESS, RIGHT...?
COULD HE HAVE BEEN THE DRIVER AT THE TIME?
YES... I THINK IT'S HIGHLY LIKELY...
I WONDER...
ガタッ
GATA (CLATTER)
CURSE-BREAKER?

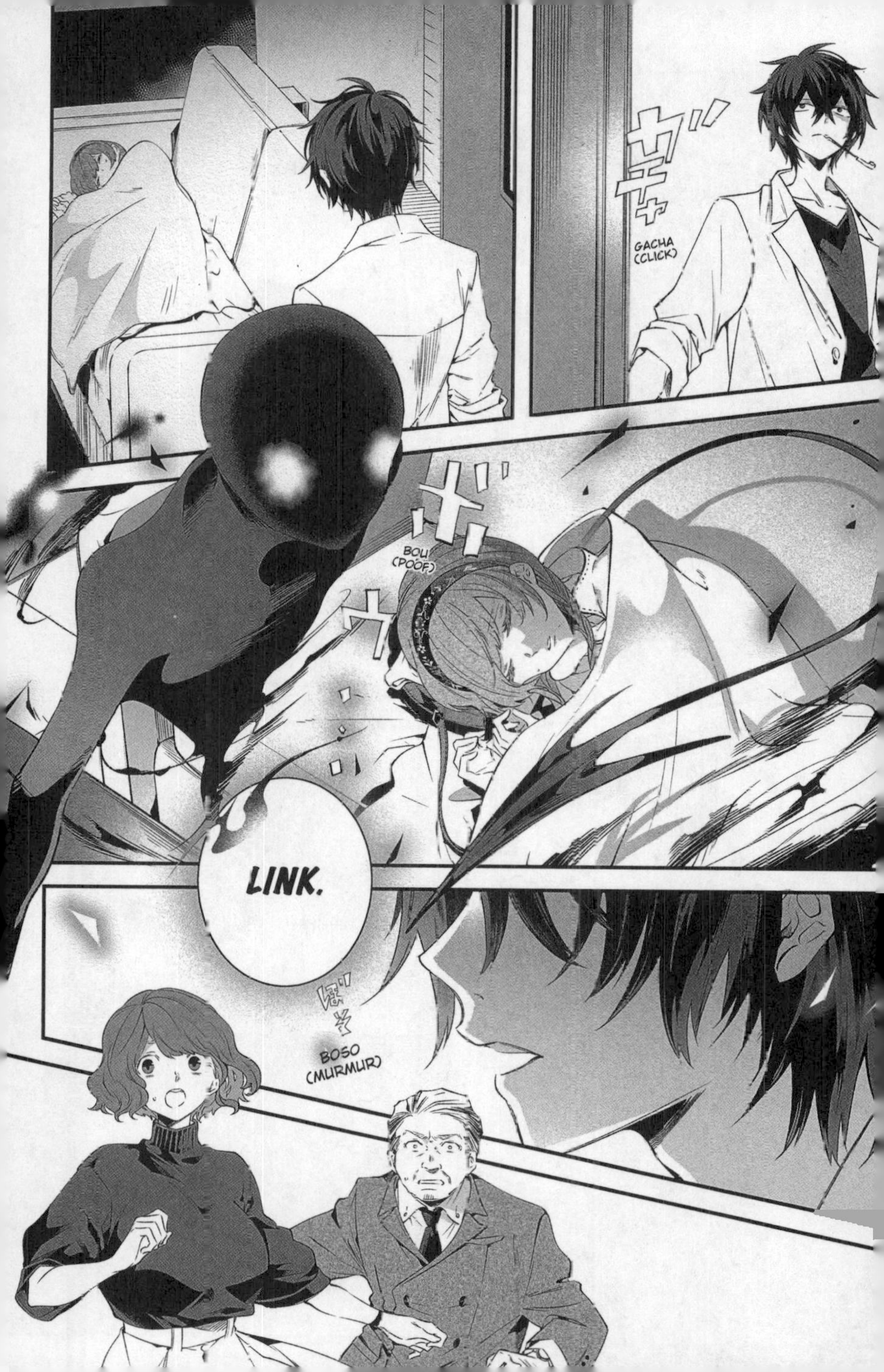
GACHA (CLICK)
BOU (POOF)
LINK.
BOSO (MURMUR)

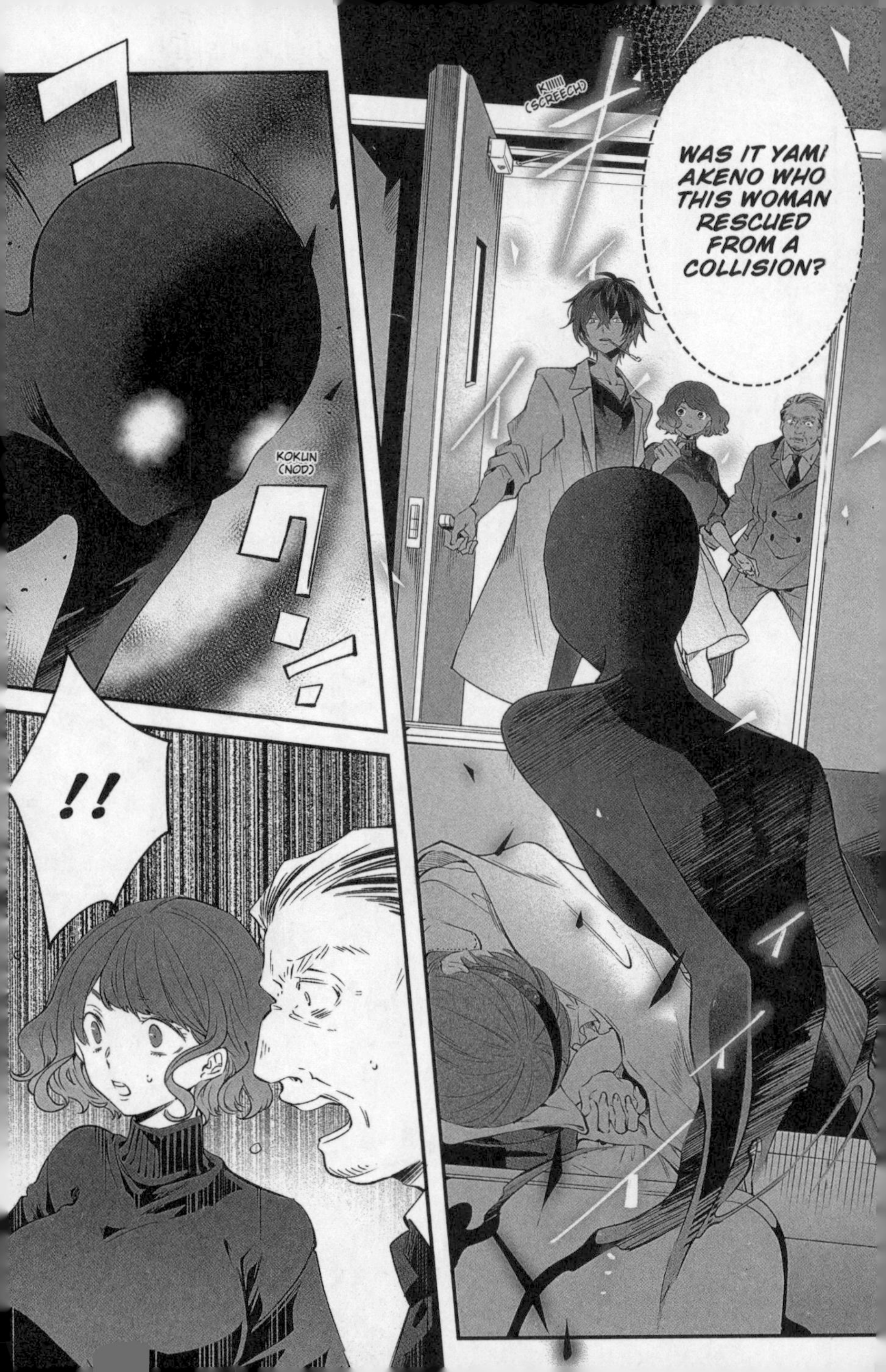
KIIIIII
(SCREECH)
WAS IT YAMI AKENO WHO THIS WOMAN RESCUED FROM A COLLISION?
KOKUN
(NOD)
!!

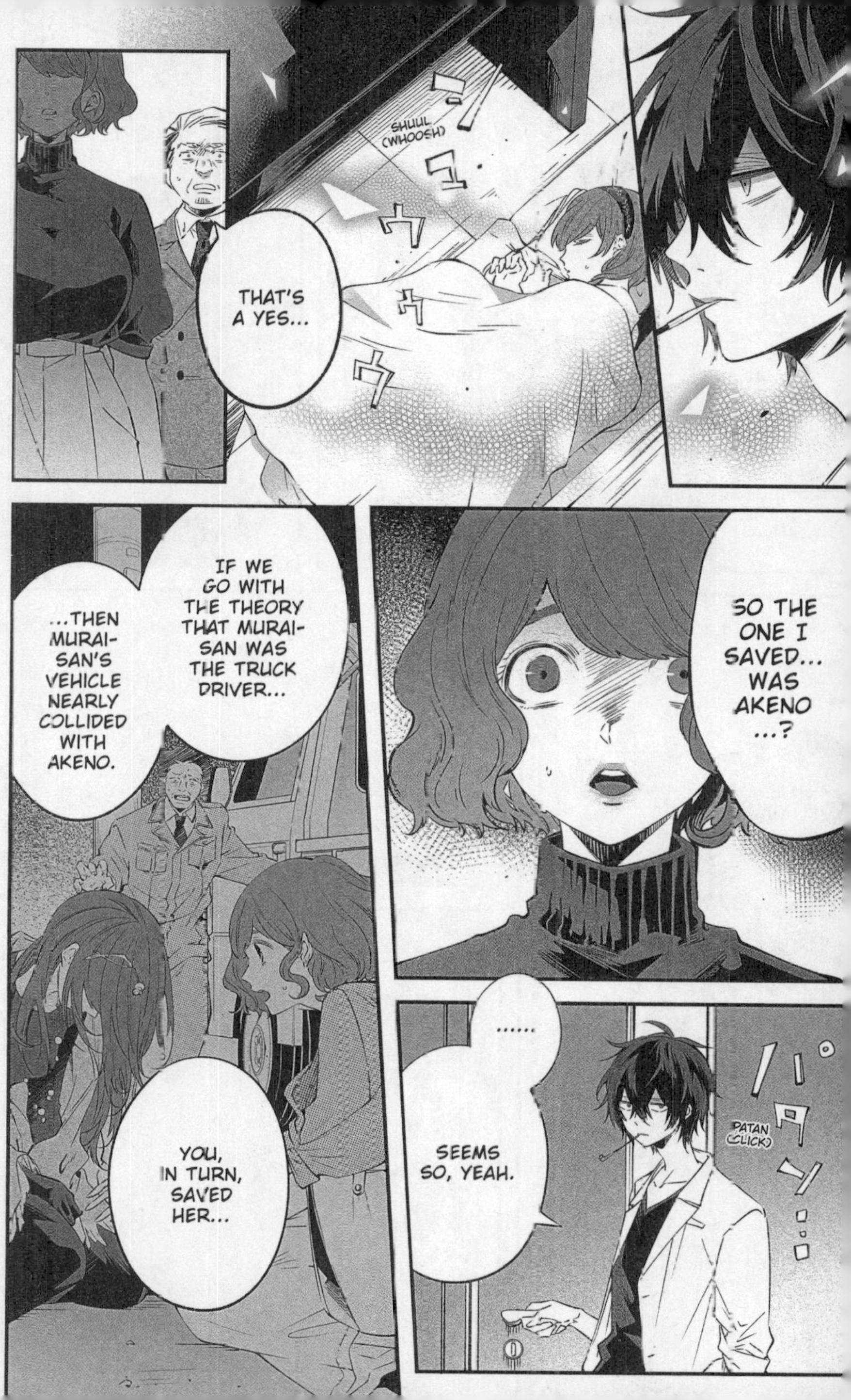
SHUUL (WHOOSH)
THAT'S A YES...
SO THE ONE I SAVED... WAS AKENO ...?
......
SEEMS SO, YEAH.
PATAN (CLICK)
IF WE GO WITH THE THEORY THAT MURAI-SAN WAS THE TRUCK DRIVER...
...THEN MURAI-SAN'S VEHICLE NEARLY COLLIDED WITH AKENO.
YOU, IN TURN, SAVED HER...

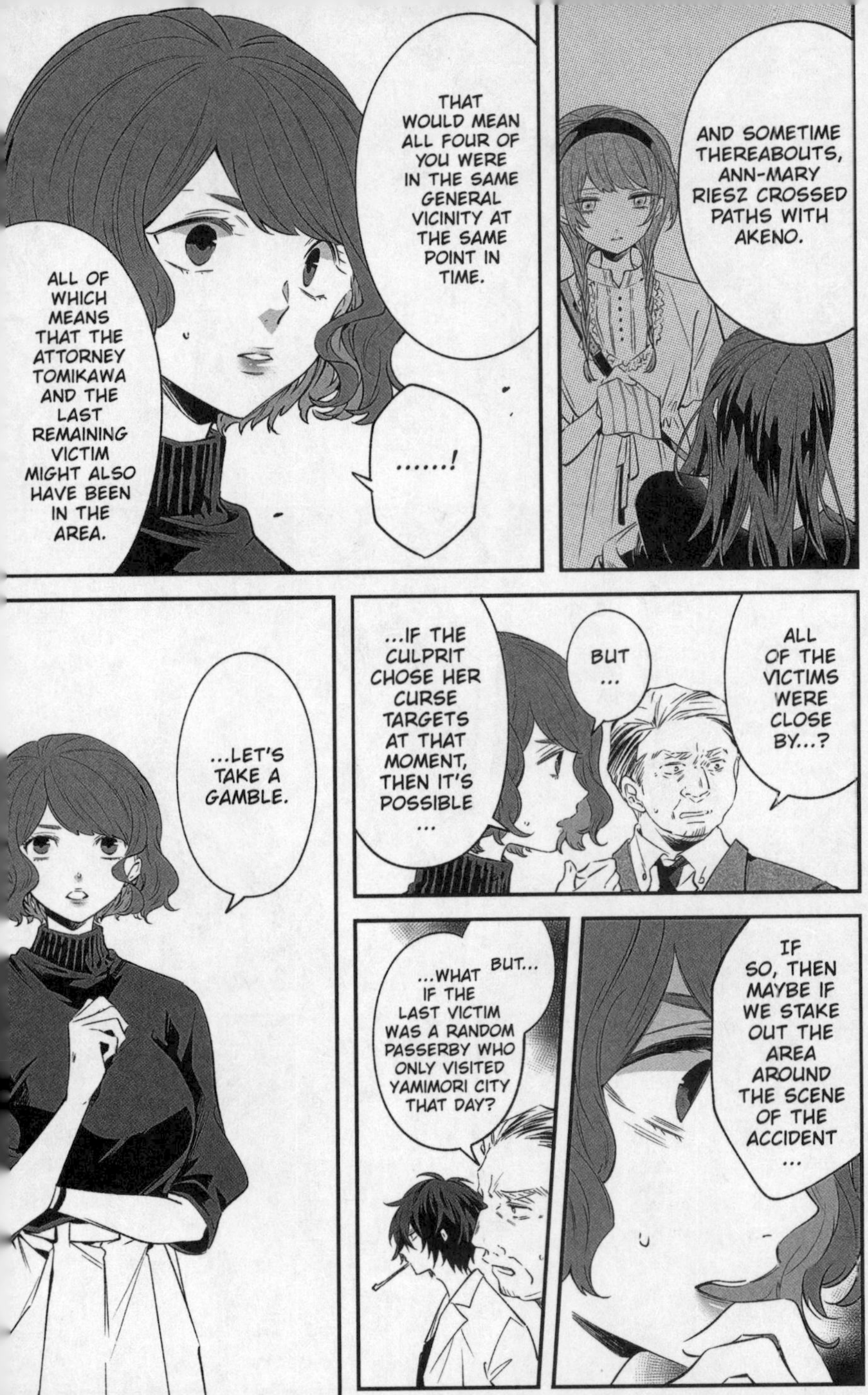
AND SOMETIME THEREABOUTS, ANN-MARY RIESZ CROSSED PATHS WITH AKENO.
THAT WOULD MEAN ALL FOUR OF YOU WERE IN THE SAME GENERAL VICINITY AT THE SAME POINT IN TIME.
......!
ALL OF WHICH MEANS THAT THE ATTORNEY TOMIKAWA AND THE LAST REMAINING VICTIM MIGHT ALSO HAVE BEEN IN THE AREA.
ALL OF THE VICTIMS WERE CLOSE BY...?
BUT ...
...IF THE CULPRIT CHOSE HER CURSE TARGETS AT THAT MOMENT, THEN IT'S POSSIBLE ...
IF SO, THEN MAYBE IF WE STAKE OUT THE AREA AROUND THE SCENE OF THE ACCIDENT ...
BUT...
...WHAT IF THE LAST VICTIM WAS A RANDOM PASSERBY WHO ONLY VISITED YAMIMORI CITY THAT DAY?
...LET'S TAKE A GAMBLE.

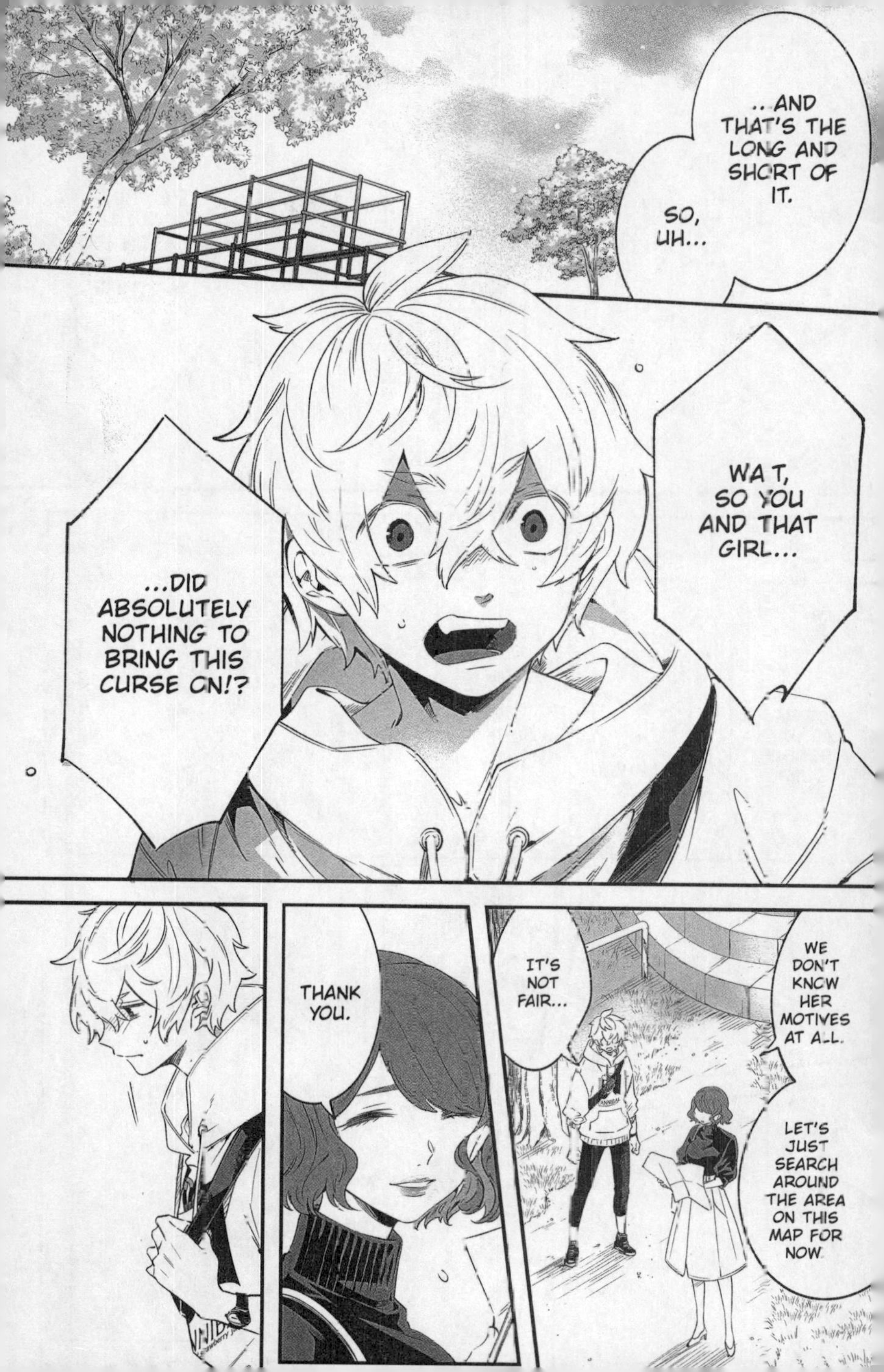
...AND THAT'S THE LONG AND SHORT OF IT.
SO, UH...
WAIT, SO YOU AND THAT GIRL...
...DID ABSOLUTELY NOTHING TO BRING THIS CURSE ON!?
WE DON'T KNOW HER MOTIVES AT ALL.
LET'S JUST SEARCH AROUND THE AREA ON THIS MAP FOR NOW.
IT'S NOT FAIR...
THANK YOU.

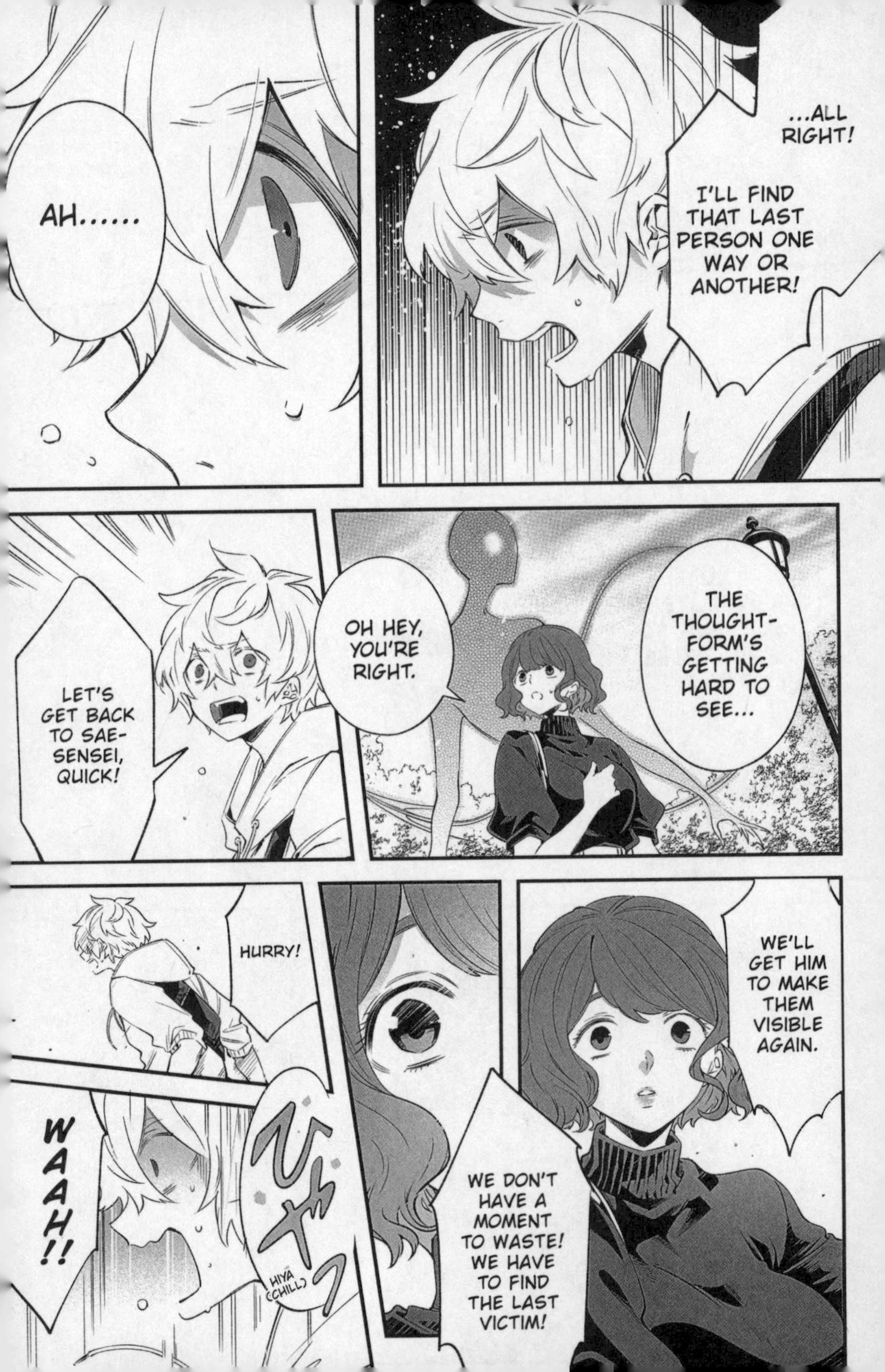
...ALL RIGHT!
I'LL FIND THAT LAST PERSON ONE WAY OR ANOTHER!
AH......
THE THOUGHT-FORM'S GETTING HARD TO SEE...
OH HEY, YOU'RE RIGHT.
LET'S GET BACK TO SAE-SENSEI, QUICK!
WE'LL GET HIM TO MAKE THEM VISIBLE AGAIN.
WE DON'T HAVE A MOMENT TO WASTE! WE HAVE TO FIND THE LAST VICTIM!
HURRY!
HIYA (CHILL)
WAAH!!

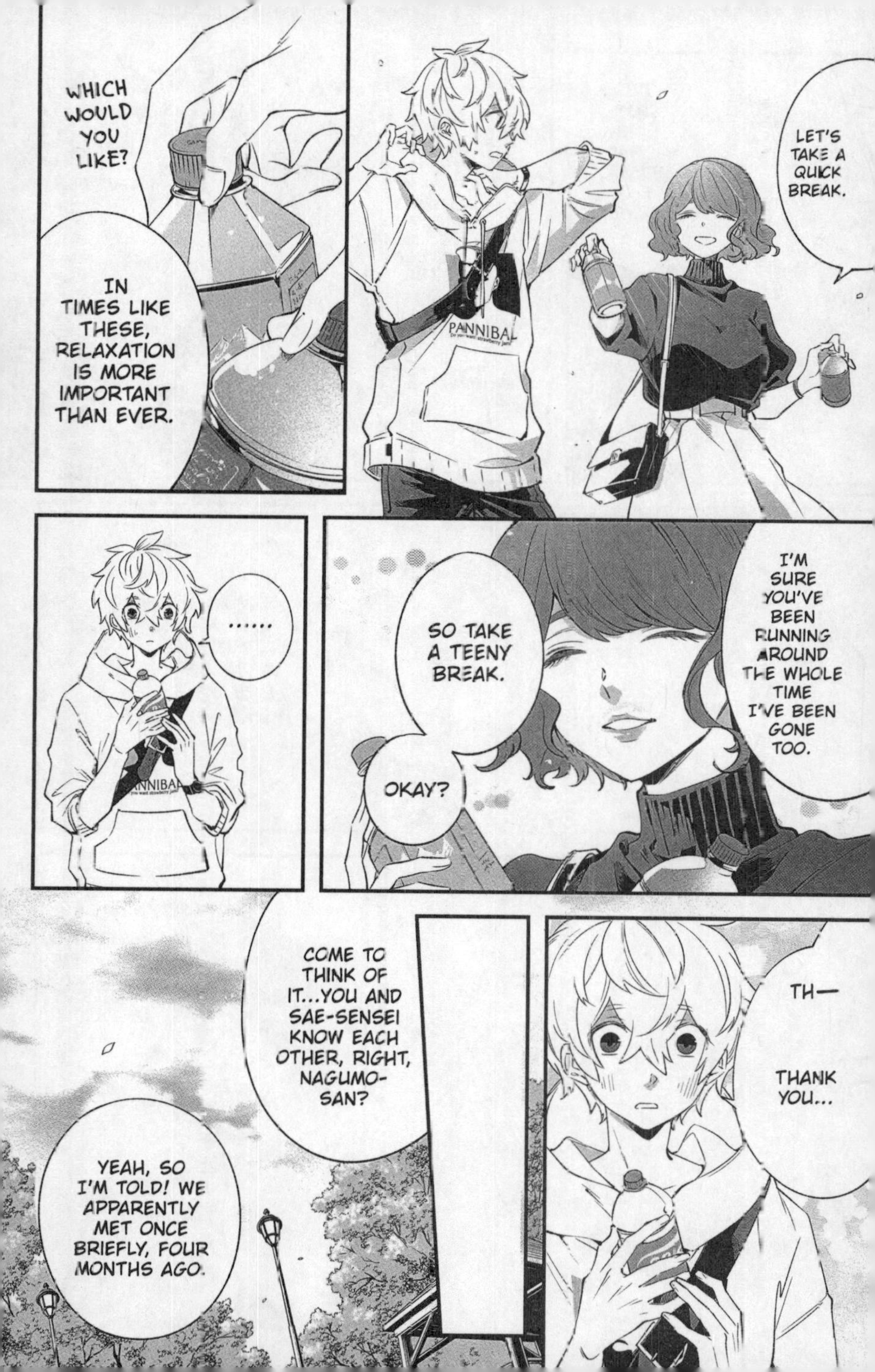
LET'S TAKE A QUICK BREAK.
WHICH WOULD YOU LIKE?
IN TIMES LIKE THESE, RELAXATION IS MORE IMPORTANT THAN EVER.
PANNIBAL
I'M SURE YOU'VE BEEN RUNNING AROUND THE WHOLE TIME I'VE BEEN GONE TOO.
SO TAKE A TEENY BREAK.
OKAY?
......
TH—
THANK YOU...
COME TO THINK OF IT...YOU AND SAE-SENSEI KNOW EACH OTHER, RIGHT, NAGUMO-SAN?
YEAH, SO I'M TOLD! WE APPARENTLY MET ONCE BRIEFLY, FOUR MONTHS AGO.

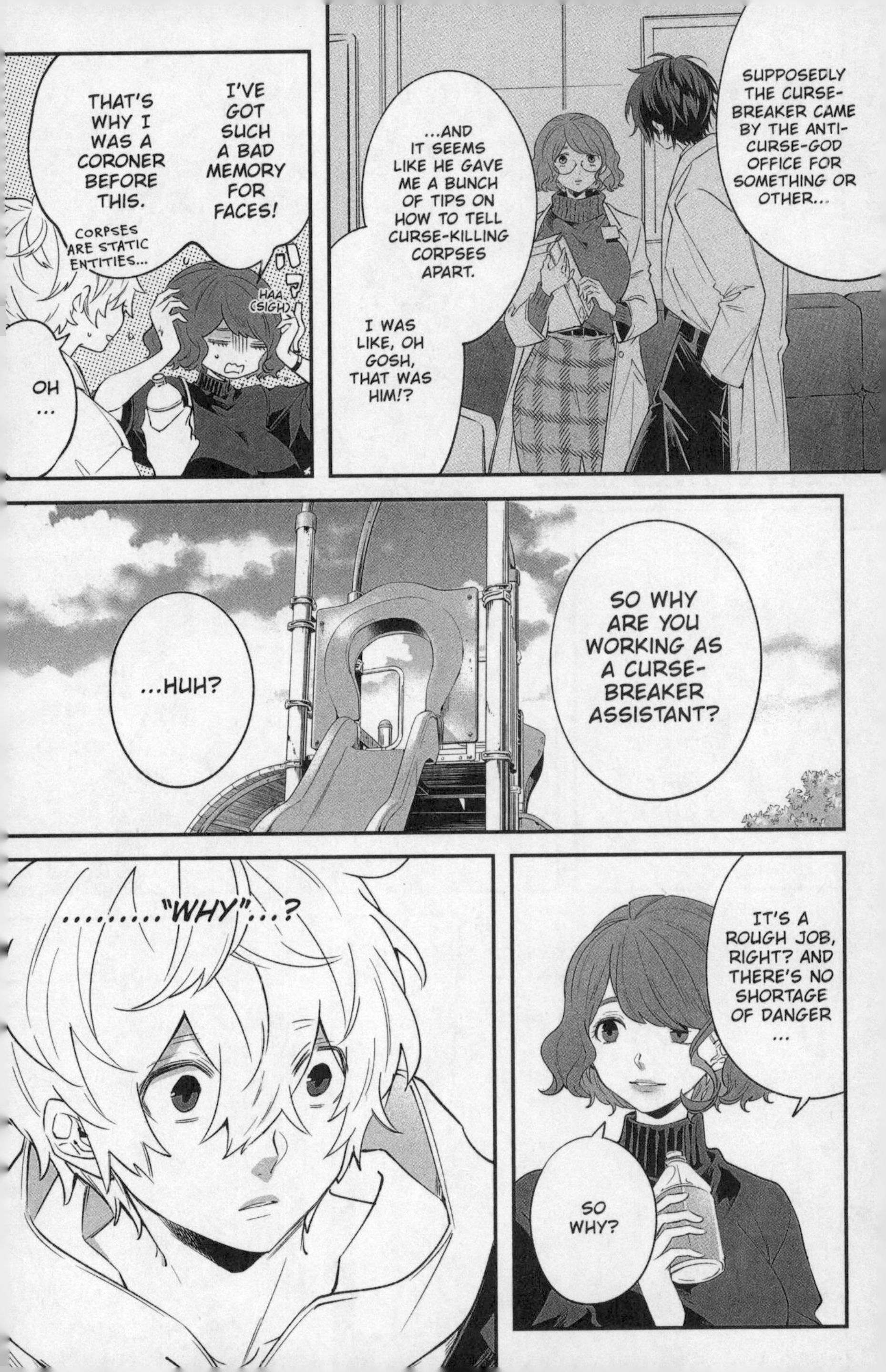
SUPPOSEDLY THE CURSE-BREAKER CAME BY THE ANTI-CURSE-GOD OFFICE FOR SOMETHING OR OTHER...
...AND IT SEEMS LIKE HE GAVE ME A BUNCH OF TIPS ON HOW TO TELL CURSE-KILLING CORPSES APART.
I WAS LIKE, OH GOSH, THAT WAS HIM!?
I'VE GOT SUCH A BAD MEMORY FOR FACES!
THAT'S WHY I WAS A CORONER BEFORE THIS.
CORPSES ARE STATIC ENTITIES...
HAA (SIGH)
OH ...
SO WHY ARE YOU WORKING AS A CURSE-BREAKER ASSISTANT?
...HUH?
IT'S A ROUGH JOB, RIGHT? AND THERE'S NO SHORTAGE OF DANGER ...
SO WHY?
........."WHY"...?

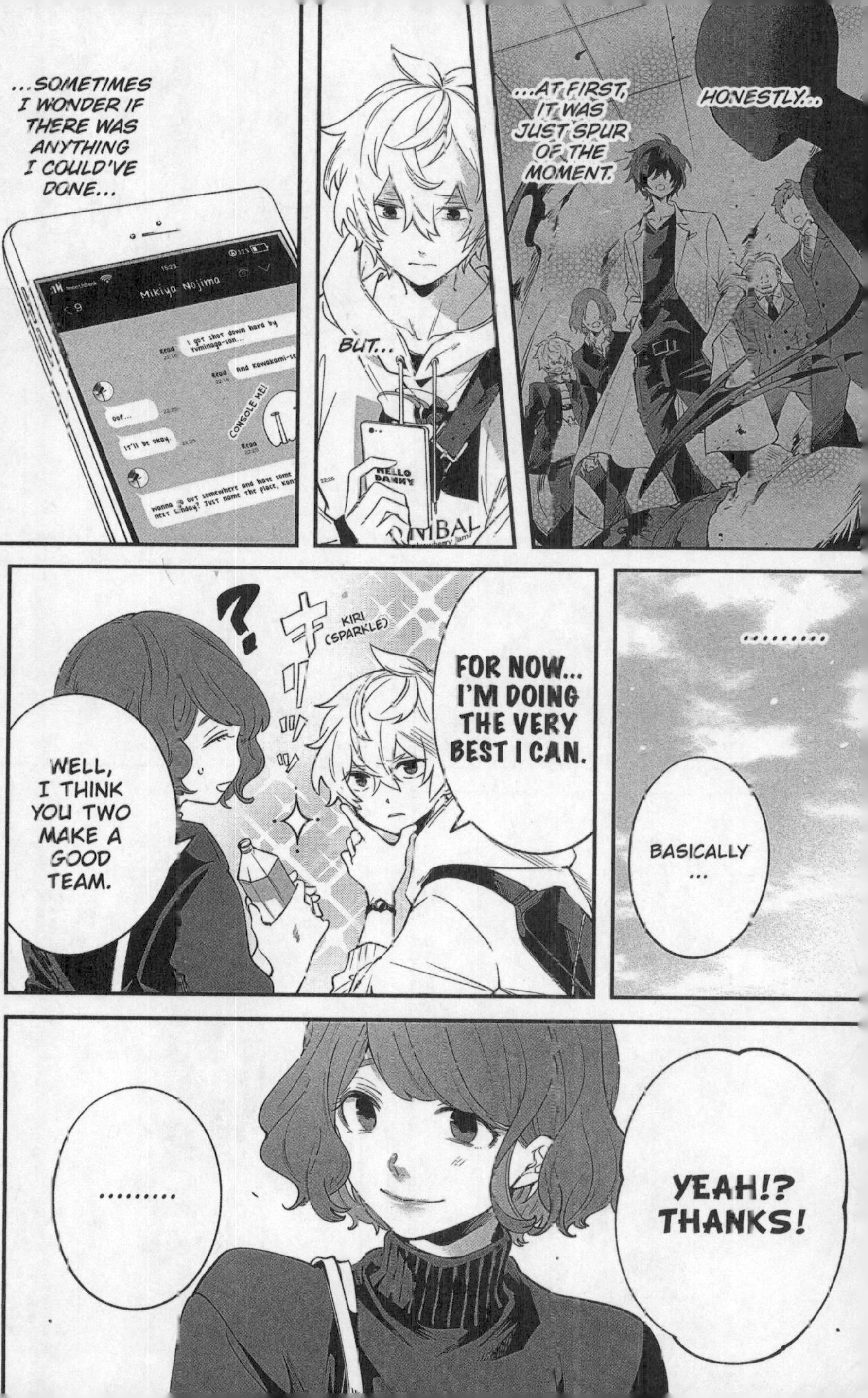
HONESTLY...
...AT FIRST, IT WAS JUST SPUR OF THE MOMENT.
BUT...
HELLO DANNY
...SOMETIMES I WONDER IF THERE WAS ANYTHING I COULD'VE DONE...
Mikiya Nojima
I got shot down hard by Yuminaga-san...
Oof...
It'll be okay.
CONSOLE ME!
....
BASICALLY ...
FOR NOW... I'M DOING THE VERY BEST I CAN.
KIRI (SPARKLE)
WELL, I THINK YOU TWO MAKE A GOOD TEAM.
YEAH!? THANKS!
....

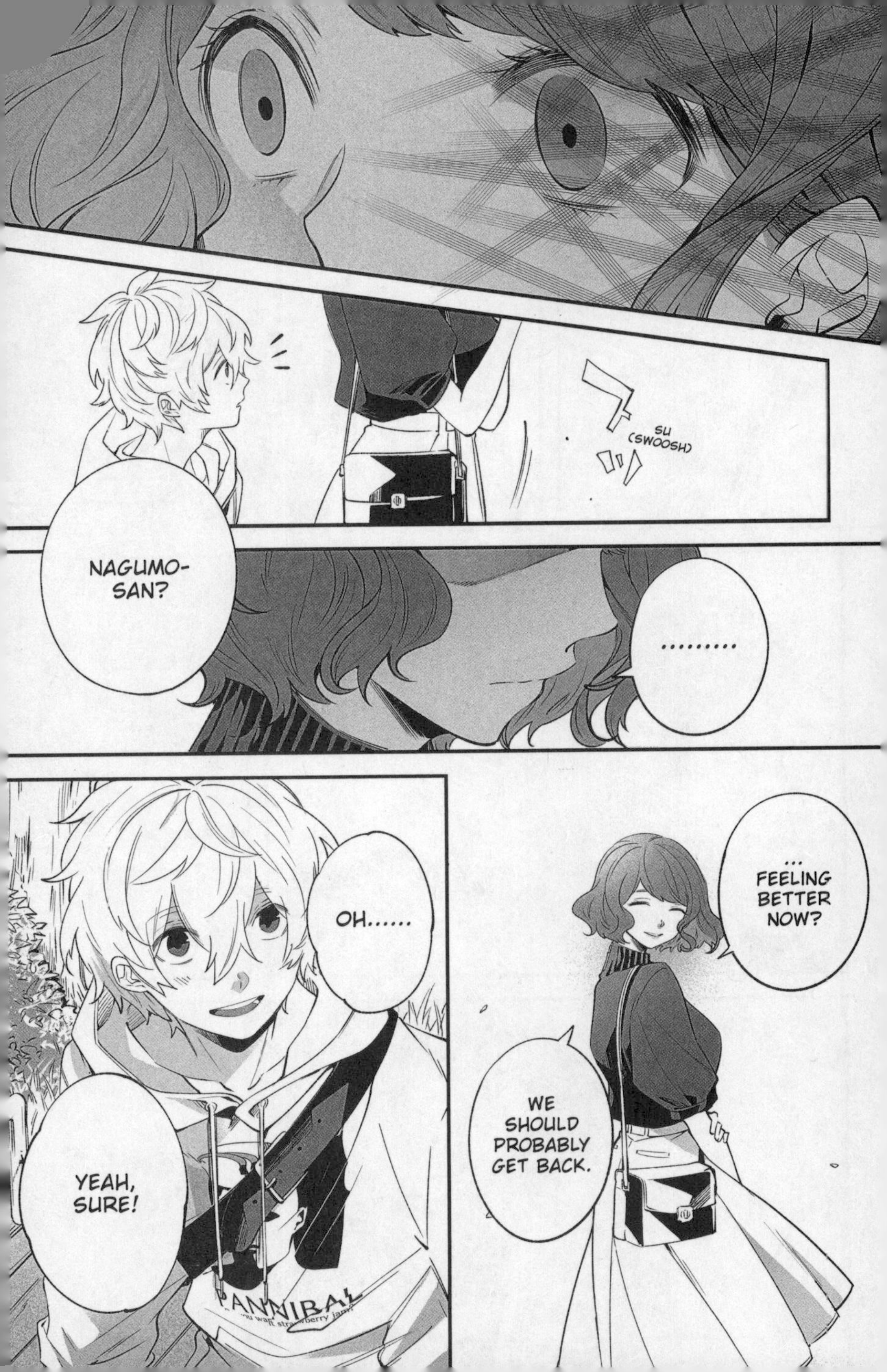
SU
(SWOOSH)
NAGUMO-SAN?
....
...
FEELING
BETTER
NOW?
WE
SHOULD
PROBABLY
GET BACK.
OH......
YEAH,
SURE!

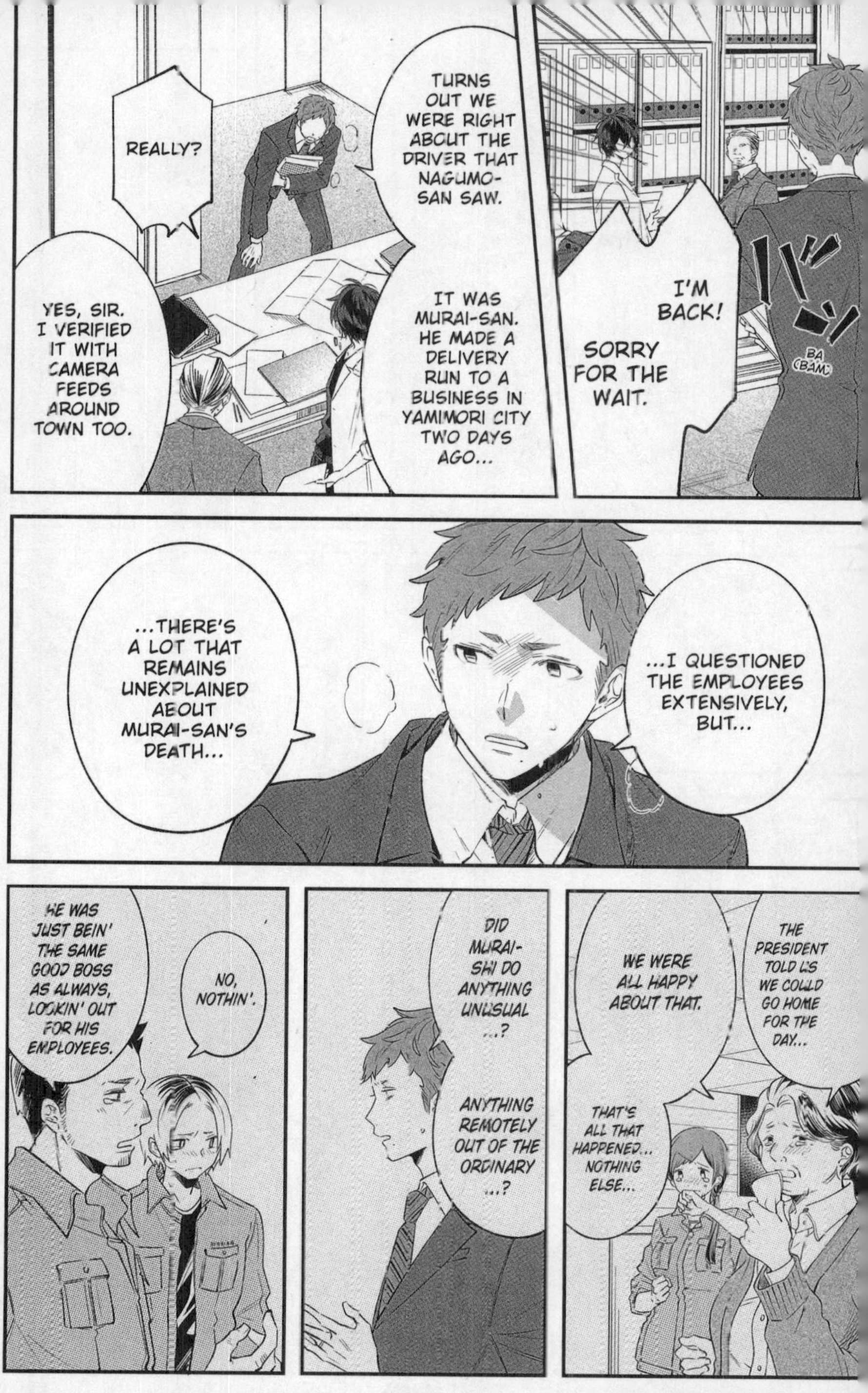
I'M BACK!
SORRY FOR THE WAIT.
BA (BAM)
TURNS OUT WE WERE RIGHT ABOUT THE DRIVER THAT NAGUMO-SAN SAW.
REALLY?
IT WAS MURAI-SAN. HE MADE A DELIVERY RUN TO A BUSINESS IN YAMIMORI CITY TWO DAYS AGO...
YES, SIR. I VERIFIED IT WITH CAMERA FEEDS AROUND TOWN TOO.
...I QUESTIONED THE EMPLOYEES EXTENSIVELY, BUT...
...THERE'S A LOT THAT REMAINS UNEXPLAINED ABOUT MURAI-SAN'S DEATH...
THE PRESIDENT TOLD US WE COULD GO HOME FOR THE DAY...
WE WERE ALL HAPPY ABOUT THAT.
THAT'S ALL THAT HAPPENED... NOTHING ELSE...
DID MURAI-SHI DO ANYTHING UNUSUAL ...?
ANYTHING REMOTELY OUT OF THE ORDINARY ...?
NO, NOTHIN'.
HE WAS JUST BEIN' THE SAME GOOD BOSS AS ALWAYS, LOOKIN' OUT FOR HIS EMPLOYEES.

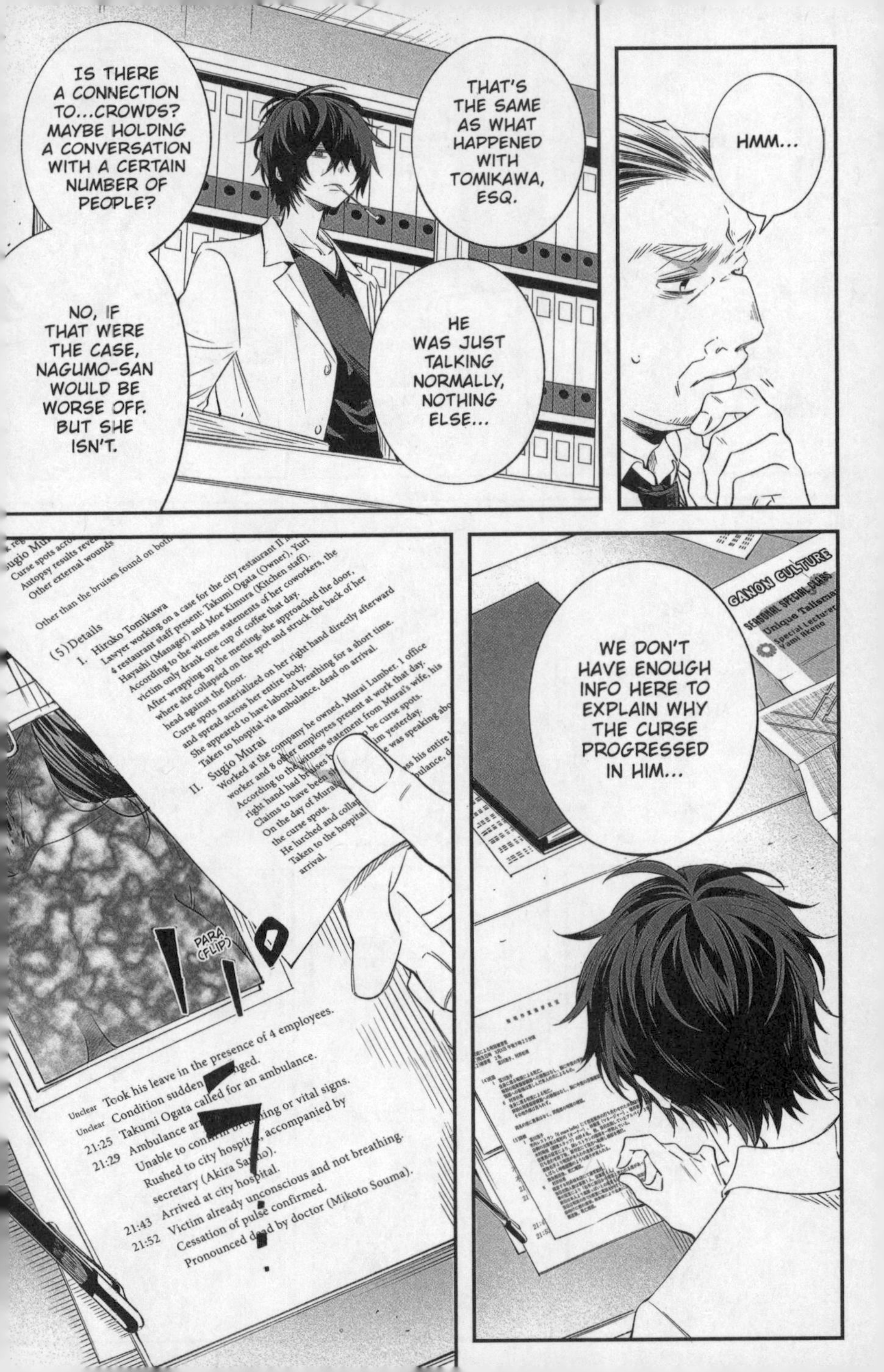
HMM...
THAT'S THE SAME AS WHAT HAPPENED WITH TOMIKAWA, ESQ.
HE WAS JUST TALKING NORMALLY, NOTHING ELSE...
IS THERE A CONNECTION TO...CROWDS? MAYBE HOLDING A CONVERSATION WITH A CERTAIN NUMBER OF PEOPLE?
NO, IF THAT WERE THE CASE, NAGUMO-SAN WOULD BE WORSE OFF. BUT SHE ISN'T.
WE DON'T HAVE ENOUGH INFO HERE TO EXPLAIN WHY THE CURSE PROGRESSED IN HIM...
GANON CULTURE
Autopsy results reve
Other external wounds
Other than the bruises found on both
(5) Details
I. Hiroko Tomikawa
Lawyer working on a case for the city restaurant
4 restaurant staff present: Takumi Ogata (Owner), Yuri
Hayashi (Manager) and Moe Kimura (Kitchen staff).
According to the witness statements of her coworkers, the
victim only drank one cup of coffee that day.
After wrapping up the meeting, she approached the door,
where she collapsed on the spot and struck the back of her
head against the floor.
Curse spots materialized on her right hand directly afterward
and spread across her entire body.
She appeared to have labored breathing for a short time.
Taken to hospital via ambulance, dead on arrival.
II. Sugio Murai
Worked at the company he owned, Murai Lumber. 1 office
worker and 8 other employees present at work that day.
According to the witness statement from Murai's wife, his
right hand had bruises
Claims to have been
On the day of Murai
the curse spots.
He lurched and colla
Taken to the hospital
arrival.
PARA (FLIP)
Unclear Took his leave in the presence of 4 employees.
Unclear Condition sudden
21:25 Takumi Ogata called for an ambulance.
21:29 Ambulance ar
Unable to confir
Rushed to city hospit
secretary (Akira Sa
21:43 Arrived at city hospital.
Victim already unconscious and not breathing.
21:52 Cessation of pulse confirmed.
Pronounced d by doctor (Mikoto Souma).

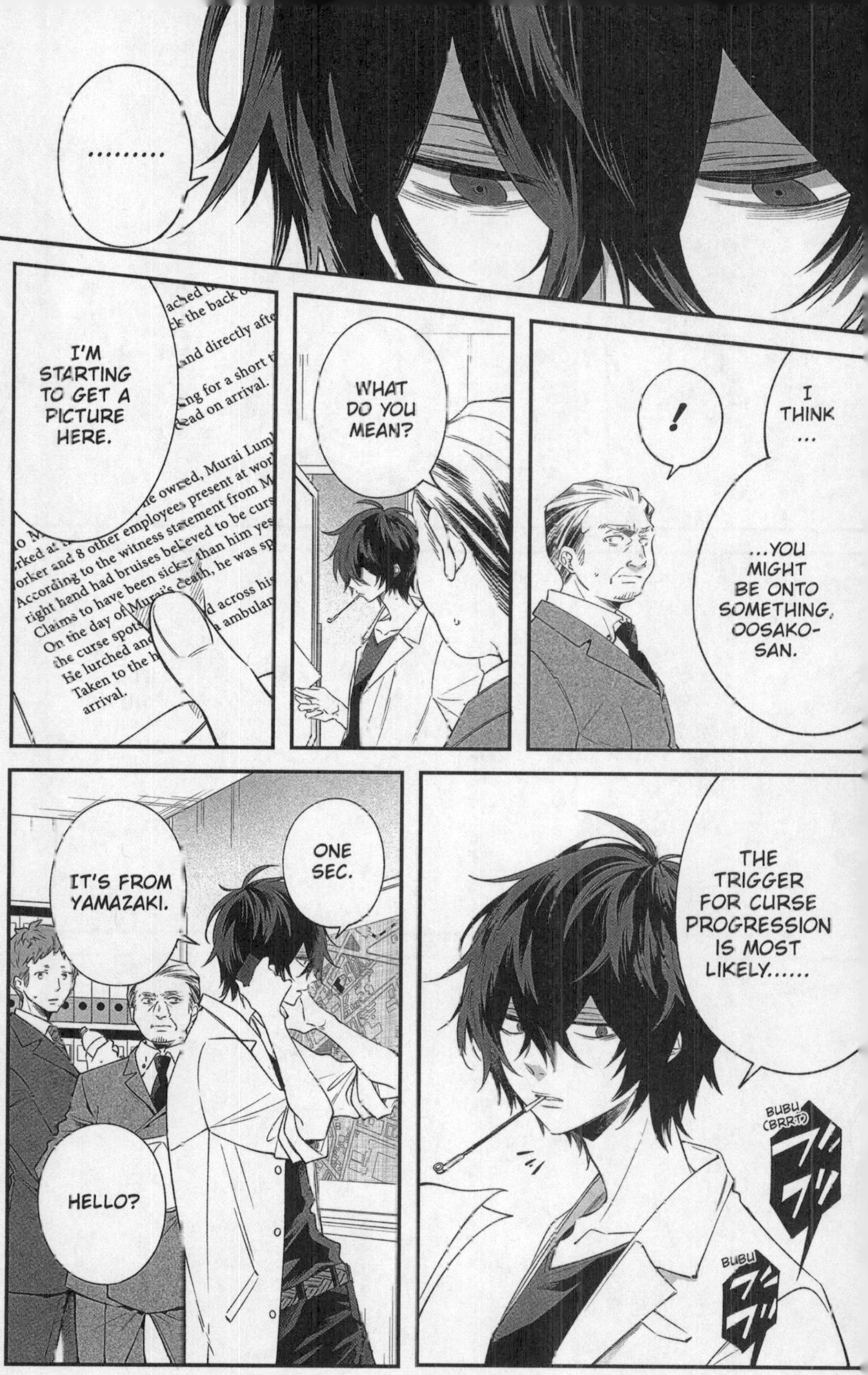
....
I THINK ...
...YOU MIGHT BE ONTO SOMETHING, OOSAKO-SAN.
!
WHAT DO YOU MEAN?
I'M STARTING TO GET A PICTURE HERE.
THE TRIGGER FOR CURSE PROGRESSION IS MOST LIKELY......
BUBU (BRRT)
BUBU
ONE SEC.
IT'S FROM YAMAZAKI.
HELLO?

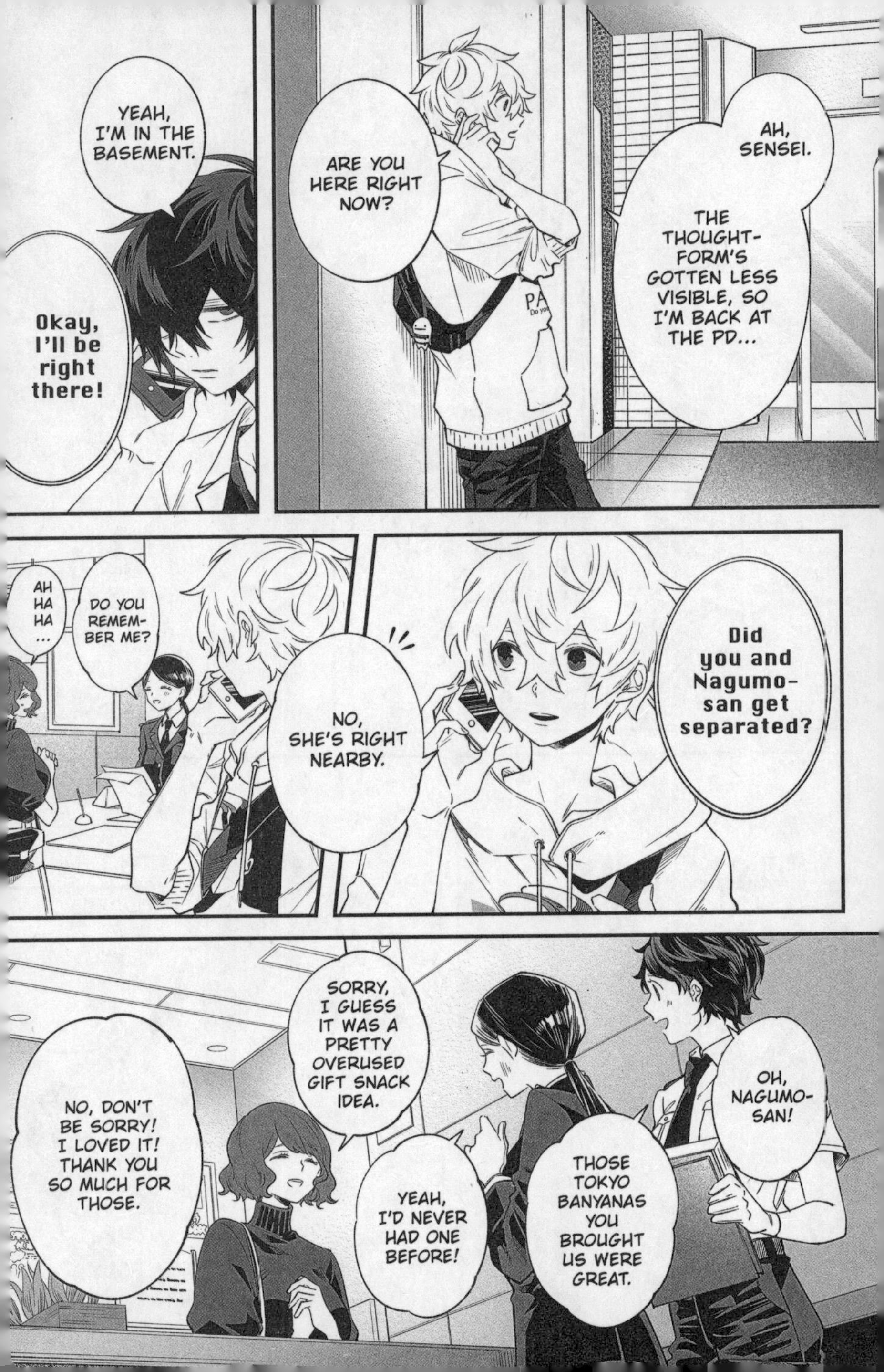
AH, SENSEI.
THE THOUGHT-FORM'S GOTTEN LESS VISIBLE, SO I'M BACK AT THE PD...
ARE YOU HERE RIGHT NOW?
YEAH, I'M IN THE BASEMENT.
Okay, I'll be right there!
Did you and Nagumo-san get separated?
NO, SHE'S RIGHT NEARBY.
DO YOU REMEMBER ME?
AH HA HA ...
OH, NAGUMO-SAN!
THOSE TOKYO BANYANAS YOU BROUGHT US WERE GREAT.
YEAH, I'D NEVER HAD ONE BEFORE!
SORRY, I GUESS IT WAS A PRETTY OVERUSED GIFT SNACK IDEA.
NO, DON'T BE SORRY! I LOVED IT! THANK YOU SO MUCH FOR THOSE.

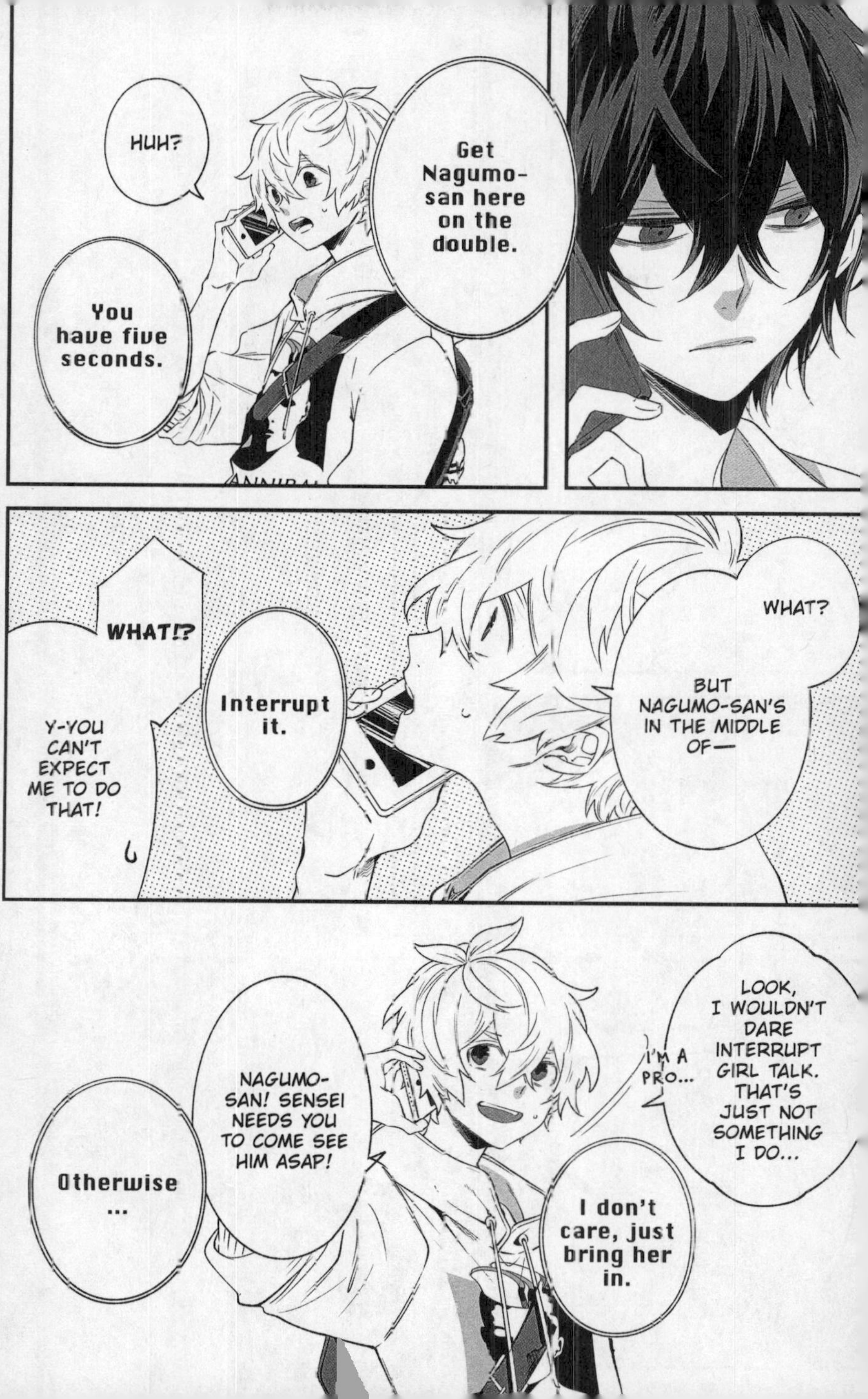
Get Nagumo-san here on the double.
HUH?
You have five seconds.
WHAT? BUT NAGUMO-SAN'S IN THE MIDDLE OF—
Interrupt it.
WHAT!?
Y-YOU CAN'T EXPECT ME TO DO THAT!
LOOK, I WOULDN'T DARE INTERRUPT GIRL TALK. THAT'S JUST NOT SOMETHING I DO...
I'M A PRO...
I don't care, just bring her in.
NAGUMO-SAN! SENSEI NEEDS YOU TO COME SEE HIM ASAP!
Otherwise ...

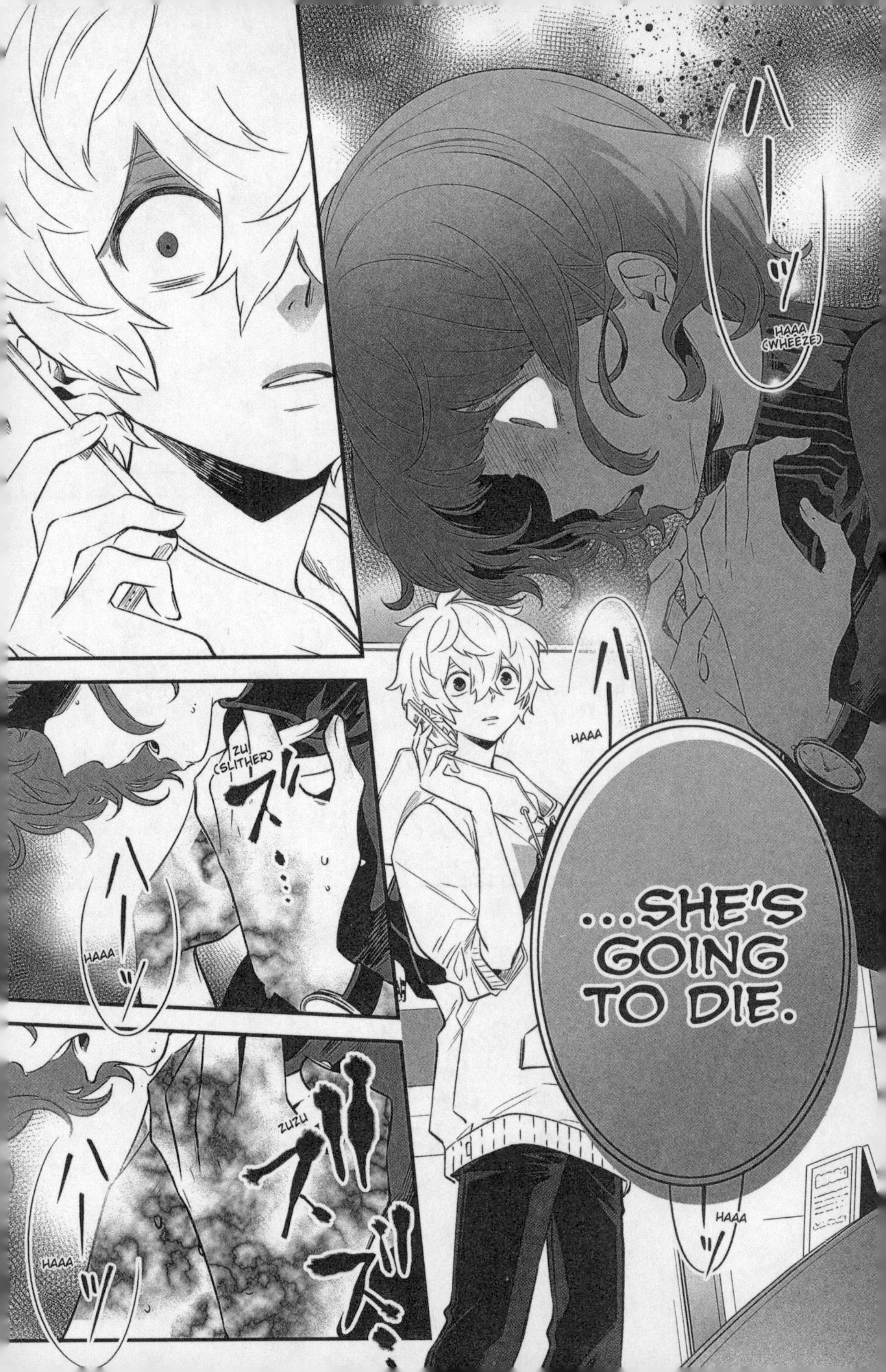
HAAA (WHEEZE)
HAAA
...SHE'S GOING TO DIE.
HAAA
ZU (SLITHER)
HAAA
ZUZU
HAAA

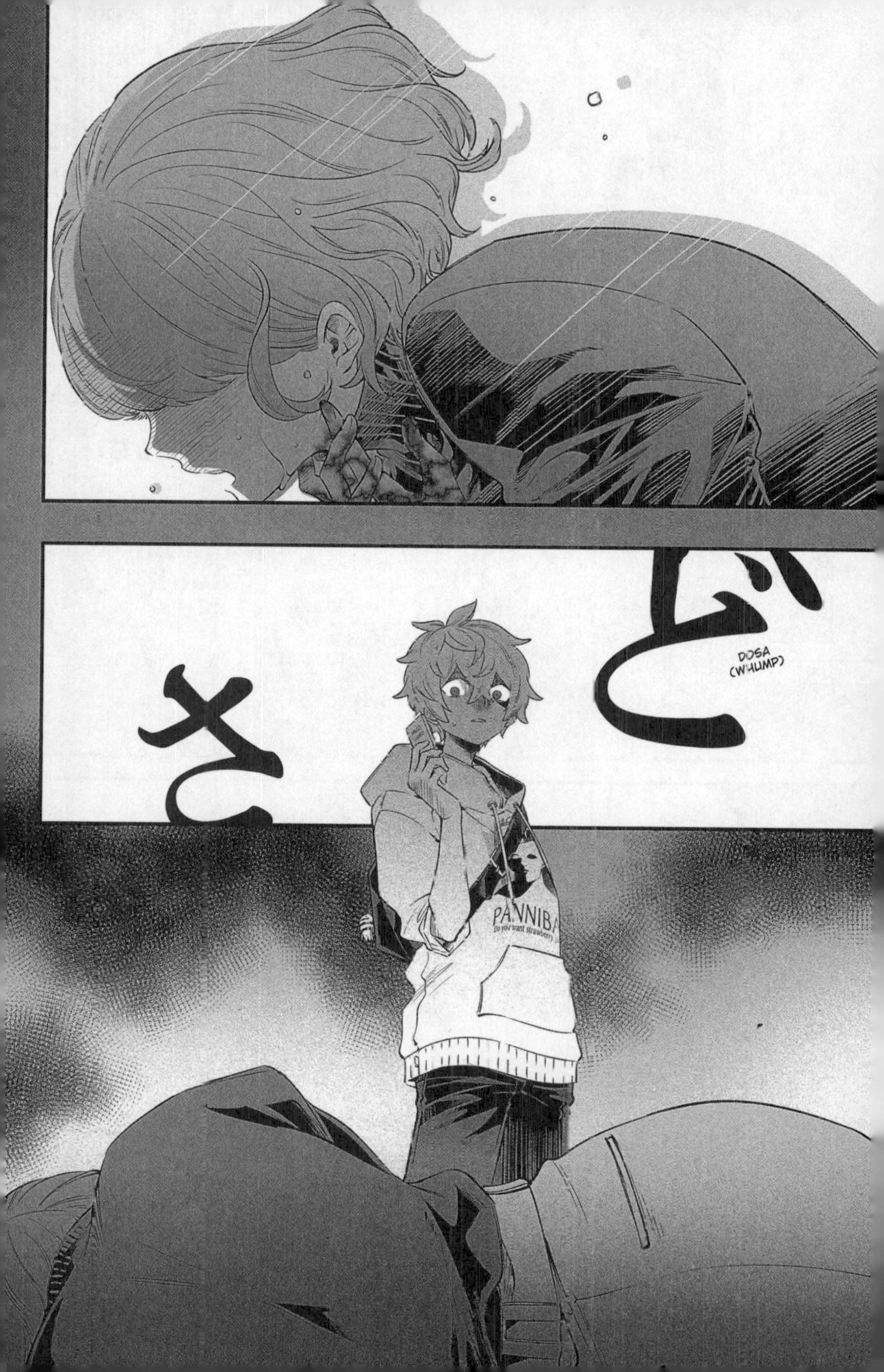
どさ
DOSA
(WHUMP)

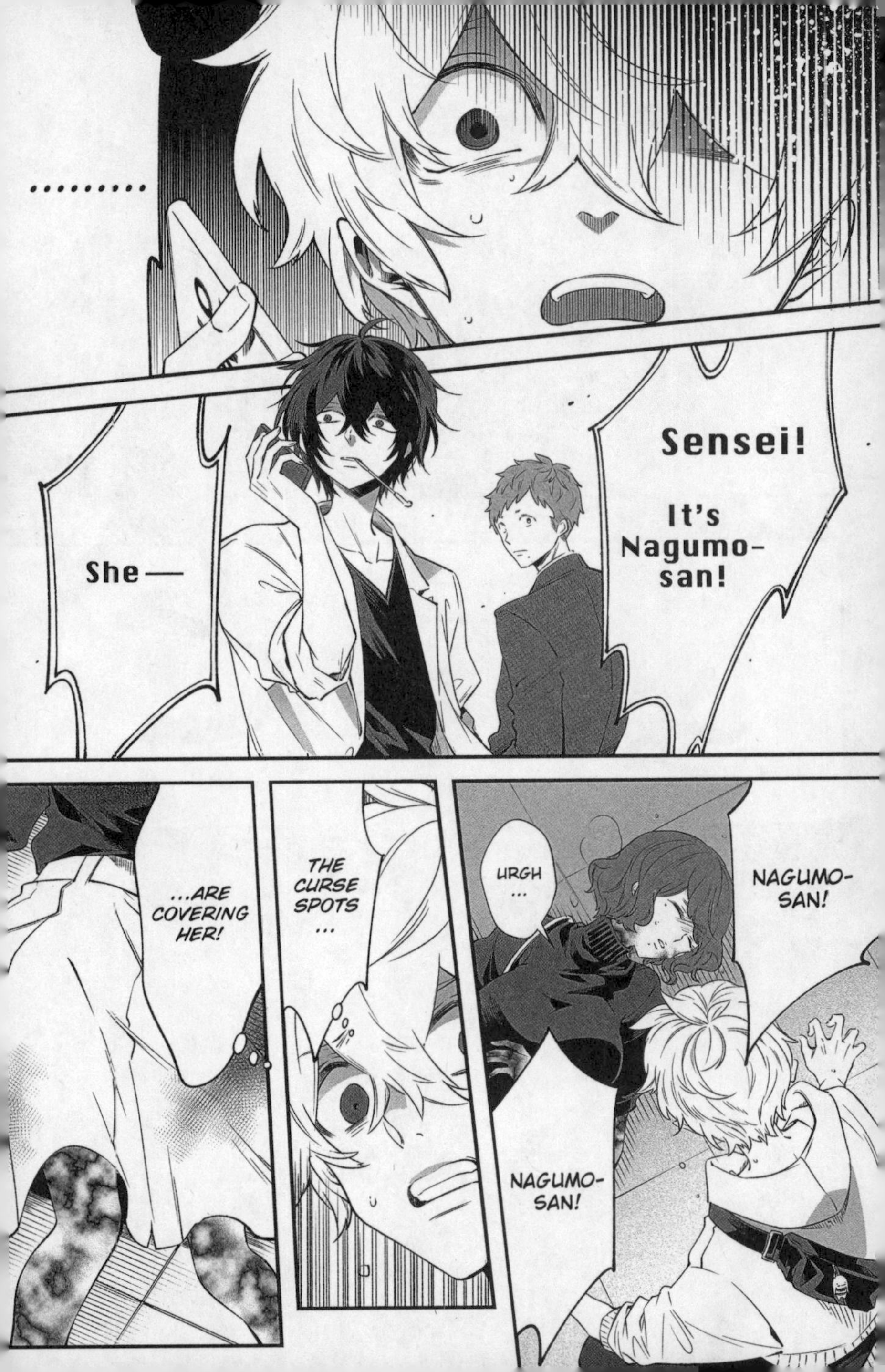
....
Sensei!
It's Nagumo-san!
She—
NAGUMO-SAN!
URGH ...
NAGUMO-SAN!
THE CURSE SPOTS ...
...ARE COVERING HER!

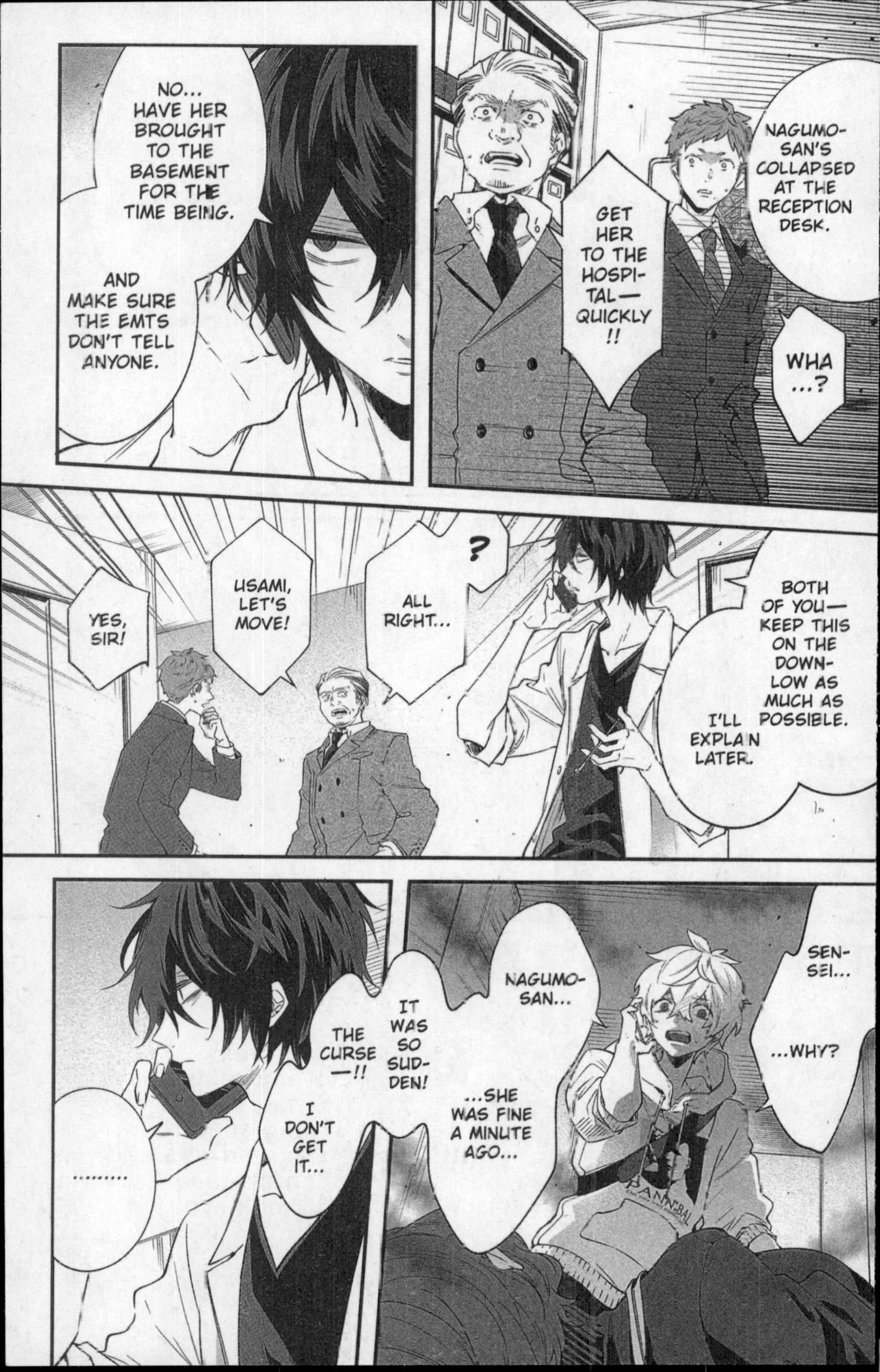
NAGUMO-SAN'S COLLAPSED AT THE RECEPTION DESK.
WHA...?
GET HER TO THE HOSPITAL—QUICKLY!!
NO... HAVE HER BROUGHT TO THE BASEMENT FOR THE TIME BEING.
AND MAKE SURE THE EMTS DON'T TELL ANYONE.
BOTH OF YOU—KEEP THIS ON THE DOWN-LOW AS MUCH AS POSSIBLE.
I'LL EXPLAIN LATER.
?
ALL RIGHT...
USAMI, LET'S MOVE!
YES, SIR!
SEN-SEI...
...WHY?
NAGUMO-SAN...
...SHE WAS FINE A MINUTE AGO...
IT WAS SO SUD-DEN!
THE CURSE—!!
I DON'T GET IT...
....

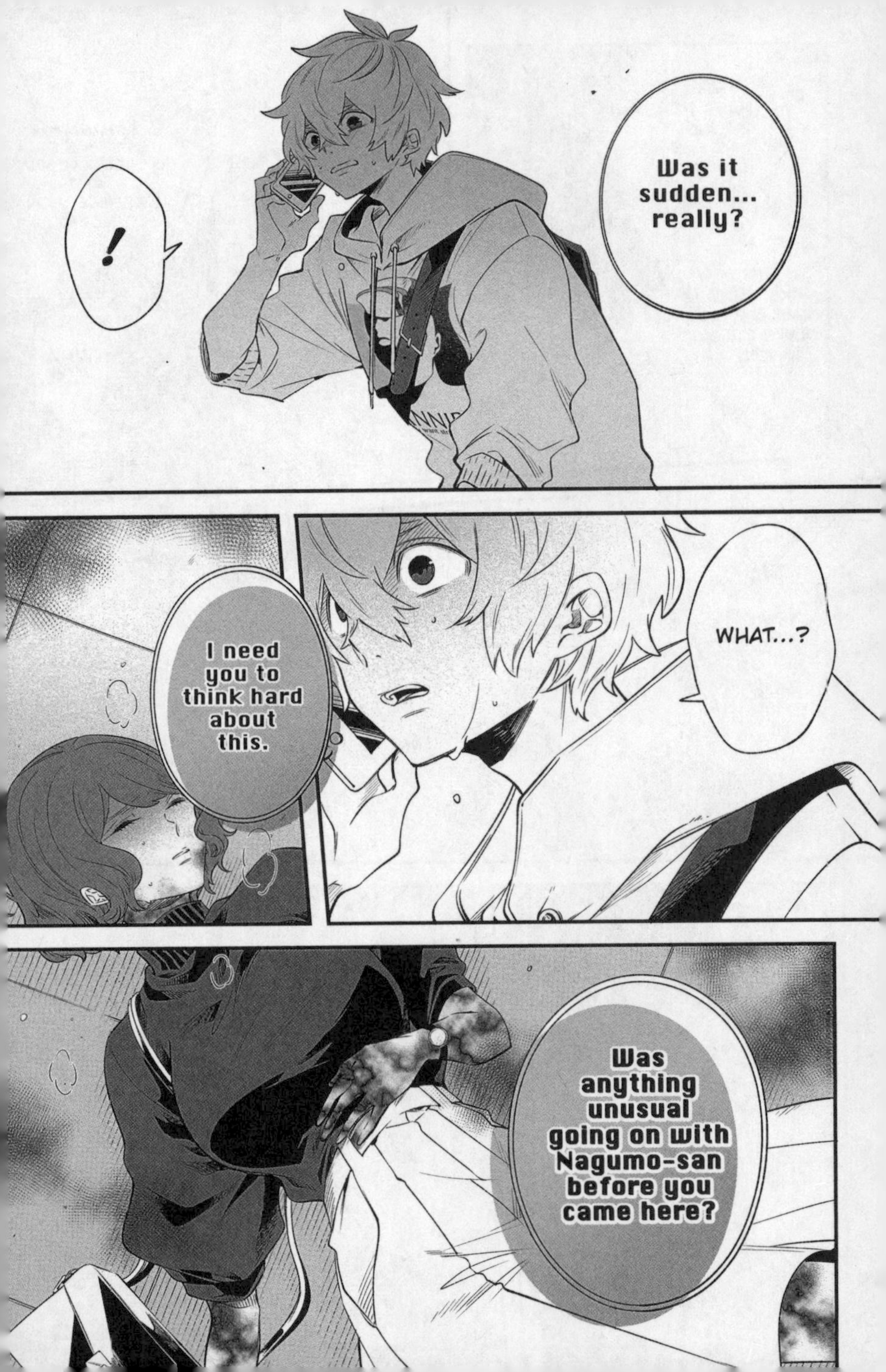
Was it sudden... really?
!
WHAT...?
I need you to think hard about this.
Was anything unusual going on with Nagumo-san before you came here?

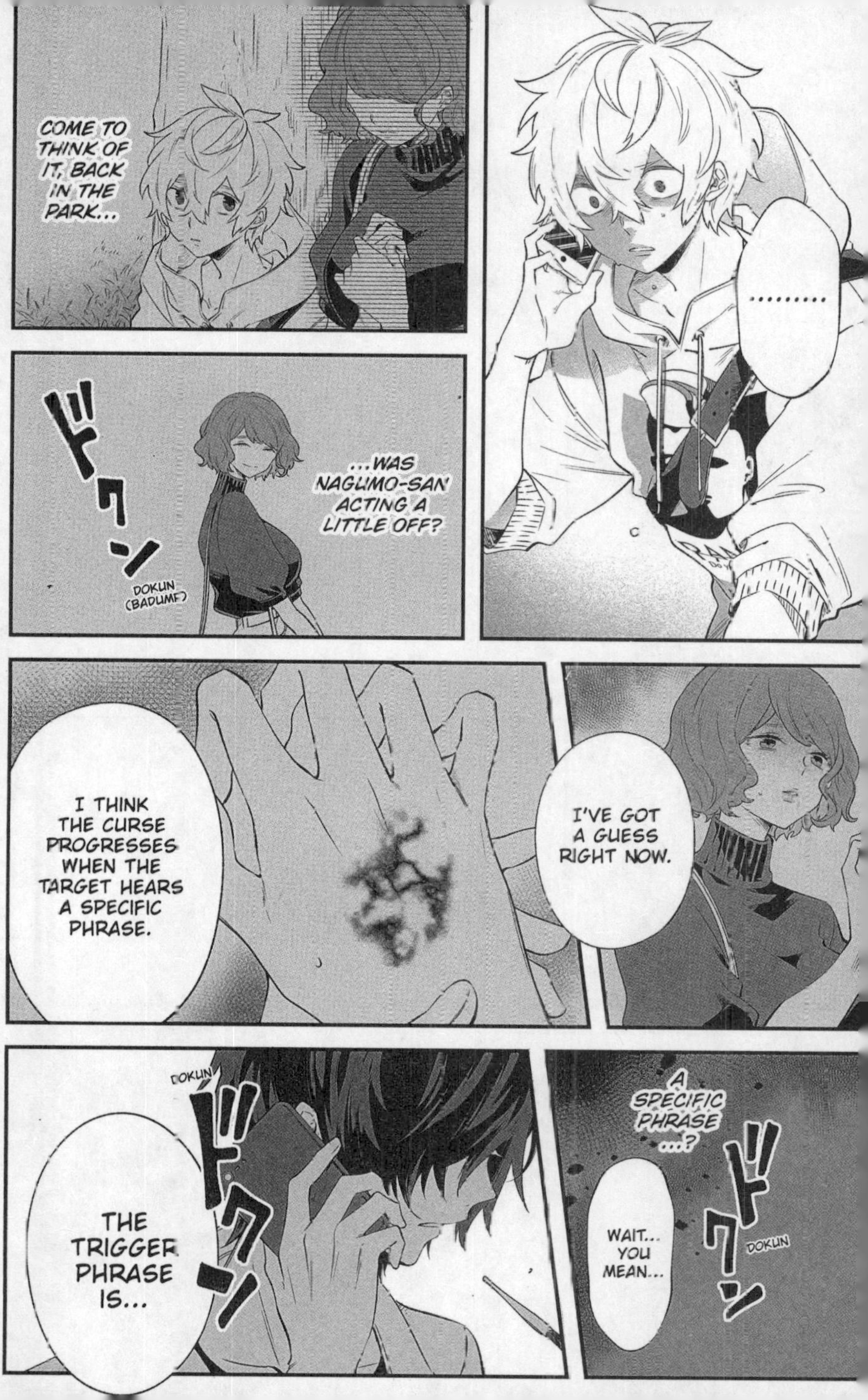
....
COME TO THINK OF IT, BACK IN THE PARK...
...WAS NAGUMO-SAN ACTING A LITTLE OFF?
ドクン
DOKUN (BADUMF)
I'VE GOT A GUESS RIGHT NOW.
I THINK THE CURSE PROGRESSES WHEN THE TARGET HEARS A SPECIFIC PHRASE.
A SPECIFIC PHRASE ...?
WAIT... YOU MEAN...
ドクン
DOKUN
ドクン
DOKUN
THE TRIGGER PHRASE IS...

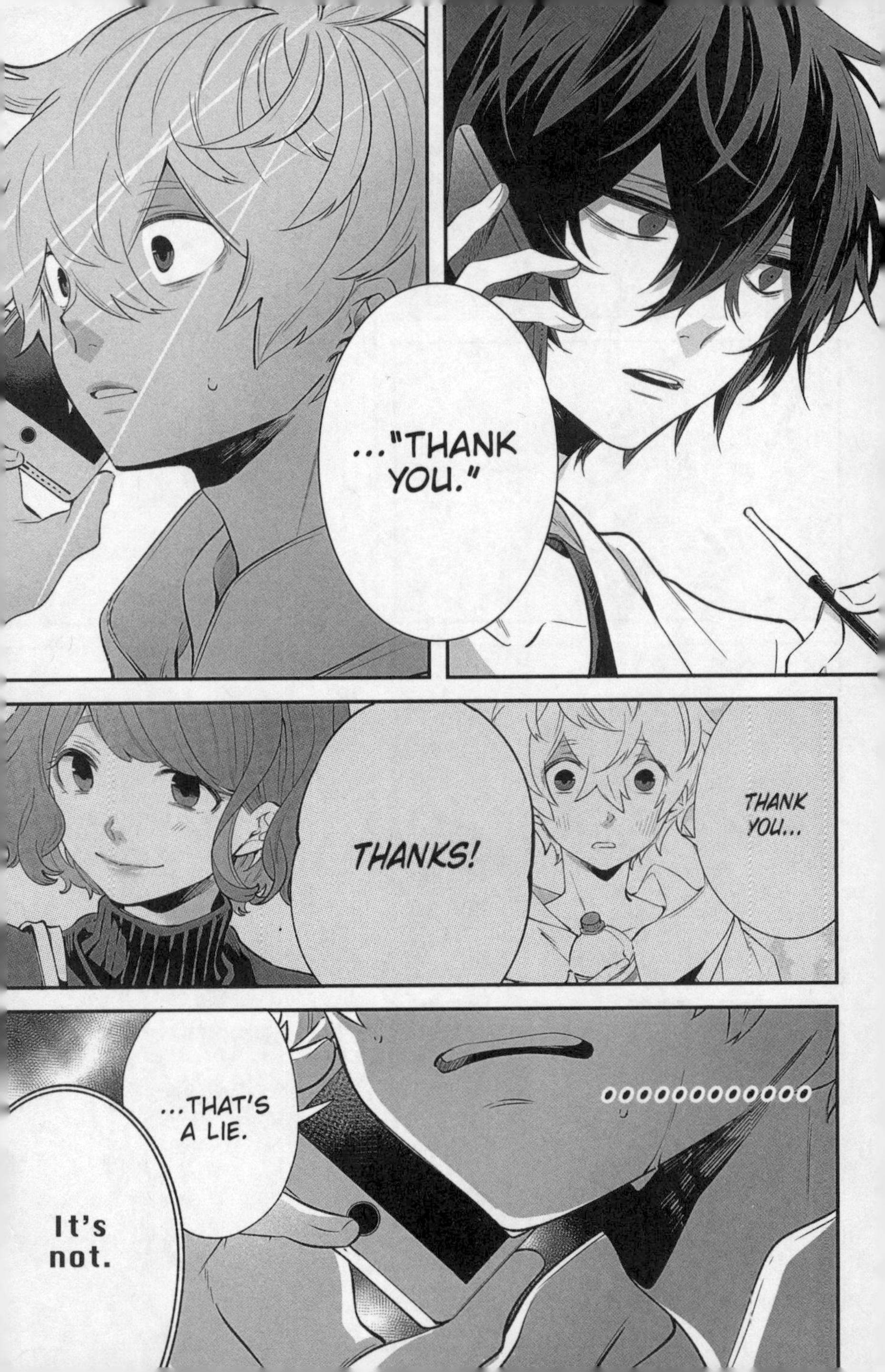
..."THANK YOU."
THANK YOU...
THANKS!
....
...THAT'S A LIE.
It's not.

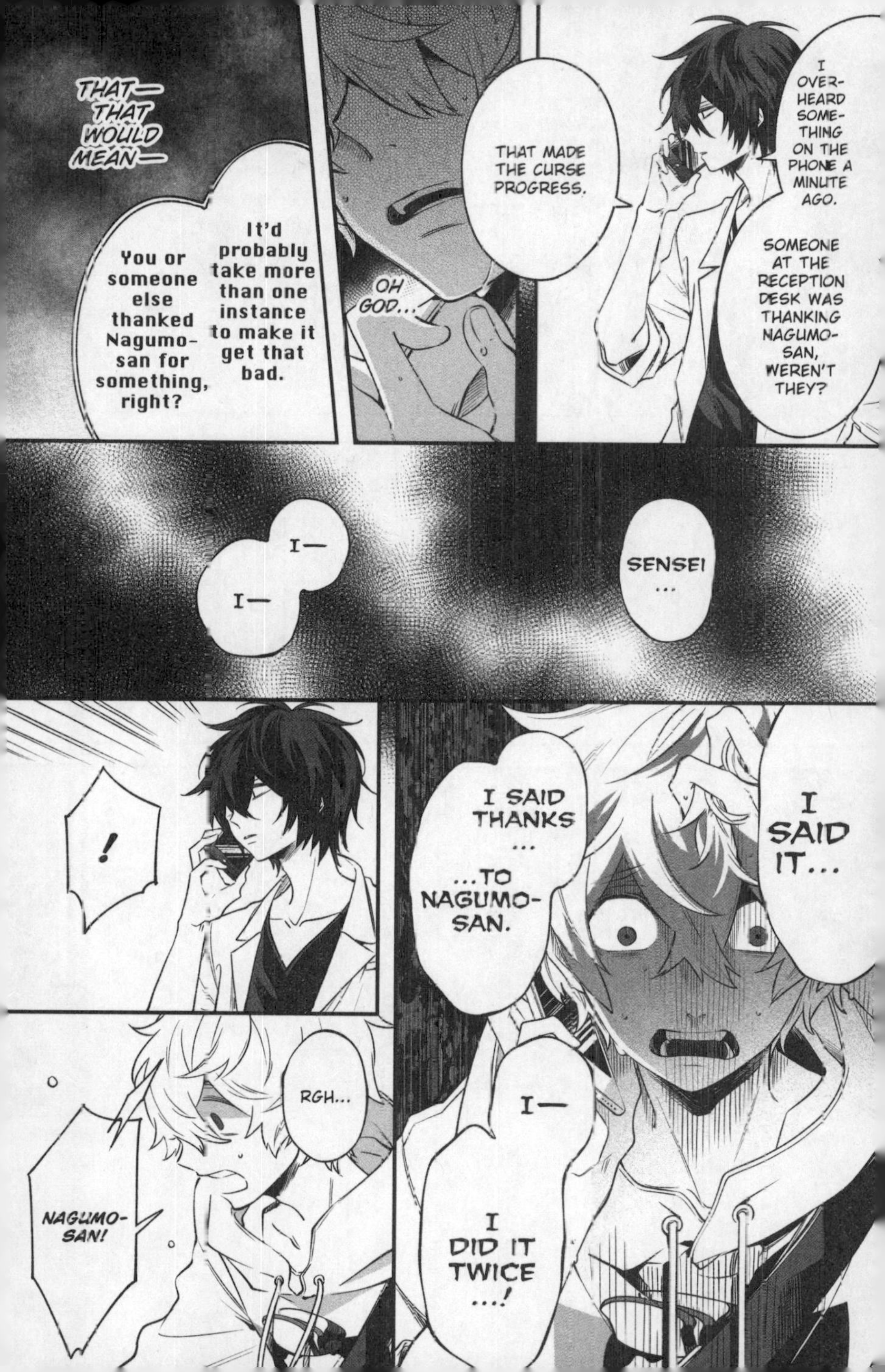
I OVERHEARD SOMETHING ON THE PHONE A MINUTE AGO.
THAT MADE THE CURSE PROGRESS.
SOMEONE AT THE RECEPTION DESK WAS THANKING NAGUMO-SAN, WEREN'T THEY?
OH GOD...
THAT—THAT WOULD MEAN—
It'd probably take more than one instance to make it get that bad.
You or someone else thanked Nagumo-san for something, right?
SENSEI...
I—
I—
I SAID IT...
I SAID THANKS...
...TO NAGUMO-SAN.
I—
I DID IT TWICE...!
!
RGH...
NAGUMO-SAN!

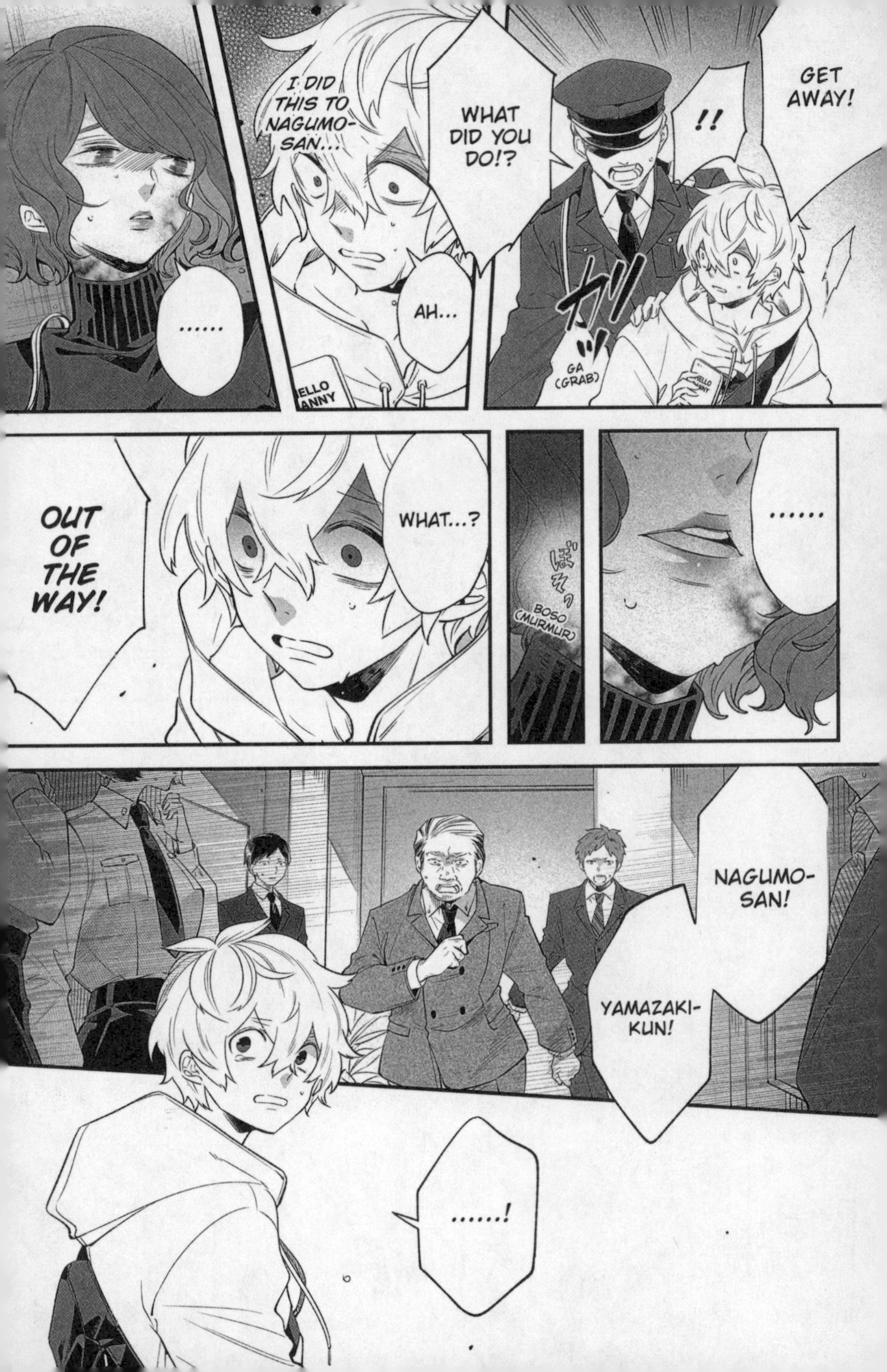
GET AWAY!
!!
WHAT DID YOU DO!?
GA (GRAB)
I DID THIS TO NAGUMO-SAN...
AH...
......
......
BOSO (MURMUR)
WHAT...?
OUT OF THE WAY!
NAGUMO-SAN!
YAMAZAKI-KUN!
......!

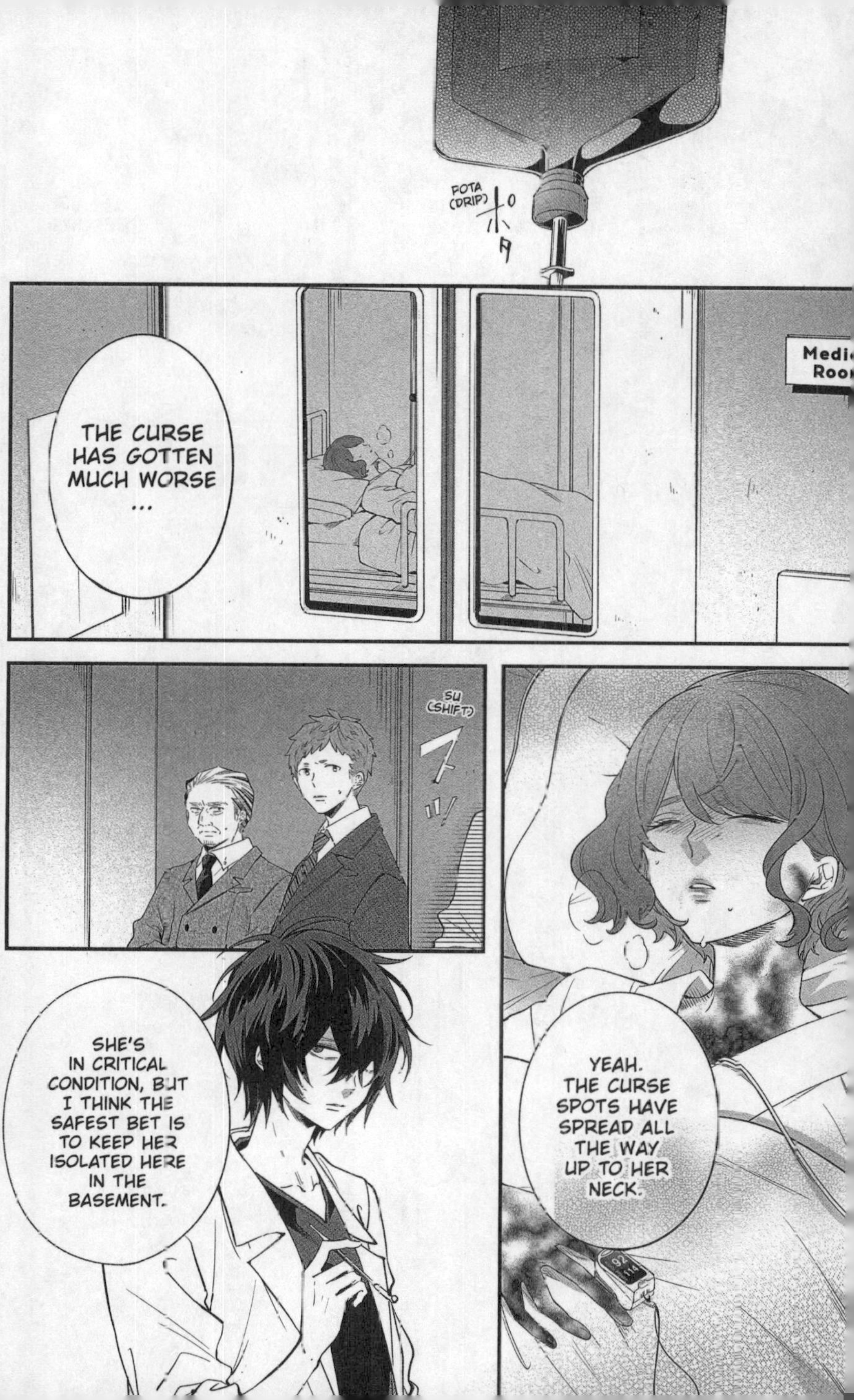
POTA (DRIP)
THE CURSE HAS GOTTEN MUCH WORSE...
YEAH. THE CURSE SPOTS HAVE SPREAD ALL THE WAY UP TO HER NECK.
SU (SHIFT)
SHE'S IN CRITICAL CONDITION, BUT I THINK THE SAFEST BET IS TO KEEP HER ISOLATED HERE IN THE BASEMENT.

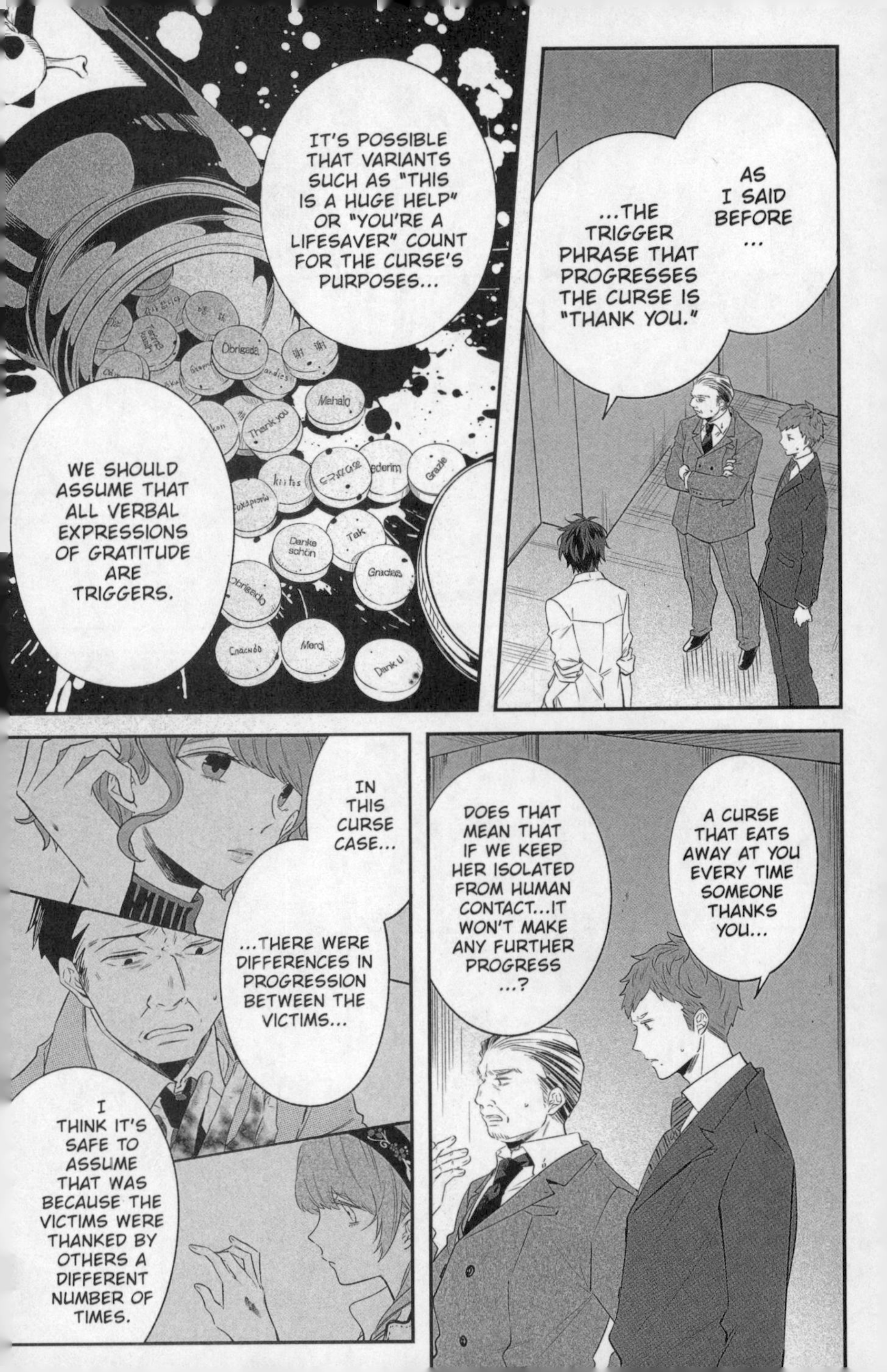
AS I SAID BEFORE...
...THE TRIGGER PHRASE THAT PROGRESSES THE CURSE IS "THANK YOU."
IT'S POSSIBLE THAT VARIANTS SUCH AS "THIS IS A HUGE HELP" OR "YOU'RE A LIFESAVER" COUNT FOR THE CURSE'S PURPOSES...
Obrigada
Mahalo
Thank you
Grazie
kiitos
Danke schön
Tak
Gracias
Merci
Dank U
WE SHOULD ASSUME THAT ALL VERBAL EXPRESSIONS OF GRATITUDE ARE TRIGGERS.
A CURSE THAT EATS AWAY AT YOU EVERY TIME SOMEONE THANKS YOU...
DOES THAT MEAN THAT IF WE KEEP HER ISOLATED FROM HUMAN CONTACT...IT WON'T MAKE ANY FURTHER PROGRESS ...?
IN THIS CURSE CASE...
...THERE WERE DIFFERENCES IN PROGRESSION BETWEEN THE VICTIMS...
I THINK IT'S SAFE TO ASSUME THAT WAS BECAUSE THE VICTIMS WERE THANKED BY OTHERS A DIFFERENT NUMBER OF TIMES.

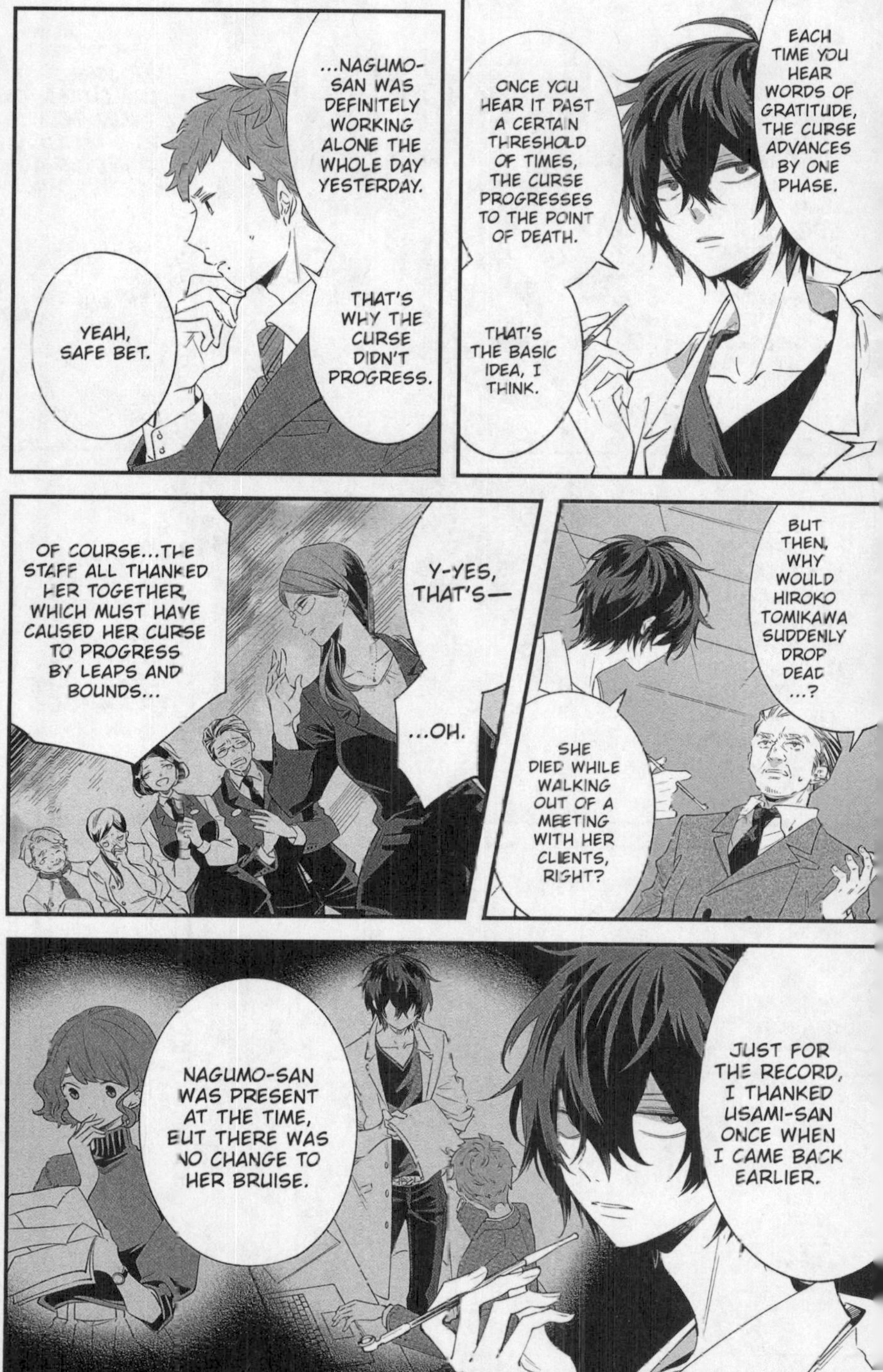
EACH TIME YOU HEAR WORDS OF GRATITUDE, THE CURSE ADVANCES BY ONE PHASE.
ONCE YOU HEAR IT PAST A CERTAIN THRESHOLD OF TIMES, THE CURSE PROGRESSES TO THE POINT OF DEATH.
THAT'S THE BASIC IDEA, I THINK.
...NAGUMO-SAN WAS DEFINITELY WORKING ALONE THE WHOLE DAY YESTERDAY.
THAT'S WHY THE CURSE DIDN'T PROGRESS.
YEAH, SAFE BET.
BUT THEN, WHY WOULD HIROKO TOMIKAWA SUDDENLY DROP DEAD ...?
SHE DIED WHILE WALKING OUT OF A MEETING WITH HER CLIENTS, RIGHT?
Y-YES, THAT'S—
...OH.
OF COURSE...THE STAFF ALL THANKED HER TOGETHER, WHICH MUST HAVE CAUSED HER CURSE TO PROGRESS BY LEAPS AND BOUNDS...
JUST FOR THE RECORD, I THANKED USAMI-SAN ONCE WHEN I CAME BACK EARLIER.
NAGUMO-SAN WAS PRESENT AT THE TIME, BUT THERE WAS NO CHANGE TO HER BRUISE.

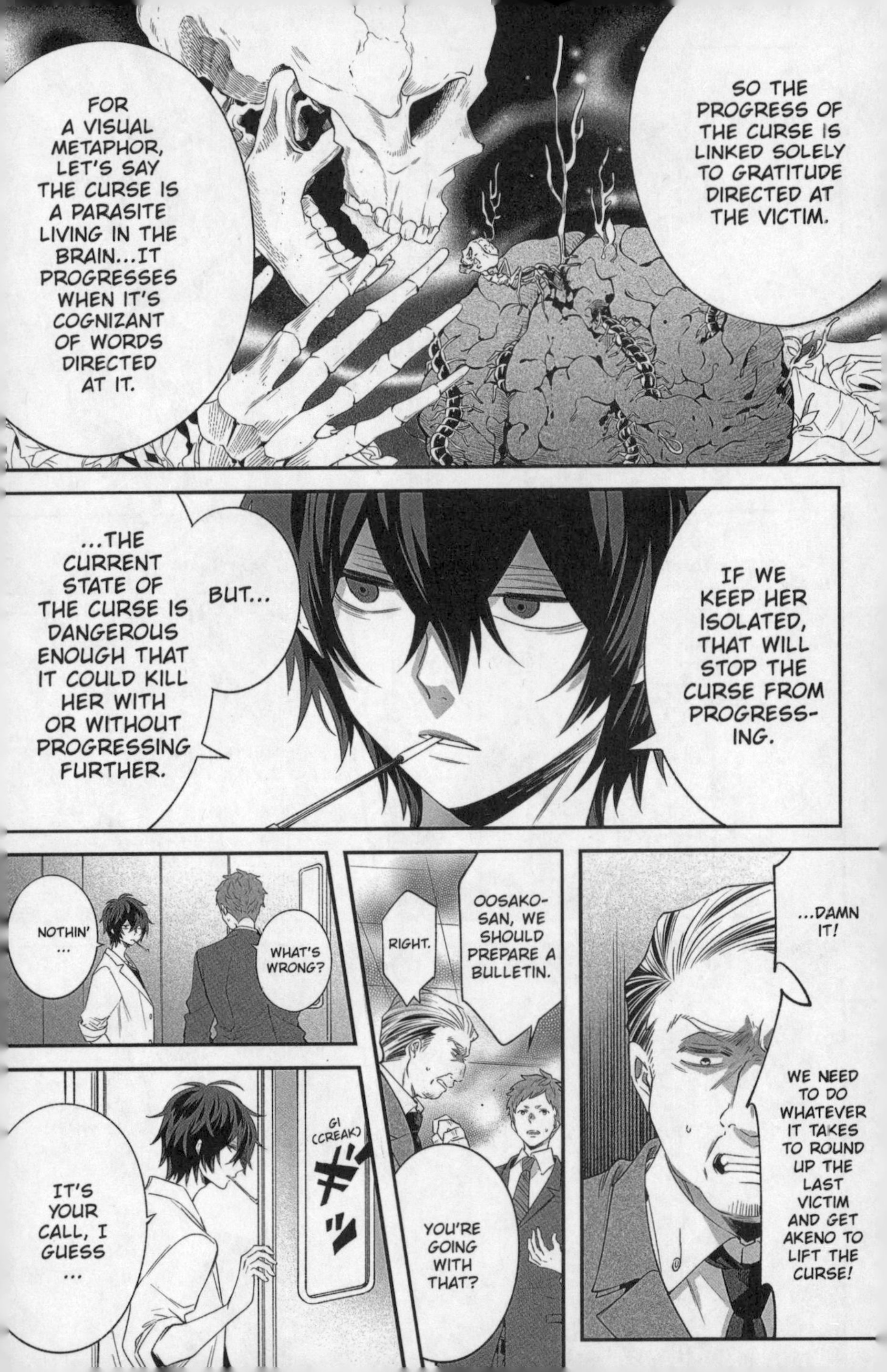
SO THE PROGRESS OF THE CURSE IS LINKED SOLELY TO GRATITUDE DIRECTED AT THE VICTIM.
FOR A VISUAL METAPHOR, LET'S SAY THE CURSE IS A PARASITE LIVING IN THE BRAIN...IT PROGRESSES WHEN IT'S COGNIZANT OF WORDS DIRECTED AT IT.
IF WE KEEP HER ISOLATED, THAT WILL STOP THE CURSE FROM PROGRESS-ING.
BUT...
...THE CURRENT STATE OF THE CURSE IS DANGEROUS ENOUGH THAT IT COULD KILL HER WITH OR WITHOUT PROGRESSING FURTHER.
...DAMN IT!
WE NEED TO DO WHATEVER IT TAKES TO ROUND UP THE LAST VICTIM AND GET AKENO TO LIFT THE CURSE!
OOSAKO-SAN, WE SHOULD PREPARE A BULLETIN.
RIGHT.
GI (CREAK)
YOU'RE GOING WITH THAT?
WHAT'S WRONG?
NOTHIN' ...
IT'S YOUR CALL, I GUESS ...

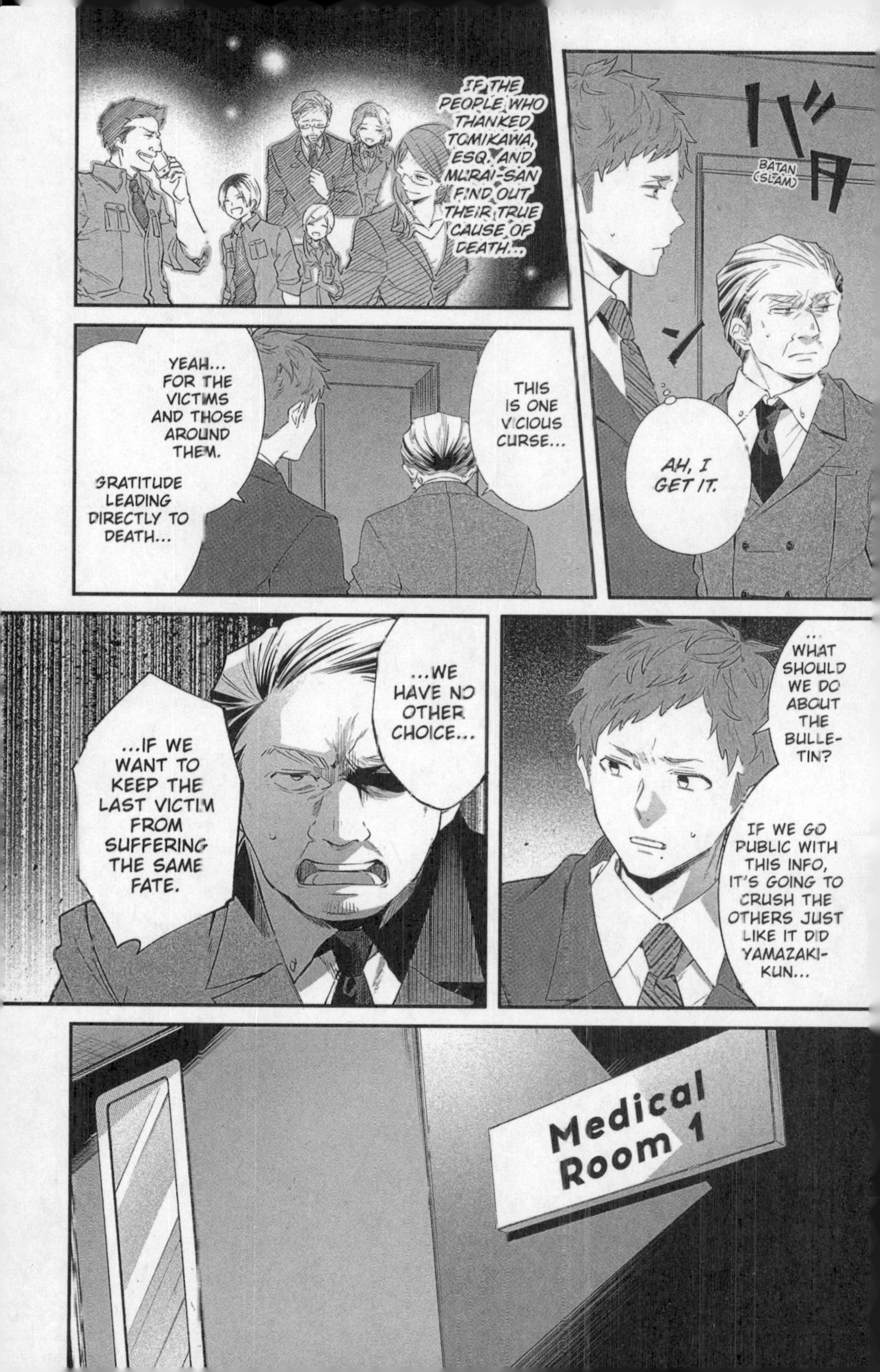
BATAN (SLAM)
AH, I GET IT.
IF THE PEOPLE WHO THANKED TOMIKAWA, ESQ. AND MURAI-SAN FIND OUT THEIR TRUE CAUSE OF DEATH...
THIS IS ONE VICIOUS CURSE...
YEAH... FOR THE VICTIMS AND THOSE AROUND THEM.
GRATITUDE LEADING DIRECTLY TO DEATH...
...WHAT SHOULD WE DO ABOUT THE BULLE-TIN?
IF WE GO PUBLIC WITH THIS INFO, IT'S GOING TO CRUSH THE OTHERS JUST LIKE IT DID YAMAZAKI-KUN...
...WE HAVE NO OTHER CHOICE...
...IF WE WANT TO KEEP THE LAST VICTIM FROM SUFFERING THE SAME FATE.
Medical Room 1

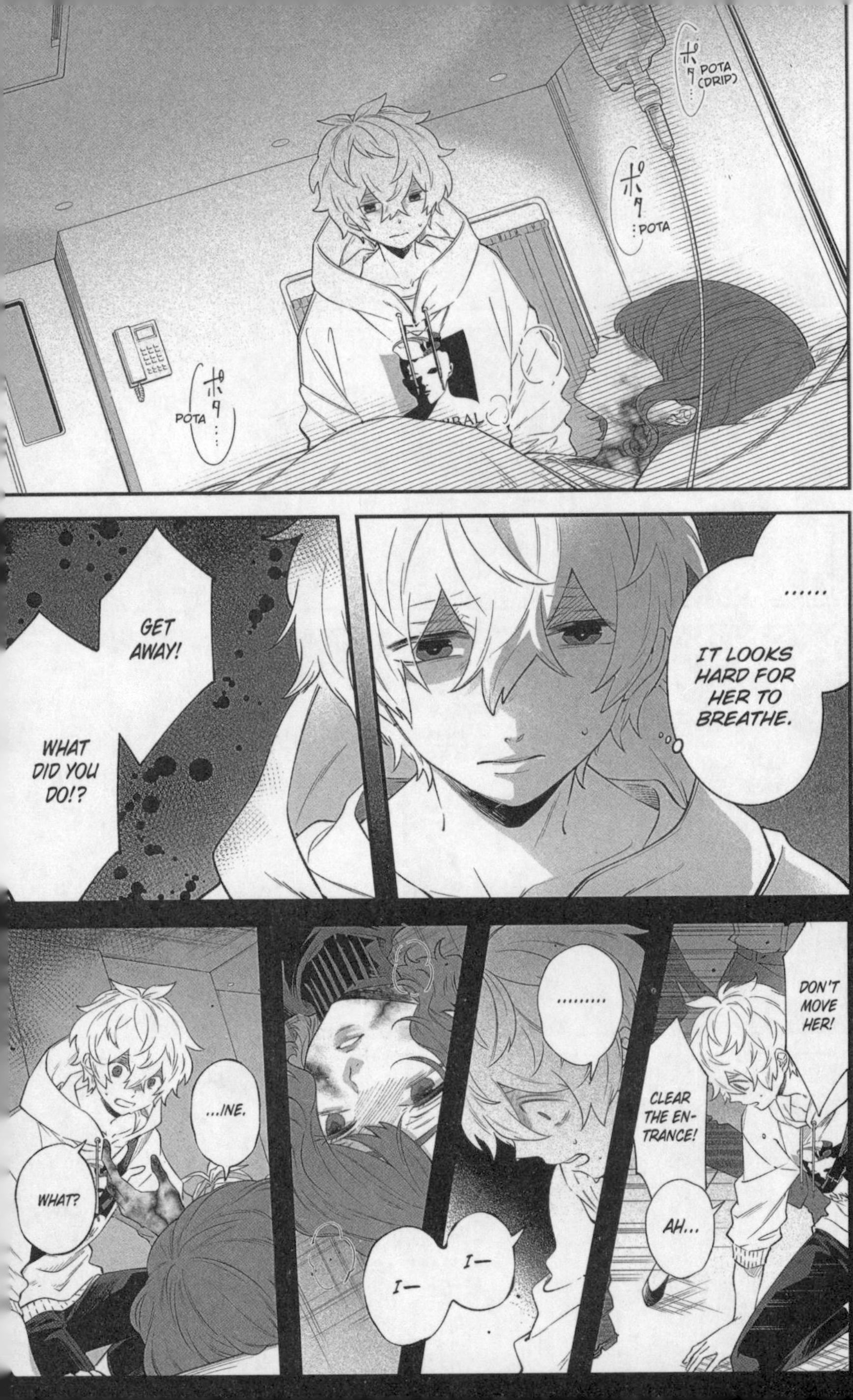
ポタ…
POTA (DRIP)
ポタ…
POTA
ポタ…
POTA
......
IT LOOKS HARD FOR HER TO BREATHE.
GET AWAY!
WHAT DID YOU DO!?
DON'T MOVE HER!
CLEAR THE EN-TRANCE!
AH...
....
I—
I—
...INE.
WHAT?

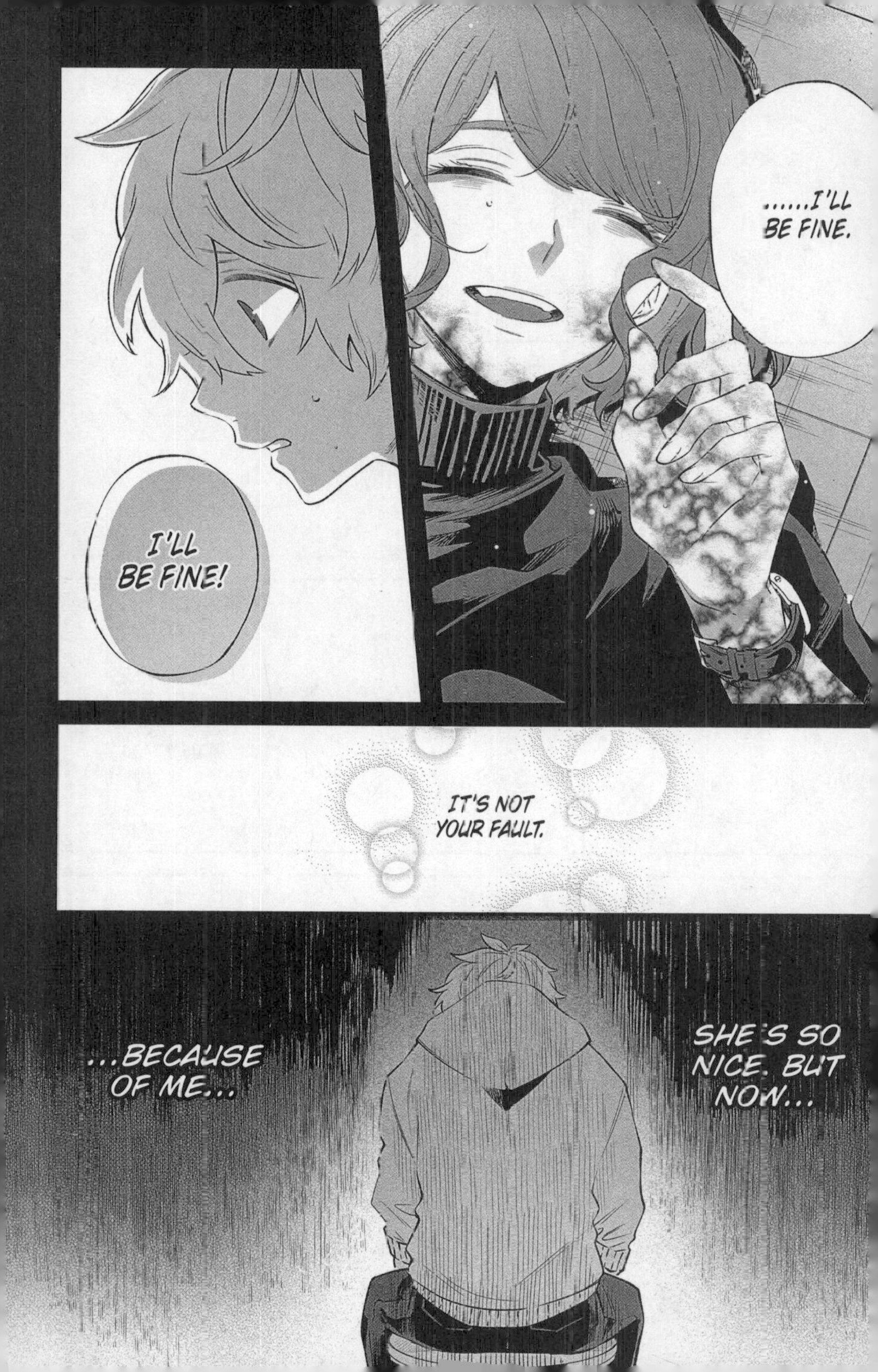
......I'LL BE FINE.
I'LL BE FINE!
IT'S NOT YOUR FAULT.
SHE'S SO NICE. BUT NOW...
...BECAUSE OF ME...

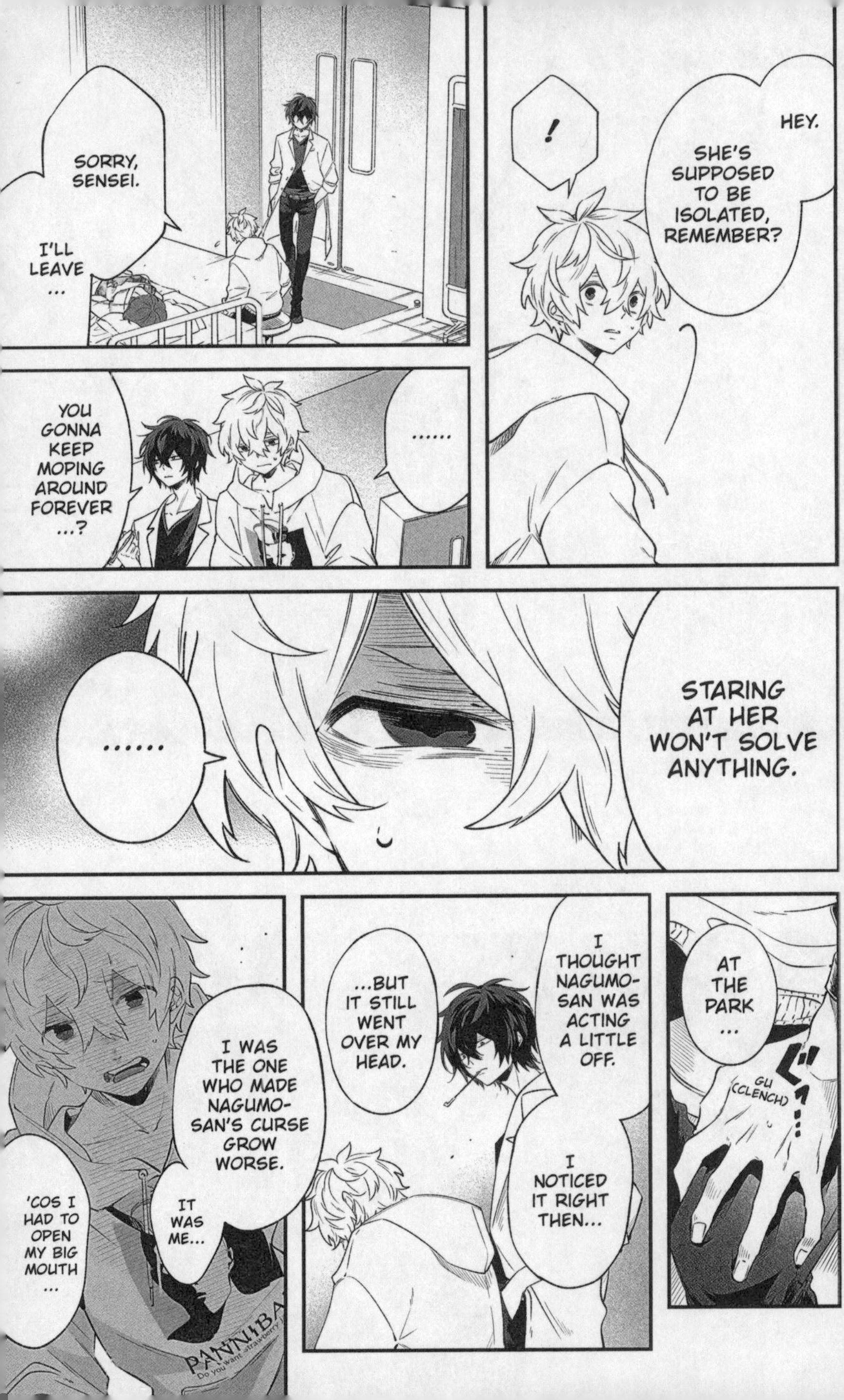
HEY.
SHE'S SUPPOSED TO BE ISOLATED, REMEMBER?
!
SORRY, SENSEI.
I'LL LEAVE ...
......
YOU GONNA KEEP MOPING AROUND FOREVER ...?
STARING AT HER WON'T SOLVE ANYTHING.
......
AT THE PARK ...
GU (CLENCH)
I THOUGHT NAGUMO-SAN WAS ACTING A LITTLE OFF.
I NOTICED IT RIGHT THEN...
...BUT IT STILL WENT OVER MY HEAD.
I WAS THE ONE WHO MADE NAGUMO-SAN'S CURSE GROW WORSE.
IT WAS ME...
'COS I HAD TO OPEN MY BIG MOUTH ...

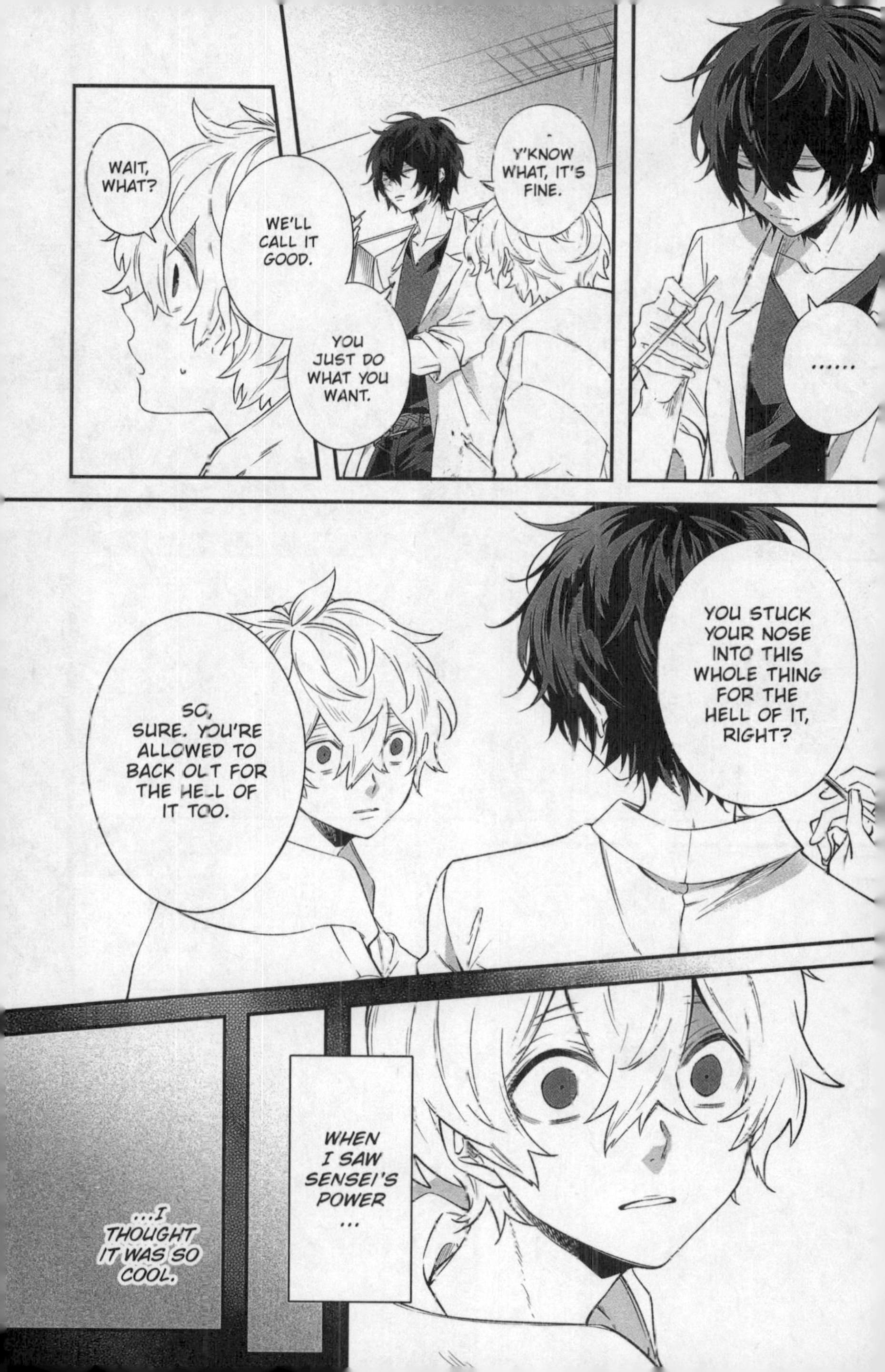
......
Y'KNOW WHAT, IT'S FINE.
WE'LL CALL IT GOOD.
YOU JUST DO WHAT YOU WANT.
WAIT, WHAT?
YOU STUCK YOUR NOSE INTO THIS WHOLE THING FOR THE HELL OF IT, RIGHT?
SO, SURE. YOU'RE ALLOWED TO BACK OUT FOR THE HELL OF IT TOO.
WHEN I SAW SENSEI'S POWER ...
...I THOUGHT IT WAS SO COOL.

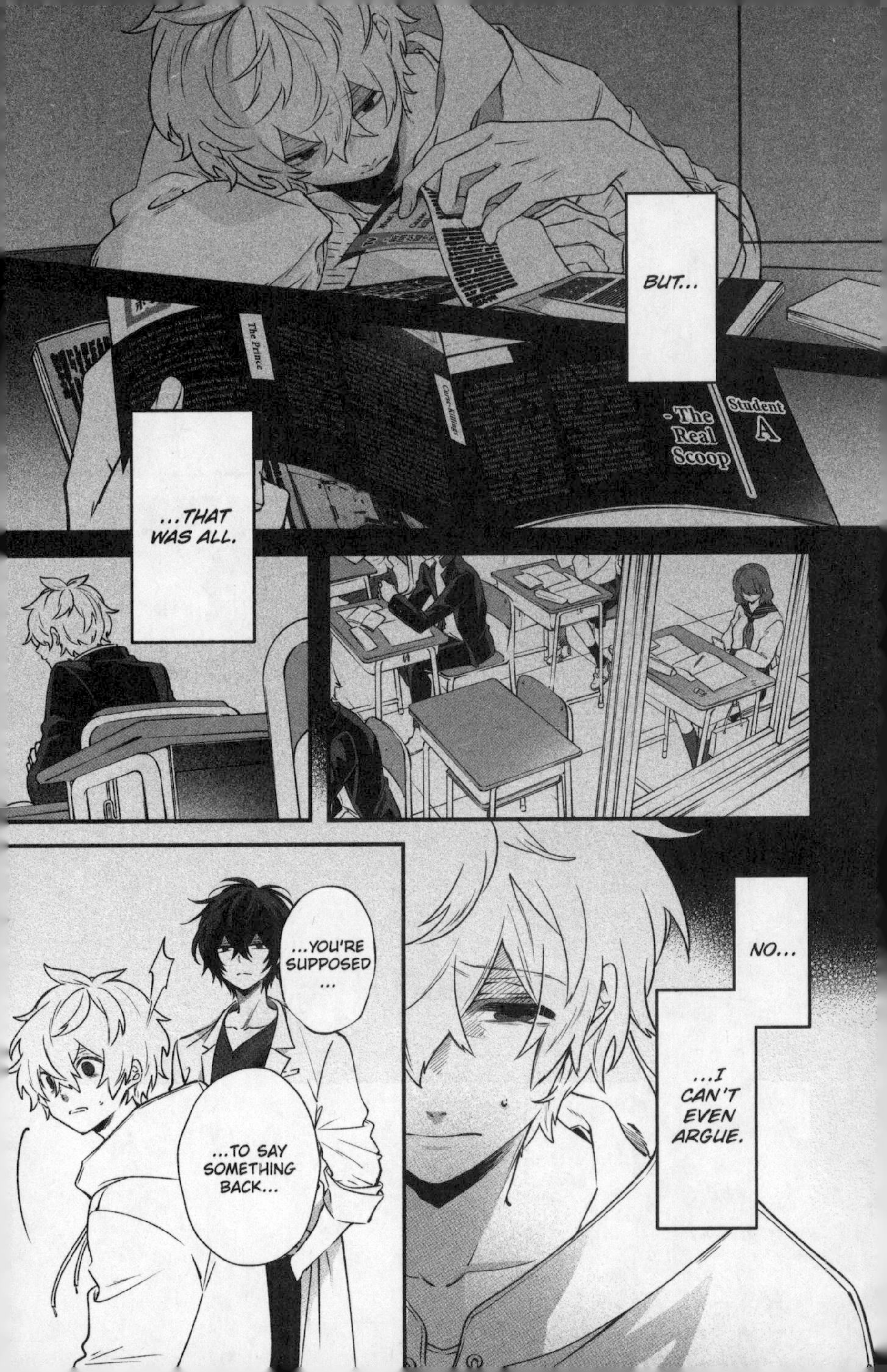
BUT...
Student A - The Real Scoop
Curse-Killing
The Prince
...THAT WAS ALL.
NO...
...I CAN'T EVEN ARGUE.
...YOU'RE SUPPOSED ...
...TO SAY SOMETHING BACK...

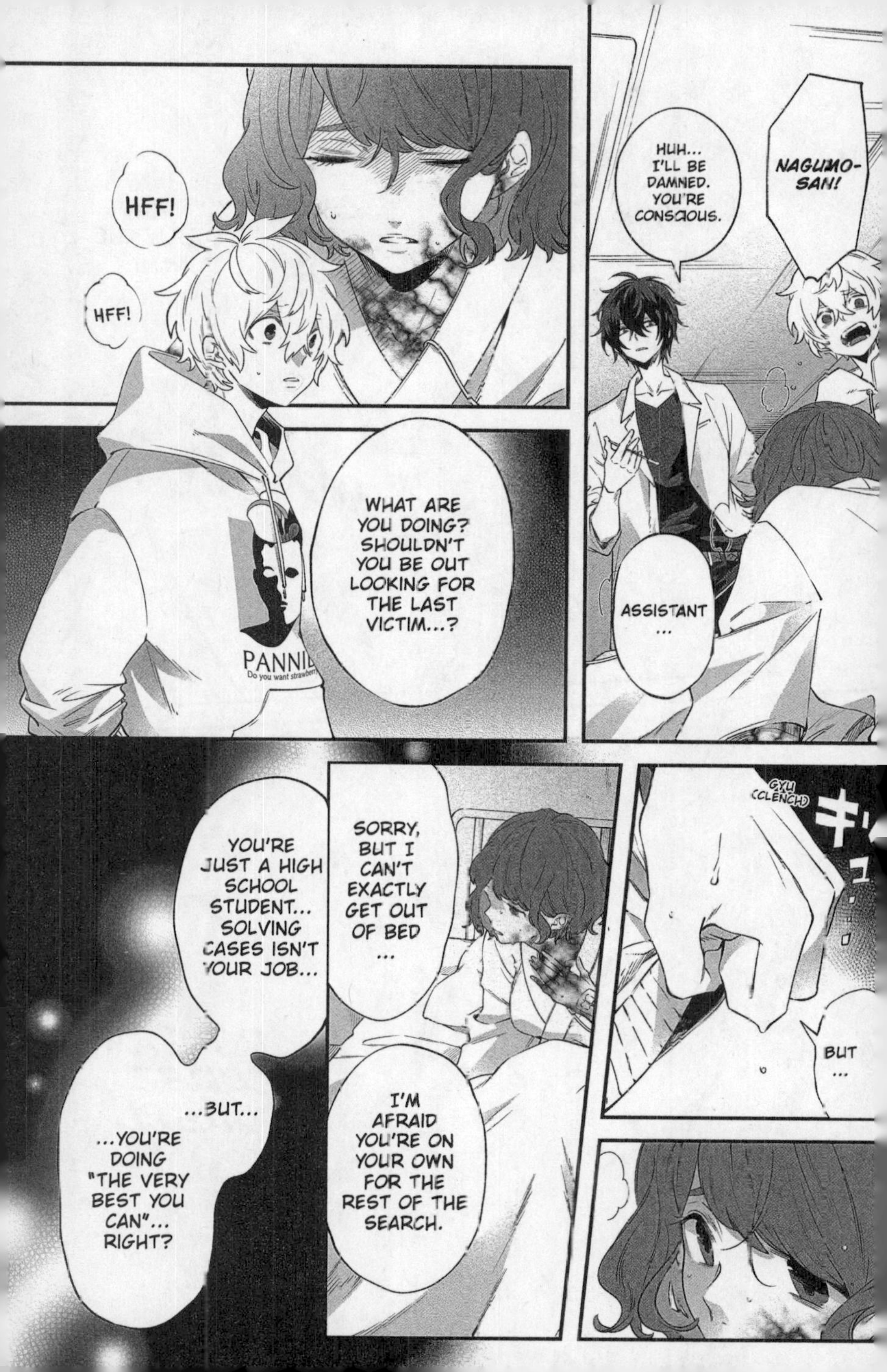
NAGUMO-SAN!
HUH... I'LL BE DAMNED. YOU'RE CONSCIOUS.
ASSISTANT ...
HFF!
HFF!
PANNIE
Do you want strawberry
WHAT ARE YOU DOING? SHOULDN'T YOU BE OUT LOOKING FOR THE LAST VICTIM...?
GYU (CLENCH)
BUT ...
SORRY, BUT I CAN'T EXACTLY GET OUT OF BED ...
I'M AFRAID YOU'RE ON YOUR OWN FOR THE REST OF THE SEARCH.
YOU'RE JUST A HIGH SCHOOL STUDENT... SOLVING CASES ISN'T YOUR JOB...
...BUT...
...YOU'RE DOING "THE VERY BEST YOU CAN"... RIGHT?

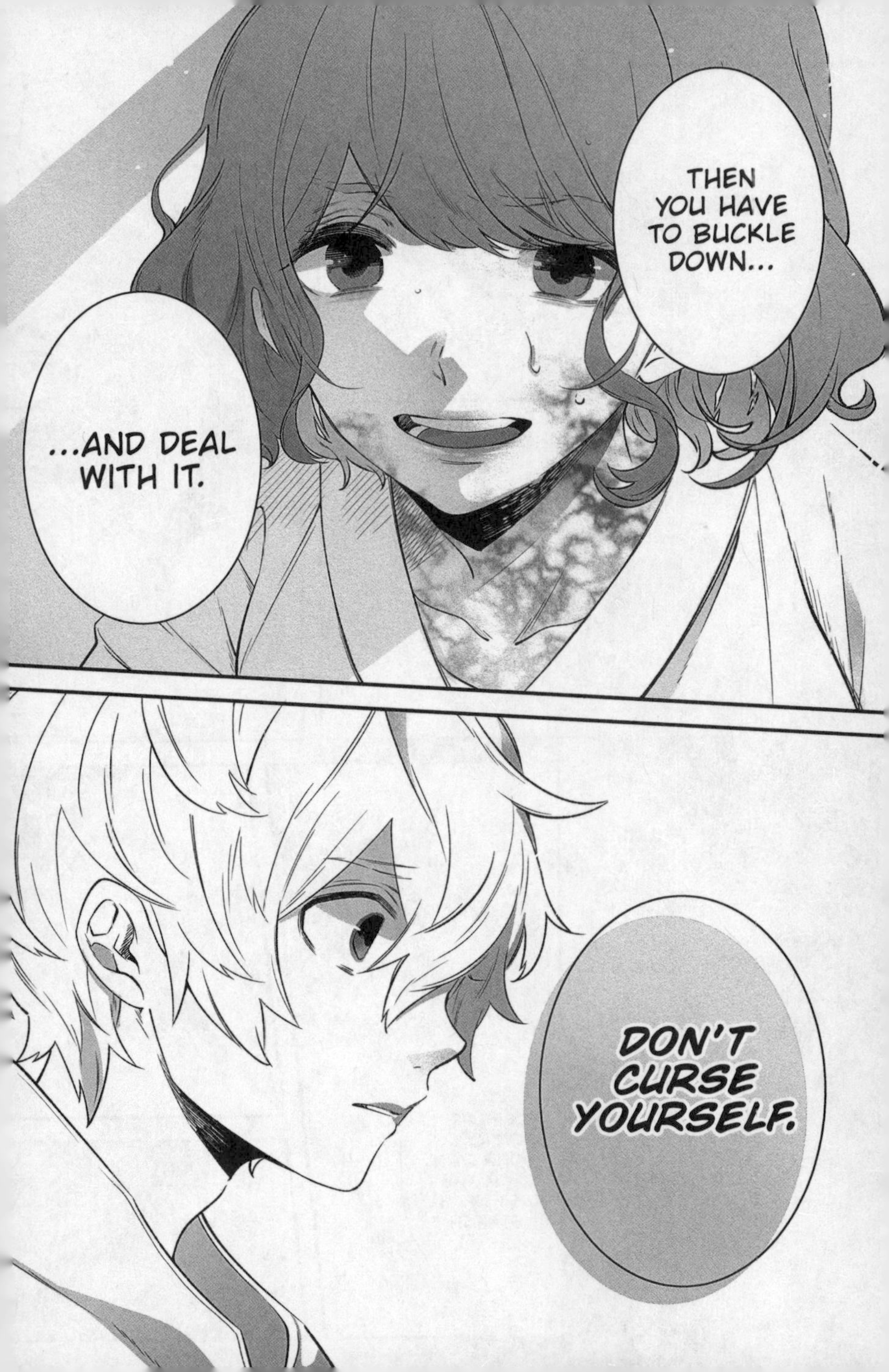
THEN YOU HAVE TO BUCKLE DOWN...
...AND DEAL WITH IT.
DON'T CURSE YOURSELF.

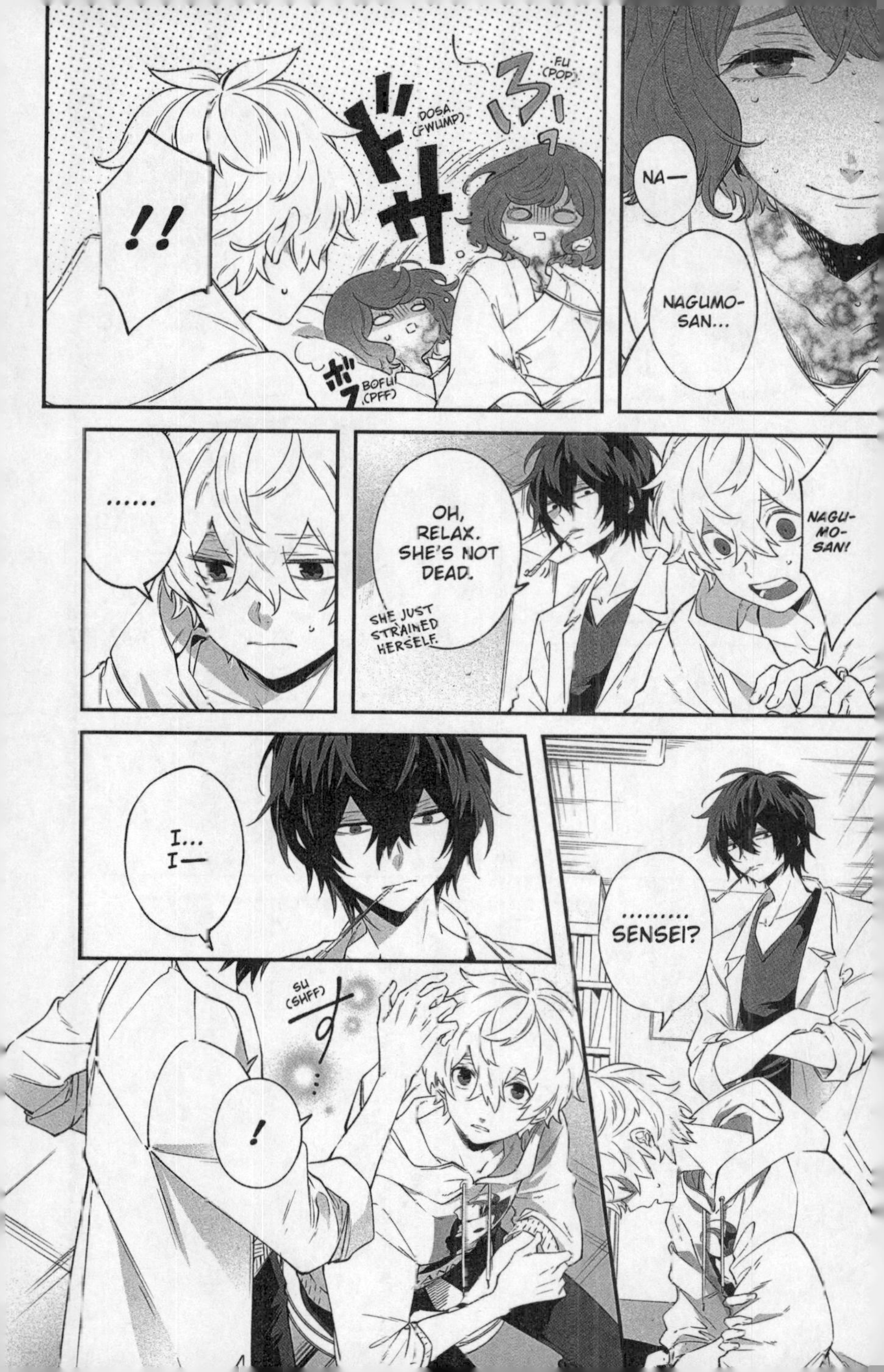

NA—
NAGUMO-SAN...
FU (POP)
DOSA (FWUMP)
!!
BOFU (PFF)
NAGUMO-SAN!
OH, RELAX. SHE'S NOT DEAD.
SHE JUST STRAINED HERSELF.
......
.... SENSEI?
I... I—
SU (SHFF)
!

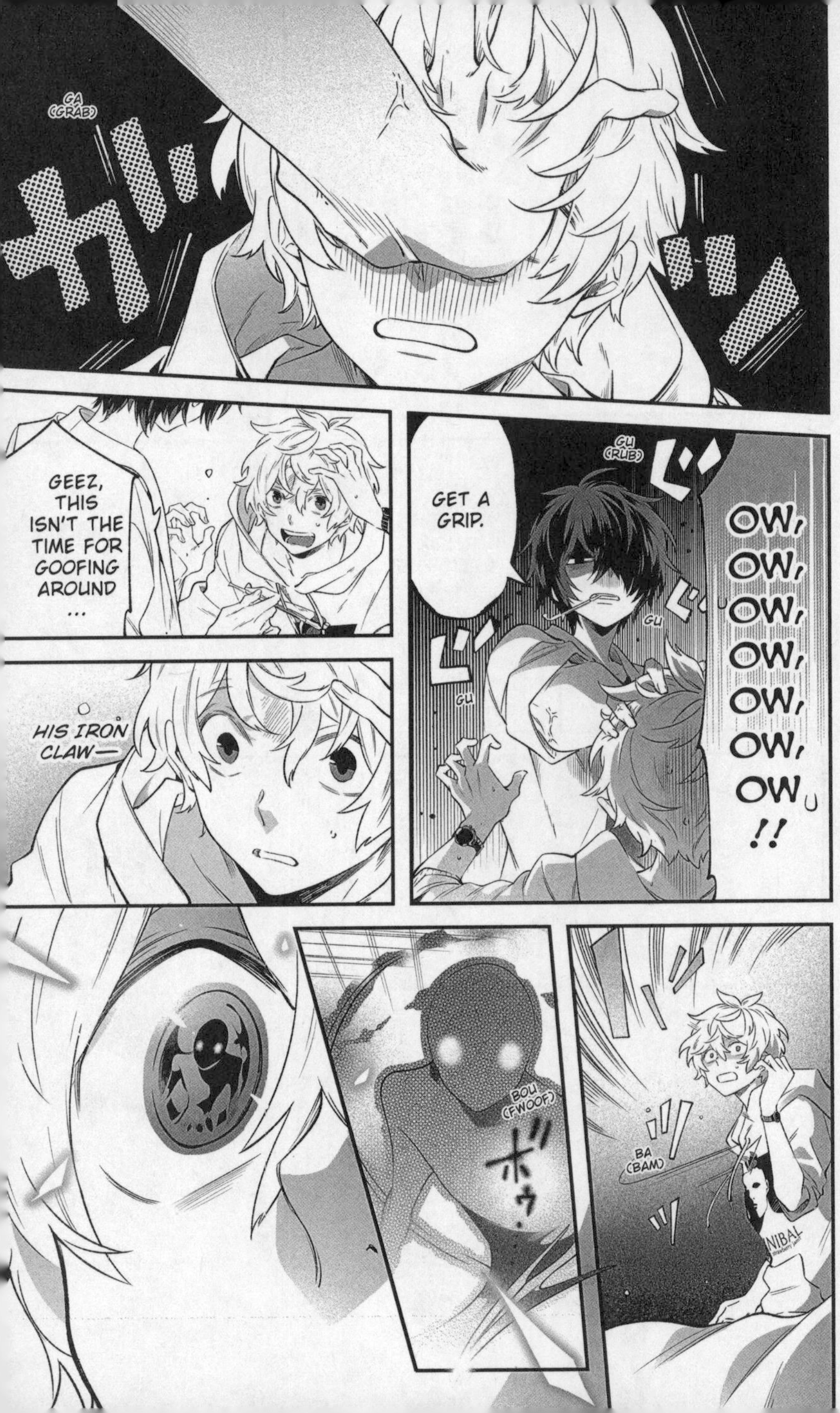
GA (GRAB)
GET A GRIP.
GU (RUB)
GU
GU
OW, OW, OW, OW, OW, OW, OW!!
GEEZ, THIS ISN'T THE TIME FOR GOOFING AROUND...
HIS IRON CLAW—
BA (BAM)
BOU (FWOOF)

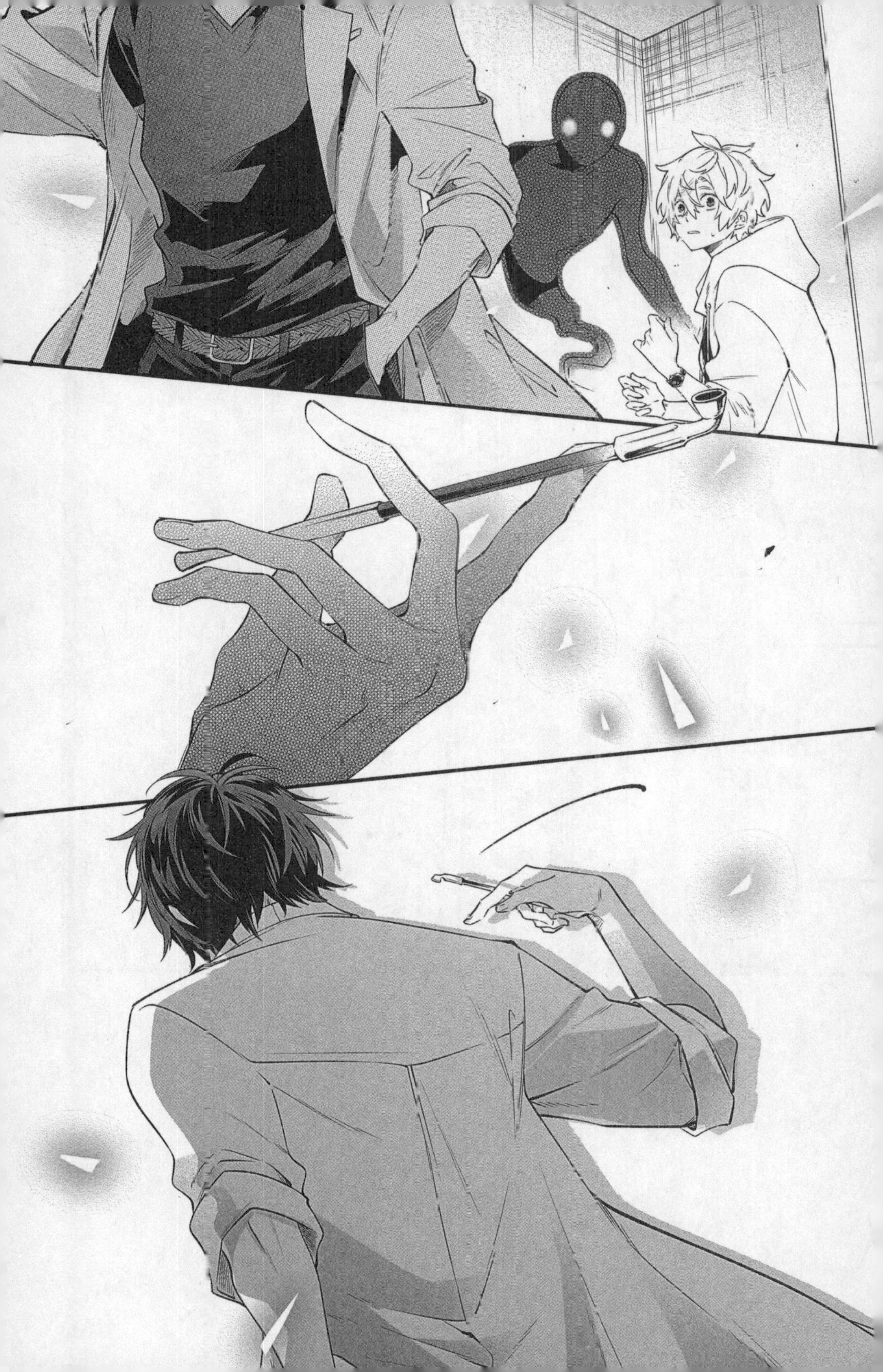

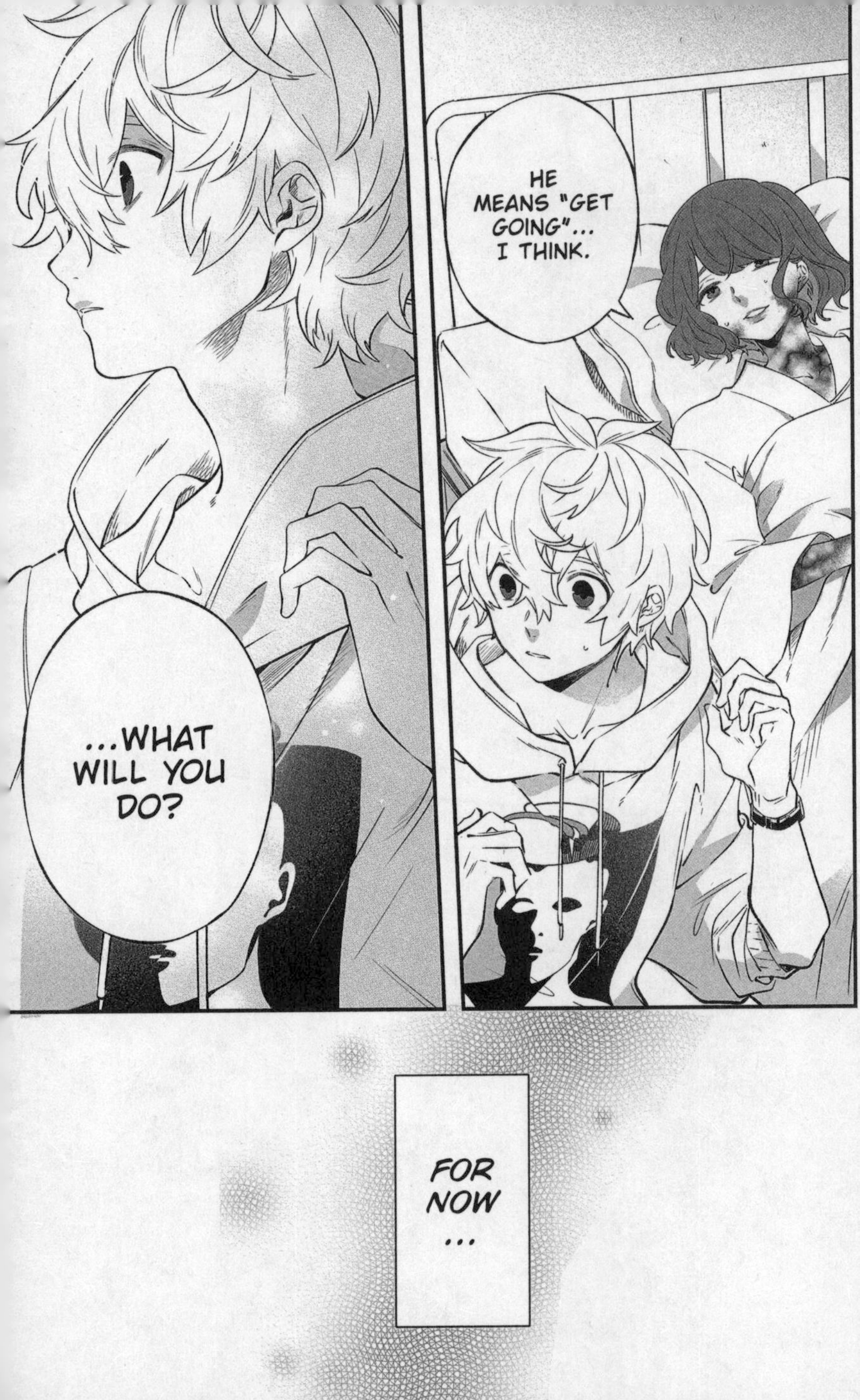
HE MEANS "GET GOING"... I THINK.
...WHAT WILL YOU DO?
FOR NOW ...

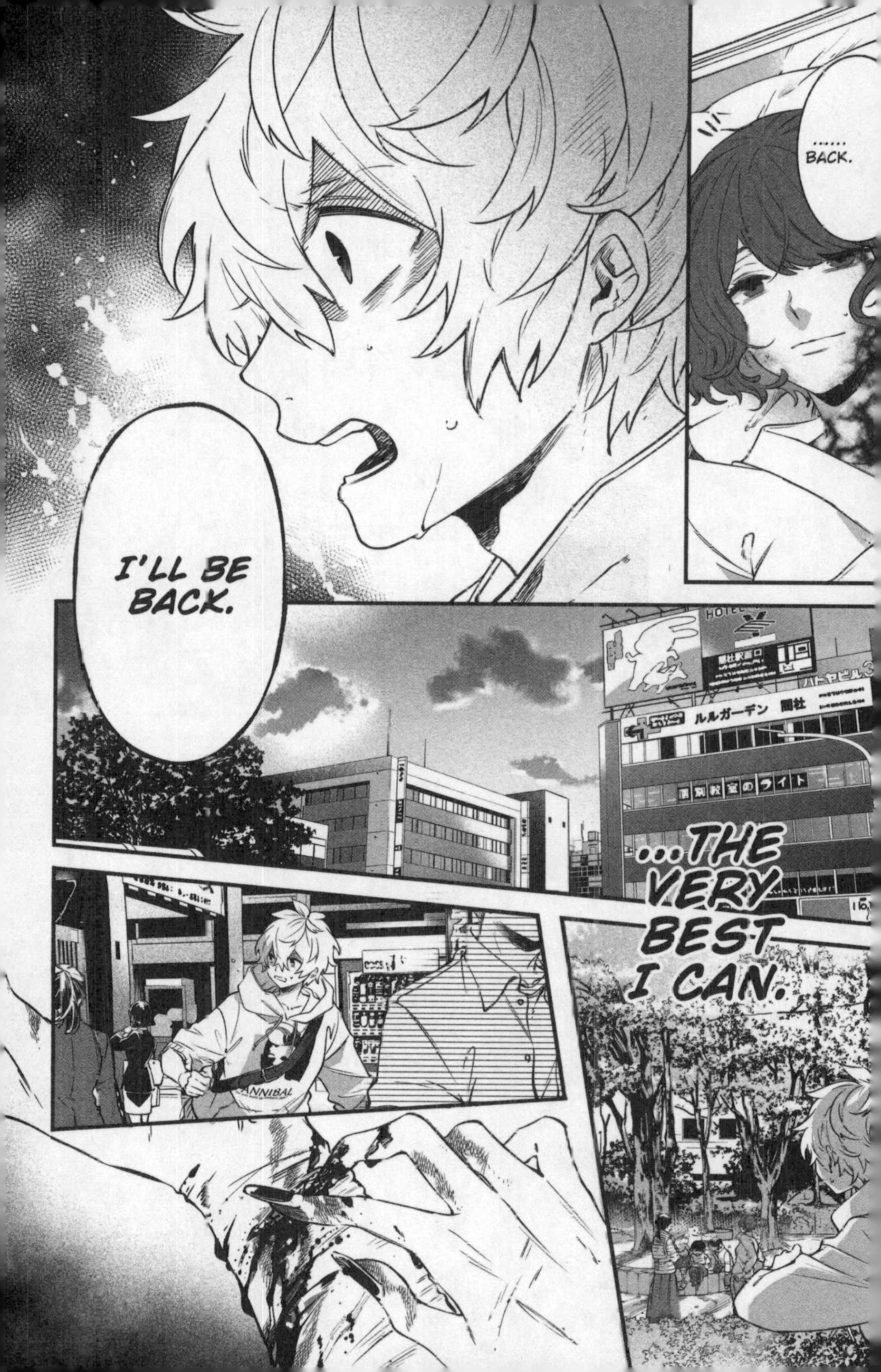

...... BACK.
I'LL BE BACK.
ルルガーデン
...THE VERY BEST I CAN.

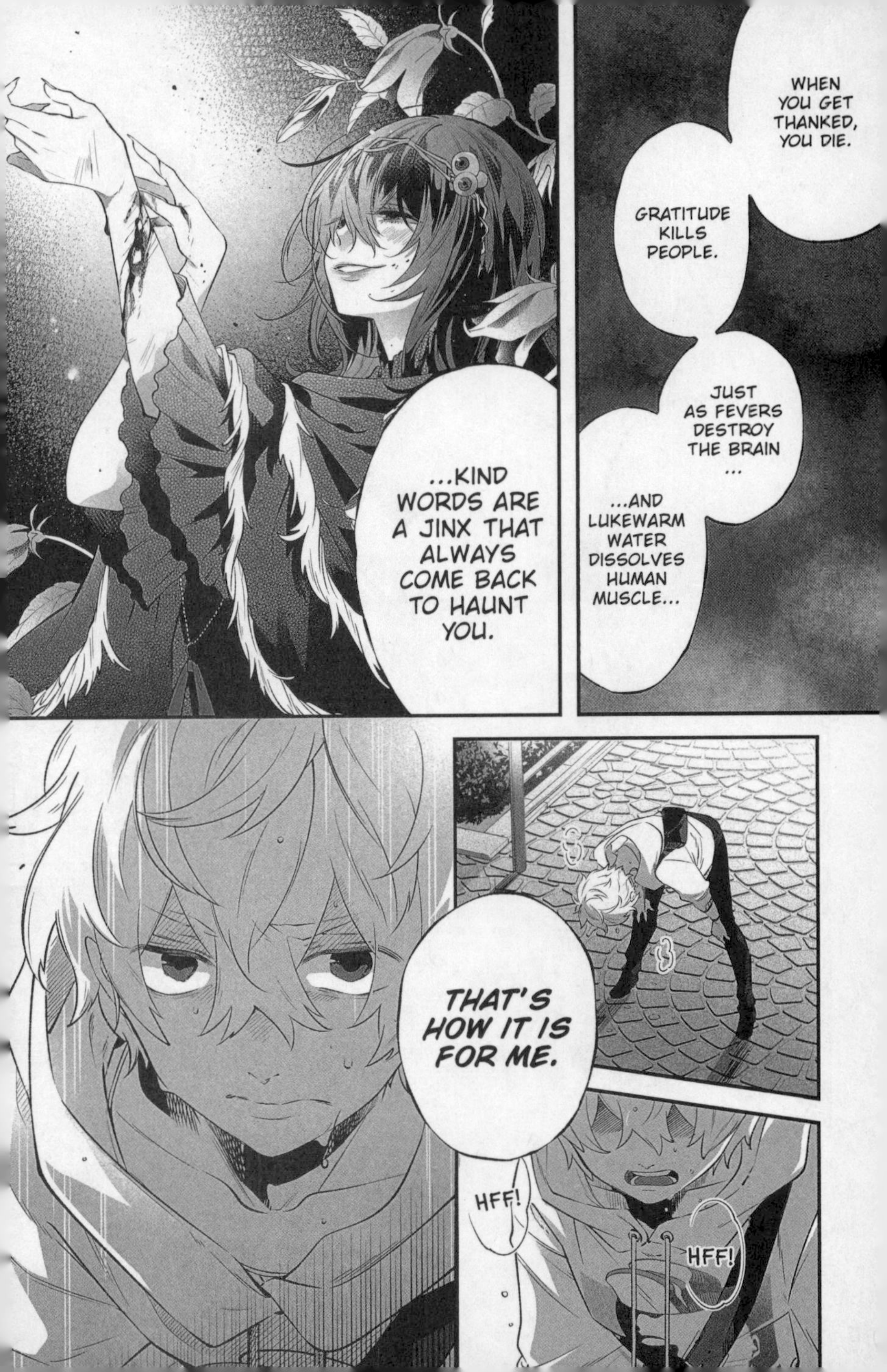
WHEN YOU GET THANKED, YOU DIE.
GRATITUDE KILLS PEOPLE.
JUST AS FEVERS DESTROY THE BRAIN...
...AND LUKEWARM WATER DISSOLVES HUMAN MUSCLE...
...KIND WORDS ARE A JINX THAT ALWAYS COME BACK TO HAUNT YOU.
HFF!
HFF!
THAT'S HOW IT IS FOR ME.

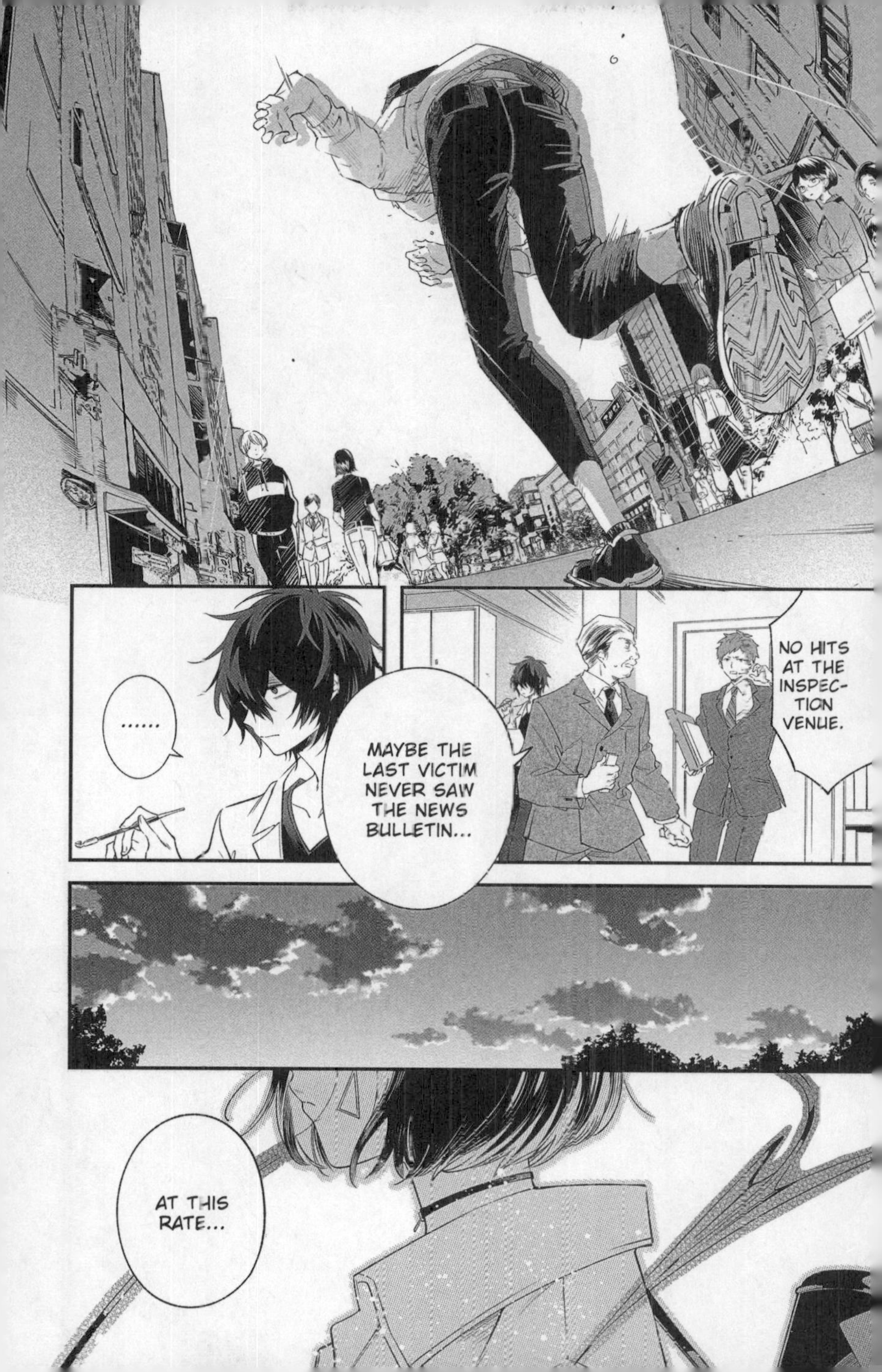
NO HITS AT THE INSPECTION VENUE.
MAYBE THE LAST VICTIM NEVER SAW THE NEWS BULLETIN...
......
AT THIS RATE...

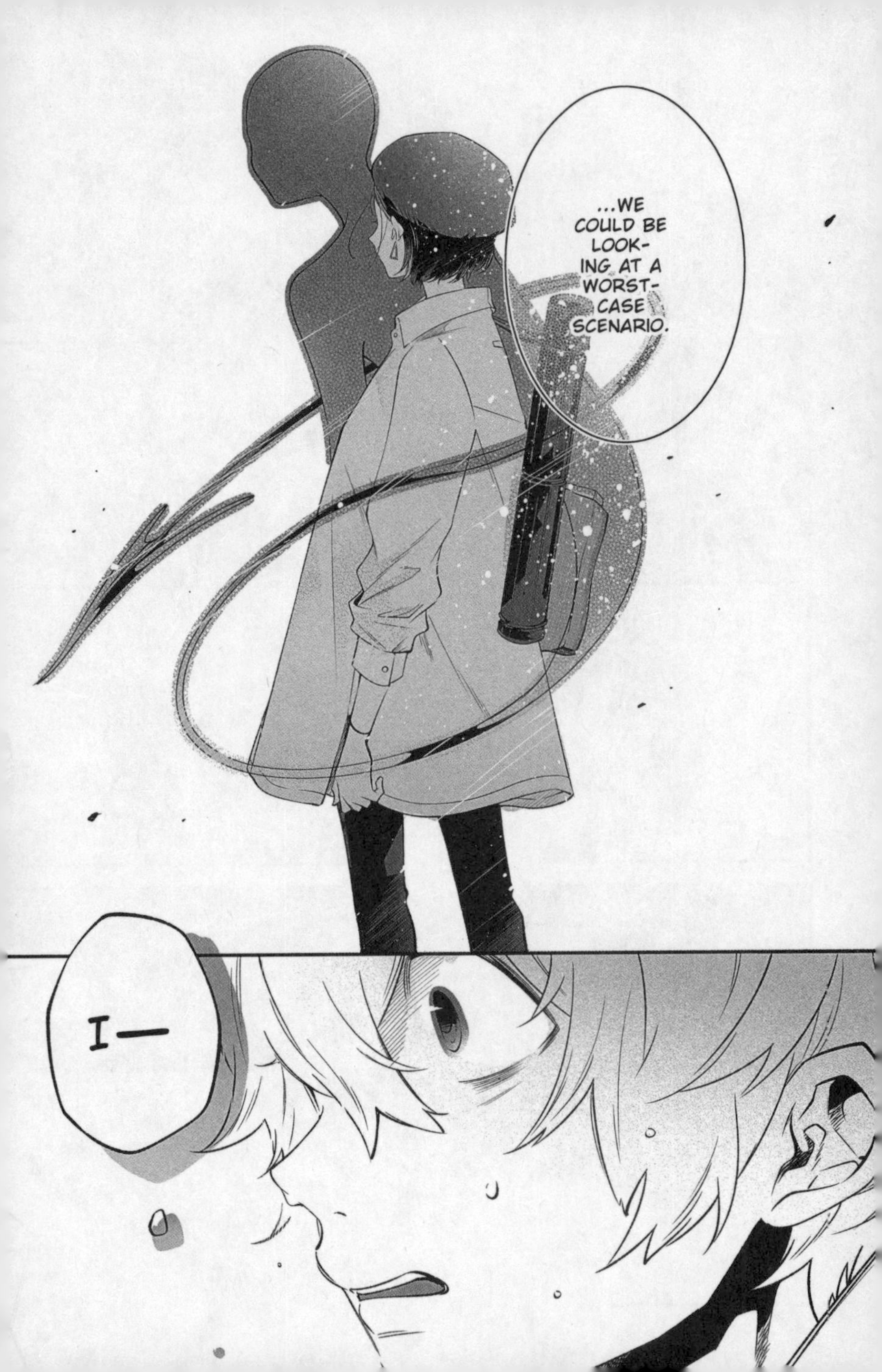
...WE COULD BE LOOKING AT A WORST-CASE SCENARIO.
I—

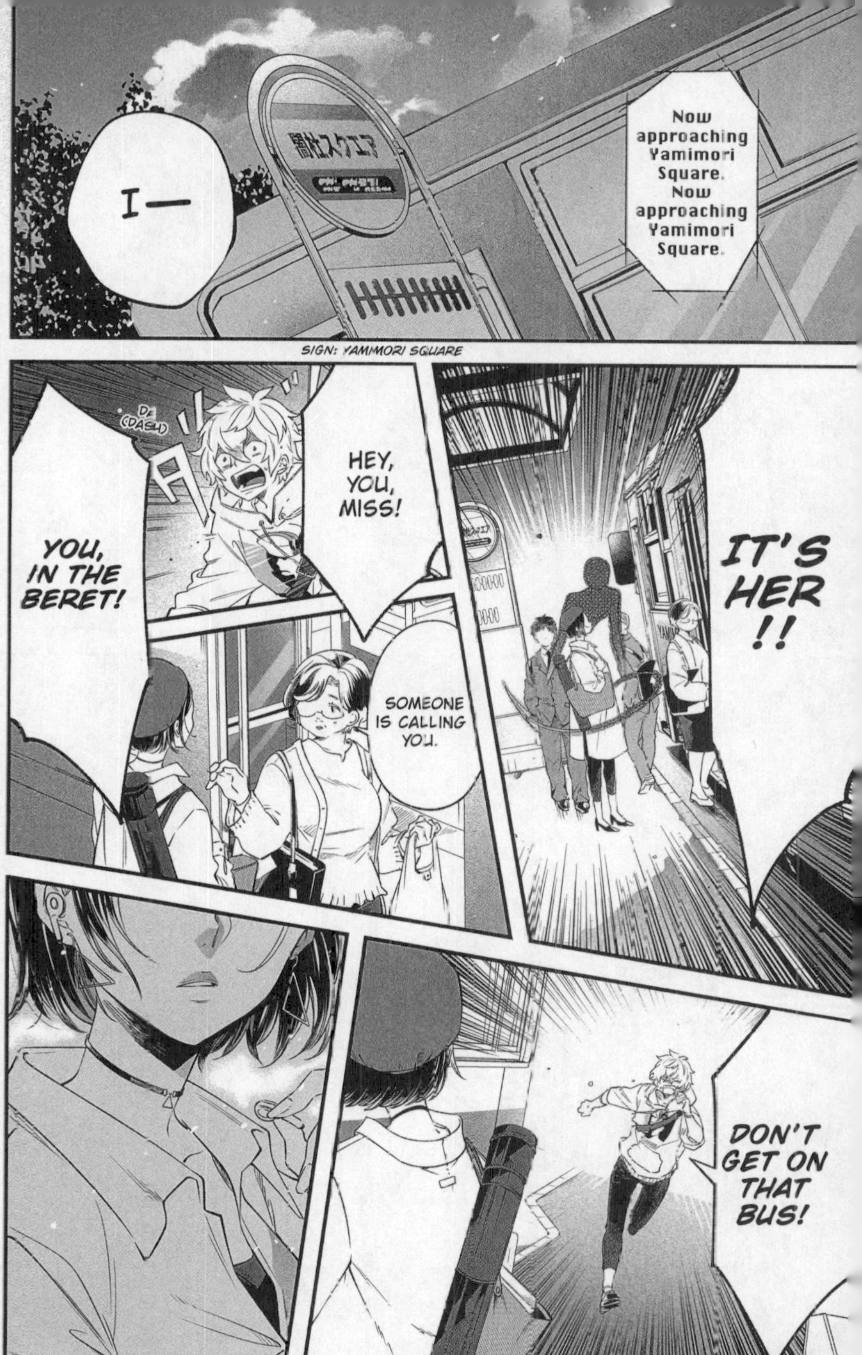
Now approaching Yamimori Square. Now approaching Yamimori Square.
I—
SIGN: YAMMORI SQUARE
IT'S HER!!
HEY, YOU, MISS!
DE (DASH)
YOU, IN THE BERET!
SOMEONE IS CALLING YOU.
DON'T GET ON THAT BUS!

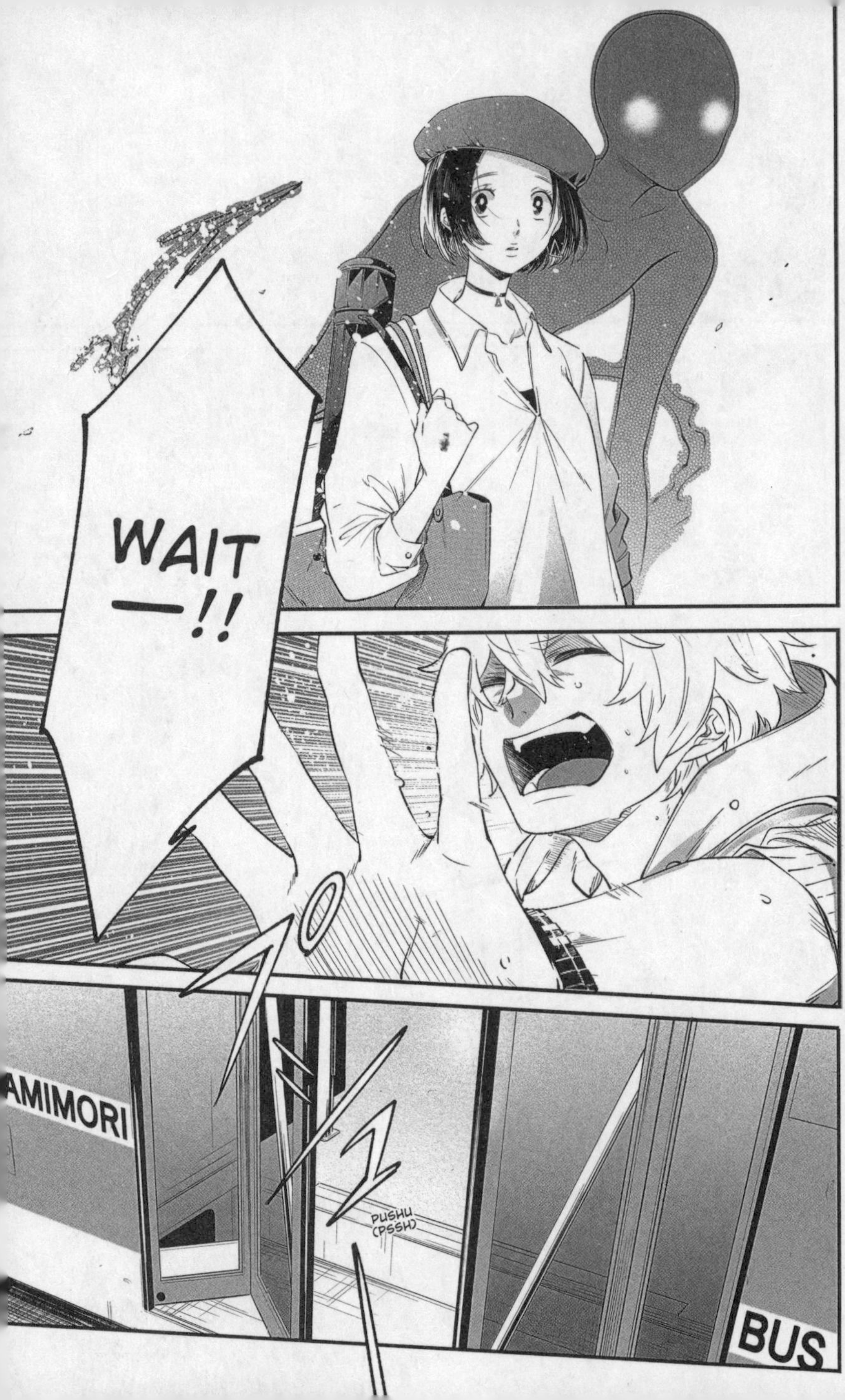
WAIT —!!
PUSHU (PSSH)
AMIMORI
BUS

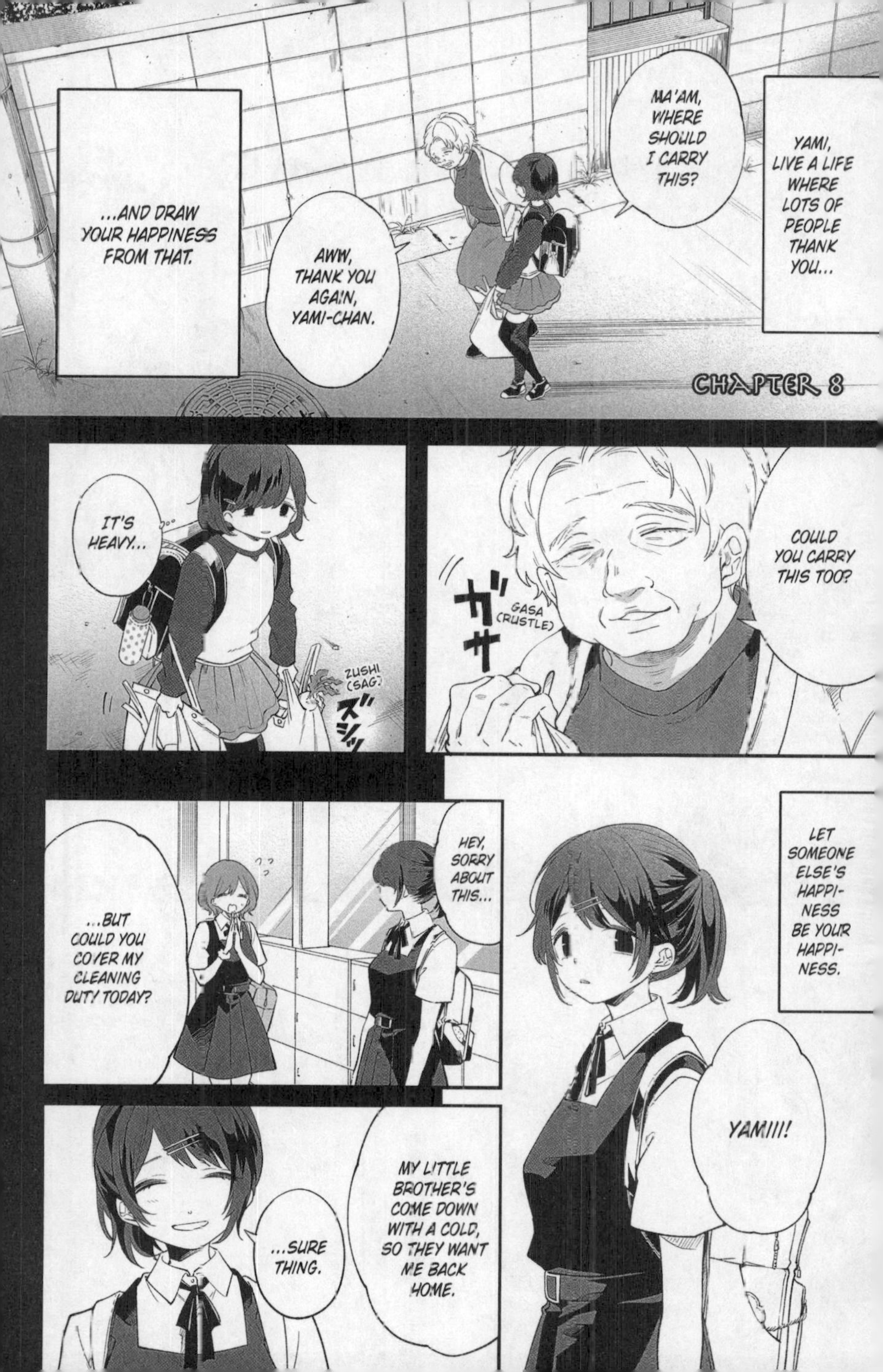
YAMI, LIVE A LIFE WHERE LOTS OF PEOPLE THANK YOU...
MA'AM, WHERE SHOULD I CARRY THIS?
AWW, THANK YOU AGAIN, YAMI-CHAN.
...AND DRAW YOUR HAPPINESS FROM THAT.
CHAPTER 8
COULD YOU CARRY THIS TOO?
ガサ
GASA (RUSTLE)
IT'S HEAVY...
ズシッ
ZUSHI (SAG)
LET SOMEONE ELSE'S HAPPI-NESS BE YOUR HAPPI-NESS.
YAMIII!
HEY, SORRY ABOUT THIS...
...BUT COULD YOU COVER MY CLEANING DUTY TODAY?
MY LITTLE BROTHER'S COME DOWN WITH A COLD, SO THEY WANT ME BACK HOME.
...SURE THING.

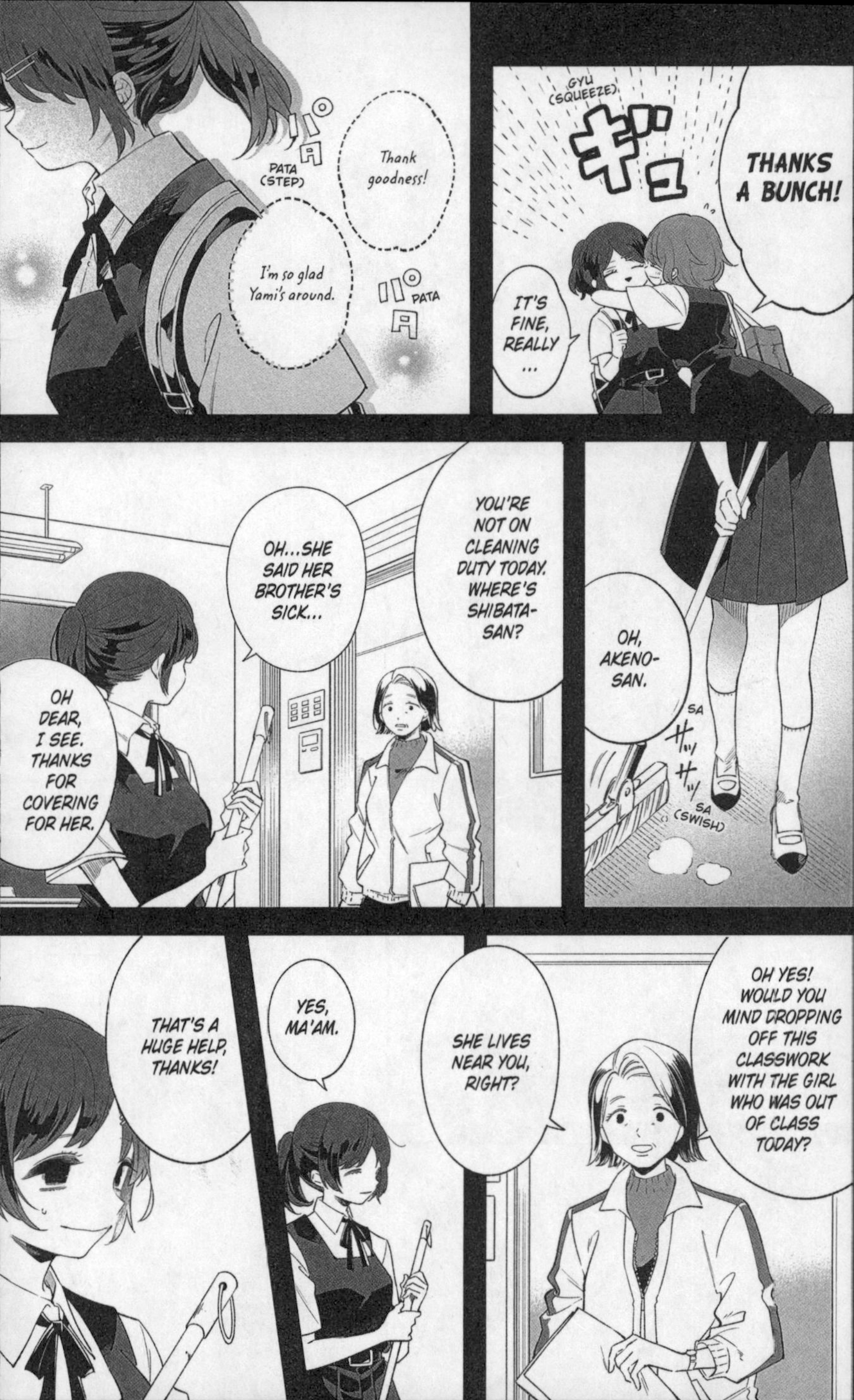

GYU (SQUEEZE)
ギュ
THANKS A BUNCH!
IT'S FINE, REALLY...
Thank goodness!
PATA (STEP)
I'm so glad Yami's around.
PATA
OH, AKENO-SAN.
SA
SA (SWISH)
YOU'RE NOT ON CLEANING DUTY TODAY. WHERE'S SHIBATA-SAN?
OH...SHE SAID HER BROTHER'S SICK...
OH DEAR, I SEE. THANKS FOR COVERING FOR HER.
OH YES! WOULD YOU MIND DROPPING OFF THIS CLASSWORK WITH THE GIRL WHO WAS OUT OF CLASS TODAY?
SHE LIVES NEAR YOU, RIGHT?
YES, MA'AM.
THAT'S A HUGE HELP, THANKS!

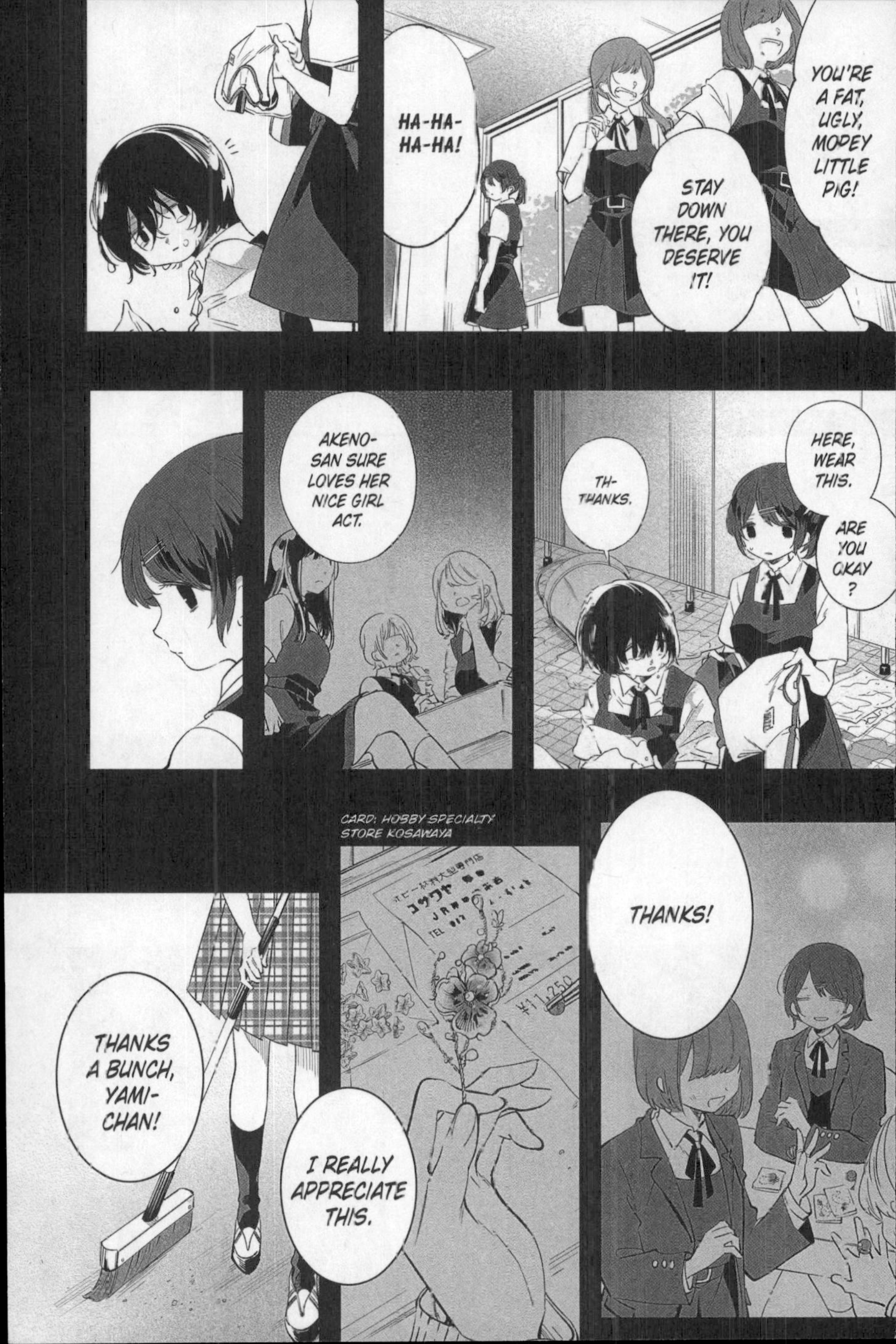
YOU'RE A FAT, UGLY, MOPEY LITTLE PIG!
STAY DOWN THERE, YOU DESERVE IT!
HA-HA-HA-HA!
HERE, WEAR THIS.
ARE YOU OKAY?
TH-THANKS.
AKENO-SAN SURE LOVES HER NICE GIRL ACT.
THANKS!
CARD: HOBBY SPECIALTY STORE KOSAWAYA
¥11,250
I REALLY APPRECIATE THIS.
THANKS A BUNCH, YAMI-CHAN!

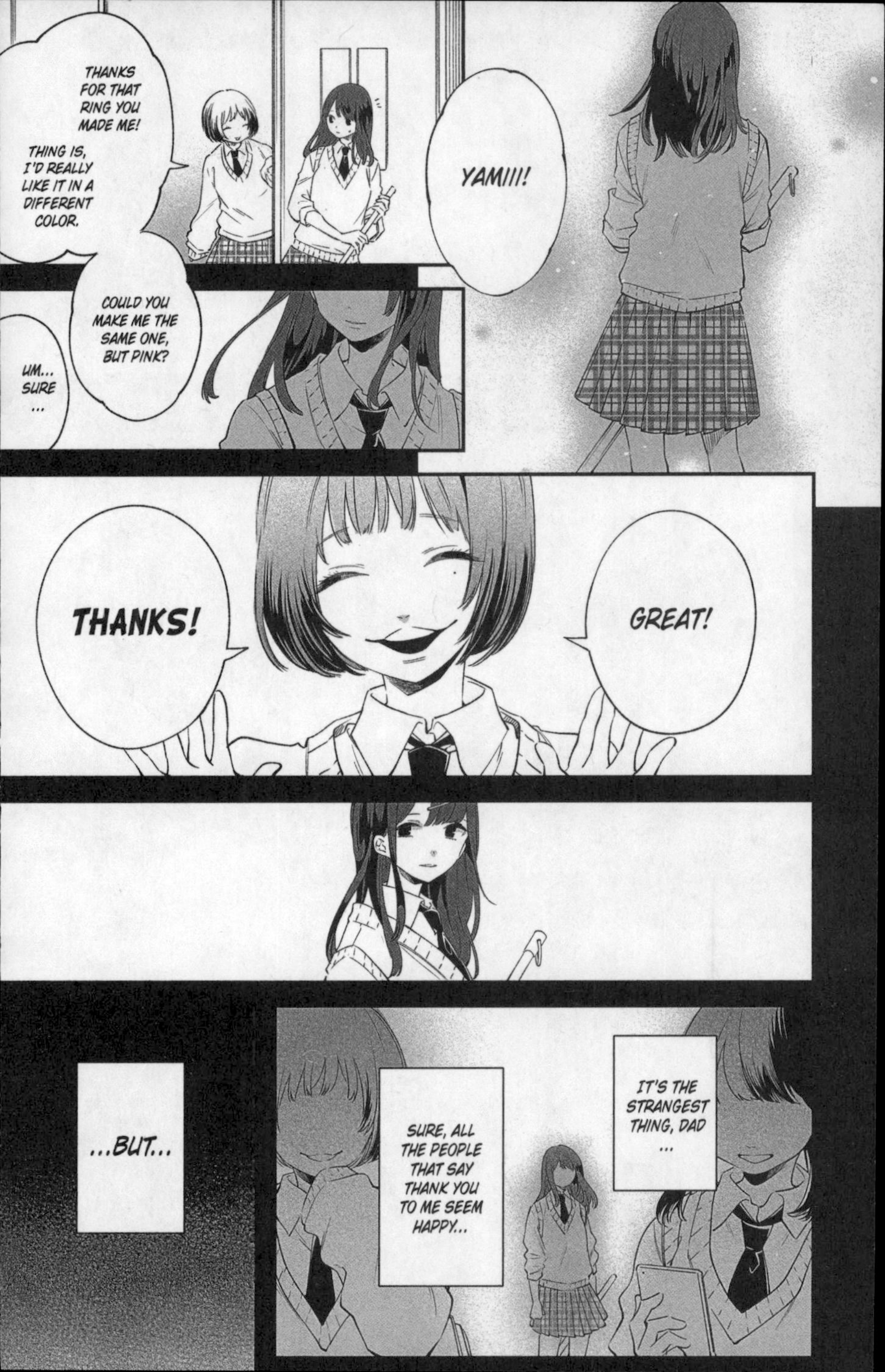
YAMIII!
THANKS FOR THAT RING YOU MADE ME!
THING IS, I'D REALLY LIKE IT IN A DIFFERENT COLOR.
COULD YOU MAKE ME THE SAME ONE, BUT PINK?
UM... SURE...
GREAT!
THANKS!
IT'S THE STRANGEST THING, DAD...
SURE, ALL THE PEOPLE THAT SAY THANK YOU TO ME SEEM HAPPY...
...BUT...

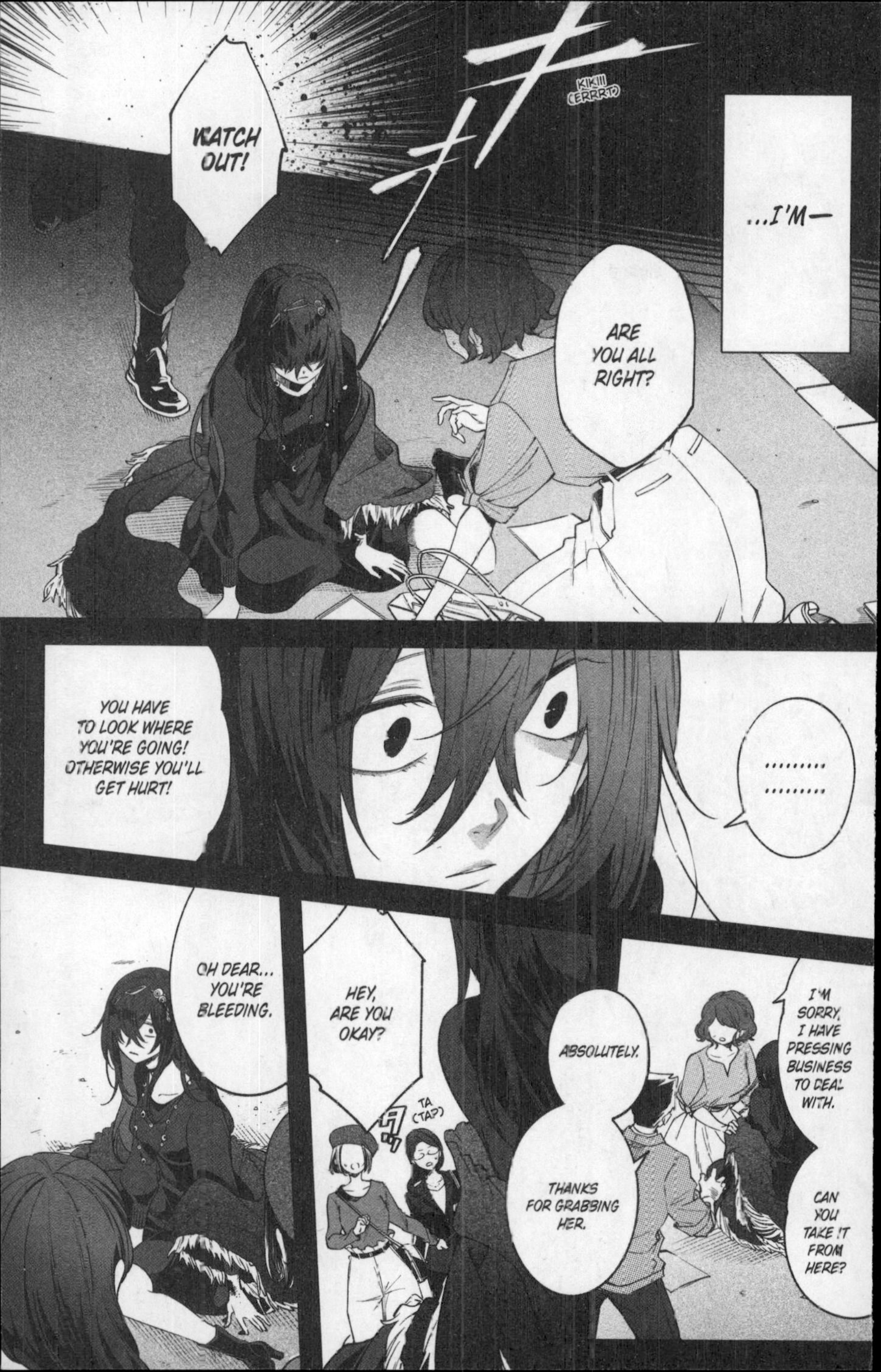
...I'M—
KIKIII (ERRRT)
WATCH OUT!
ARE YOU ALL RIGHT?
....
YOU HAVE TO LOOK WHERE YOU'RE GOING! OTHERWISE YOU'LL GET HURT!
I'M SORRY, I HAVE PRESSING BUSINESS TO DEAL WITH.
ABSOLUTELY.
CAN YOU TAKE IT FROM HERE?
THANKS FOR GRABBING HER.
HEY, ARE YOU OKAY?
TA (TAP)
OH DEAR... YOU'RE BLEEDING.

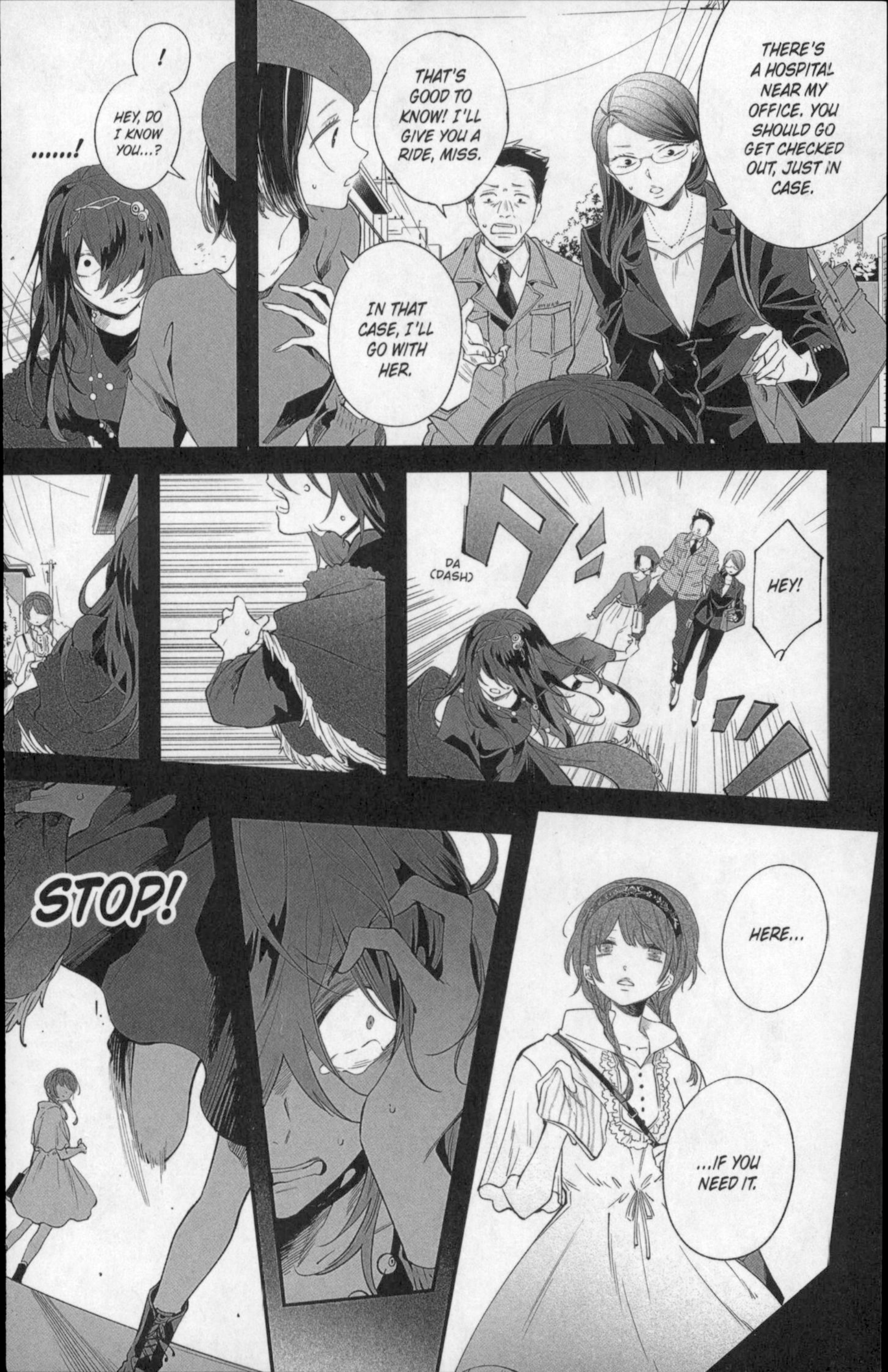
THERE'S A HOSPITAL NEAR MY OFFICE. YOU SHOULD GO GET CHECKED OUT, JUST IN CASE.
THAT'S GOOD TO KNOW! I'LL GIVE YOU A RIDE, MISS.
IN THAT CASE, I'LL GO WITH HER.
!
HEY, DO I KNOW YOU...?
......!
HEY!
DA (DASH)
HERE...
...IF YOU NEED IT.
STOP!

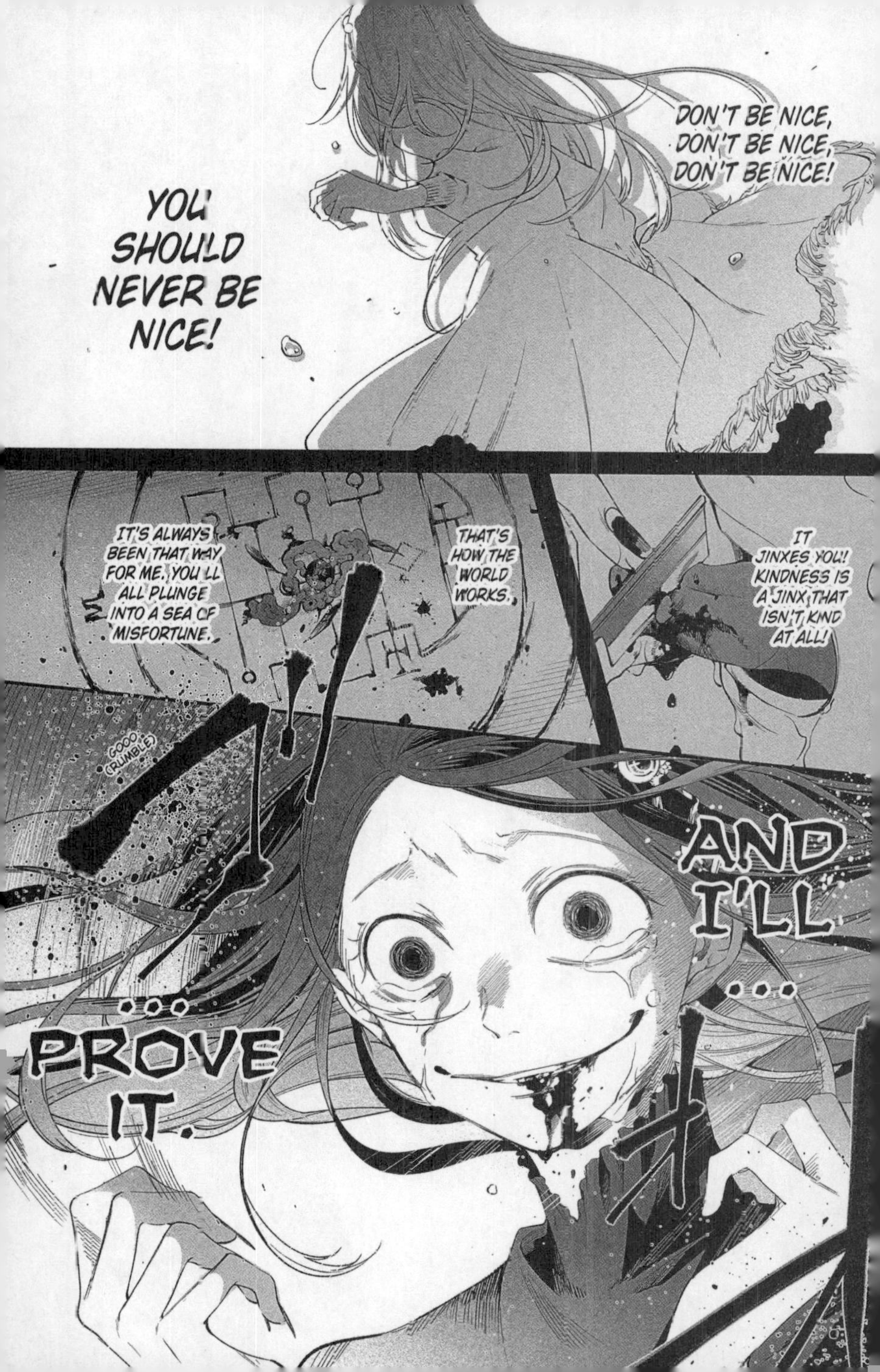
DON'T BE NICE, DON'T BE NICE, DON'T BE NICE!
YOU SHOULD NEVER BE NICE!
IT JINXES YOU! KINDNESS IS A JINX THAT ISN'T KIND AT ALL!
THAT'S HOW THE WORLD WORKS.
IT'S ALWAYS BEEN THAT WAY FOR ME. YOU'LL ALL PLUNGE INTO A SEA OF MISFORTUNE.
AND I'LL...
...PROVE IT.
GOOO (RUMBLE)

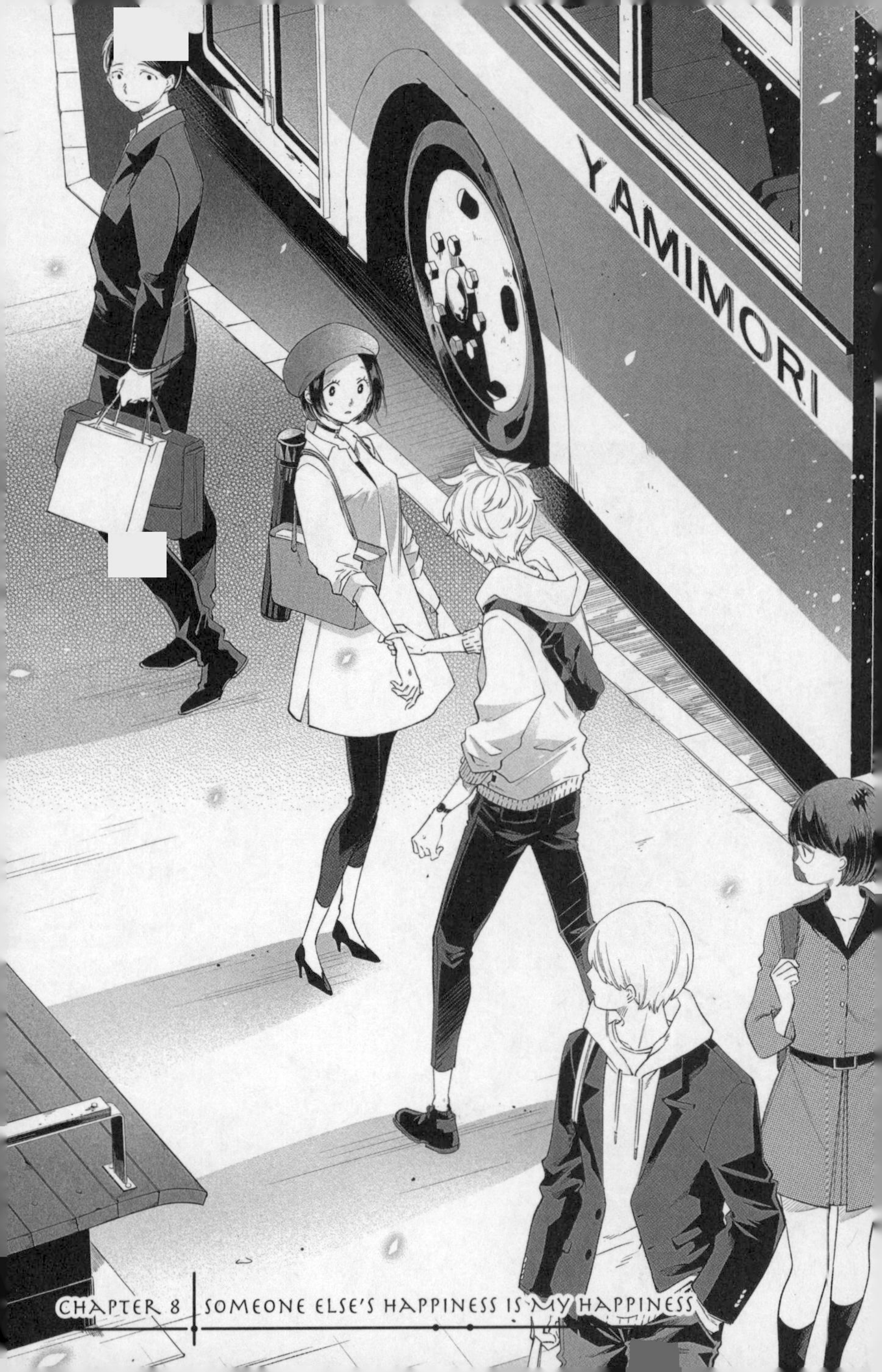
YAMIMORI

Chapter 8 | Someone Else's Happiness Is My Happiness

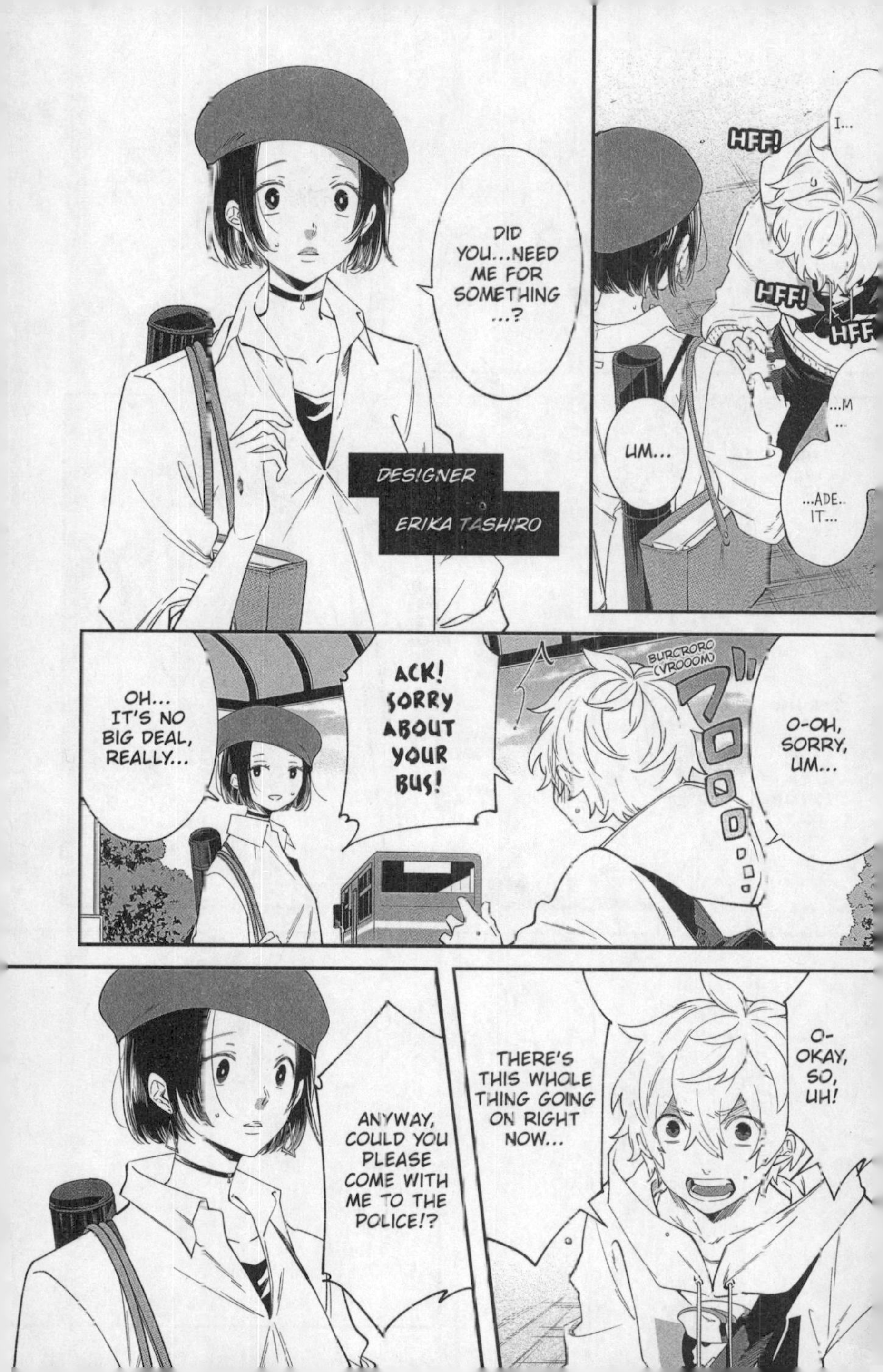
I...
HFF!
HFF!
HFF
...M
...
...ADE..
IT...
UM...
DID YOU...NEED ME FOR SOMETHING...?
DESIGNER
ERIKA TASHIRO
O-OH, SORRY, UM...
BURORORO (VROOOM)
ACK! SORRY ABOUT YOUR BUS!
OH... IT'S NO BIG DEAL, REALLY...
O-OKAY, SO, UH!
THERE'S THIS WHOLE THING GOING ON RIGHT NOW...
ANYWAY, COULD YOU PLEASE COME WITH ME TO THE POLICE!?

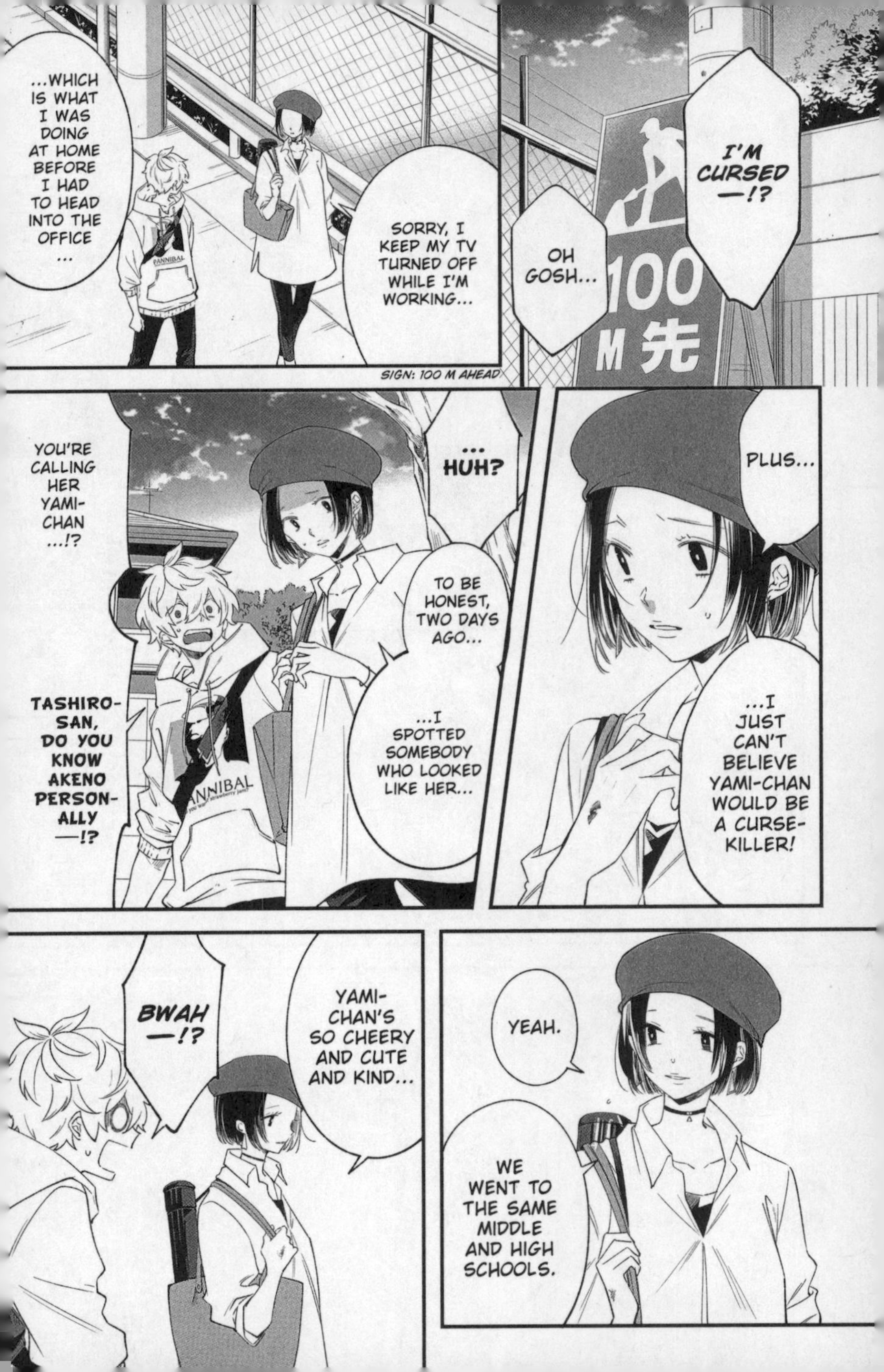
I'M CURSED—!?
OH GOSH...
100 M 先
SIGN: 100 M AHEAD
SORRY, I KEEP MY TV TURNED OFF WHILE I'M WORKING...
...WHICH IS WHAT I WAS DOING AT HOME BEFORE I HAD TO HEAD INTO THE OFFICE...
PLUS...
...I JUST CAN'T BELIEVE YAMI-CHAN WOULD BE A CURSE-KILLER!
...HUH?
YOU'RE CALLING HER YAMI-CHAN...!?
TO BE HONEST, TWO DAYS AGO...
...I SPOTTED SOMEBODY WHO LOOKED LIKE HER...
TASHIRO-SAN, DO YOU KNOW AKENO PERSONALLY—!?
YEAH.
WE WENT TO THE SAME MIDDLE AND HIGH SCHOOLS.
YAMI-CHAN'S SO CHEERY AND CUTE AND KIND...
BWAH—!?

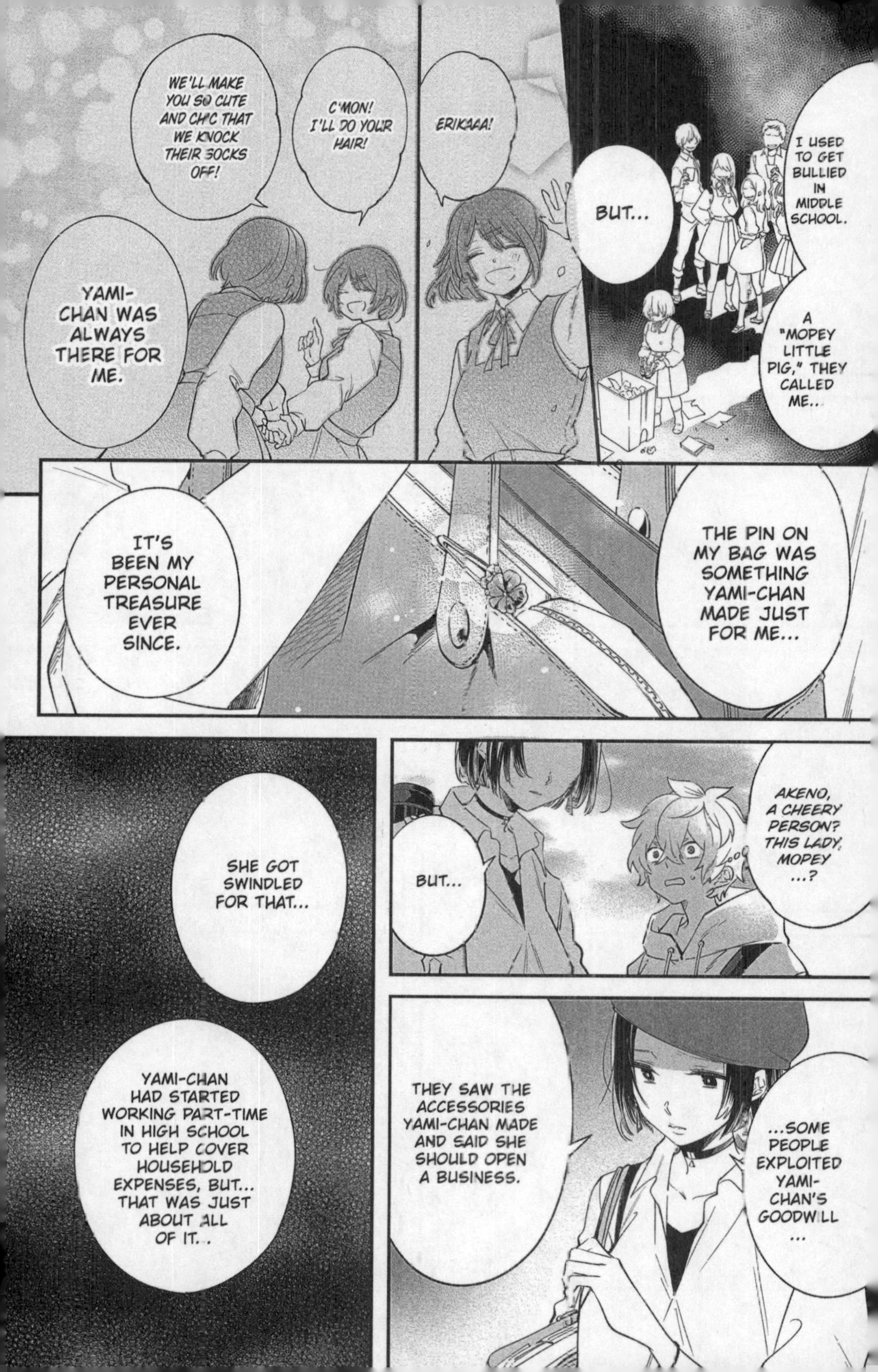

I USED TO GET BULLIED IN MIDDLE SCHOOL.
A "MOPEY LITTLE PIG," THEY CALLED ME...
BUT...
ERIKAAA!
C'MON! I'LL DO YOUR HAIR!
WE'LL MAKE YOU SO CUTE AND CHIC THAT WE KNOCK THEIR SOCKS OFF!
YAMI-CHAN WAS ALWAYS THERE FOR ME.
THE PIN ON MY BAG WAS SOMETHING YAMI-CHAN MADE JUST FOR ME...
IT'S BEEN MY PERSONAL TREASURE EVER SINCE.
AKENO, A CHEERY PERSON? THIS LADY, MOPEY ...?
BUT...
...SOME PEOPLE EXPLOITED YAMI-CHAN'S GOODWILL ...
THEY SAW THE ACCESSORIES YAMI-CHAN MADE AND SAID SHE SHOULD OPEN A BUSINESS.
SHE GOT SWINDLED FOR THAT...
YAMI-CHAN HAD STARTED WORKING PART-TIME IN HIGH SCHOOL TO HELP COVER HOUSEHOLD EXPENSES, BUT... THAT WAS JUST ABOUT ALL OF IT...

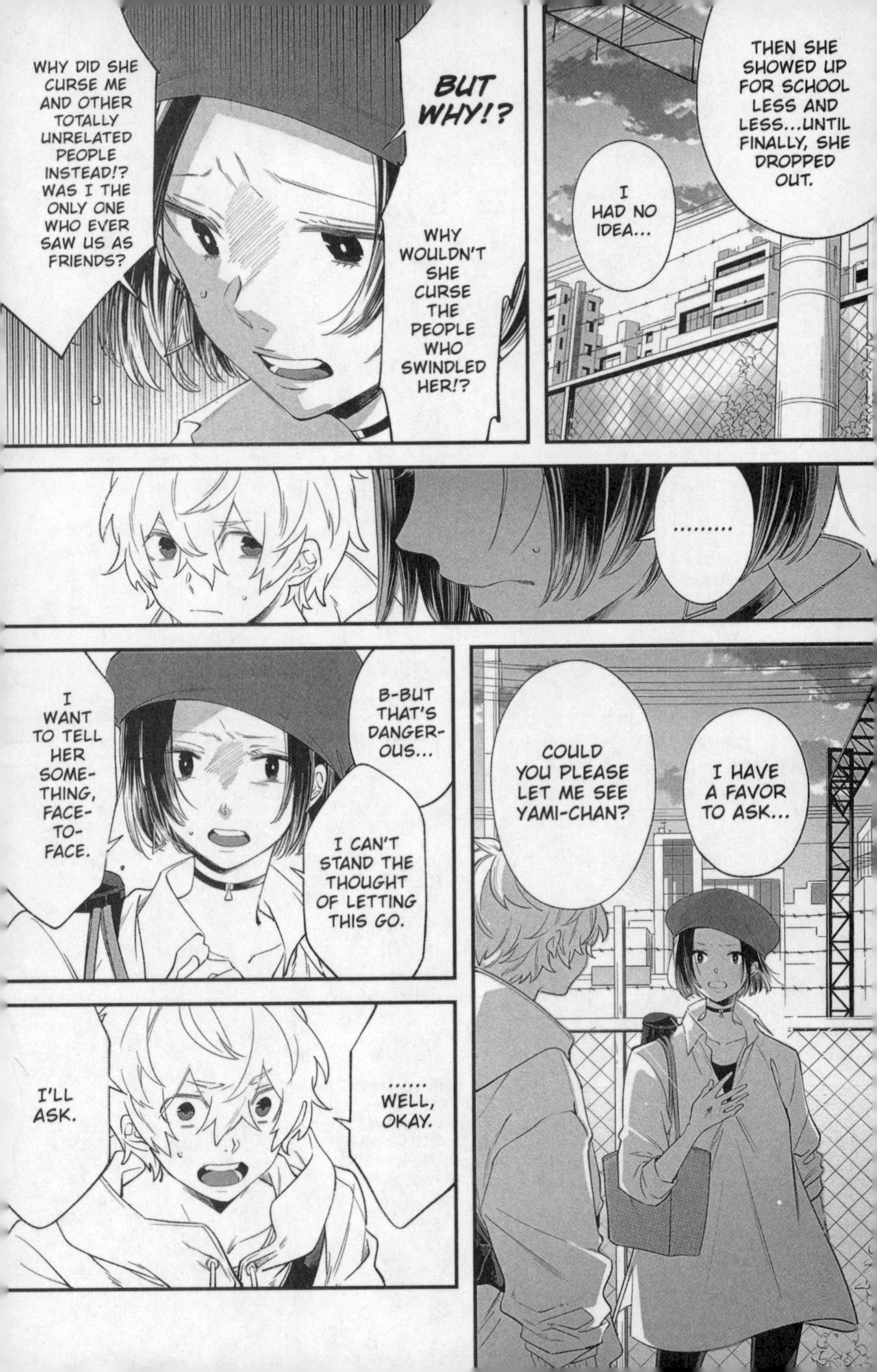
THEN SHE SHOWED UP FOR SCHOOL LESS AND LESS...UNTIL FINALLY, SHE DROPPED OUT.
I HAD NO IDEA...
BUT WHY!?
WHY WOULDN'T SHE CURSE THE PEOPLE WHO SWINDLED HER!?
WHY DID SHE CURSE ME AND OTHER TOTALLY UNRELATED PEOPLE INSTEAD!? WAS I THE ONLY ONE WHO EVER SAW US AS FRIENDS?
....
I HAVE A FAVOR TO ASK...
COULD YOU PLEASE LET ME SEE YAMI-CHAN?
B-BUT THAT'S DANGER-OUS...
I WANT TO TELL HER SOME-THING, FACE-TO-FACE.
I CAN'T STAND THE THOUGHT OF LETTING THIS GO.
......WELL, OKAY.
I'LL ASK.

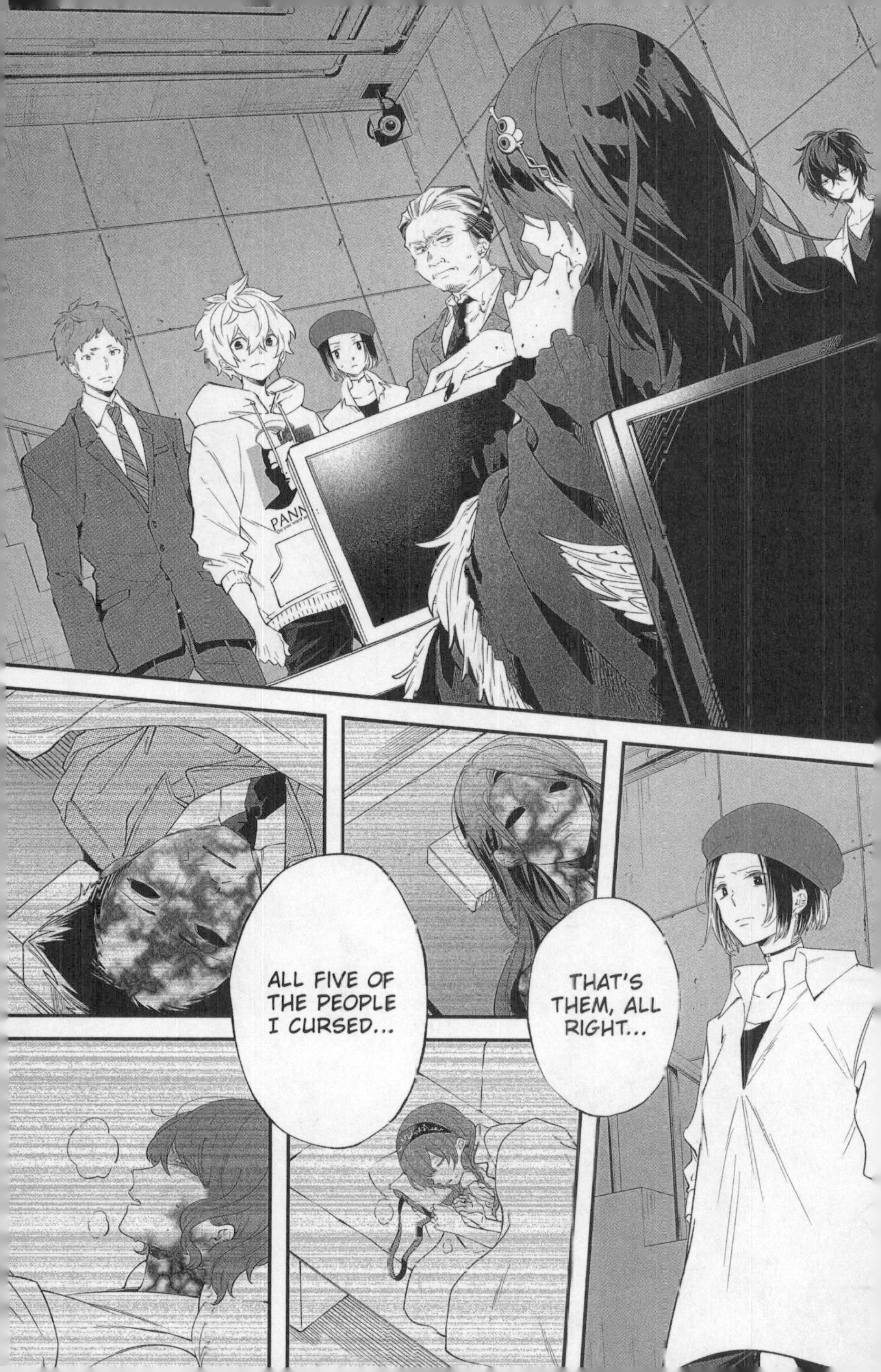
PANN
THAT'S THEM, ALL RIGHT...
ALL FIVE OF THE PEOPLE I CURSED...

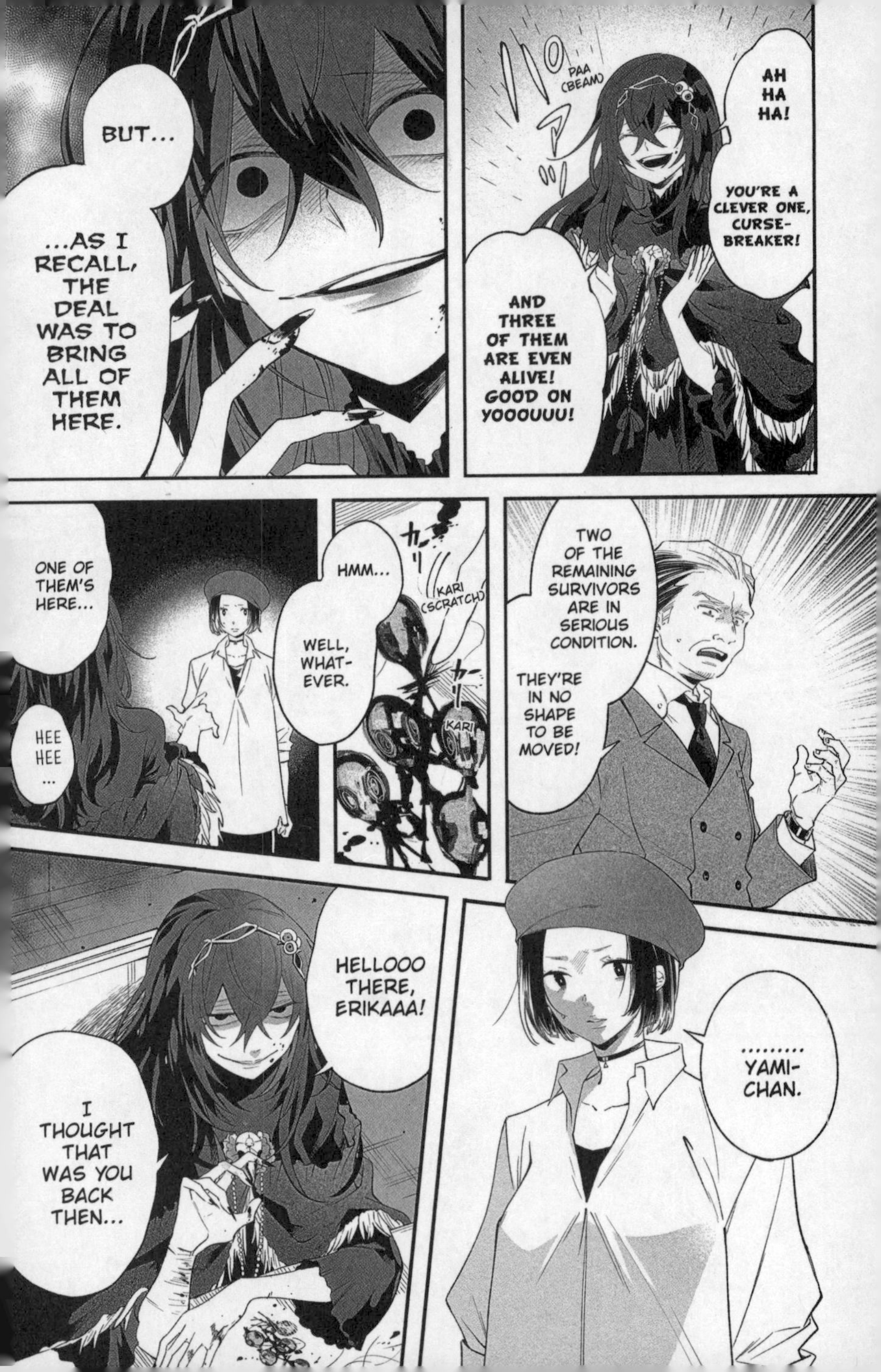
PAA (BEAM)
AH HA HA!
YOU'RE A CLEVER ONE, CURSE-BREAKER!
AND THREE OF THEM ARE EVEN ALIVE! GOOD ON YOOOUUU!
BUT...
...AS I RECALL, THE DEAL WAS TO BRING ALL OF THEM HERE.
TWO OF THE REMAINING SURVIVORS ARE IN SERIOUS CONDITION.
THEY'RE IN NO SHAPE TO BE MOVED!
KARI (SCRATCH)
KARI
HMM...
WELL, WHAT-EVER.
ONE OF THEM'S HERE...
HEE HEE ...
....
YAMI-CHAN.
HELLOOO THERE, ERIKAAA!
I THOUGHT THAT WAS YOU BACK THEN...

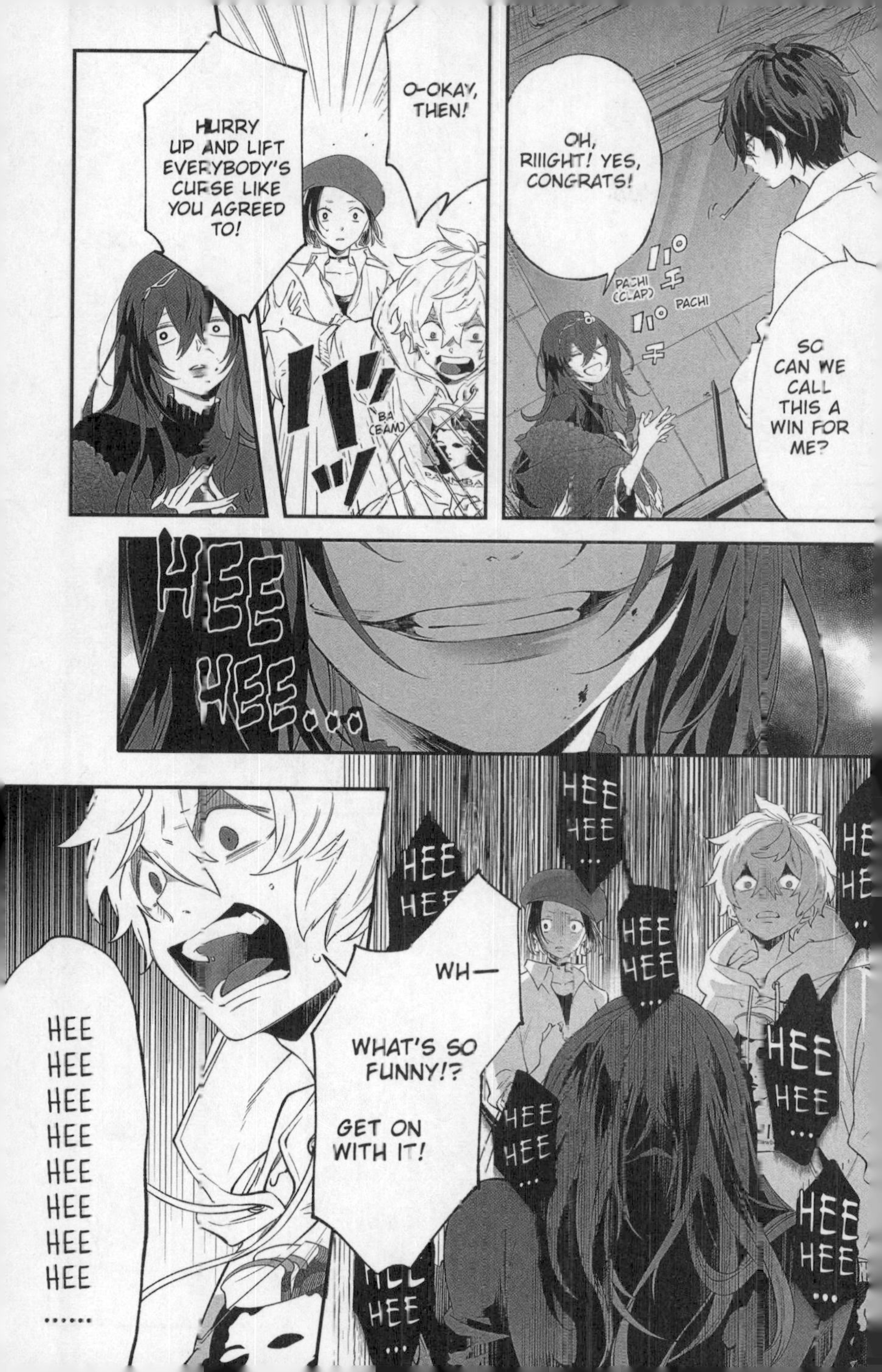
SO CAN WE CALL THIS A WIN FOR ME?
OH, RIIIGHT! YES, CONGRATS!
PACHI (CLAP) PACHI
O-OKAY, THEN!
HURRY UP AND LIFT EVERYBODY'S CURSE LIKE YOU AGREED TO!
BA (BAM)
HEE HEE...
HEE HEE...
HEE HEE...
HEE HEE...
HEE HEE
HEE HEE...
WH—
WHAT'S SO FUNNY!?
GET ON WITH IT!
HEE HEE...
HEE HEE...
HEE HEE...
HEE HEE HEE HEE HEE HEE HEE HEE ......

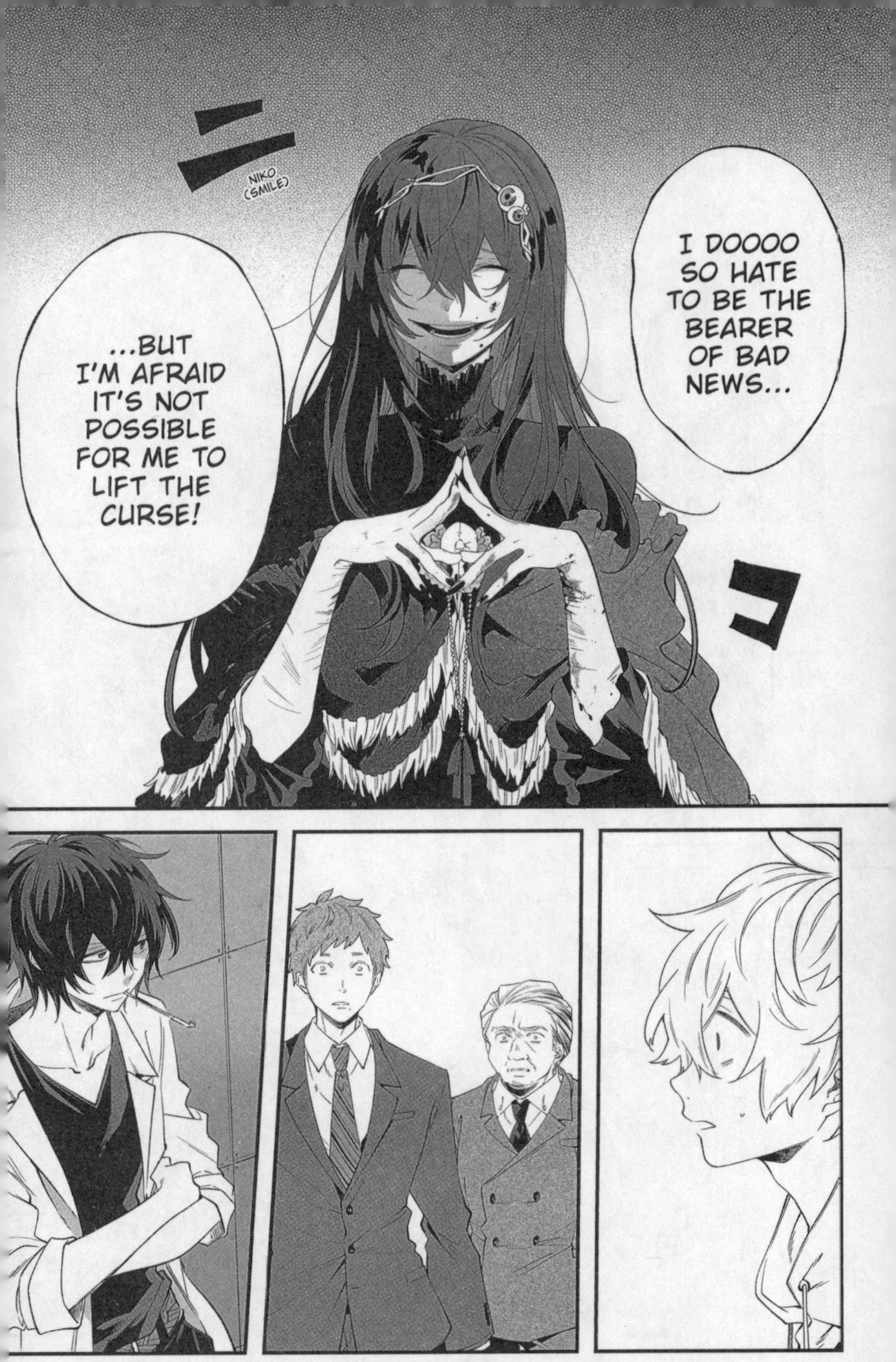
NIKO (SMILE)
I DOOOO SO HATE TO BE THE BEARER OF BAD NEWS...
...BUT I'M AFRAID IT'S NOT POSSIBLE FOR ME TO LIFT THE CURSE!

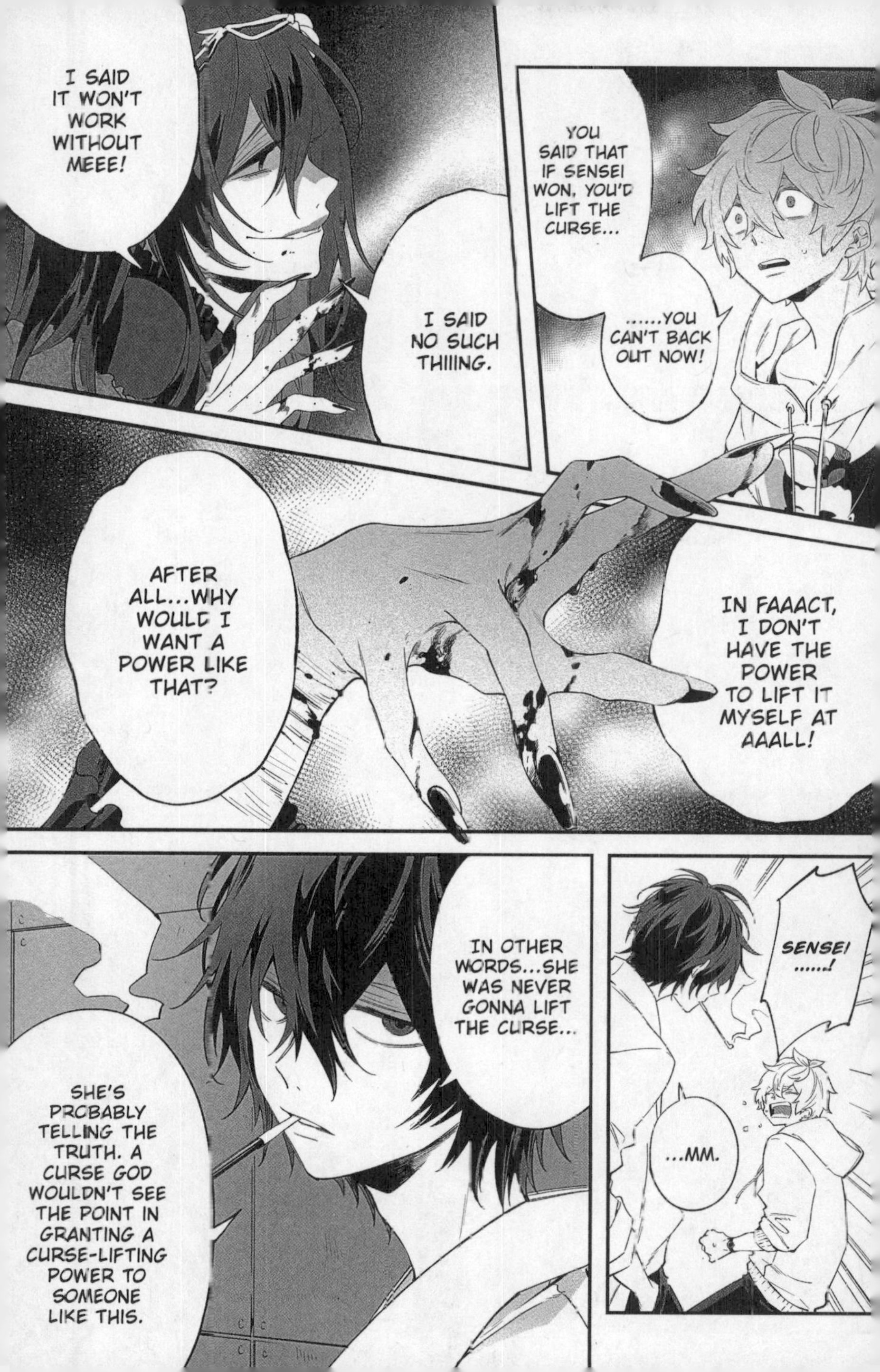

YOU SAID THAT IF SENSEI WON, YOU'D LIFT THE CURSE...
......YOU CAN'T BACK OUT NOW!
I SAID NO SUCH THIIING.
I SAID IT WON'T WORK WITHOUT MEEE!
IN FAAACT, I DON'T HAVE THE POWER TO LIFT IT MYSELF AT AAALL!
AFTER ALL...WHY WOULD I WANT A POWER LIKE THAT?
SENSEI ......!
...MM.
IN OTHER WORDS...SHE WAS NEVER GONNA LIFT THE CURSE...
SHE'S PROBABLY TELLING THE TRUTH. A CURSE GOD WOULDN'T SEE THE POINT IN GRANTING A CURSE-LIFTING POWER TO SOMEONE LIKE THIS.

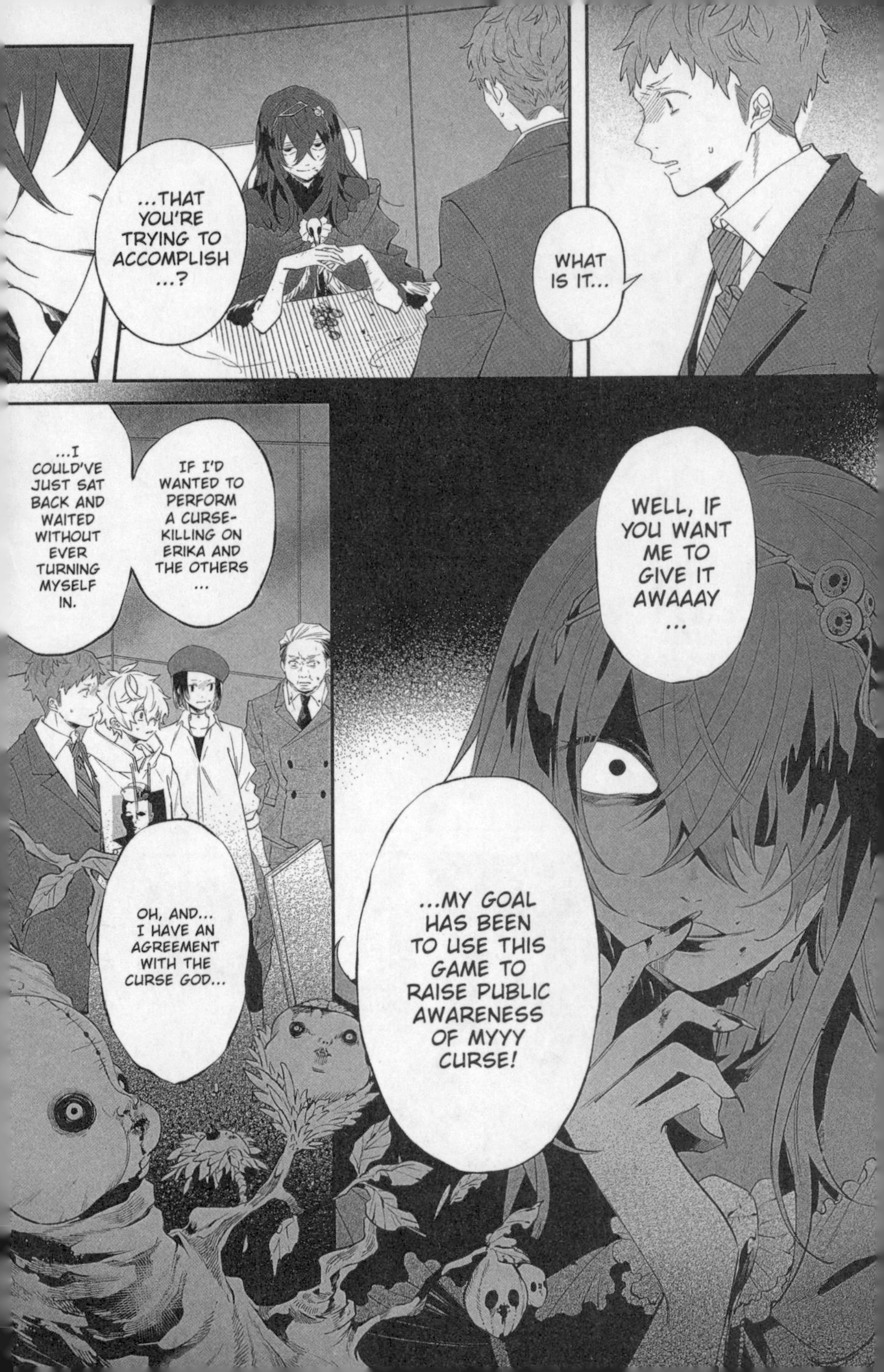
WHAT IS IT...
...THAT YOU'RE TRYING TO ACCOMPLISH ...?
WELL, IF YOU WANT ME TO GIVE IT AWAAAY ...
...MY GOAL HAS BEEN TO USE THIS GAME TO RAISE PUBLIC AWARENESS OF MYYY CURSE!
IF I'D WANTED TO PERFORM A CURSE-KILLING ON ERIKA AND THE OTHERS ...
...I COULD'VE JUST SAT BACK AND WAITED WITHOUT EVER TURNING MYSELF IN.
OH, AND... I HAVE AN AGREEMENT WITH THE CURSE GOD...

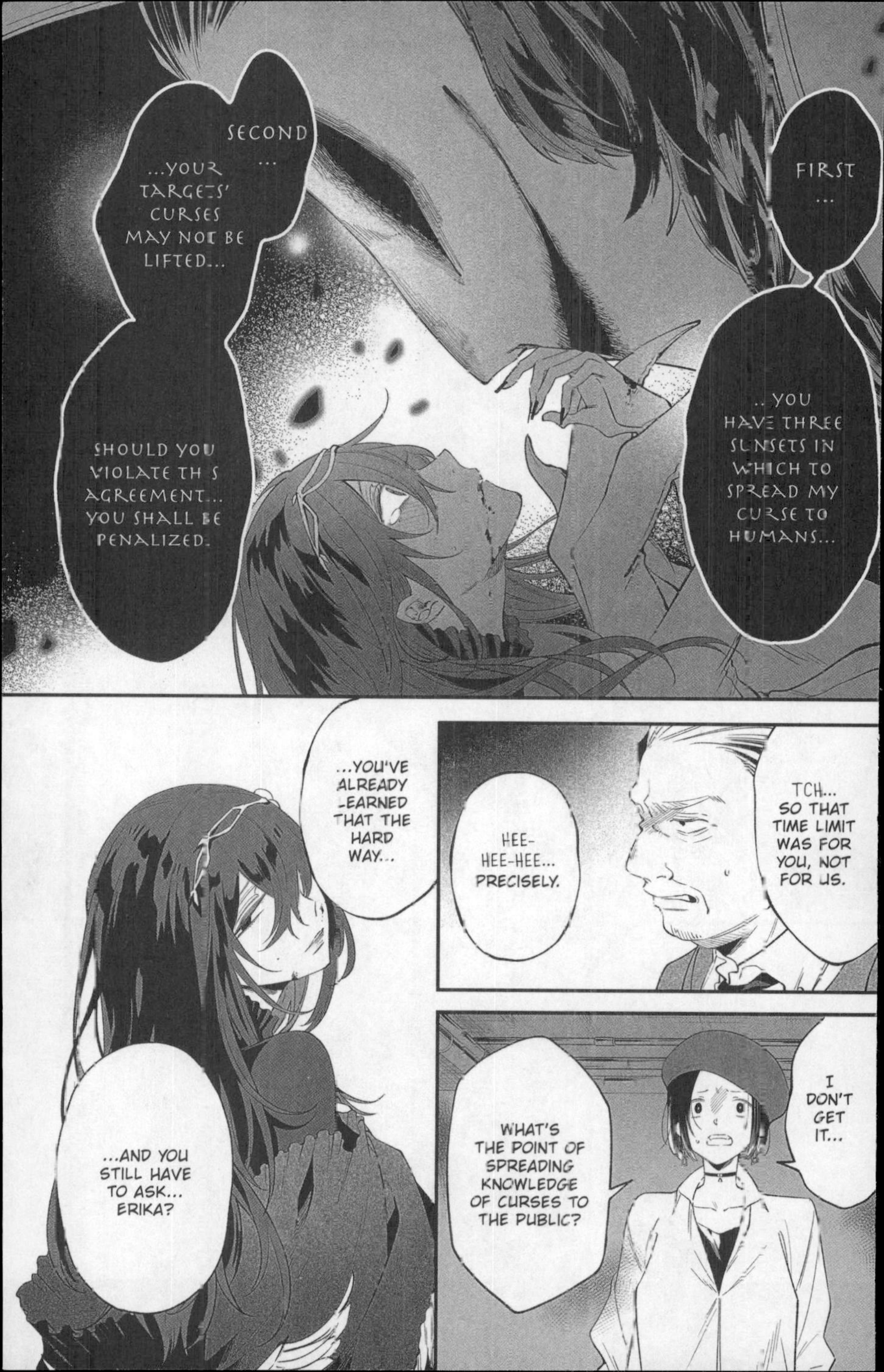
FIRST ...
.. YOU HAVE THREE SUNSETS IN WHICH TO SPREAD MY CURSE TO HUMANS...
SECOND ...
...YOUR TARGETS' CURSES MAY NOT BE LIFTED...
SHOULD YOU VIOLATE THIS AGREEMENT... YOU SHALL BE PENALIZED.
TCH... SO THAT TIME LIMIT WAS FOR YOU, NOT FOR US.
HEE-HEE-HEE... PRECISELY.
I DON'T GET IT...
WHAT'S THE POINT OF SPREADING KNOWLEDGE OF CURSES TO THE PUBLIC?
...YOU'VE ALREADY LEARNED THAT THE HARD WAY...
...AND YOU STILL HAVE TO ASK... ERIKA?

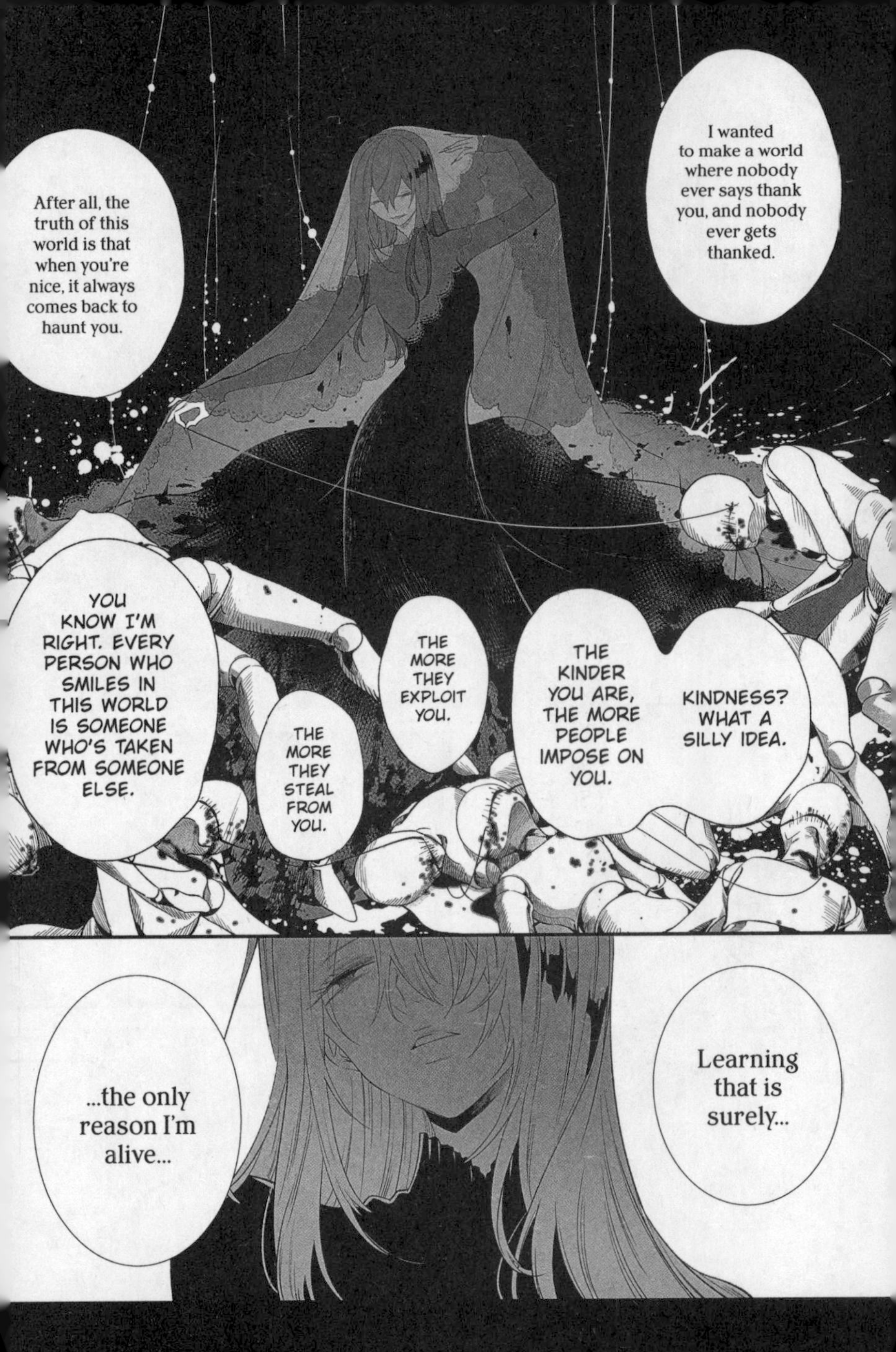
I wanted to make a world where nobody ever says thank you, and nobody ever gets thanked.
After all, the truth of this world is that when you're nice, it always comes back to haunt you.
KINDNESS? WHAT A SILLY IDEA.
THE KINDER YOU ARE, THE MORE PEOPLE IMPOSE ON YOU.
THE MORE THEY EXPLOIT YOU.
THE MORE THEY STEAL FROM YOU.
YOU KNOW I'M RIGHT. EVERY PERSON WHO SMILES IN THIS WORLD IS SOMEONE WHO'S TAKEN FROM SOMEONE ELSE.
Learning that is surely...
...the only reason I'm alive...

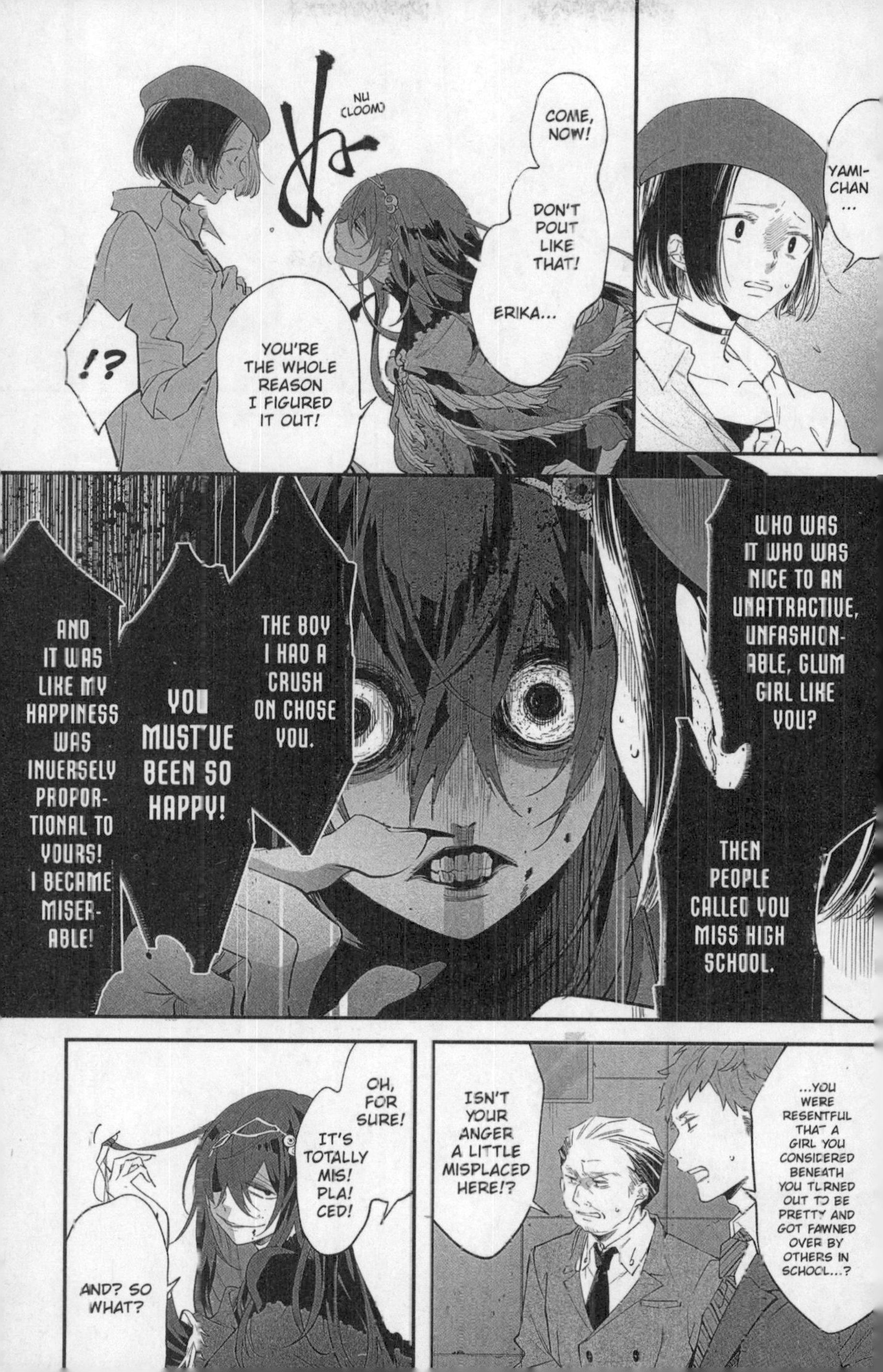
YAMI-CHAN...
COME, NOW!
DON'T POUT LIKE THAT!
ERIKA...
NU (LOOM)
YOU'RE THE WHOLE REASON I FIGURED IT OUT!
!?
WHO WAS IT WHO WAS NICE TO AN UNATTRACTIVE, UNFASHION-ABLE, GLUM GIRL LIKE YOU?
THEN PEOPLE CALLED YOU MISS HIGH SCHOOL.
THE BOY I HAD A CRUSH ON CHOSE YOU.
YOU MUST'VE BEEN SO HAPPY!
AND IT WAS LIKE MY HAPPINESS WAS INVERSELY PROPOR-TIONAL TO YOURS! I BECAME MISER-ABLE!
...YOU WERE RESENTFUL THAT A GIRL YOU CONSIDERED BENEATH YOU TURNED OUT TO BE PRETTY AND GOT FAWNED OVER BY OTHERS IN SCHOOL...?
ISN'T YOUR ANGER A LITTLE MISPLACED HERE!?
OH, FOR SURE!
IT'S TOTALLY MIS! PLA! CED!
AND? SO WHAT?

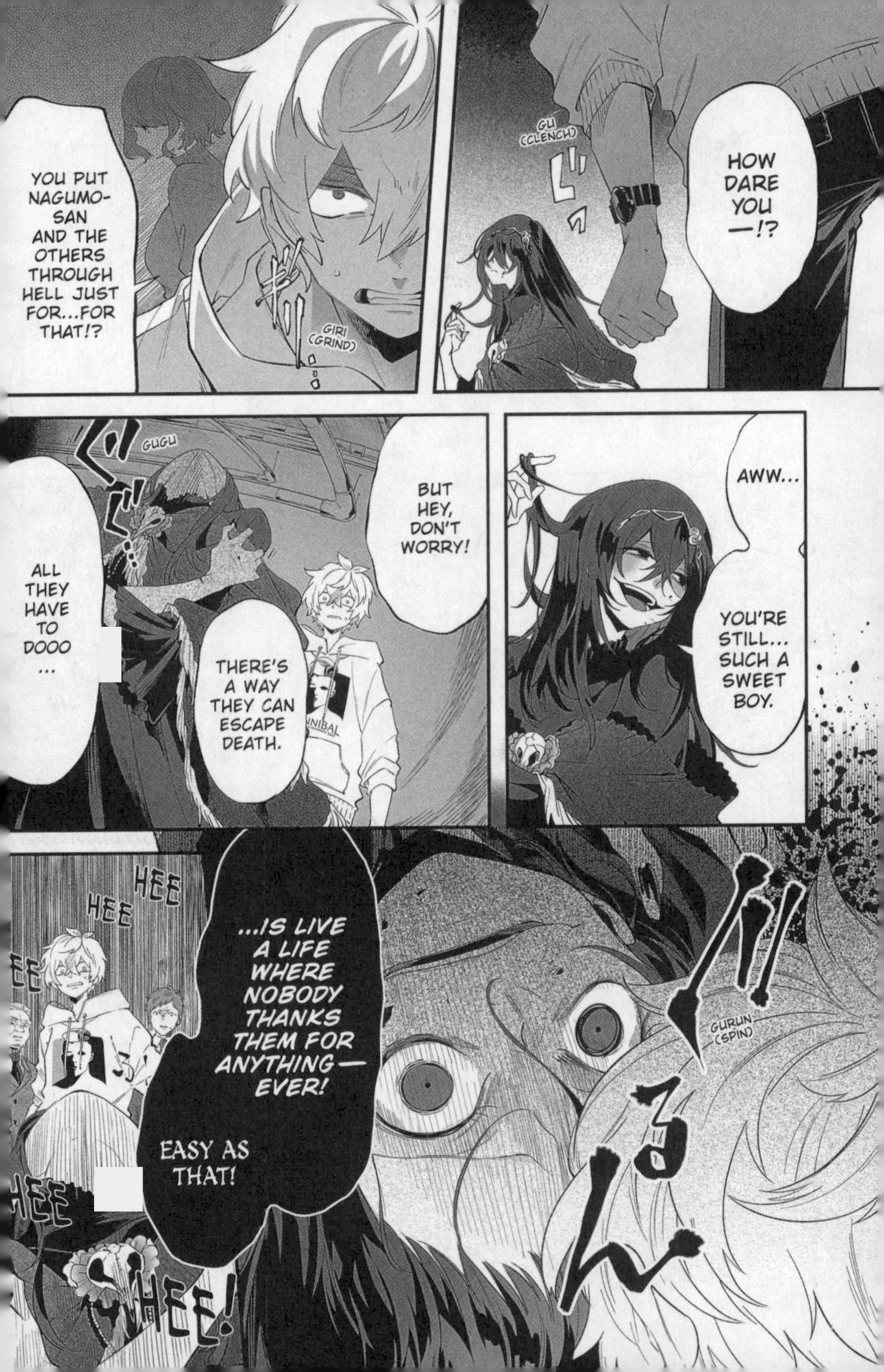
HOW DARE YOU—!?
GU (CLENCH)
YOU PUT NAGUMO-SAN AND THE OTHERS THROUGH HELL JUST FOR...FOR THAT!?
GIRI (GRIND)
AWW...
YOU'RE STILL... SUCH A SWEET BOY.
BUT HEY, DON'T WORRY!
THERE'S A WAY THEY CAN ESCAPE DEATH.
GUGU
ALL THEY HAVE TO DOOO ...
GURUN (SPIN)
...IS LIVE A LIFE WHERE NOBODY THANKS THEM FOR ANYTHING—EVER!
EASY AS THAT!
HEE
HEE
HEE
HEE
SHEE!

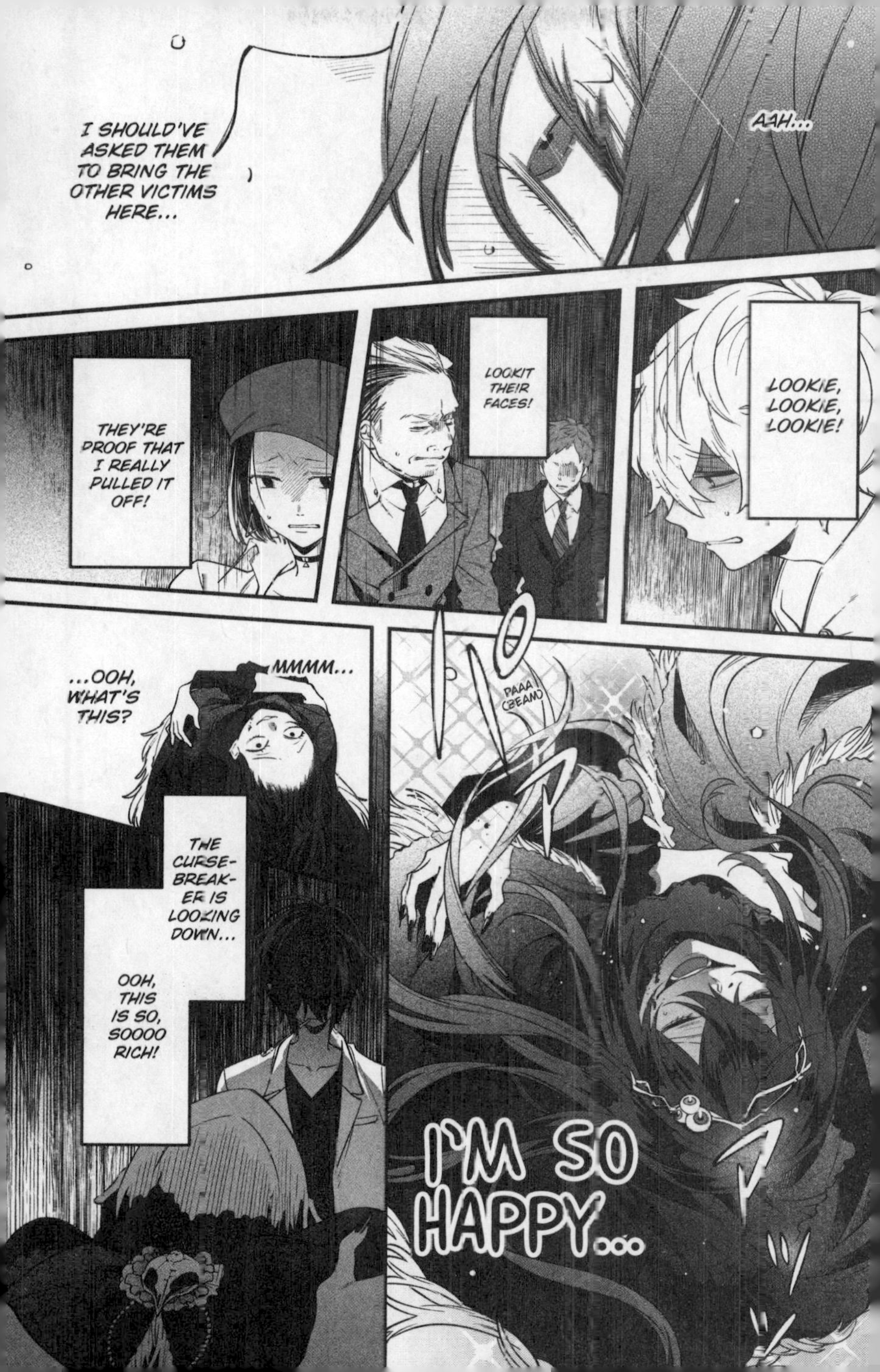
AAH...
I SHOULD'VE ASKED THEM TO BRING THE OTHER VICTIMS HERE...
LOOKIE, LOOKIE, LOOKIE!
LOOKIT THEIR FACES!
THEY'RE PROOF THAT I REALLY PULLED IT OFF!
PAAA (BEAM)
I'M SO HAPPY...
MMMM...
...OOH, WHAT'S THIS?
THE CURSE-BREAKER IS LOOKING DOWN...
OOH, THIS IS SO, SOOOO RICH!

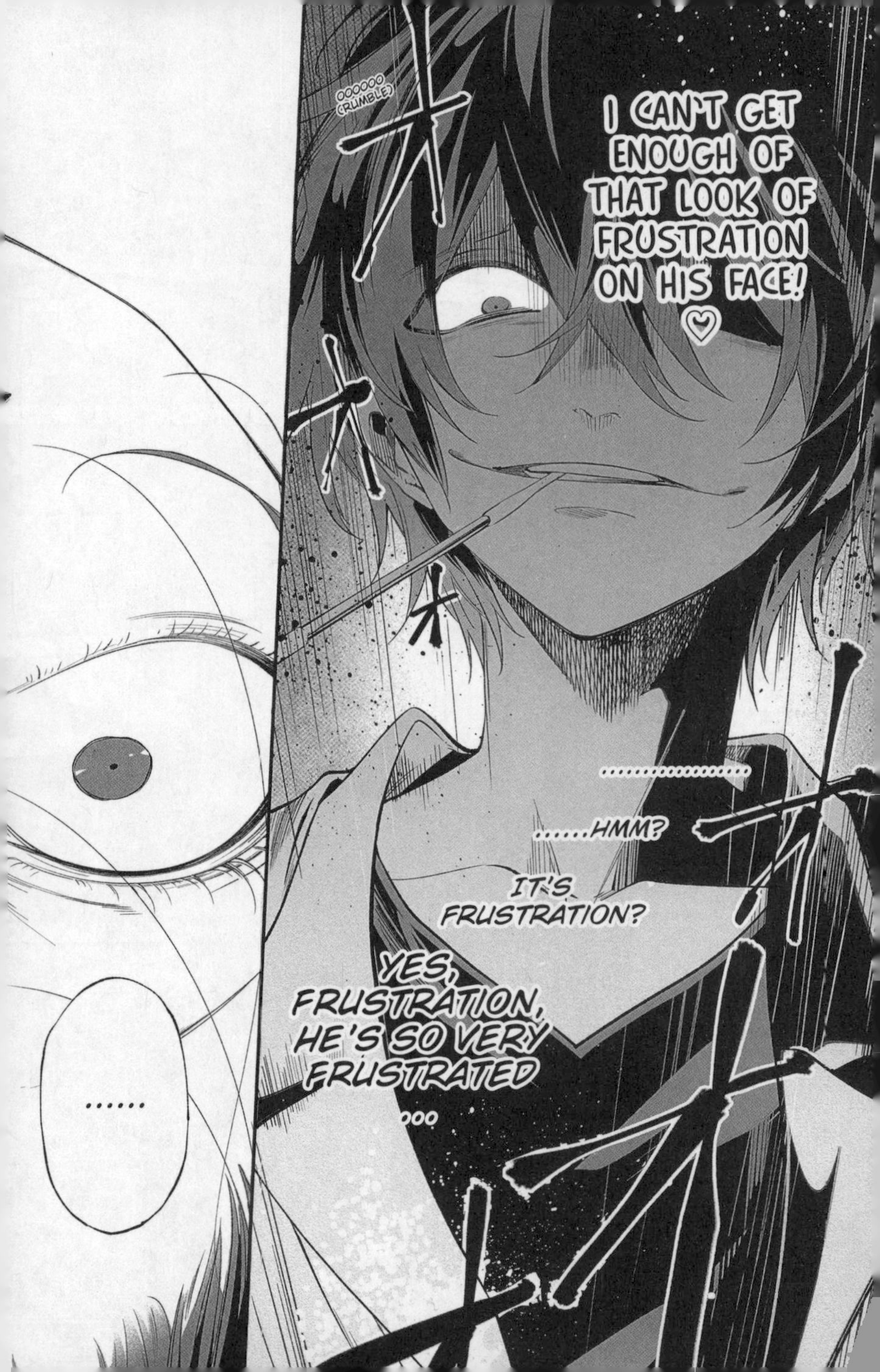
I CAN'T GET ENOUGH OF THAT LOOK OF FRUSTRATION ON HIS FACE! ♡
OOOOOO (RUMBLE)
....
......HMM?
IT'S FRUSTRATION?
YES, FRUSTRATION, HE'S SO VERY FRUSTRATED...
......

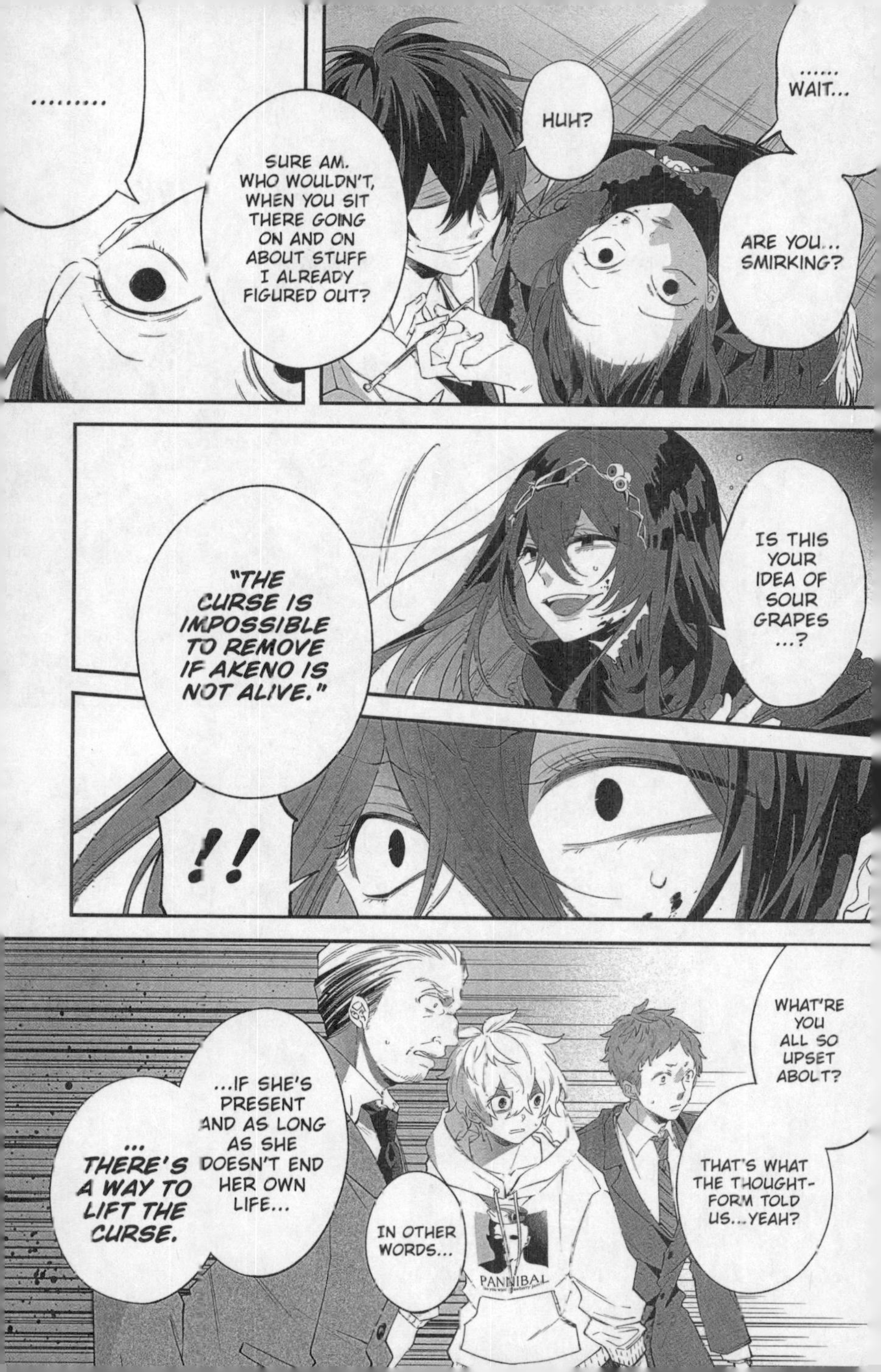

...... WAIT...
ARE YOU... SMIRKING?
HUH?
SURE AM. WHO WOULDN'T, WHEN YOU SIT THERE GOING ON AND ON ABOUT STUFF I ALREADY FIGURED OUT?
....
IS THIS YOUR IDEA OF SOUR GRAPES ...?
"THE CURSE IS IMPOSSIBLE TO REMOVE IF AKENO IS NOT ALIVE."
!!
WHAT'RE YOU ALL SO UPSET ABOUT?
THAT'S WHAT THE THOUGHT-FORM TOLD US...YEAH?
IN OTHER WORDS...
...IF SHE'S PRESENT AND AS LONG AS SHE DOESN'T END HER OWN LIFE...
... THERE'S A WAY TO LIFT THE CURSE.
PANNIBAL

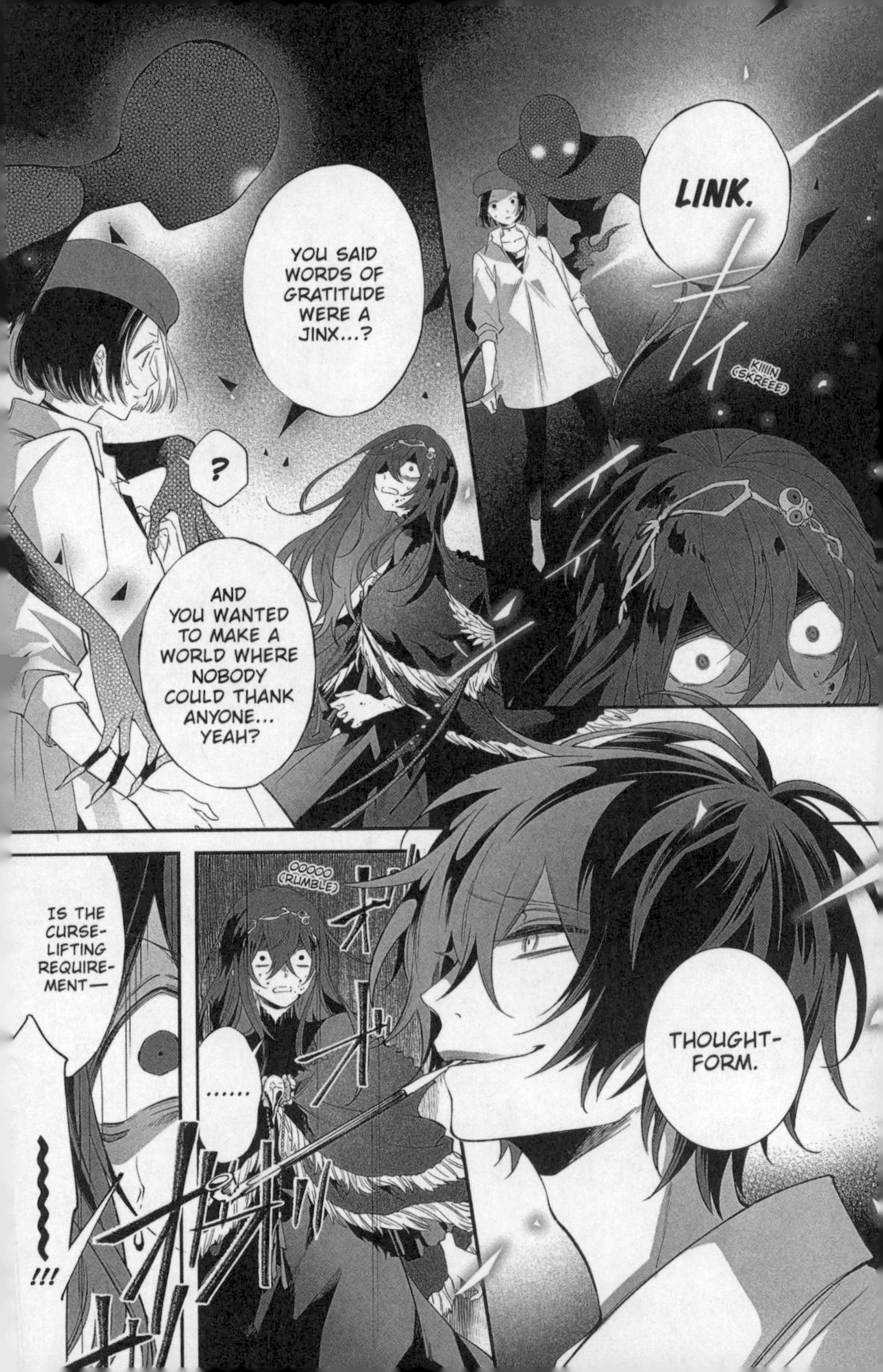

LINK.
KIIIN (SKREEE)
YOU SAID WORDS OF GRATITUDE WERE A JINX...?
?
AND YOU WANTED TO MAKE A WORLD WHERE NOBODY COULD THANK ANYONE... YEAH?
THOUGHT-FORM.
OOOOO (RUMBLE)
......
IS THE CURSE-LIFTING REQUIREMENT—
~~~!!!
~~~

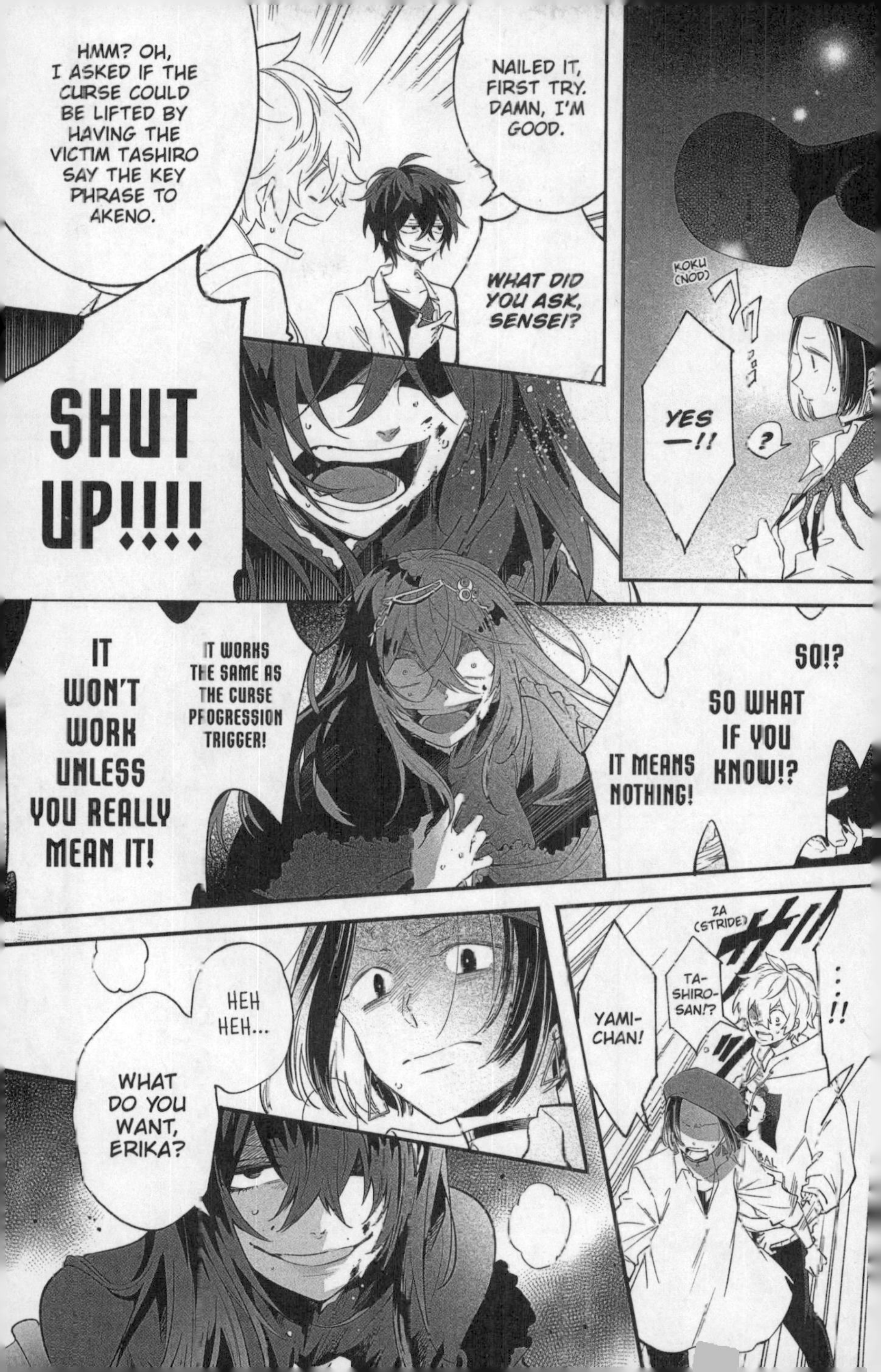
KOKU (NOD)
YES—!!
?
NAILED IT, FIRST TRY. DAMN, I'M GOOD.
WHAT DID YOU ASK, SENSEI?
HMM? OH, I ASKED IF THE CURSE COULD BE LIFTED BY HAVING THE VICTIM TASHIRO SAY THE KEY PHRASE TO AKENO.
SHUT UP!!!!
SO!?
SO WHAT IF YOU KNOW!?
IT MEANS NOTHING!
IT WORKS THE SAME AS THE CURSE PROGRESSION TRIGGER!
IT WON'T WORK UNLESS YOU REALLY MEAN IT!
ZA (STRIDE)
...!!
TA-SHIRO-SAN!?
YAMI-CHAN!
HEH HEH...
WHAT DO YOU WANT, ERIKA?

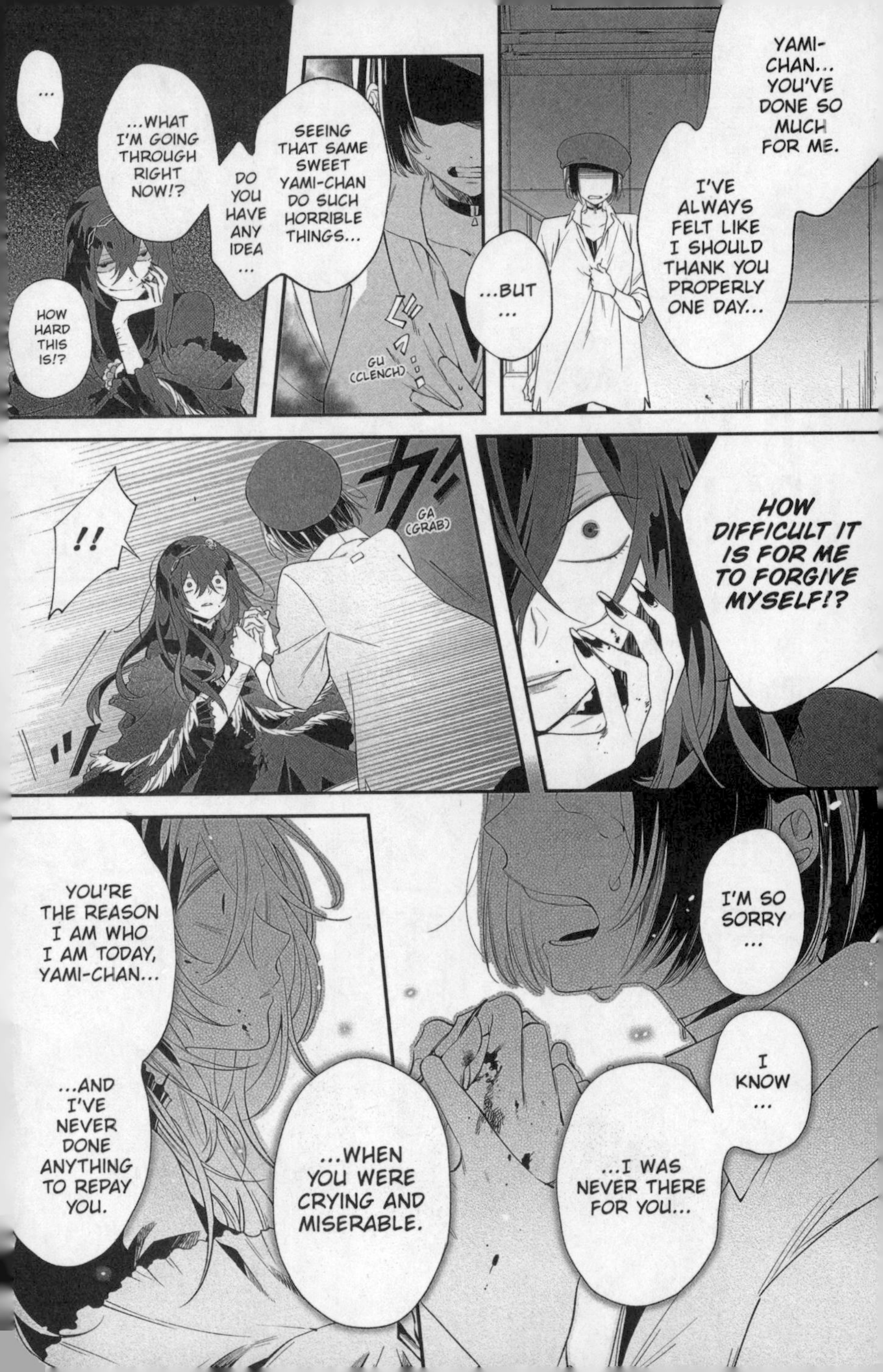
YAMI-CHAN... YOU'VE DONE SO MUCH FOR ME.
I'VE ALWAYS FELT LIKE I SHOULD THANK YOU PROPERLY ONE DAY...
...BUT ...
GU (CLENCH)
SEEING THAT SAME SWEET YAMI-CHAN DO SUCH HORRIBLE THINGS...
DO YOU HAVE ANY IDEA ...
...WHAT I'M GOING THROUGH RIGHT NOW!?
HOW HARD THIS IS!?
...
HOW DIFFICULT IT IS FOR ME TO FORGIVE MYSELF!?
GA (GRAB)
!!
I'M SO SORRY ...
I KNOW ...
...I WAS NEVER THERE FOR YOU...
...WHEN YOU WERE CRYING AND MISERABLE.
YOU'RE THE REASON I AM WHO I AM TODAY, YAMI-CHAN...
...AND I'VE NEVER DONE ANYTHING TO REPAY YOU.

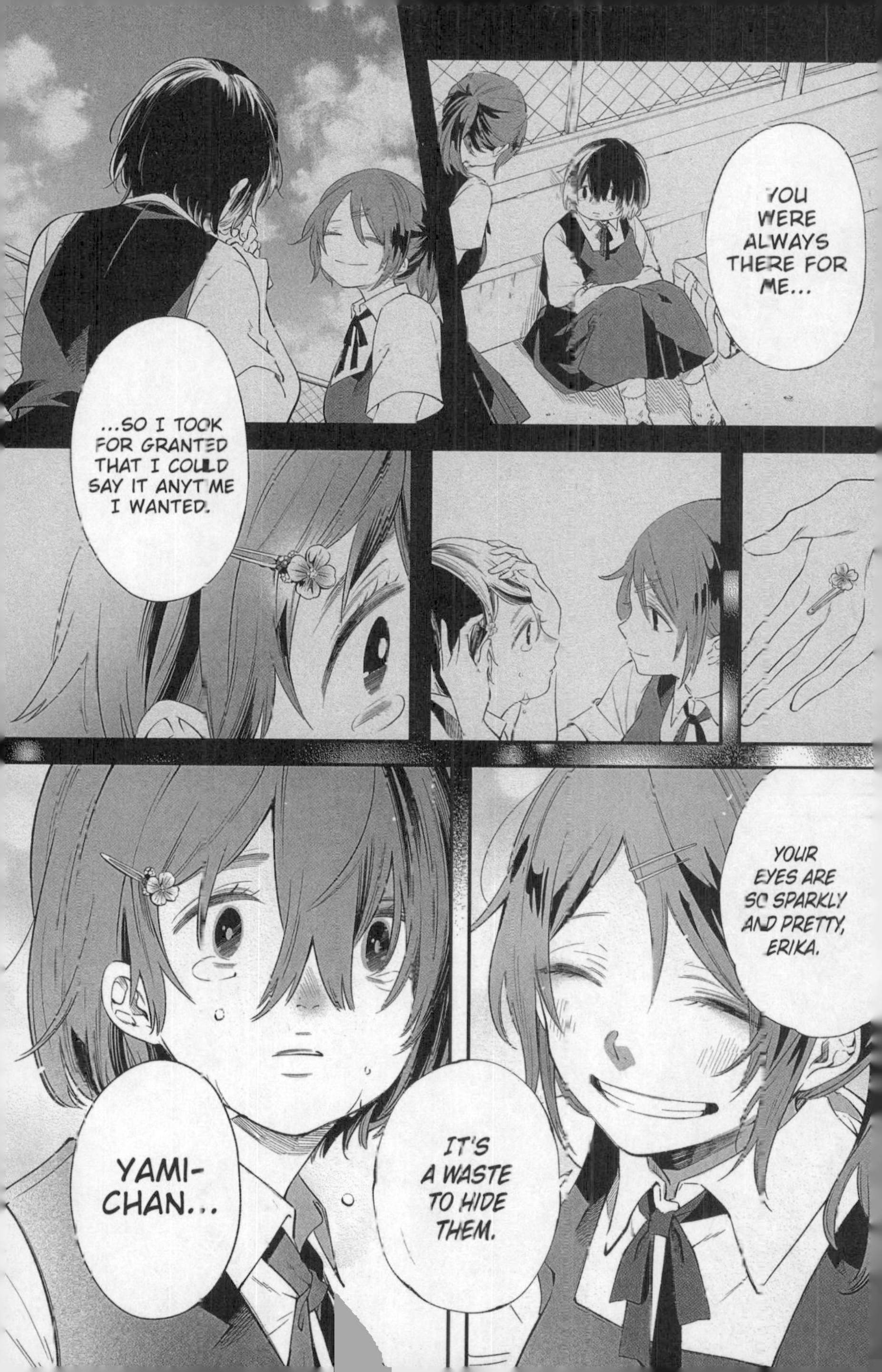

YOU WERE ALWAYS THERE FOR ME...
...SO I TOOK FOR GRANTED THAT I COULD SAY IT ANYTIME I WANTED.
YOUR EYES ARE SO SPARKLY AND PRETTY, ERIKA.
IT'S A WASTE TO HIDE THEM.
YAMI-CHAN...

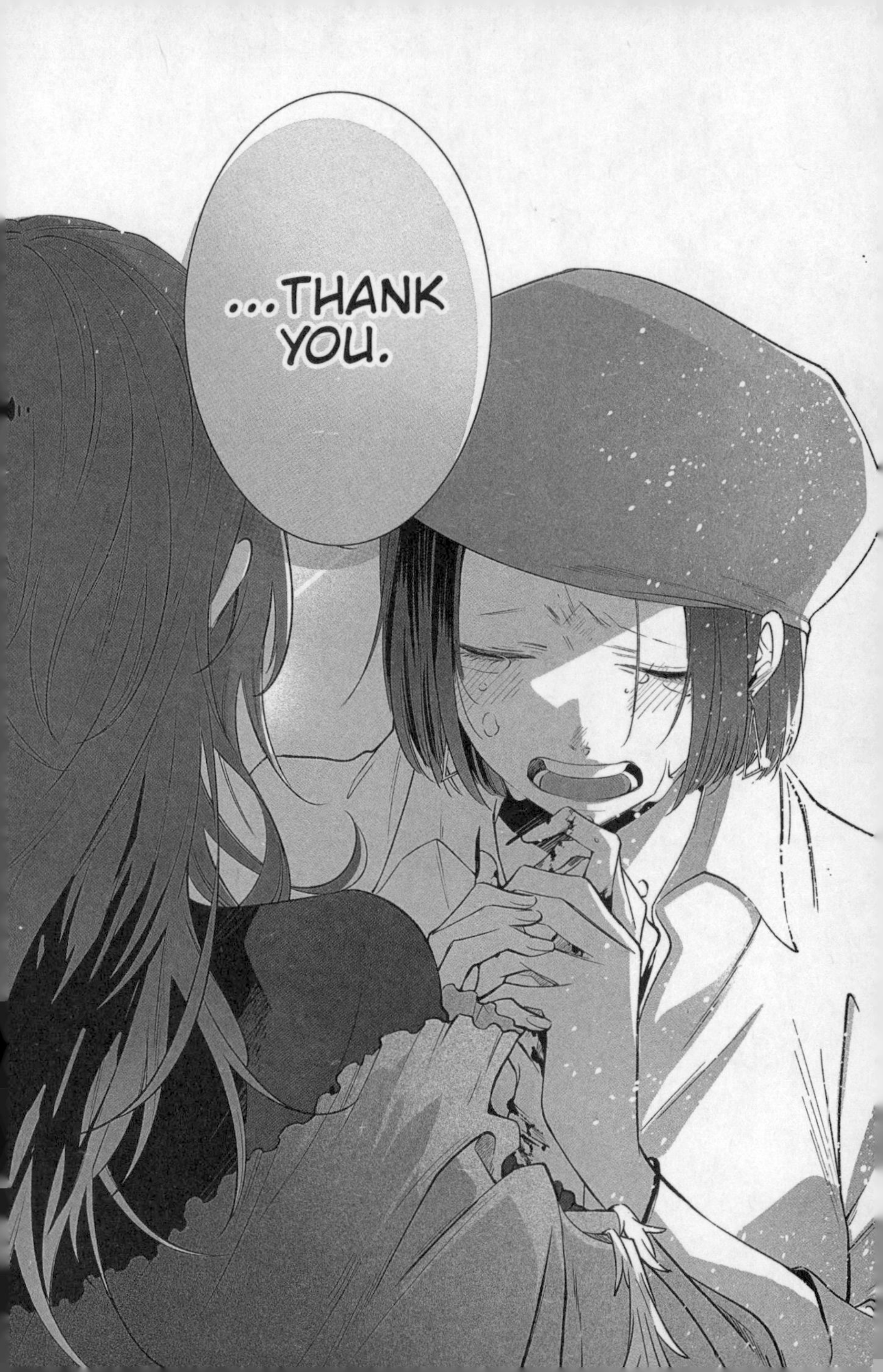
...THANK YOU.

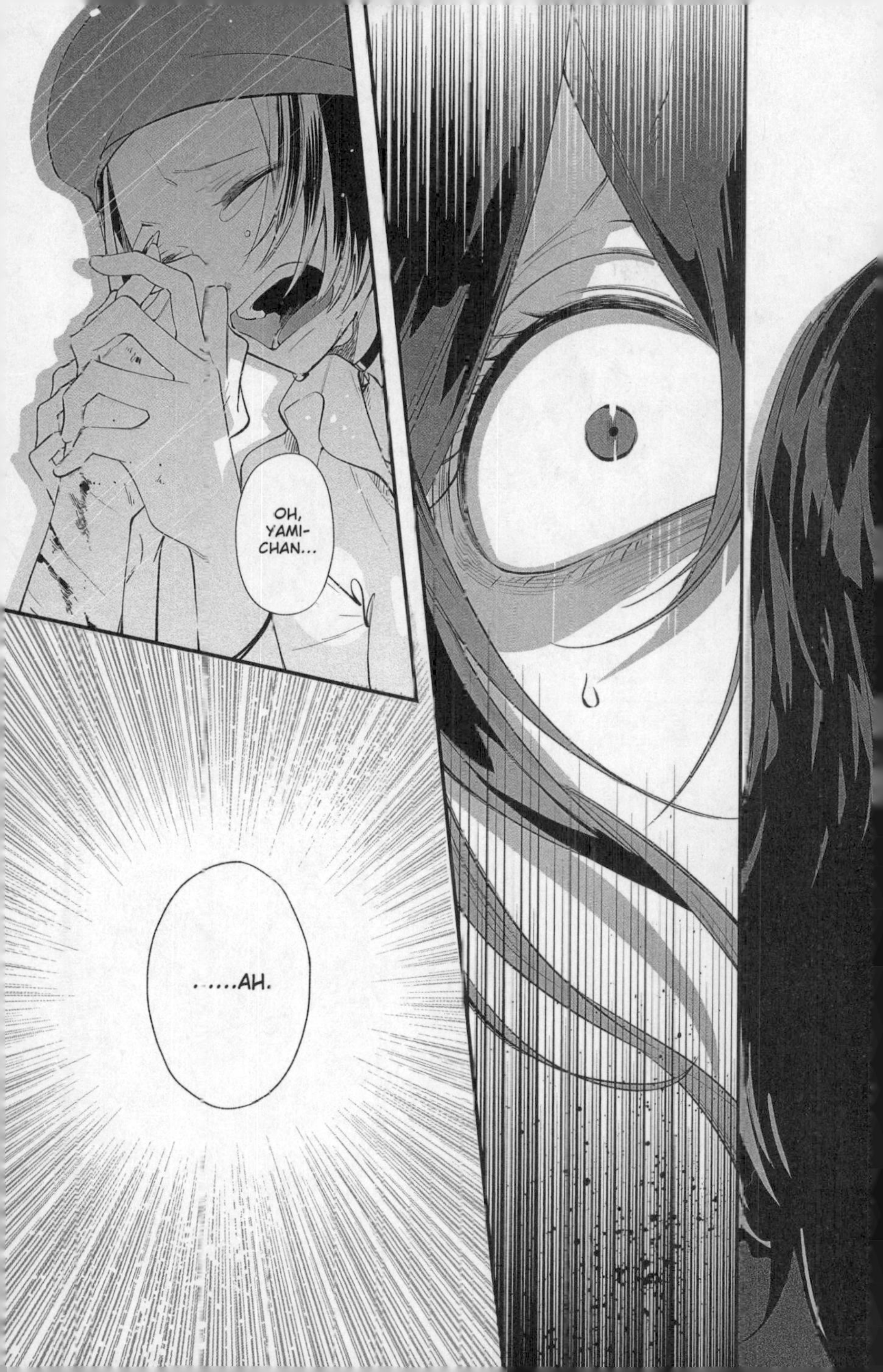
OH, YAMI-CHAN...
......AH.

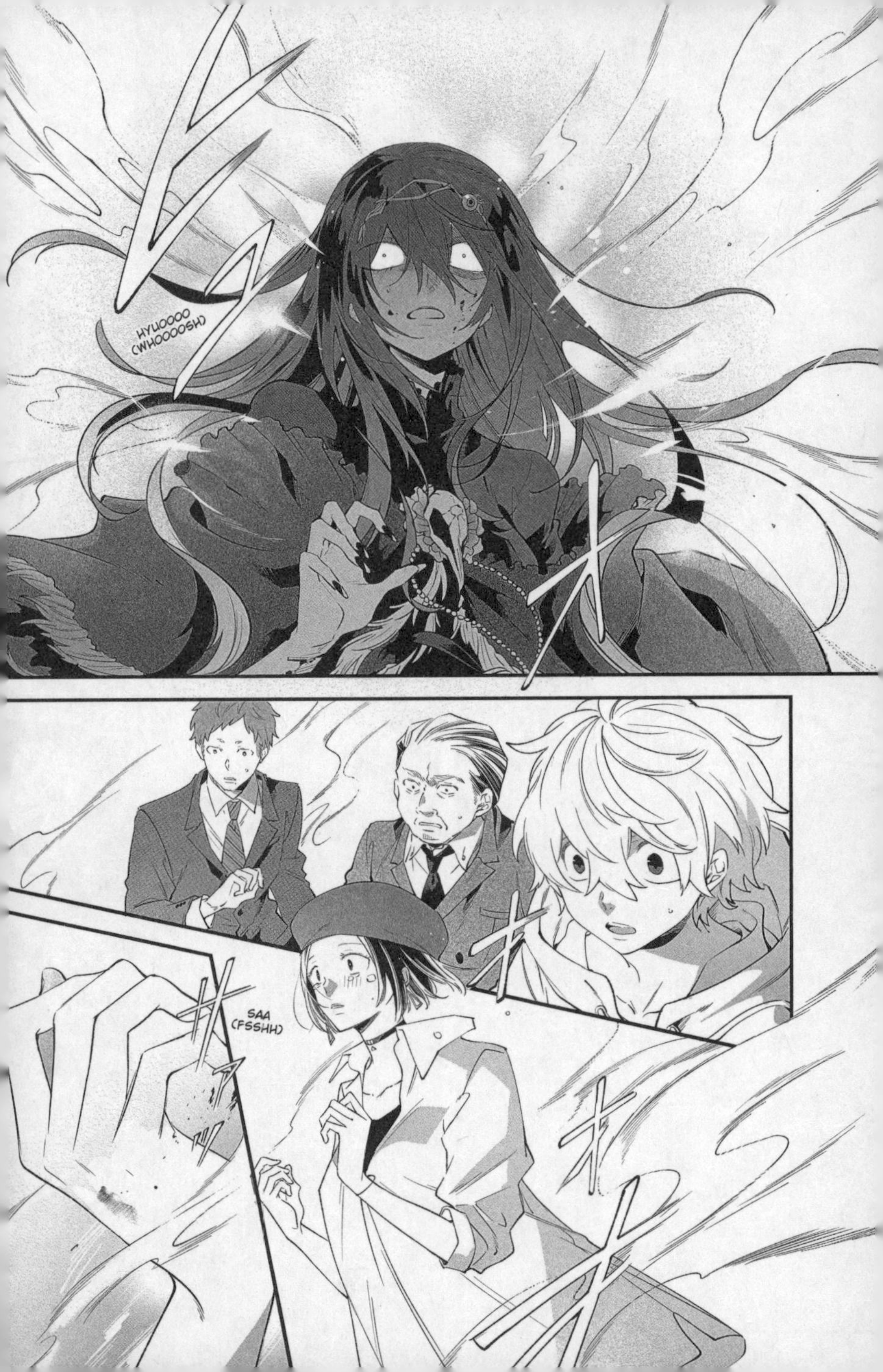
HYUOOOO
(WHOOOOSH)
SAA
(FSSHH)

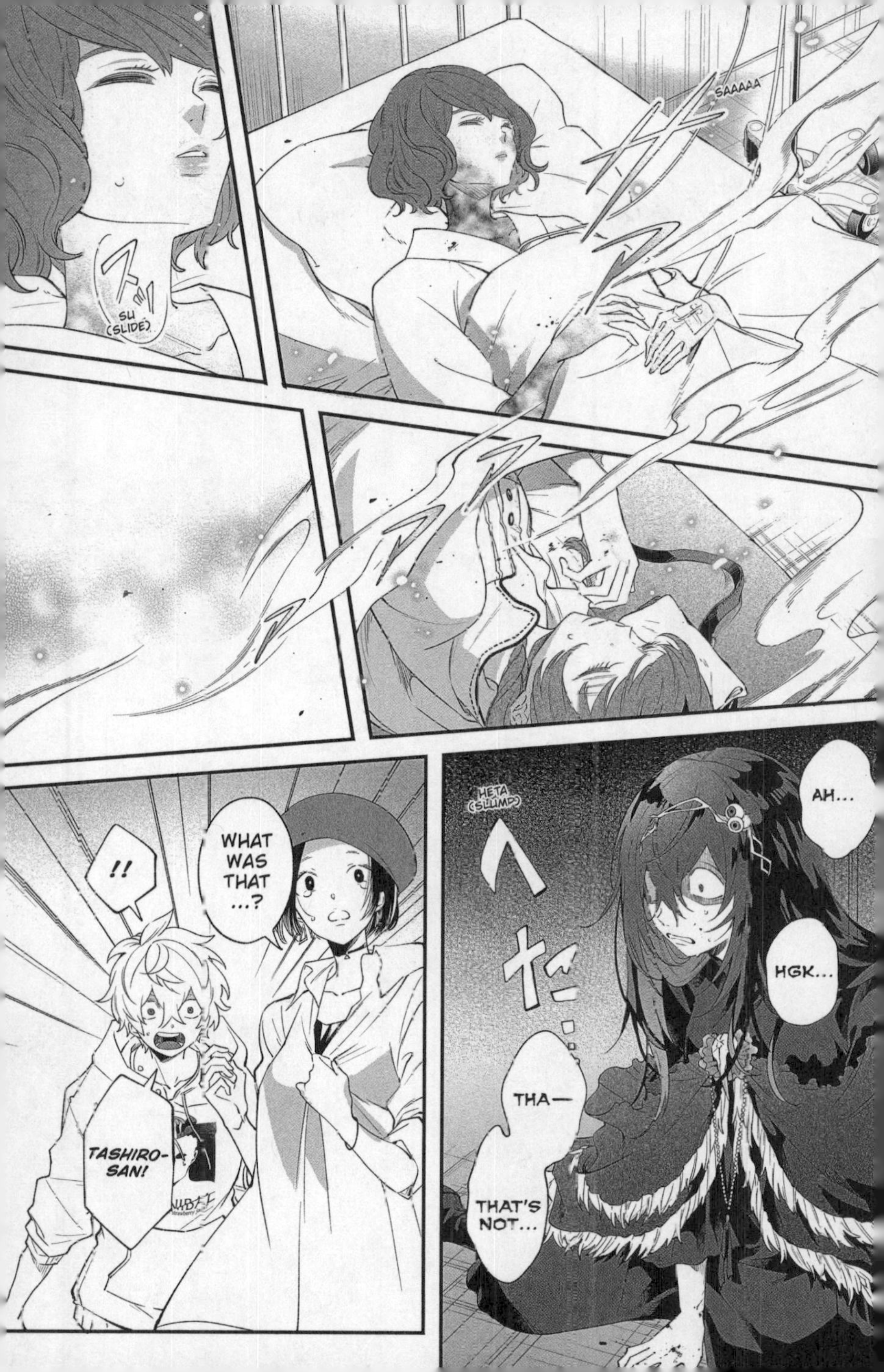
SAAAAA
SU (SLIDE)
AH...
HETA (SLUMP)
HGK...
THA—
THAT'S NOT...
WHAT WAS THAT ...?
!!
TASHIRO-SAN!

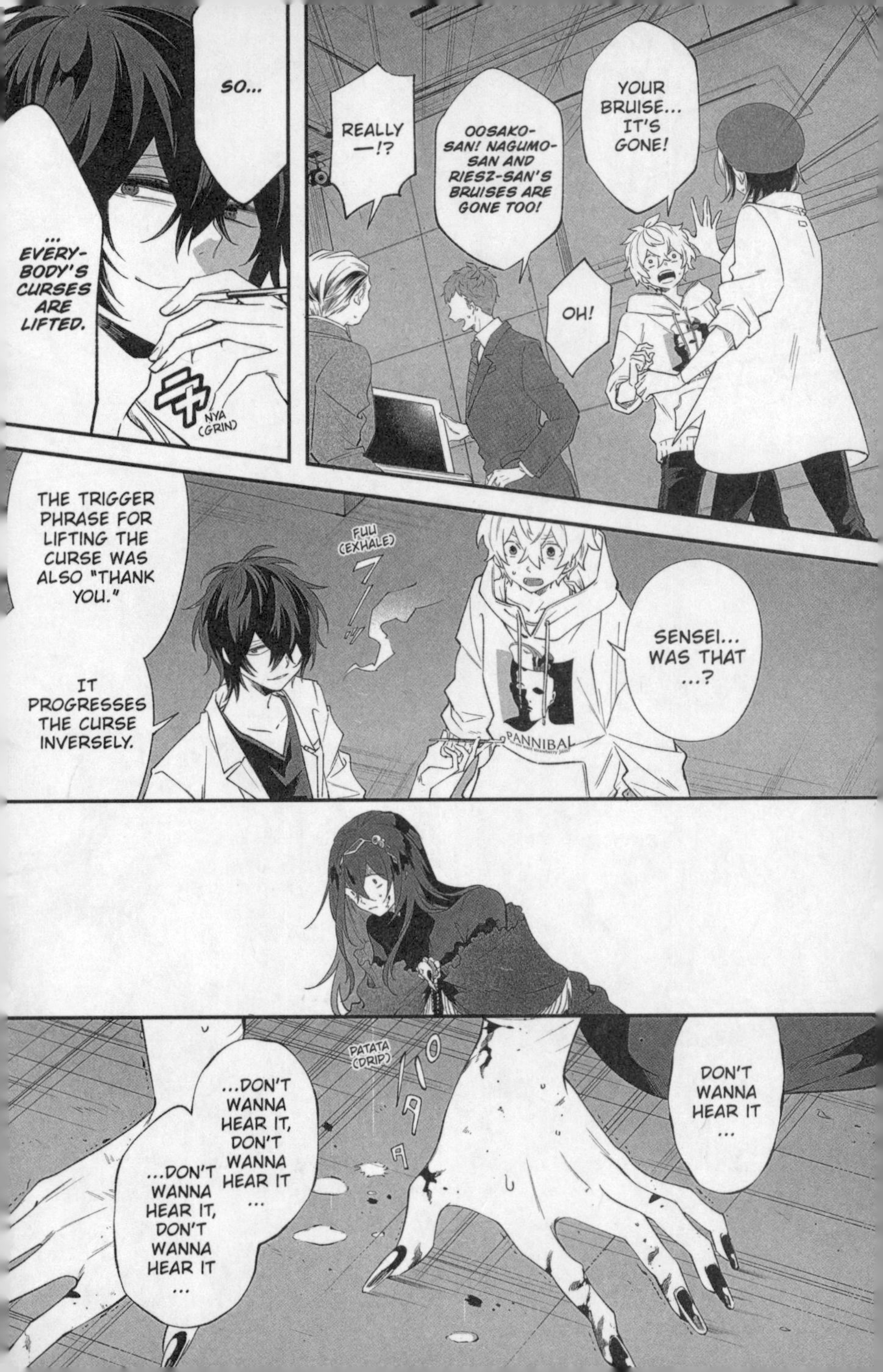

YOUR BRUISE... IT'S GONE!
OOSAKO-SAN! NAGUMO-SAN AND RIESZ-SAN'S BRUISES ARE GONE TOO!
REALLY—!?
OH!
SO...
...EVERYBODY'S CURSES ARE LIFTED.
NYA (GRIN)
SENSEI... WAS THAT ...?
FUU (EXHALE)
THE TRIGGER PHRASE FOR LIFTING THE CURSE WAS ALSO "THANK YOU."
IT PROGRESSES THE CURSE INVERSELY.
DON'T WANNA HEAR IT ...
PATATA (DRIP)
...DON'T WANNA HEAR IT, DON'T WANNA HEAR IT ...
...DON'T WANNA HEAR IT, DON'T WANNA HEAR IT ...

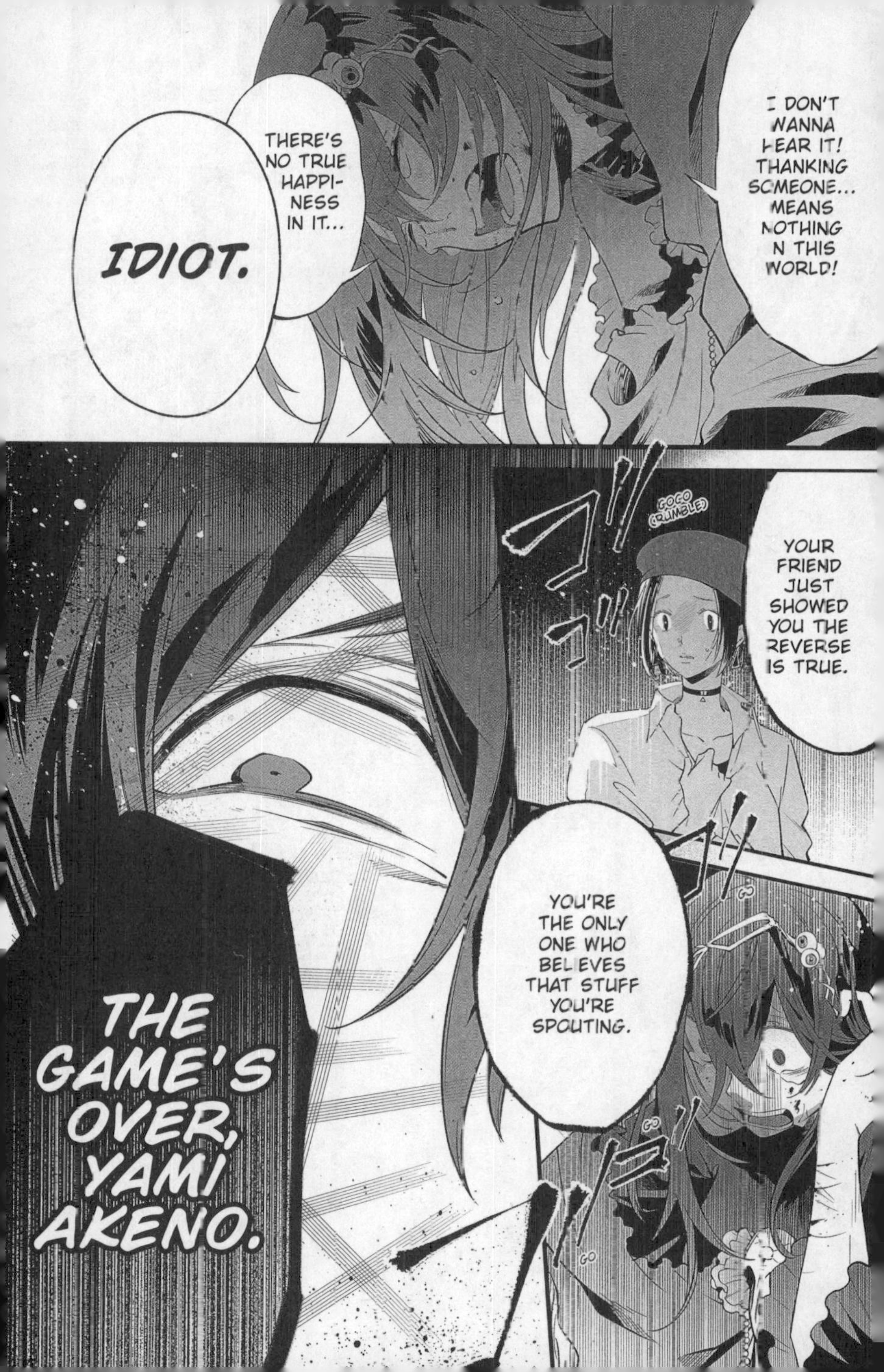
I DON'T WANNA HEAR IT! THANKING SOMEONE... MEANS NOTHING IN THIS WORLD!
THERE'S NO TRUE HAPPINESS IN IT...
IDIOT.
GOGO (RUMBLE)
YOUR FRIEND JUST SHOWED YOU THE REVERSE IS TRUE.
GO
YOU'RE THE ONLY ONE WHO BELIEVES THAT STUFF YOU'RE SPOUTING.
GO
GO
THE GAME'S OVER, YAMI AKENO.

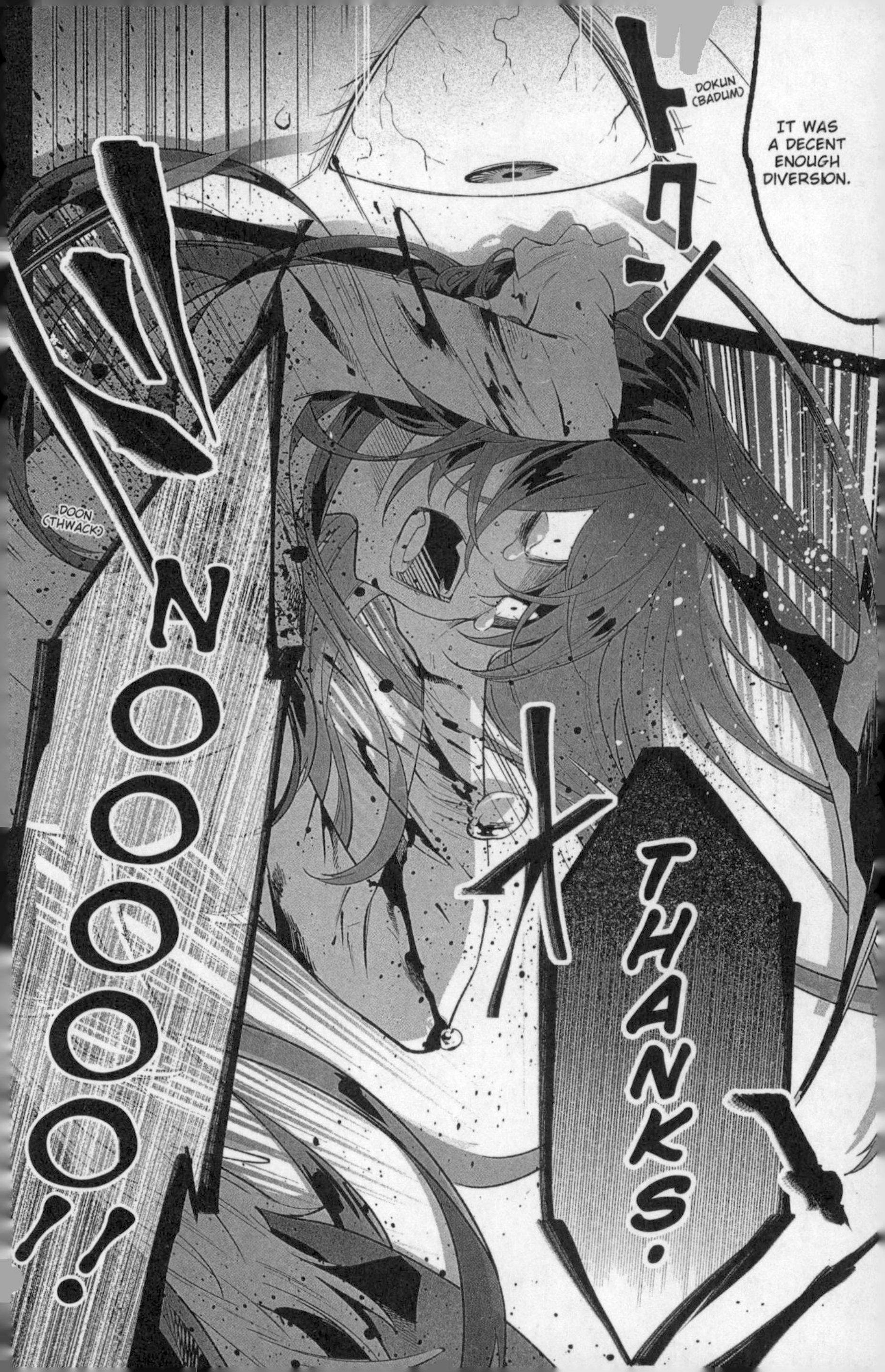
IT WAS A DECENT ENOUGH DIVERSION.
DOKUN (BADUM)
THANKS.
NOOOOO!!
DOON (THWACK)

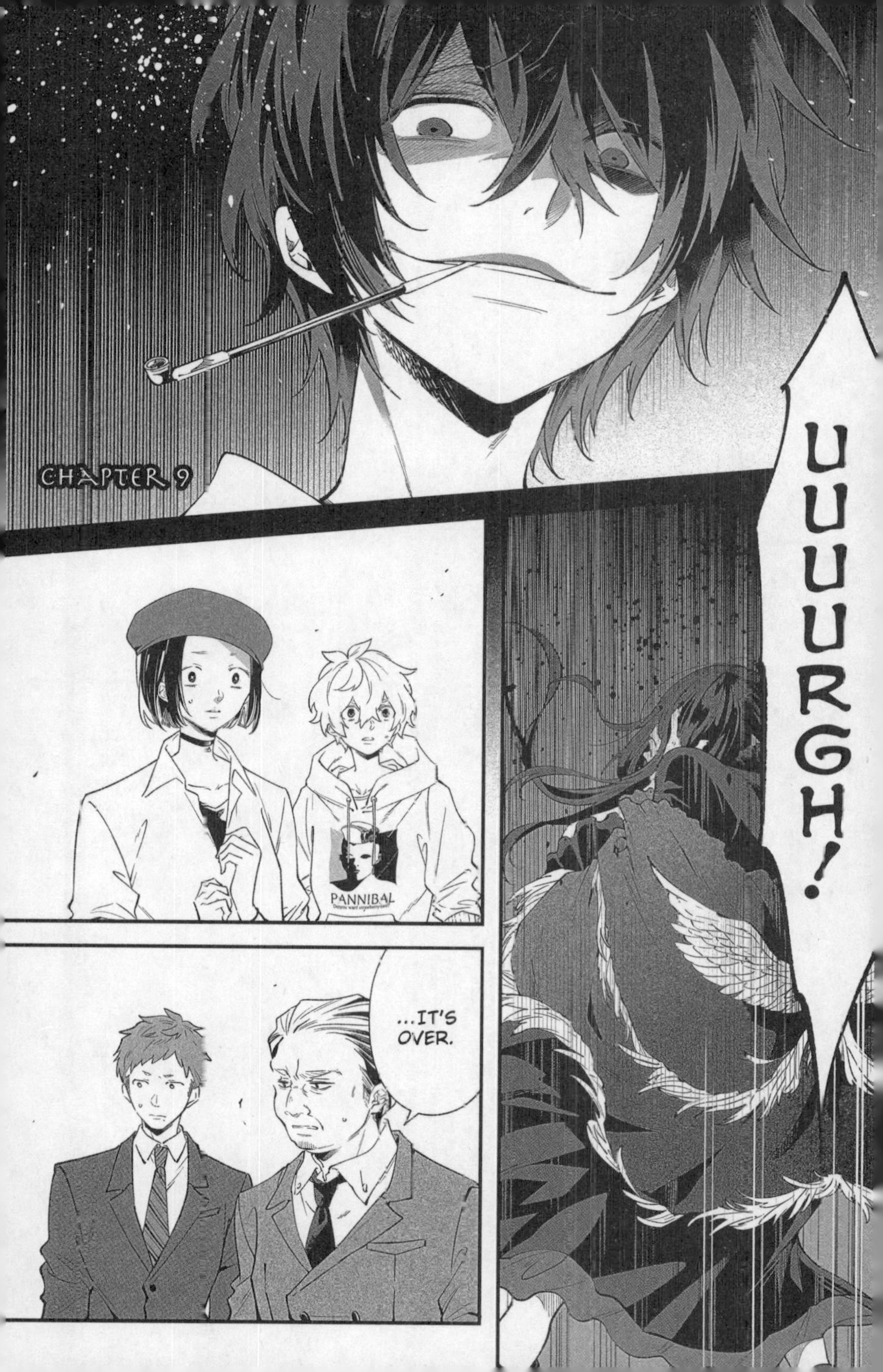
CHAPTER 9
UUUURGH!
PANNIBAL
...IT'S OVER.

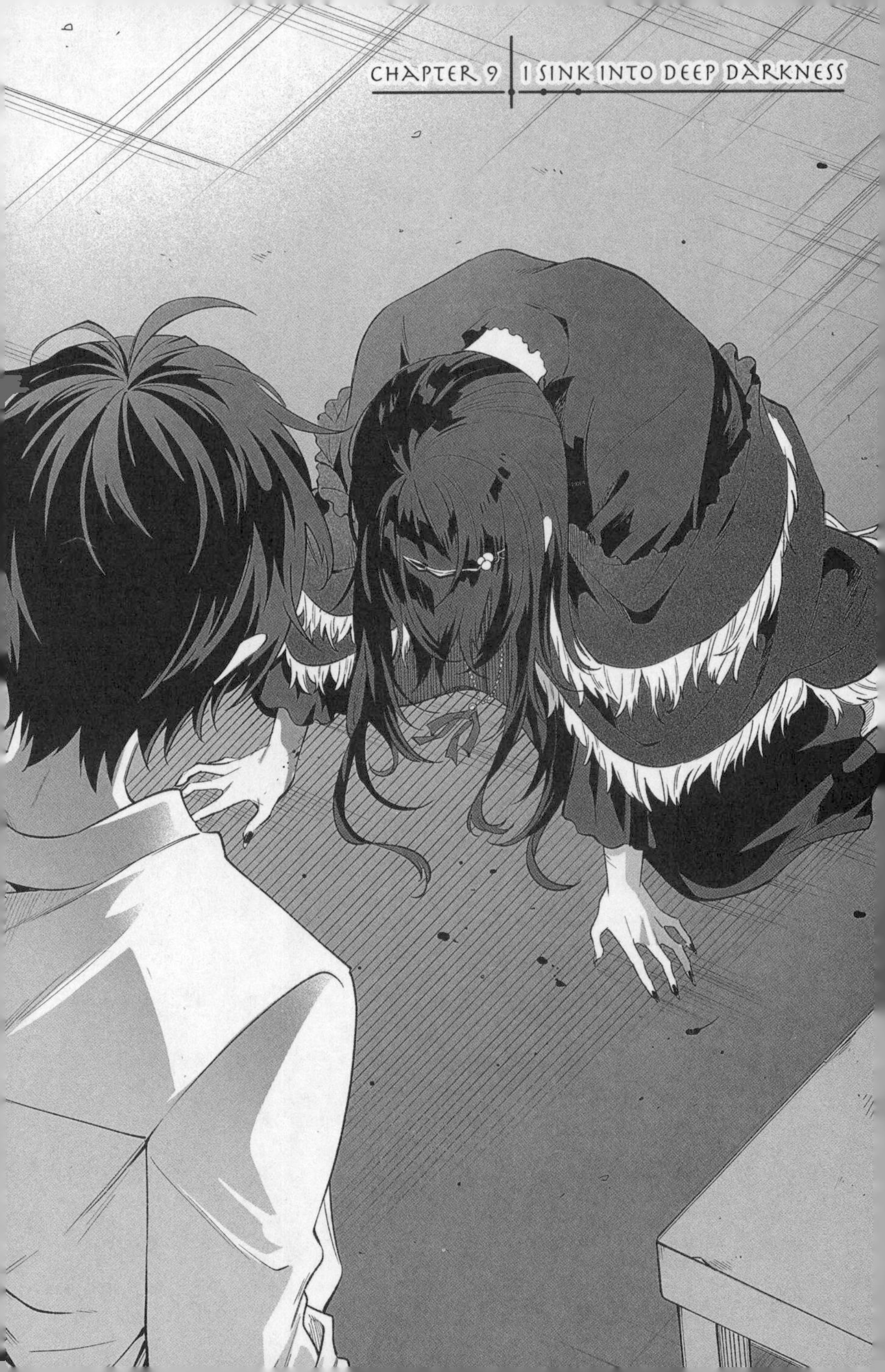
CHAPTER 9 I SINK INTO DEEP DARKNESS

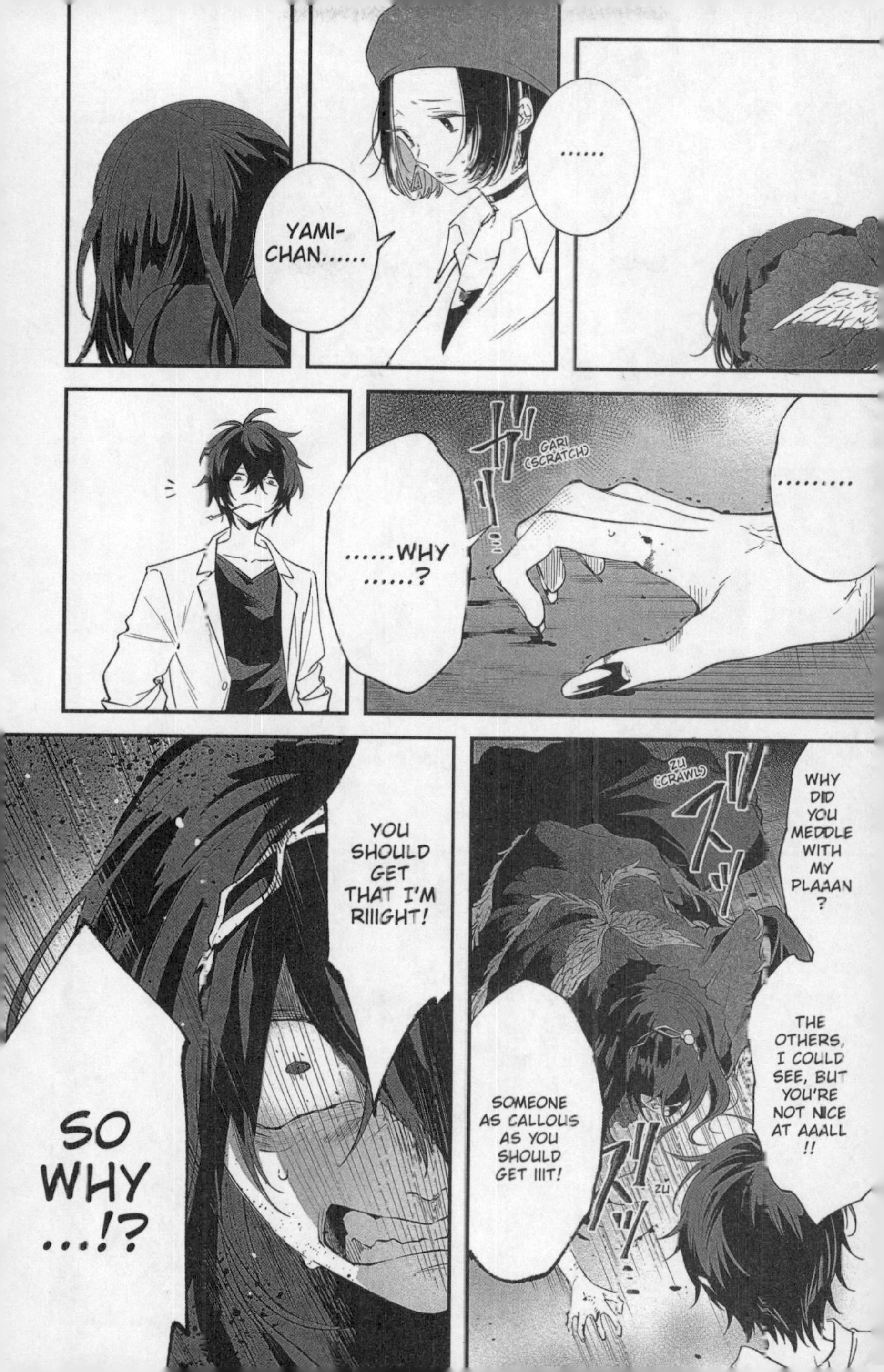
......
YAMI-CHAN......
....
GARI (SCRATCH)
......WHY ......?
WHY DID YOU MEDDLE WITH MY PLAAAN?
ZU (CRAWL)
THE OTHERS, I COULD SEE, BUT YOU'RE NOT NICE AT AAALL!!
SOMEONE AS CALLOUS AS YOU SHOULD GET IIIT!
ZU
YOU SHOULD GET THAT I'M RIIIGHT!
SO WHY...!?

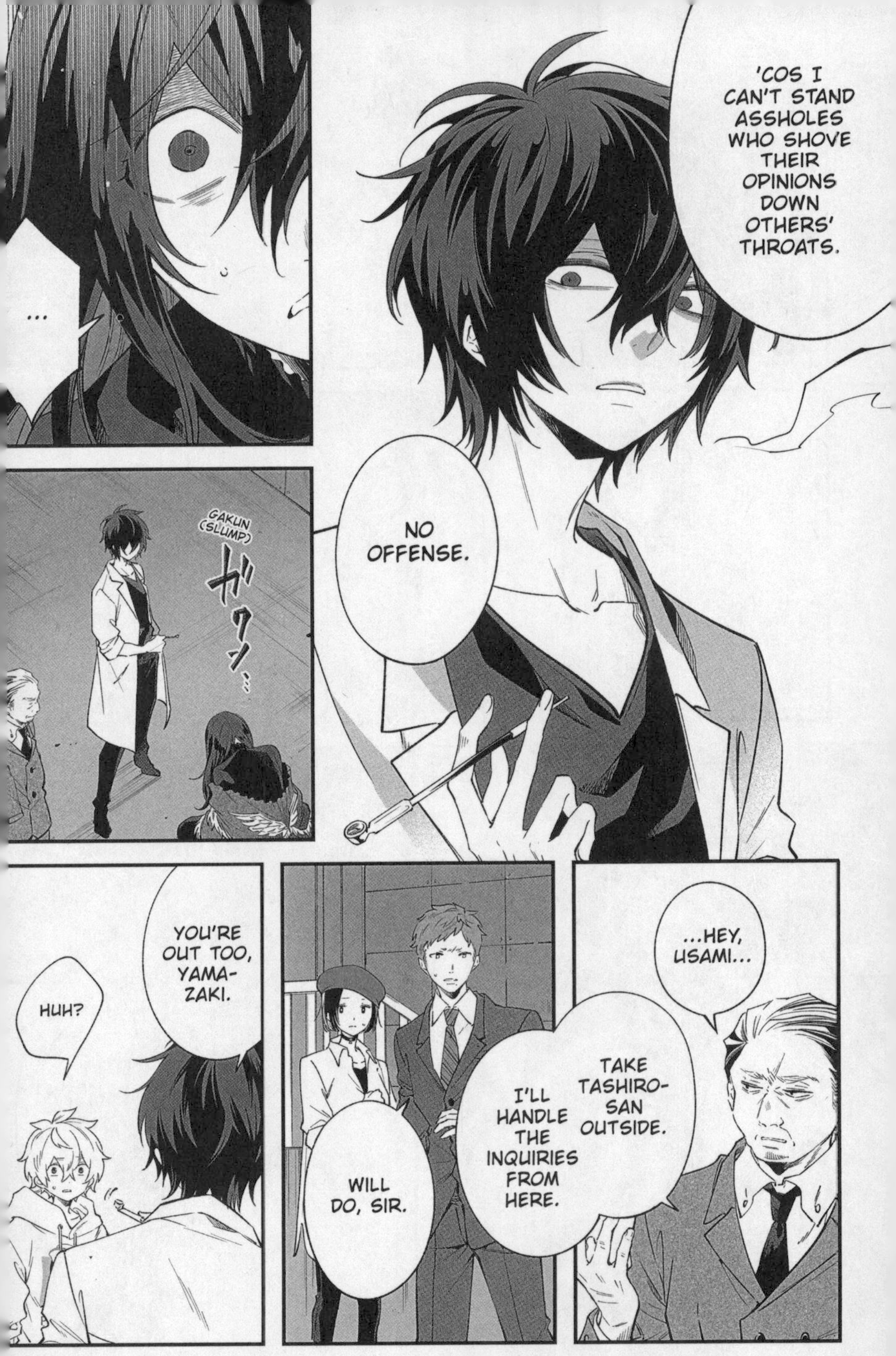
'COS I CAN'T STAND ASSHOLES WHO SHOVE THEIR OPINIONS DOWN OTHERS' THROATS.
NO OFFENSE.
...
GAKUN (SLUMP)
ガクン
...HEY, USAMI...
TAKE TASHIRO-SAN OUTSIDE.
I'LL HANDLE THE INQUIRIES FROM HERE.
WILL DO, SIR.
YOU'RE OUT TOO, YAMA-ZAKI.
HUH?

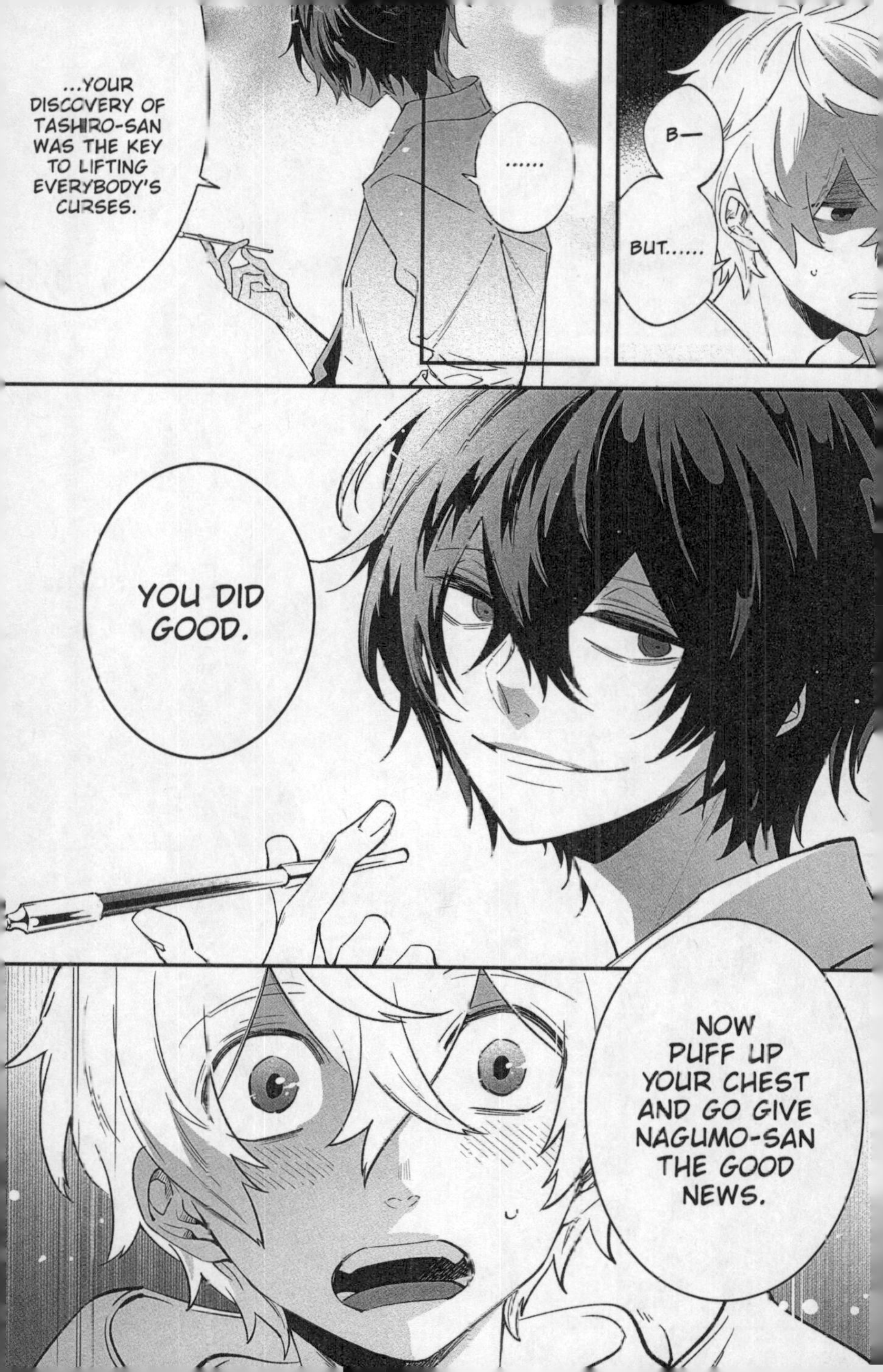
B—
BUT......
......
...YOUR DISCOVERY OF TASHIRO-SAN WAS THE KEY TO LIFTING EVERYBODY'S CURSES.
YOU DID GOOD.
NOW PUFF UP YOUR CHEST AND GO GIVE NAGUMO-SAN THE GOOD NEWS.

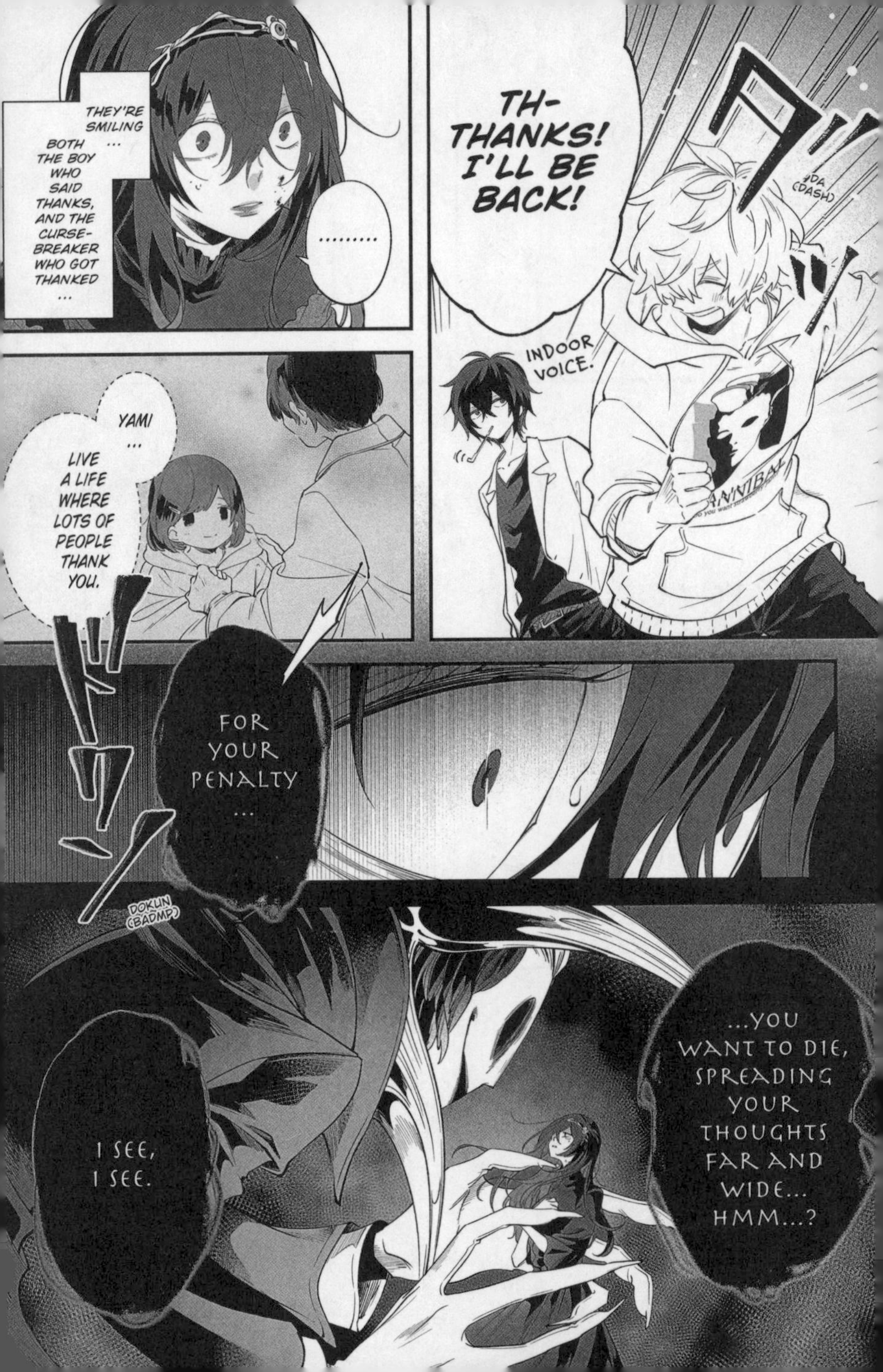
DA (DASH)
TH-THANKS! I'LL BE BACK!
INDOOR VOICE.
CANNIBAL
THEY'RE SMILING ... BOTH THE BOY WHO SAID THANKS, AND THE CURSE-BREAKER WHO GOT THANKED ...
....
YAMI ... LIVE A LIFE WHERE LOTS OF PEOPLE THANK YOU.
FOR YOUR PENALTY ...
DOKUN (BADMP)
...YOU WANT TO DIE, SPREADING YOUR THOUGHTS FAR AND WIDE... HMM...?
I SEE, I SEE.

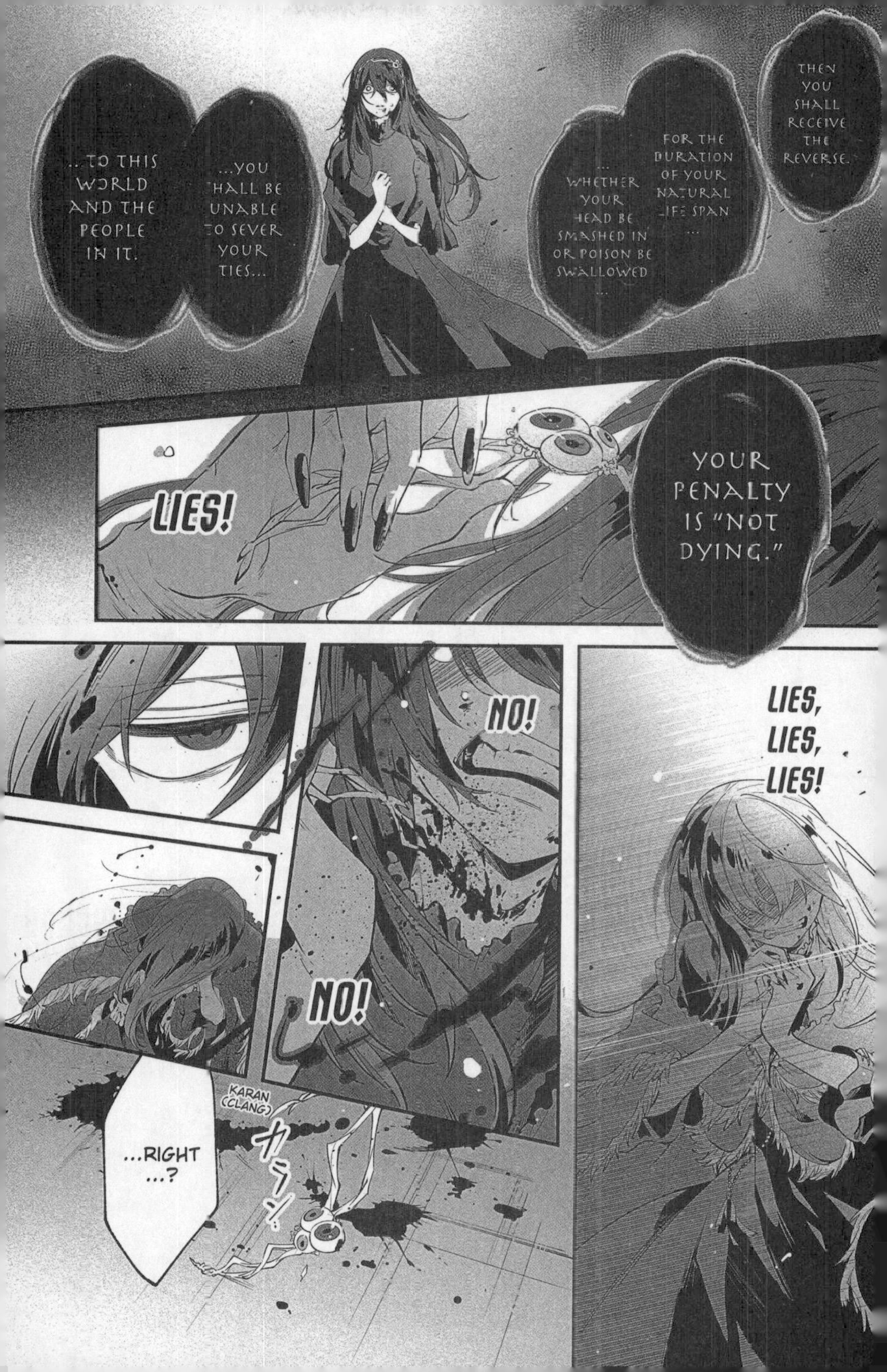
THEN YOU SHALL RECEIVE THE REVERSE.
FOR THE DURATION OF YOUR NATURAL LIFE SPAN...
...WHETHER YOUR HEAD BE SMASHED IN OR POISON BE SWALLOWED...
...YOU SHALL BE UNABLE TO SEVER YOUR TIES...
...TO THIS WORLD AND THE PEOPLE IN IT.
YOUR PENALTY IS "NOT DYING."
LIES!
LIES, LIES, LIES!
NO!
NO!
KARAN (CLANG)
...RIGHT ...?

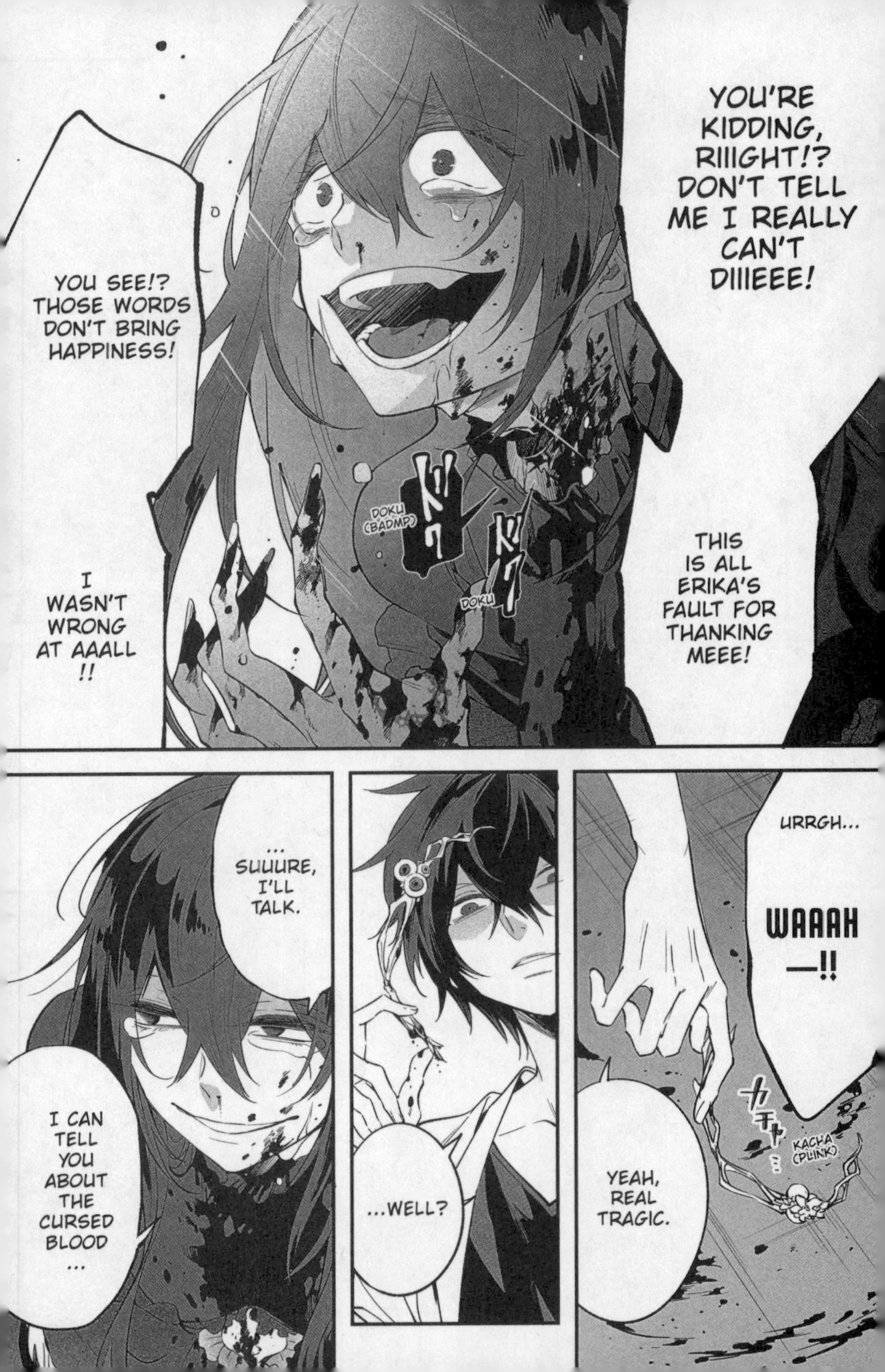
YOU'RE KIDDING, RIIIGHT!? DON'T TELL ME I REALLY CAN'T DIIIEEE!
YOU SEE!? THOSE WORDS DON'T BRING HAPPINESS!
DOKU (BADMP)
DOKU
THIS IS ALL ERIKA'S FAULT FOR THANKING MEEE!
I WASN'T WRONG AT AAALL!!
URRGH...
WAAAH—!!
KACHA (PLINK)
YEAH, REAL TRAGIC.
...WELL?
...SUUURE, I'LL TALK.
I CAN TELL YOU ABOUT THE CURSED BLOOD...

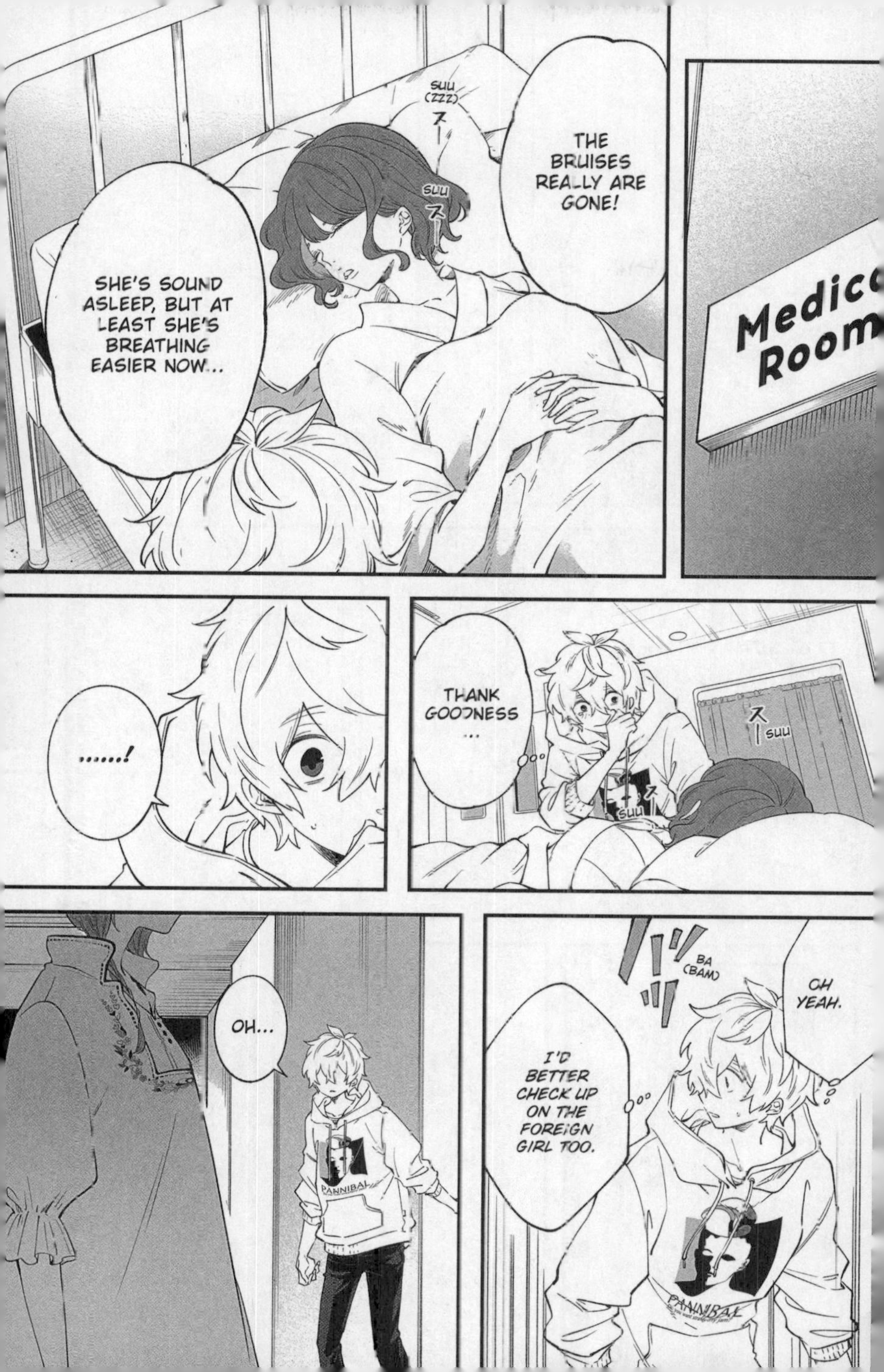
Medic
Room
THE BRUISES REALLY ARE GONE!
SUU (ZZZ)
SUU
SHE'S SOUND ASLEEP, BUT AT LEAST SHE'S BREATHING EASIER NOW...
THANK GOODNESS ...
SUU
SUU
......!
OH YEAH.
BA (BAM)
I'D BETTER CHECK UP ON THE FOREIGN GIRL TOO.
OH...

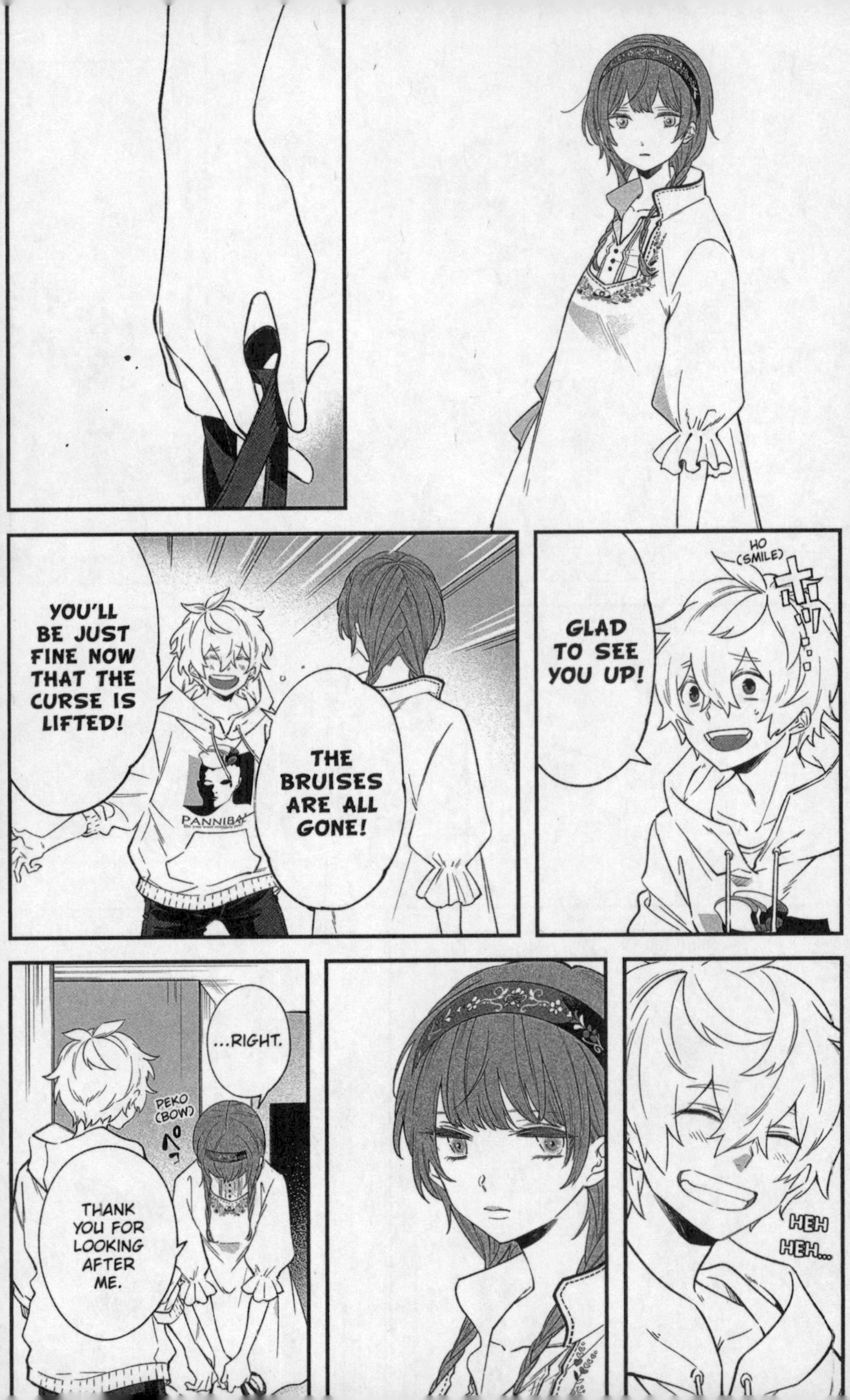
HO (SMILE)
GLAD TO SEE YOU UP!
THE BRUISES ARE ALL GONE!
YOU'LL BE JUST FINE NOW THAT THE CURSE IS LIFTED!
HEH HEH...
...RIGHT.
PEKO (BOW)
THANK YOU FOR LOOKING AFTER ME.

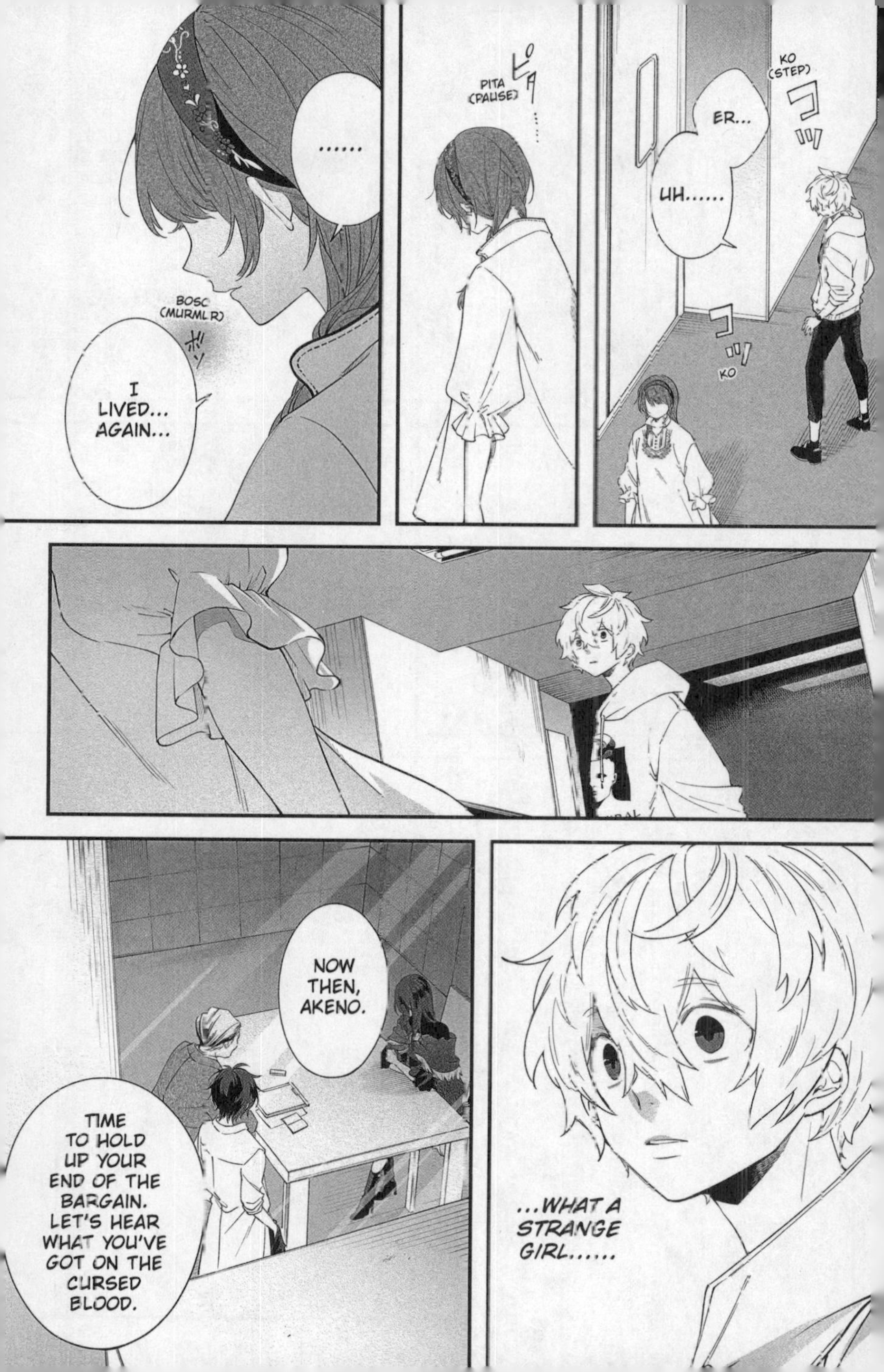
KO (STEP)
コッ
ER...
UH......
コッ
KO
PITA (PAUSE)
ピタ
......
......
BOSO (MURMUR)
ボソ
I LIVED... AGAIN...
...WHAT A STRANGE GIRL......
NOW THEN, AKENO.
TIME TO HOLD UP YOUR END OF THE BARGAIN. LET'S HEAR WHAT YOU'VE GOT ON THE CURSED BLOOD.

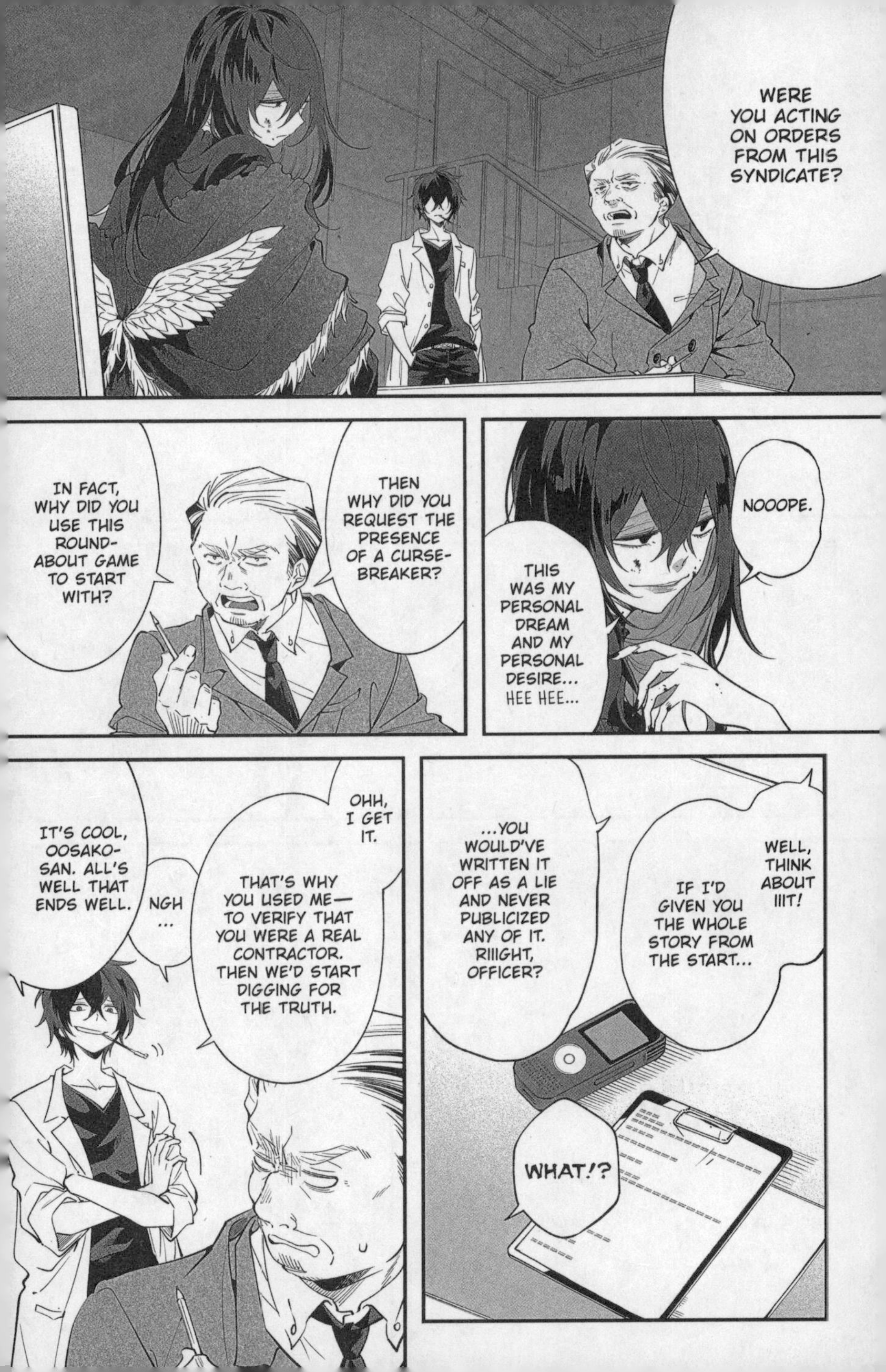
WERE YOU ACTING ON ORDERS FROM THIS SYNDICATE?
NOOOPE.
THIS WAS MY PERSONAL DREAM AND MY PERSONAL DESIRE... HEE HEE...
THEN WHY DID YOU REQUEST THE PRESENCE OF A CURSE-BREAKER?
IN FACT, WHY DID YOU USE THIS ROUND-ABOUT GAME TO START WITH?
WELL, THINK ABOUT IIIT!
IF I'D GIVEN YOU THE WHOLE STORY FROM THE START...
...YOU WOULD'VE WRITTEN IT OFF AS A LIE AND NEVER PUBLICIZED ANY OF IT. RIIIGHT, OFFICER?
WHAT!?
OHH, I GET IT.
THAT'S WHY YOU USED ME— TO VERIFY THAT YOU WERE A REAL CONTRACTOR. THEN WE'D START DIGGING FOR THE TRUTH.
NGH ...
IT'S COOL, OOSAKO-SAN. ALL'S WELL THAT ENDS WELL.

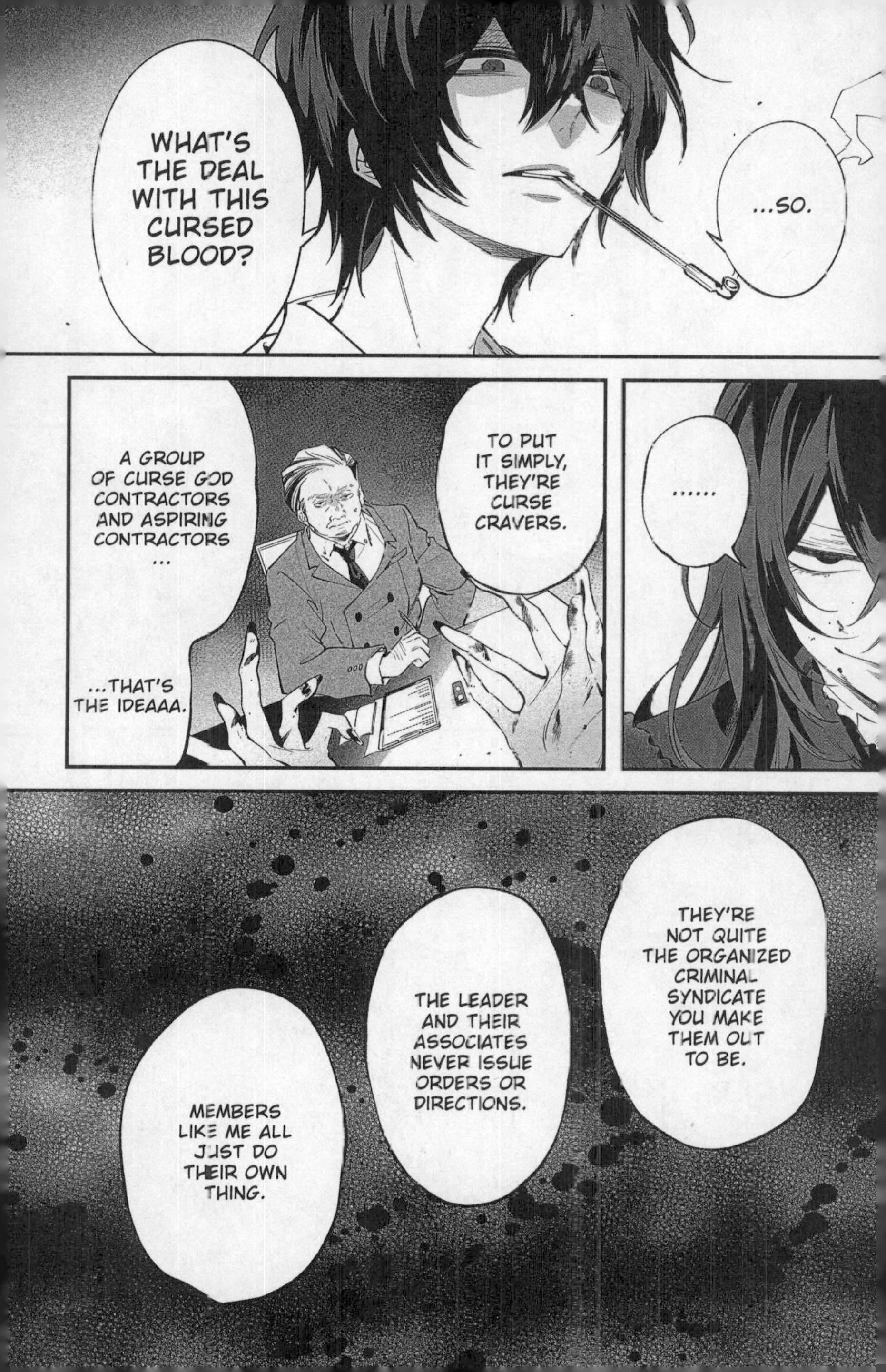
...SO.
WHAT'S THE DEAL WITH THIS CURSED BLOOD?
......
TO PUT IT SIMPLY, THEY'RE CURSE CRAVERS.
A GROUP OF CURSE GOD CONTRACTORS AND ASPIRING CONTRACTORS ...
...THAT'S THE IDEAAA.
THEY'RE NOT QUITE THE ORGANIZED CRIMINAL SYNDICATE YOU MAKE THEM OUT TO BE.
THE LEADER AND THEIR ASSOCIATES NEVER ISSUE ORDERS OR DIRECTIONS.
MEMBERS LIKE ME ALL JUST DO THEIR OWN THING.

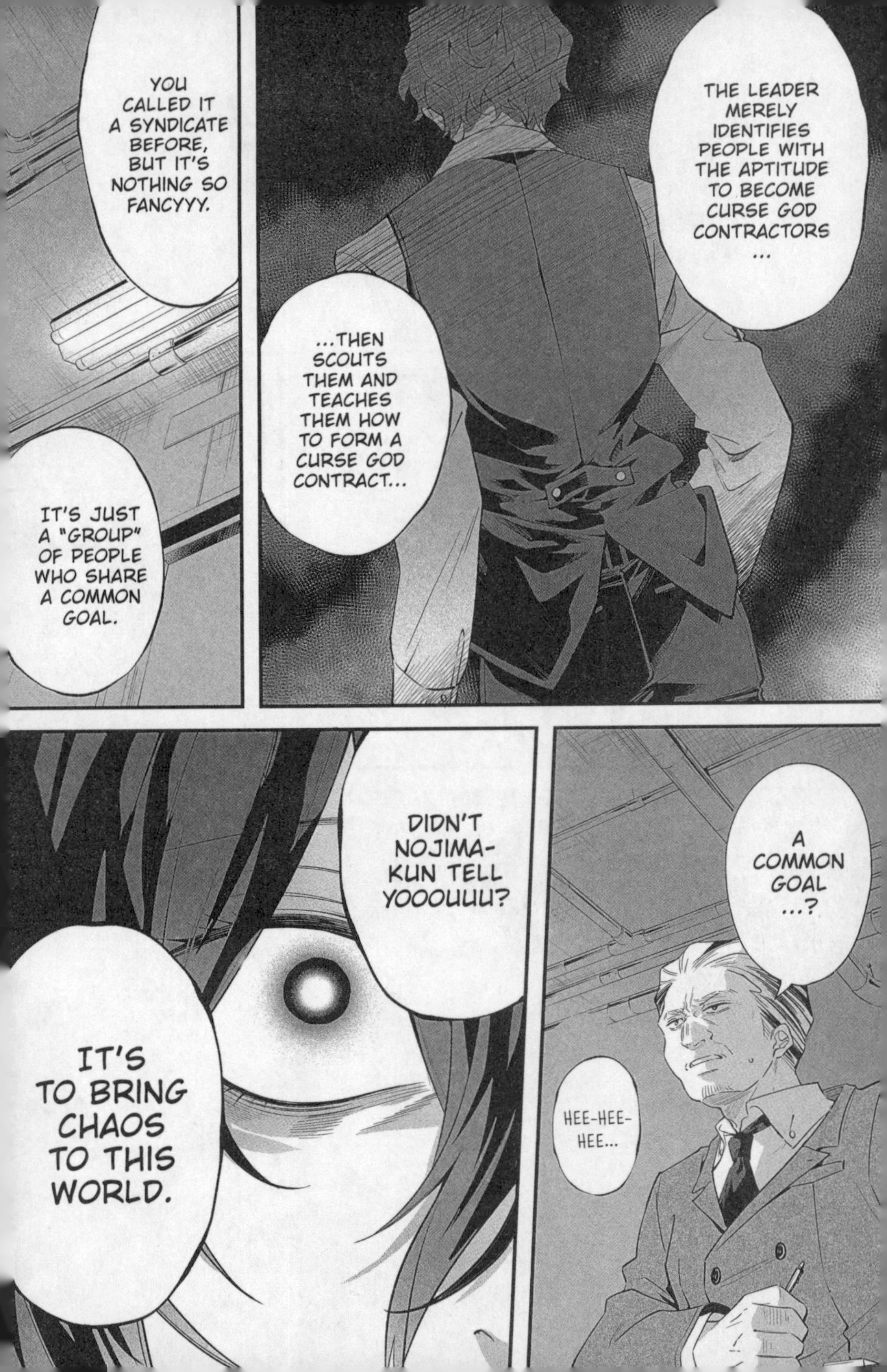
THE LEADER MERELY IDENTIFIES PEOPLE WITH THE APTITUDE TO BECOME CURSE GOD CONTRACTORS ...
...THEN SCOUTS THEM AND TEACHES THEM HOW TO FORM A CURSE GOD CONTRACT...
YOU CALLED IT A SYNDICATE BEFORE, BUT IT'S NOTHING SO FANCYYY.
IT'S JUST A "GROUP" OF PEOPLE WHO SHARE A COMMON GOAL.
A COMMON GOAL ...?
HEE-HEE-HEE...
DIDN'T NOJIMA-KUN TELL YOOOUUU?
IT'S TO BRING CHAOS TO THIS WORLD.

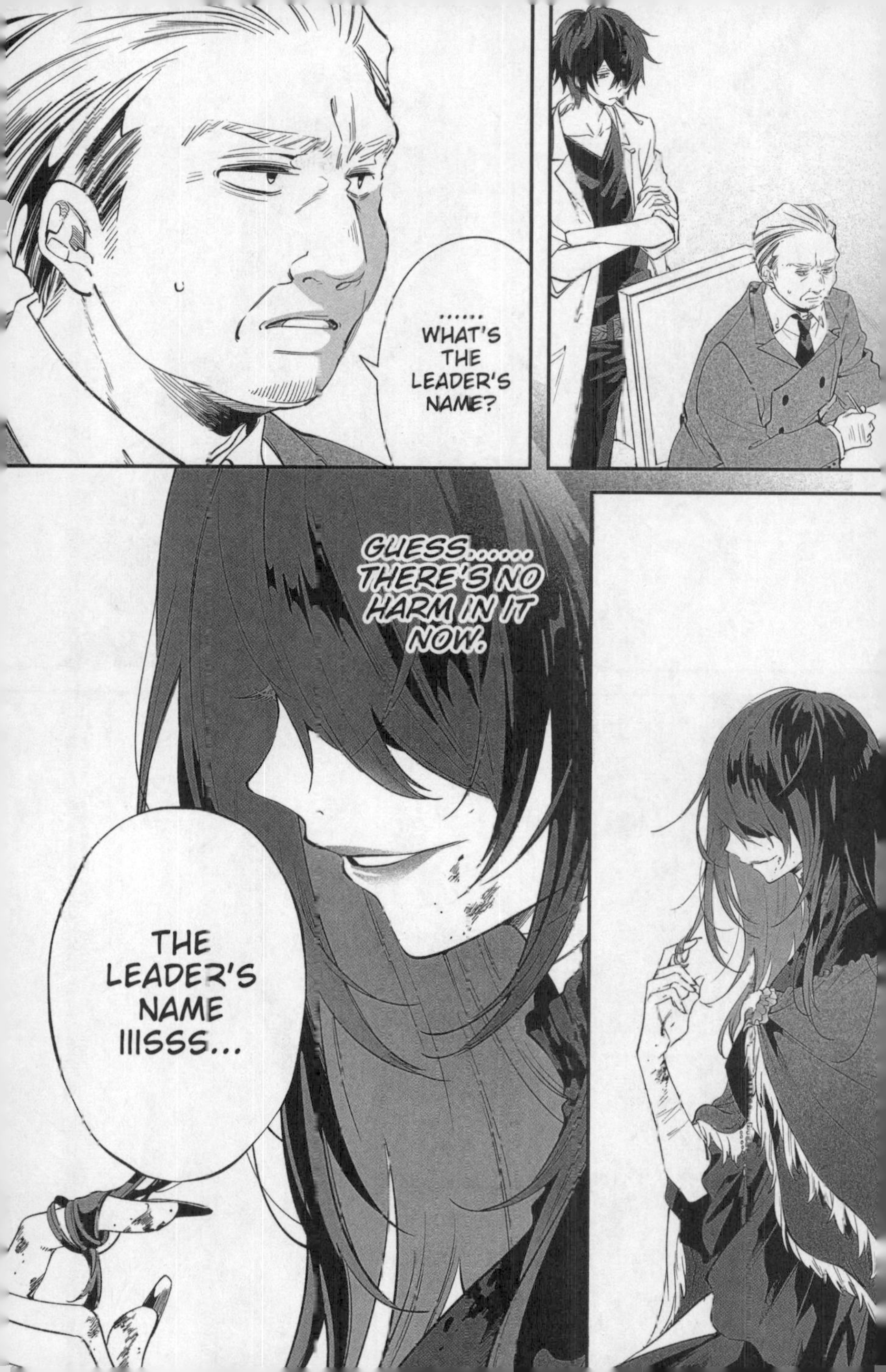
...... WHAT'S THE LEADER'S NAME?
GUESS...... THERE'S NO HARM IN IT NOW.
THE LEADER'S NAME IIISSS...

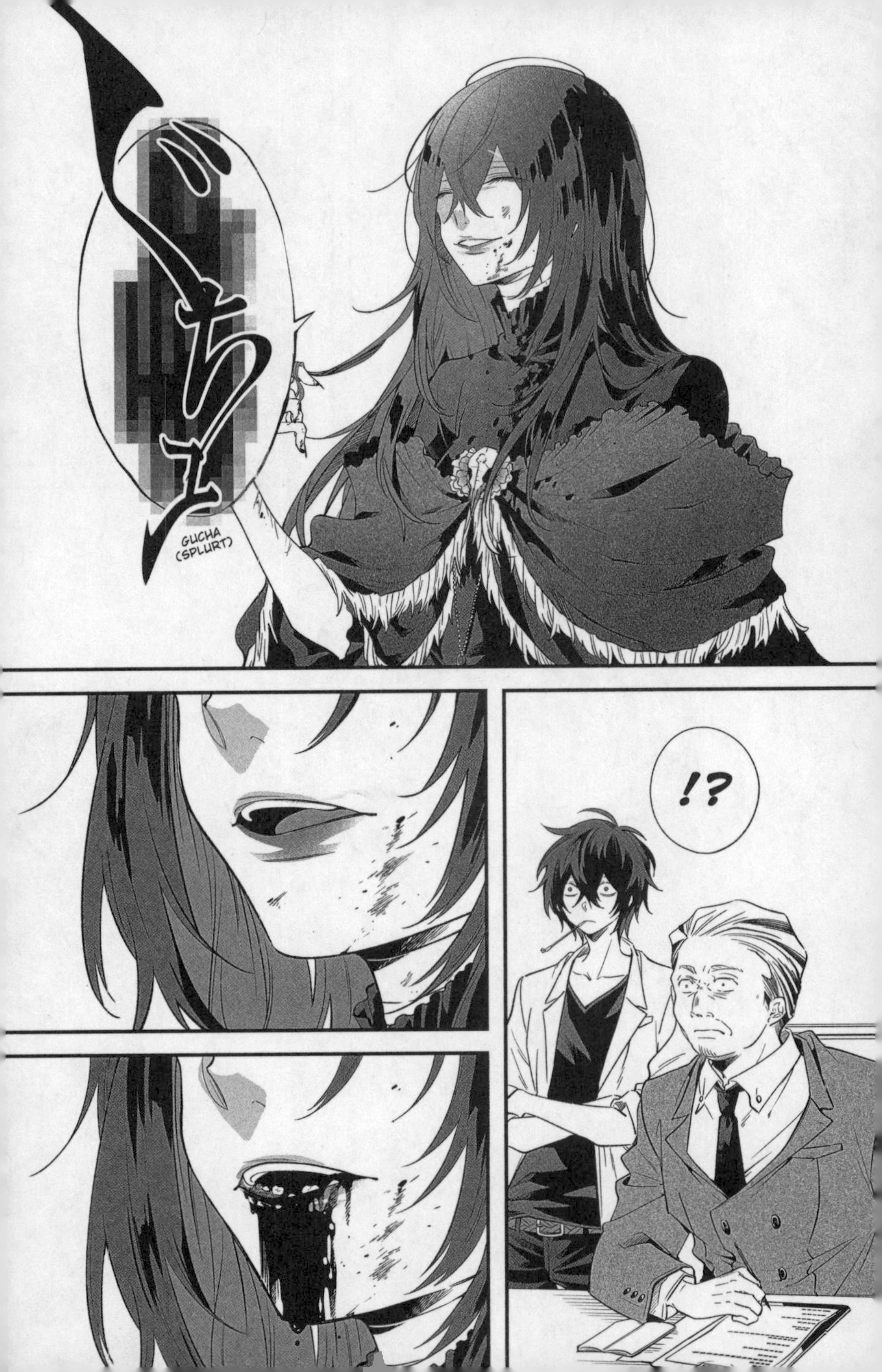
GUCHA
(SPLURT)
!?

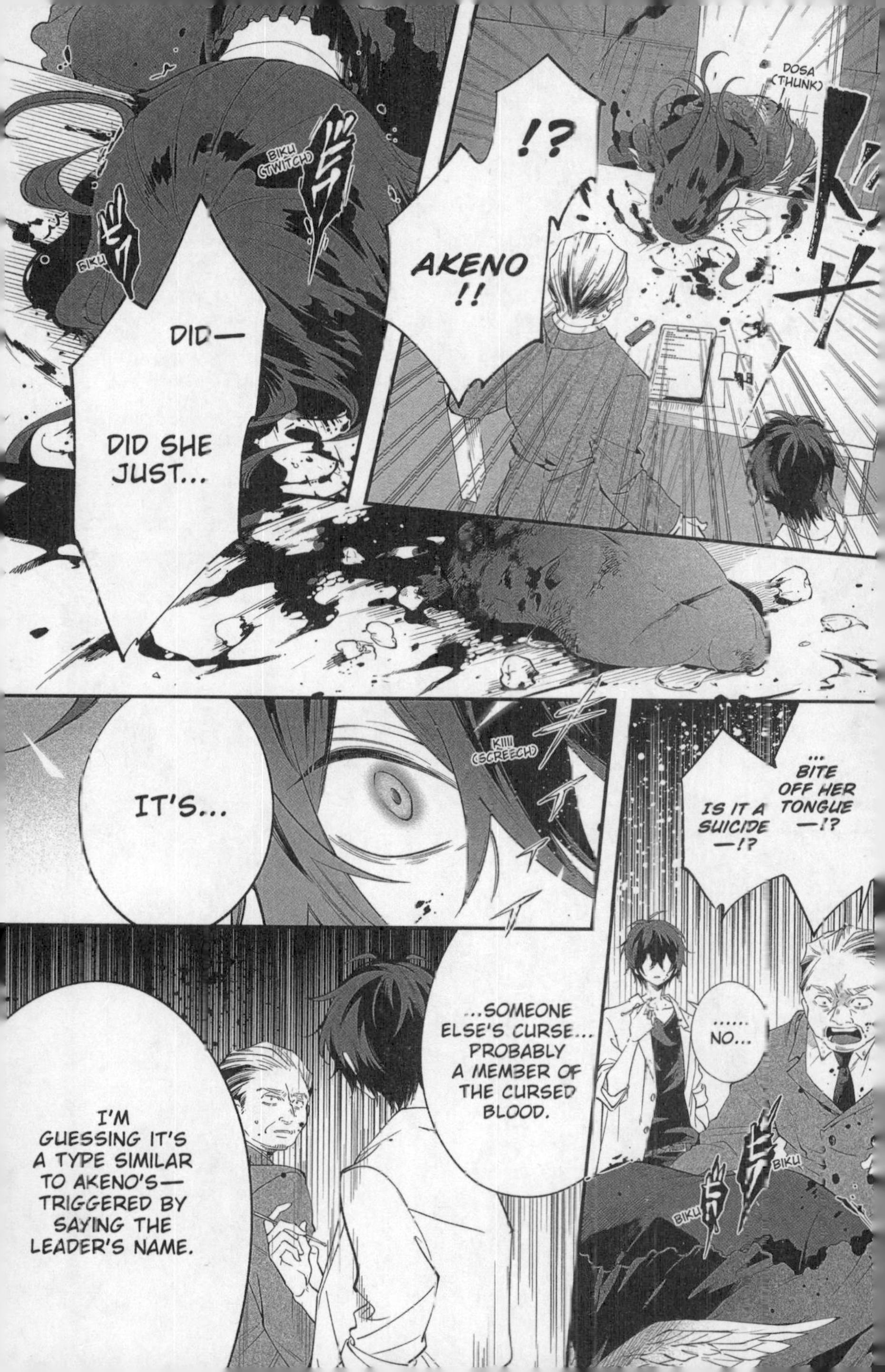
DOSA (THUNK)
!?
AKENO !!
BIKU (TWITCH)
BIKU
DID—
DID SHE JUST...
...BITE OFF HER TONGUE—!?
IS IT A SUICIDE—!?
KIIII (SCREECH)
IT'S...
......NO...
BIKU
BIKU
...SOMEONE ELSE'S CURSE... PROBABLY A MEMBER OF THE CURSED BLOOD.
I'M GUESSING IT'S A TYPE SIMILAR TO AKENO'S—TRIGGERED BY SAYING THE LEADER'S NAME.

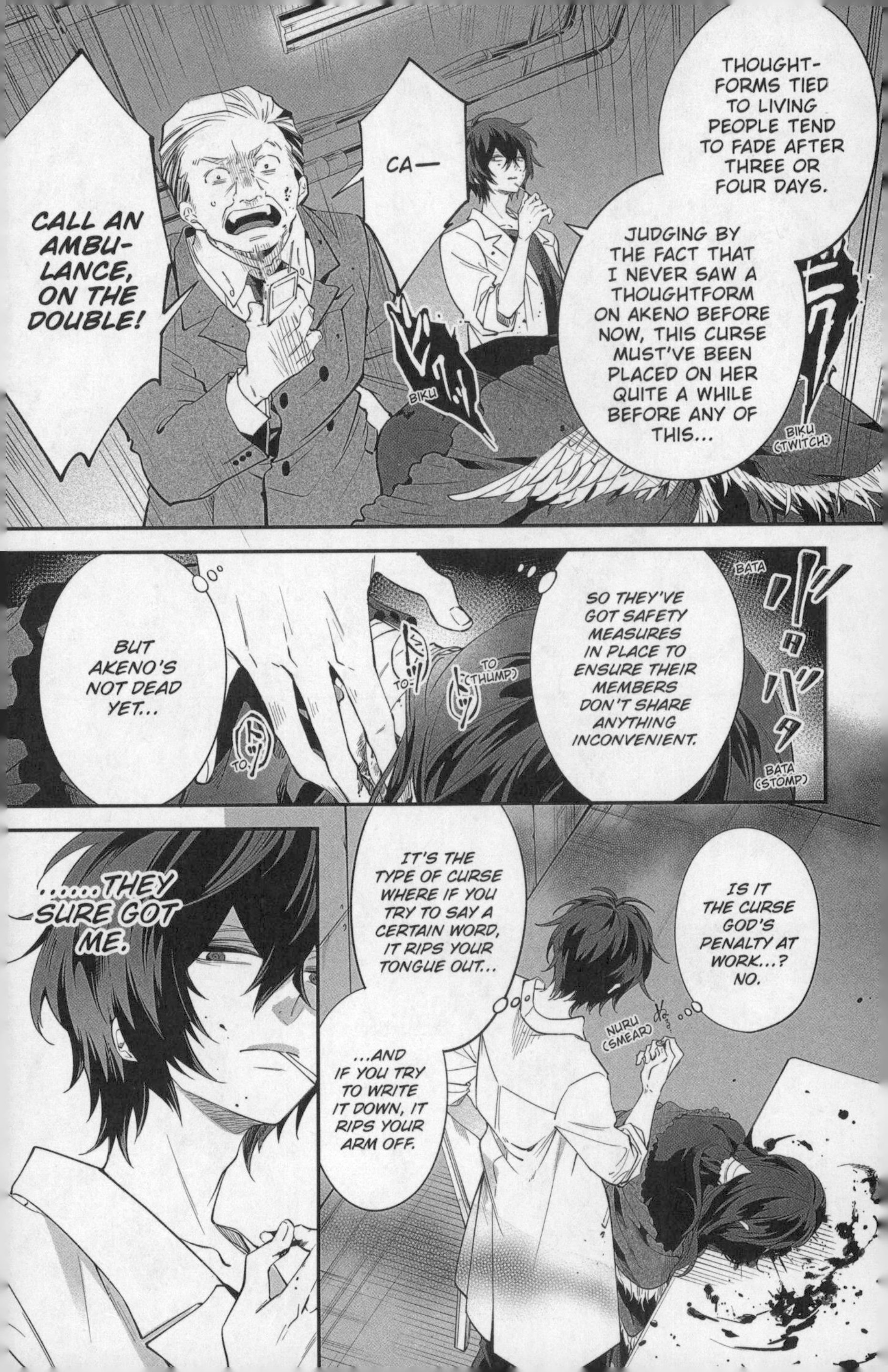
THOUGHT-FORMS TIED TO LIVING PEOPLE TEND TO FADE AFTER THREE OR FOUR DAYS.
JUDGING BY THE FACT THAT I NEVER SAW A THOUGHTFORM ON AKENO BEFORE NOW, THIS CURSE MUST'VE BEEN PLACED ON HER QUITE A WHILE BEFORE ANY OF THIS...
BIKU (TWITCH)
CA—
BIKU
CALL AN AMBU-LANCE, ON THE DOUBLE!
BATA
BATA (STOMP)
SO THEY'VE GOT SAFETY MEASURES IN PLACE TO ENSURE THEIR MEMBERS DON'T SHARE ANYTHING INCONVENIENT.
TO (THUMP)
TO
TO
BUT AKENO'S NOT DEAD YET...
IS IT THE CURSE GOD'S PENALTY AT WORK...? NO.
NURU (SMEAR)
IT'S THE TYPE OF CURSE WHERE IF YOU TRY TO SAY A CERTAIN WORD, IT RIPS YOUR TONGUE OUT...
...AND IF YOU TRY TO WRITE IT DOWN, IT RIPS YOUR ARM OFF.
......THEY SURE GOT ME.

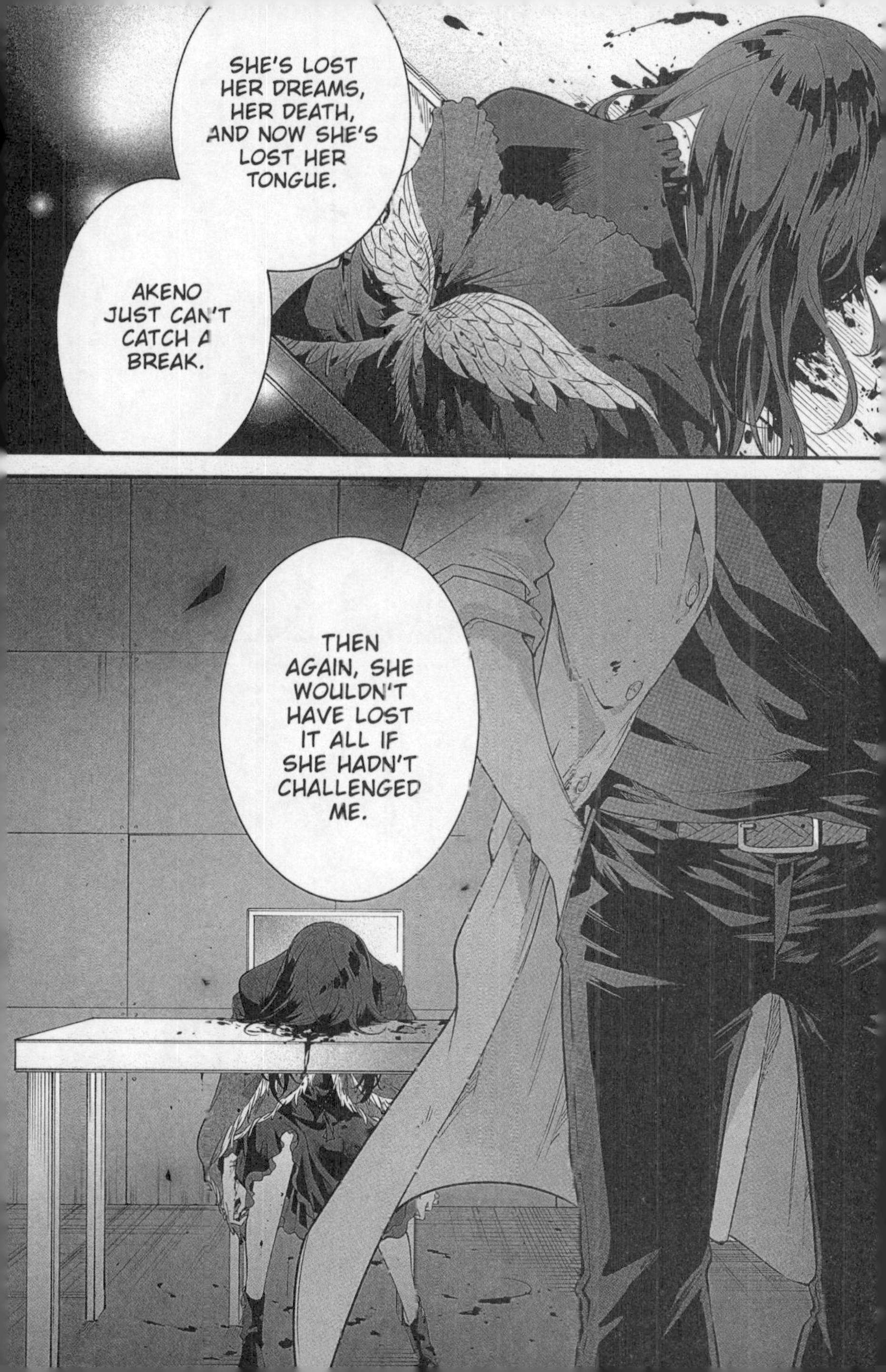
SHE'S LOST HER DREAMS, HER DEATH, AND NOW SHE'S LOST HER TONGUE.
AKENO JUST CAN'T CATCH A BREAK.
THEN AGAIN, SHE WOULDN'T HAVE LOST IT ALL IF SHE HADN'T CHALLENGED ME.

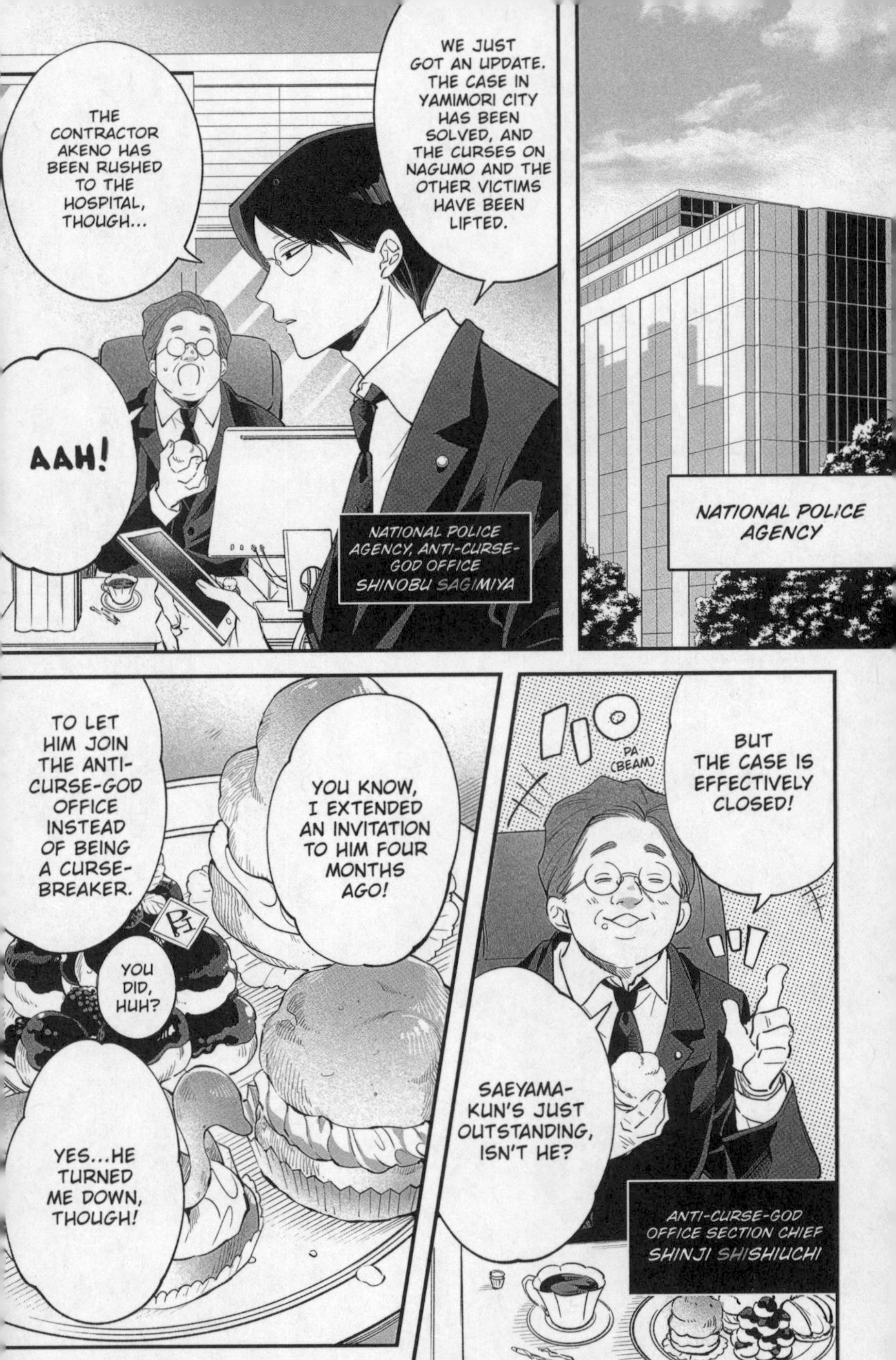
NATIONAL POLICE AGENCY
WE JUST GOT AN UPDATE. THE CASE IN YAMIMORI CITY HAS BEEN SOLVED, AND THE CURSES ON NAGUMO AND THE OTHER VICTIMS HAVE BEEN LIFTED.
THE CONTRACTOR AKENO HAS BEEN RUSHED TO THE HOSPITAL, THOUGH...
NATIONAL POLICE AGENCY, ANTI-CURSE-GOD OFFICE SHINOBU SAGIMIYA
AAH!
PA (BEAM)
BUT THE CASE IS EFFECTIVELY CLOSED!
SAEYAMA-KUN'S JUST OUTSTANDING, ISN'T HE?
ANTI-CURSE-GOD OFFICE SECTION CHIEF SHINJI SHISHIUCHI
YOU KNOW, I EXTENDED AN INVITATION TO HIM FOUR MONTHS AGO!
TO LET HIM JOIN THE ANTI-CURSE-GOD OFFICE INSTEAD OF BEING A CURSE-BREAKER.
YOU DID, HUH?
YES...HE TURNED ME DOWN, THOUGH!

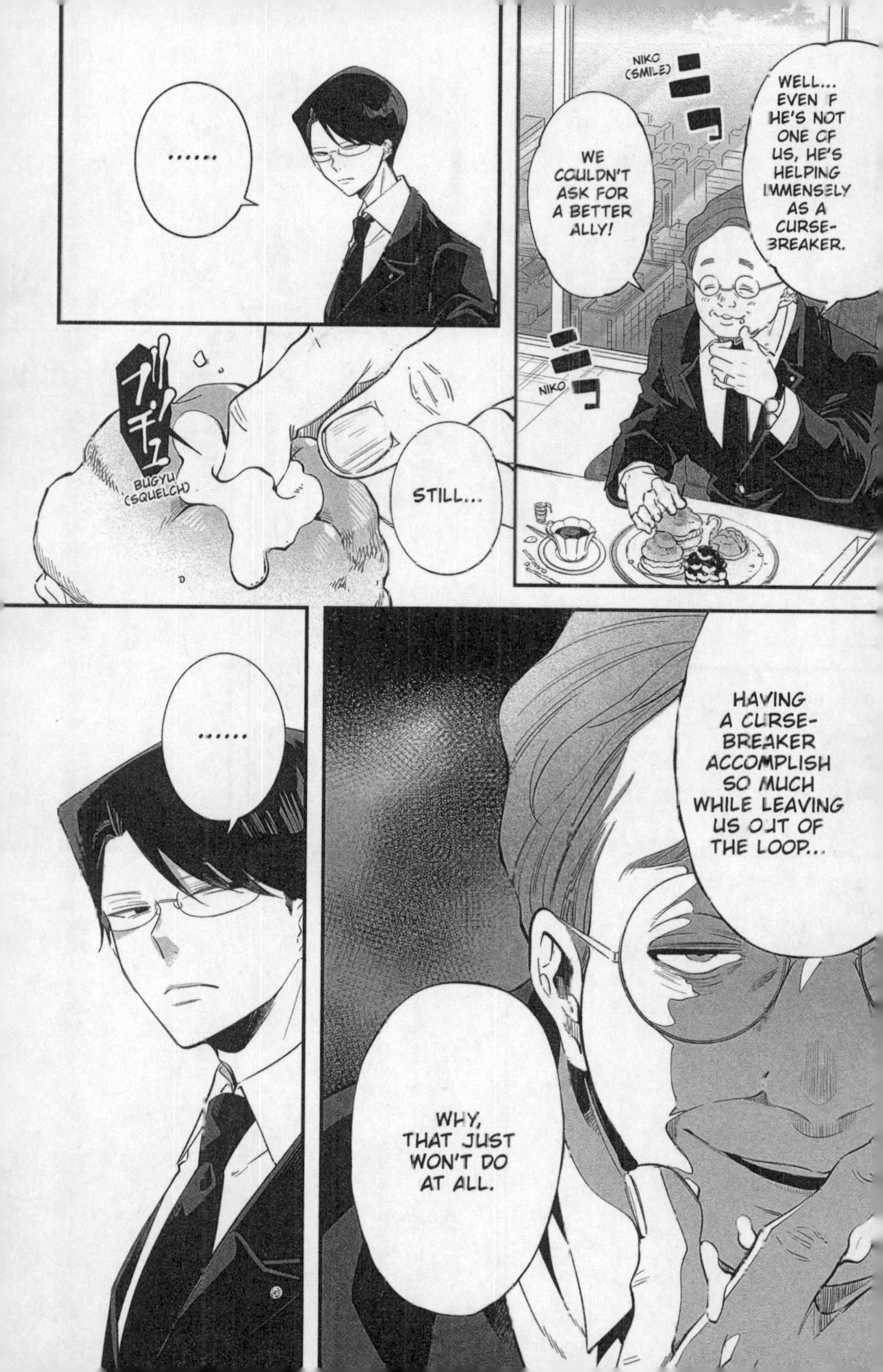
NIKO (SMILE)
WELL... EVEN IF HE'S NOT ONE OF US, HE'S HELPING IMMENSELY AS A CURSE-BREAKER.
WE COULDN'T ASK FOR A BETTER ALLY!
NIKO
......
ブチュ
BUGYU (SQUELCH)
STILL...
HAVING A CURSE-BREAKER ACCOMPLISH SO MUCH WHILE LEAVING US OUT OF THE LOOP...
WHY, THAT JUST WON'T DO AT ALL.
......

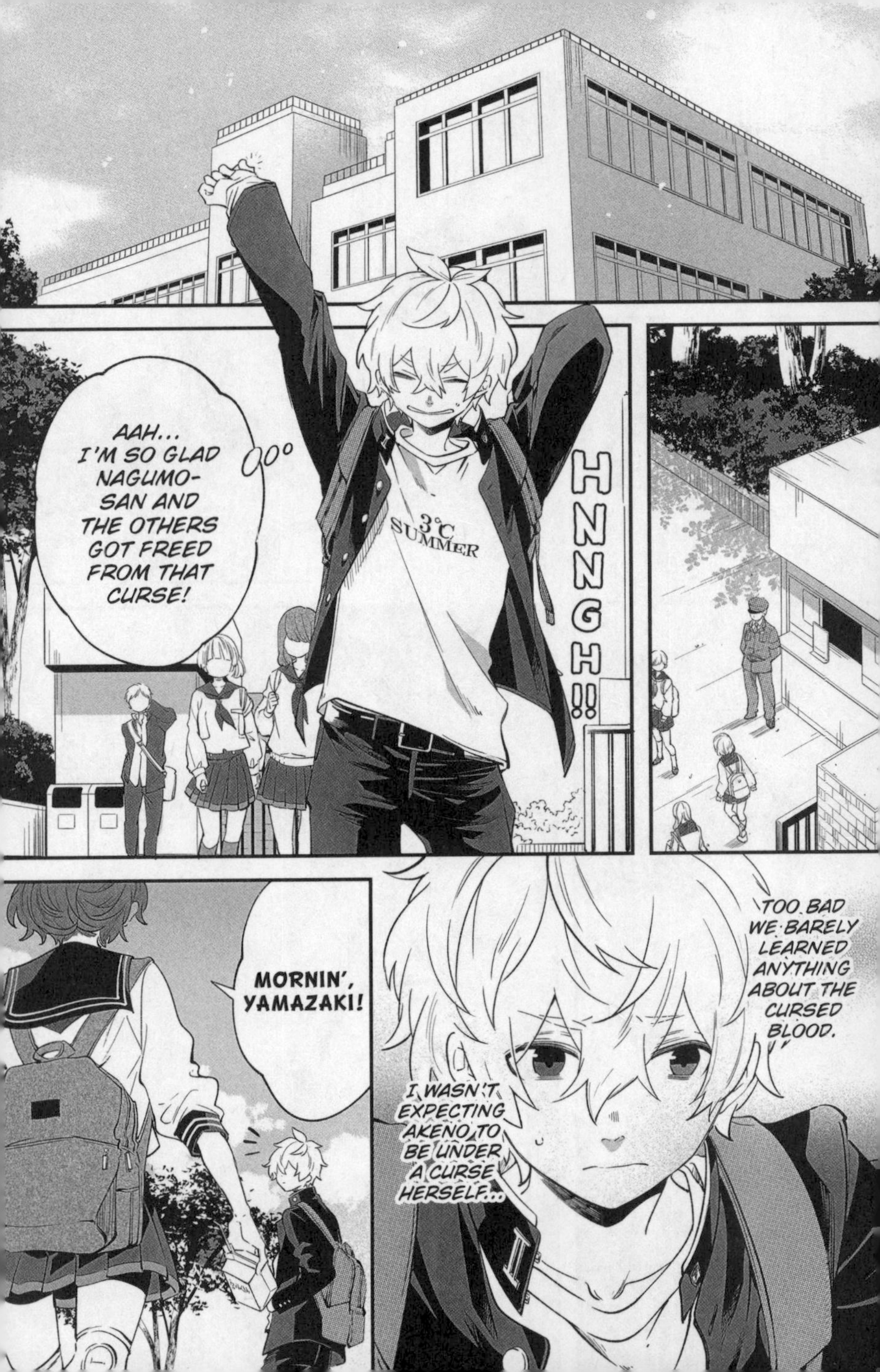
AAH... I'M SO GLAD NAGUMO-SAN AND THE OTHERS GOT FREED FROM THAT CURSE!
3°C SUMMER
HNNGH!!
TOO BAD WE BARELY LEARNED ANYTHING ABOUT THE CURSED BLOOD.
I WASN'T EXPECTING AKENO TO BE UNDER A CURSE HERSELF...
MORNIN', YAMAZAKI!

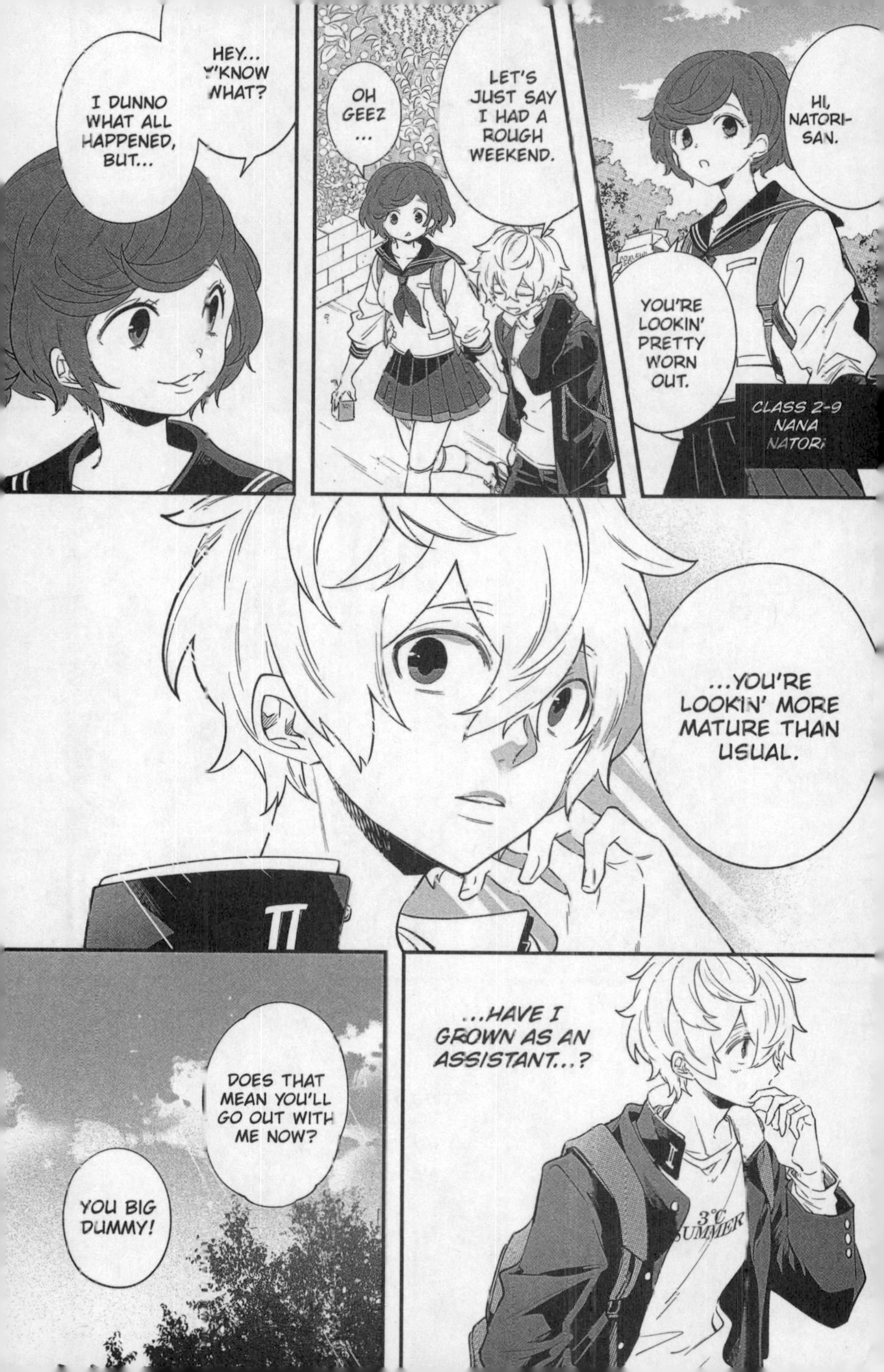
HI, NATORI-SAN.
YOU'RE LOOKIN' PRETTY WORN OUT.
CLASS 2-9 NANA NATORI
LET'S JUST SAY I HAD A ROUGH WEEKEND.
OH GEEZ ...
HEY... Y'KNOW WHAT?
I DUNNO WHAT ALL HAPPENED, BUT...
...YOU'RE LOOKIN' MORE MATURE THAN USUAL.
...HAVE I GROWN AS AN ASSISTANT...?
3°C SUMMER
DOES THAT MEAN YOU'LL GO OUT WITH ME NOW?
YOU BIG DUMMY!

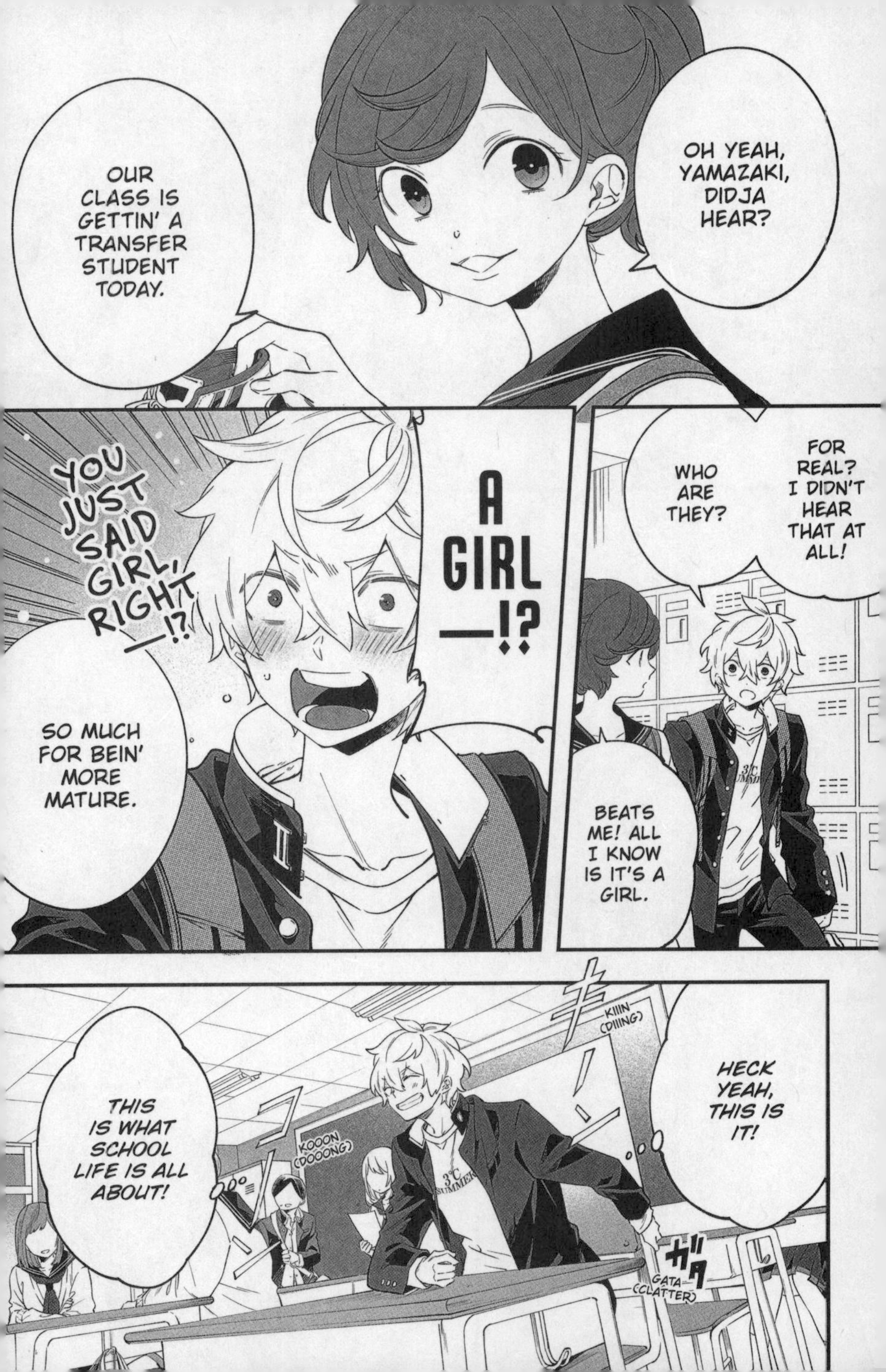
OH YEAH, YAMAZAKI, DIDJA HEAR?
OUR CLASS IS GETTIN' A TRANSFER STUDENT TODAY.
FOR REAL? I DIDN'T HEAR THAT AT ALL!
WHO ARE THEY?
BEATS ME! ALL I KNOW IS IT'S A GIRL.
A GIRL —!?
YOU JUST SAID GIRL, RIGHT —!?
SO MUCH FOR BEIN' MORE MATURE.
KIIIN (DIIING)
HECK YEAH, THIS IS IT!
GATA (CLATTER)
KOOON (DOOONG)
THIS IS WHAT SCHOOL LIFE IS ALL ABOUT!

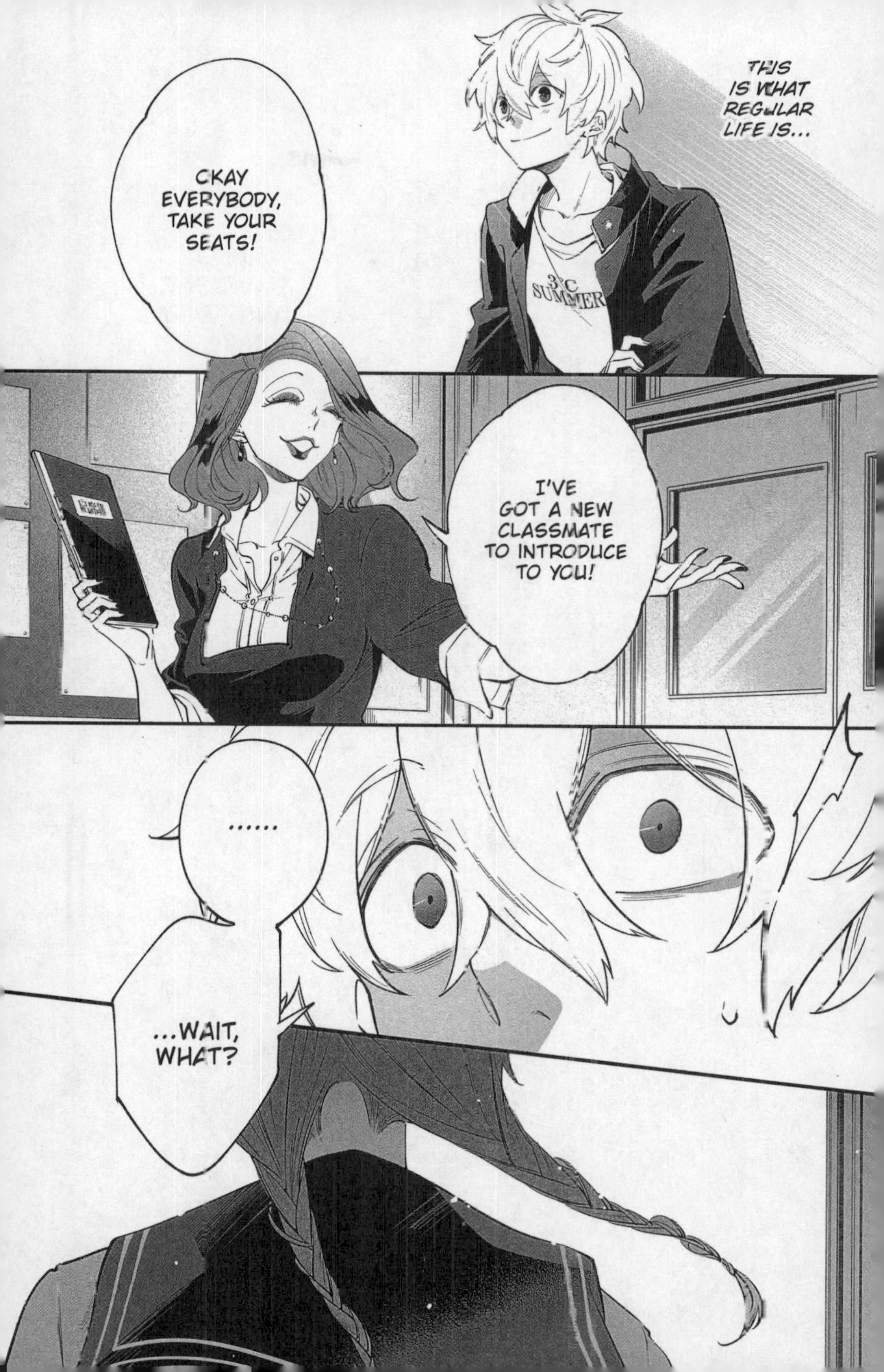
THIS IS WHAT REGULAR LIFE IS...
OKAY EVERYBODY, TAKE YOUR SEATS!
I'VE GOT A NEW CLASSMATE TO INTRODUCE TO YOU!
......
...WAIT, WHAT?

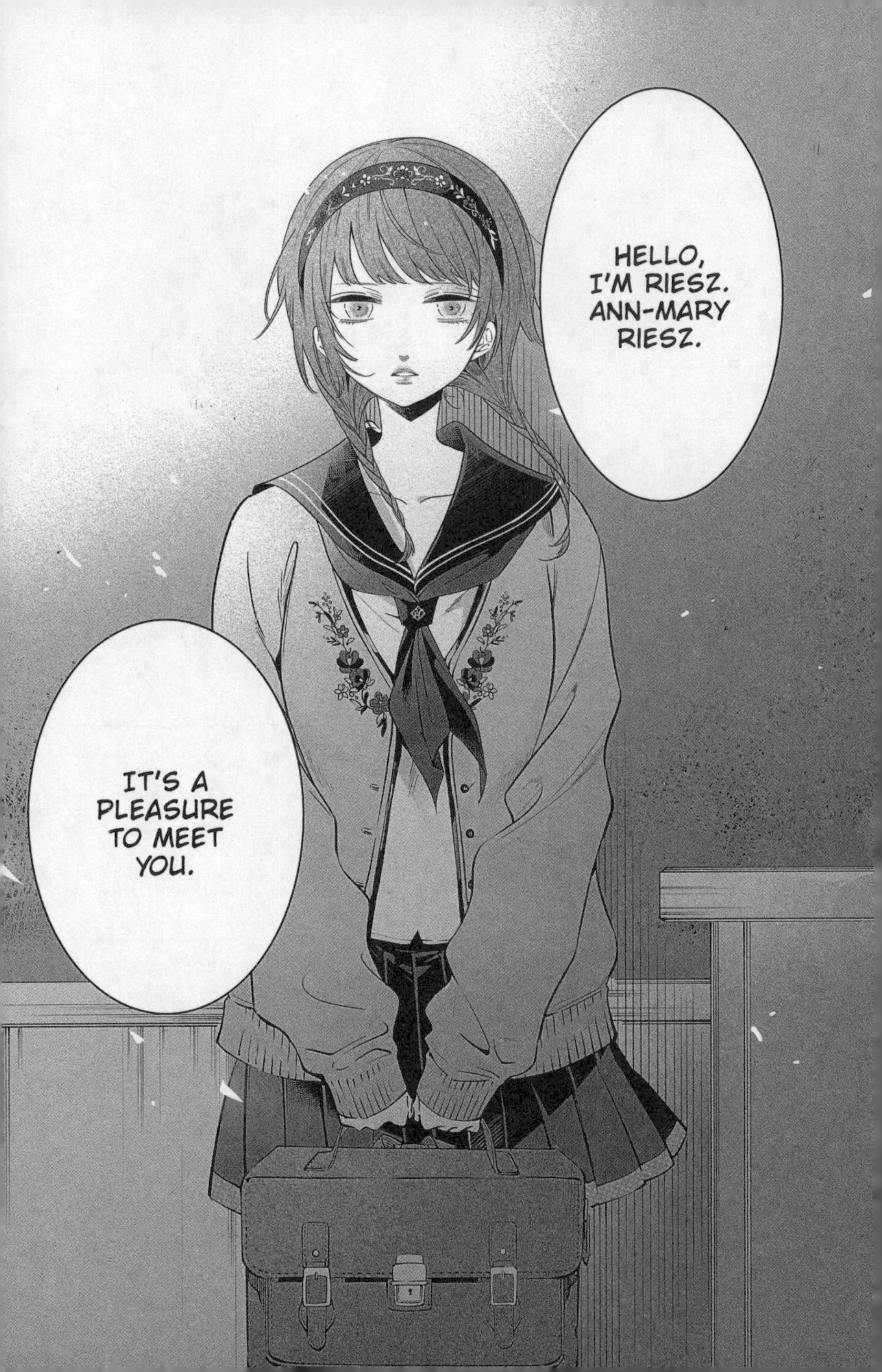
HELLO, I'M RIESZ. ANN-MARY RIESZ.
IT'S A PLEASURE TO MEET YOU.

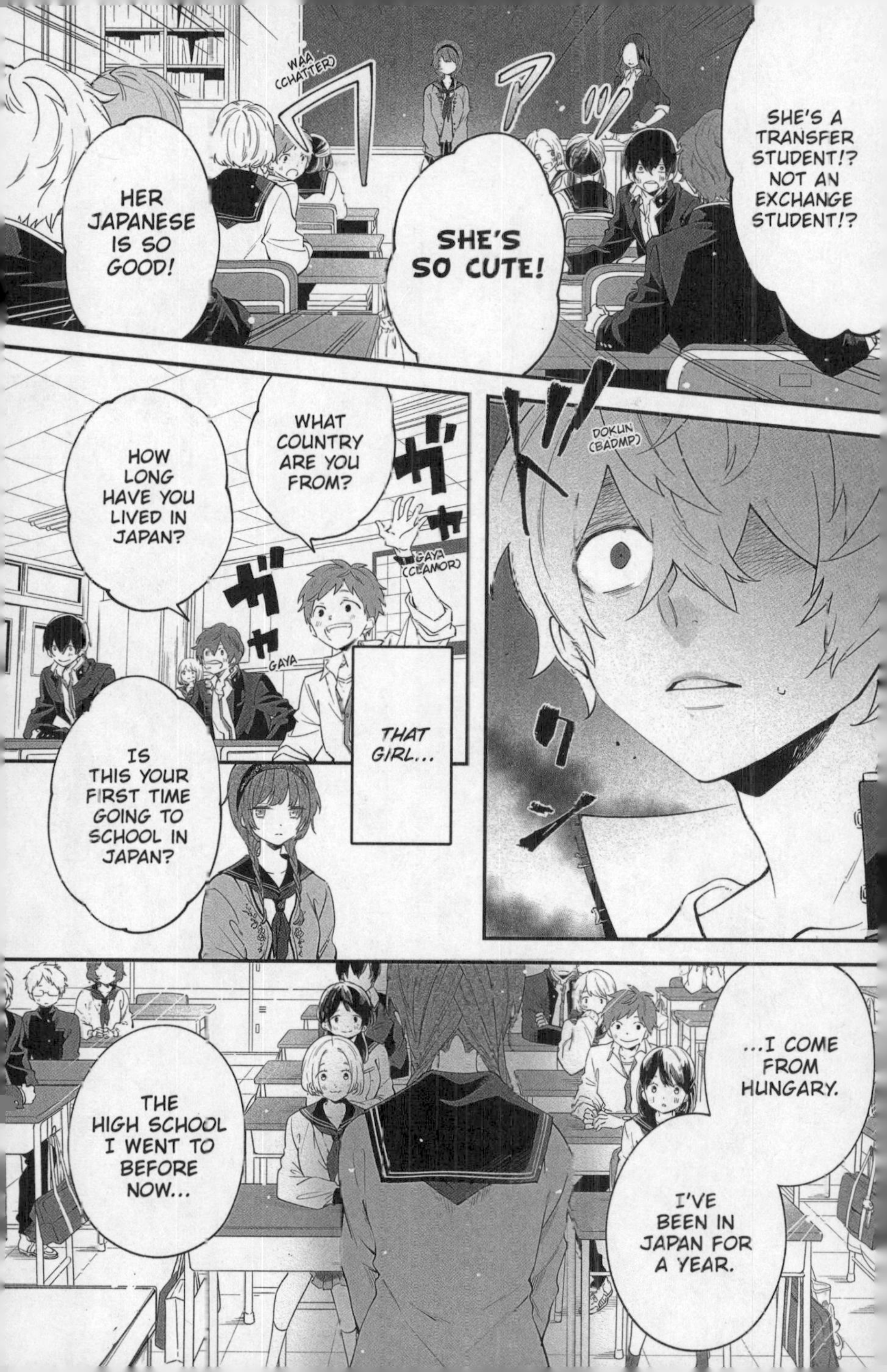
SHE'S A TRANSFER STUDENT!? NOT AN EXCHANGE STUDENT!?
SHE'S SO CUTE!
WAA (CHATTER)
HER JAPANESE IS SO GOOD!
DOKUN (BADMP)
WHAT COUNTRY ARE YOU FROM?
HOW LONG HAVE YOU LIVED IN JAPAN?
GAYA (CLAMOR)
GAYA
THAT GIRL...
IS THIS YOUR FIRST TIME GOING TO SCHOOL IN JAPAN?
...I COME FROM HUNGARY.
I'VE BEEN IN JAPAN FOR A YEAR.
THE HIGH SCHOOL I WENT TO BEFORE NOW...

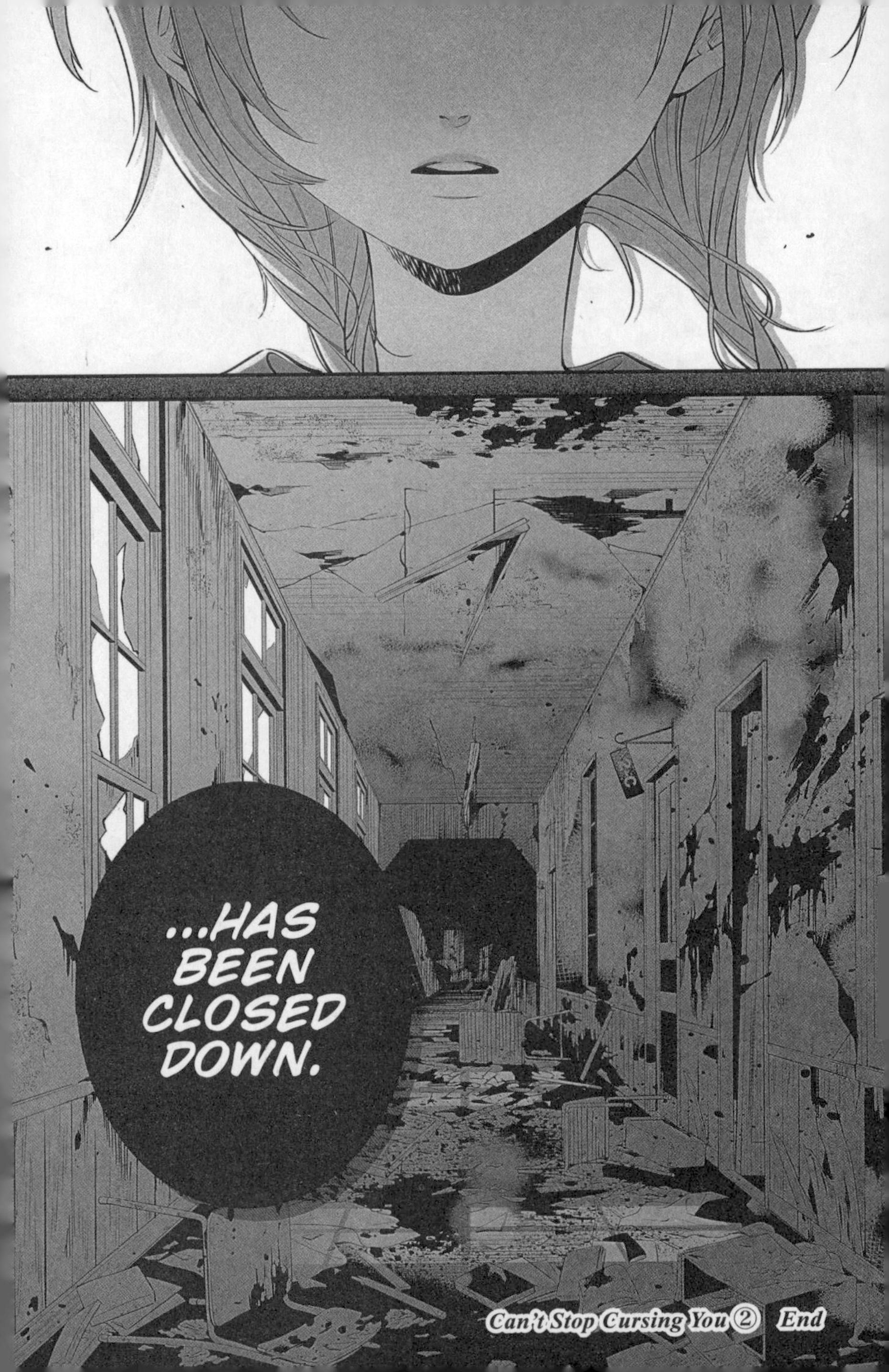
...HAS BEEN CLOSED DOWN.
Can't Stop Cursing You ② End

A fehér liliomnak is lehet fekete az árnyéka.
(Even the white lily casts a black shadow.)

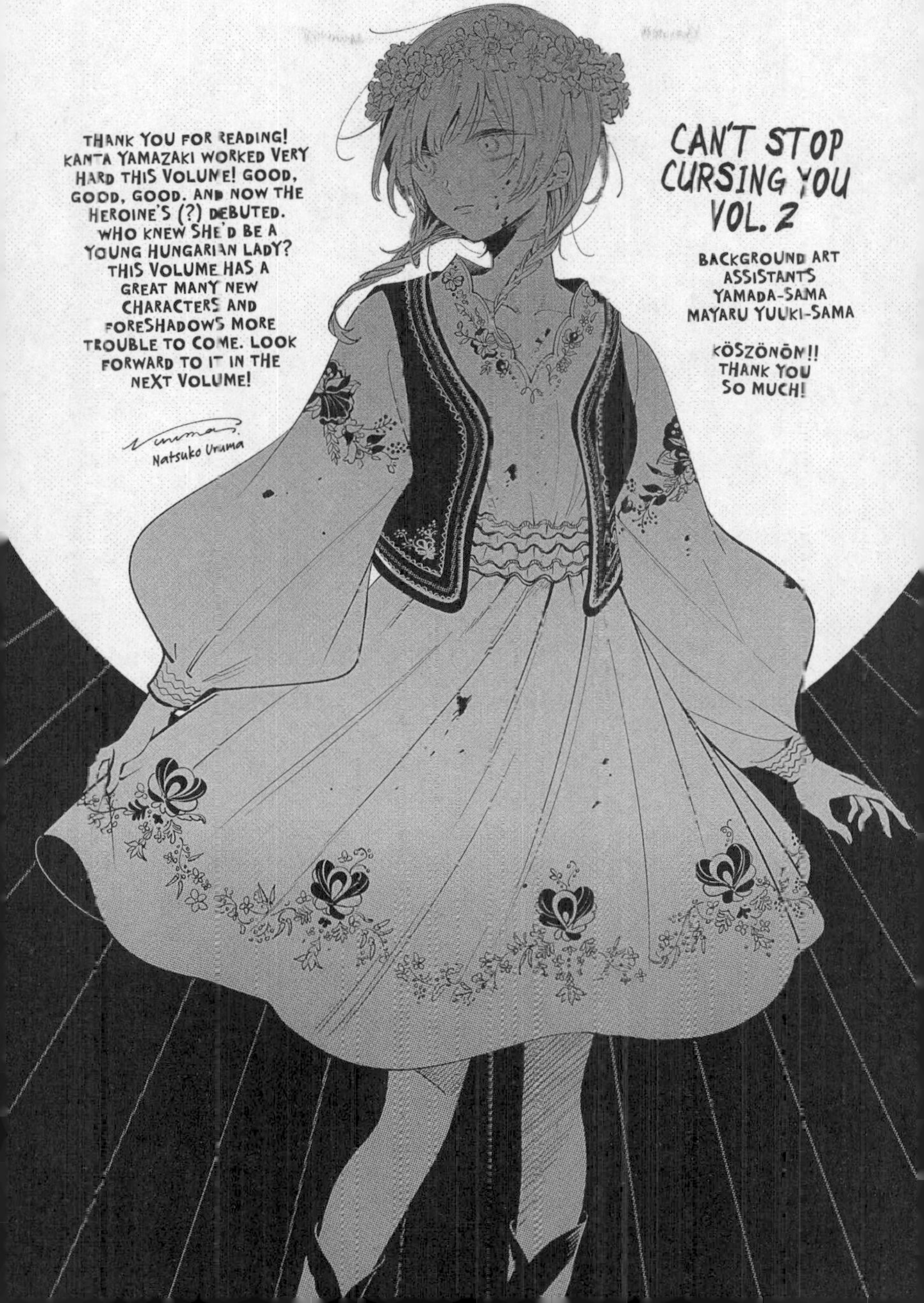
THANK YOU FOR READING! KANTA YAMAZAKI WORKED VERY HARD THIS VOLUME! GOOD, GOOD, GOOD. AND NOW THE HEROINE'S (?) DEBUTED. WHO KNEW SHE'D BE A YOUNG HUNGARIAN LADY? THIS VOLUME HAS A GREAT MANY NEW CHARACTERS AND FORESHADOWS MORE TROUBLE TO COME. LOOK FORWARD TO IT IN THE NEXT VOLUME!
Natsuko Uruma
CAN'T STOP CURSING YOU VOL. 2
BACKGROUND ART ASSISTANTS
YAMADA-SAMA
MAYARU YUUKI-SAMA
KÖSZÖNÖM!! THANK YOU SO MUCH!

Research is an act of blasphemy,
an ordeal,
and a genuine delight.

I study not for the sake of someone else.

Even if my work is derided as the product of insanity...
O curse god,
I shall quantify you.

In pursuit of that end,
no amount of sacrifice will sway my heart in the slightest.

From the notes of Dr. Rózsa,
researcher at the Curse God
Research Institute

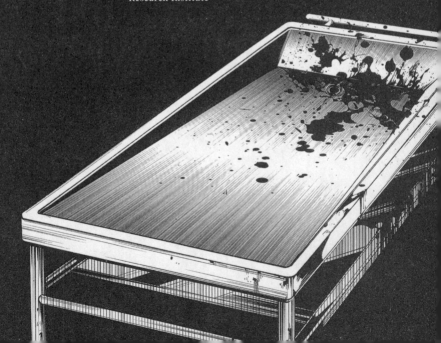

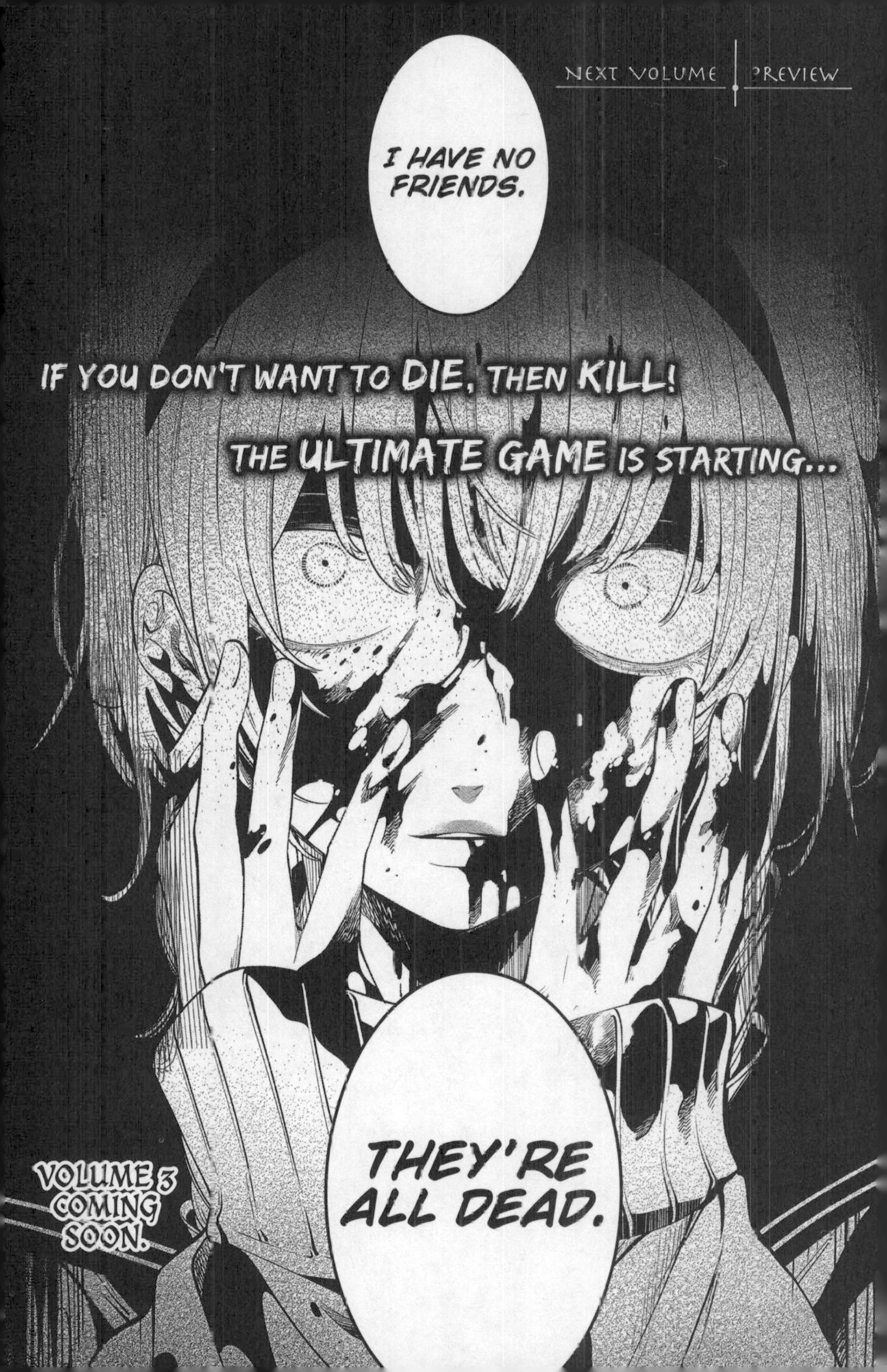
NEXT VOLUME PREVIEW
I HAVE NO FRIENDS.
IF YOU DON'T WANT TO DIE, THEN KILL!
THE ULTIMATE GAME IS STARTING...
THEY'RE ALL DEAD.
VOLUME 3 COMING SOON.

CAN'T STOP Cursing YOU 2

Art: NATSUKO URUMA

Original Story: KENSUKE KOBA

Translation: Christina Rose

Lettering: Rachel J. Pierce

DAREKA WO NOROWAZUNI IRARENAI KONO SEKAI DE Volume 2
©2020 Kensuke Koba, Natsuko Uruma/ SQUARE ENIX CO., LTD. First published in Japan in 2020 by SQUARE ENIX CO., LTD. English translation rights arranged with SQUARE ENIX CO., LTD. and Yen Press, LLC through Tuttle-Mori Agency, Inc.

Yen Press
150 West 30th Street, 19th Floor
New York, NY 10001

Visit us at yenpress.com ✳ facebook.com/yenpress ✳ twitter.com/yenpress ✳ yenpress.tumblr.com ✳ instagram.com/yenpress

First Yen Press Edition: July 2021

Yen Press is an imprint of Yen Press, LLC. The Yen Press name and logo are trademarks of Yen Press, LLC.

The publisher is not responsible for websites (or their content) that are not owned by the publisher.

Library of Congress Control Number: 2020951852

ISBNs: 978-1-9753-2170-3 (paperback)
       978-1-9753-2171-0 (ebook)

10 9 8 7 6 5 4 3 2 1

BVG

Printed in the United States of America